ERIC BUTTERWORTH was born in 1929 and educated at
Cambridge University, where he gained a B.A. in 1953 and
M.A. in 1956. From 1956 to 1966 he was a lecturer in the
Leeds Department of Adult Education and Extra-Mural
Studies, and from 1966 a Senior Research Fellow
at York University in the Department of Social
Administration and Social Work. In 1970 he was
appointed Reader in Community Work at York. His
publications include *A Muslim Community in Britain* (1967),
Immigrants in West Yorkshire (1967) and *Scope Handbook
1: The Social Background of Immigrant Children from India,
Pakistan and Cyprus* (1970) on which he collaborated with
Donald Kinnirugh. With David Weir he is the editor of the
Fontana *Modern Britain* series.

DAVID WEIR was born in 1939 and educated at Bradford
Grammar School and at Queen's College, Oxford. He
subsequently held the post of Research Sociologist at
Aberdeen University (1961–2), and from 1962–3 was
attached to the Extra-Mural Department of Leeds
University. He then joined the Sociology Department of
Hull University as Research Assistant (1963–5), and from
1965–6 was Assistant Lecturer in the Sociology Department
of Manchester University; from 1966–71 he held the post of
Lecturer there. His present position is Senior Lecturer in
Sociology at Manchester Business School and at
Manchester University.

Modern Britain Series

Edited by Eric Butterworth and David Weir
The Sociology of Modern Britain

Edited by David Weir
Men and Work in Modern Britain

Edited by
Eric Butterworth and David Weir

Social Problems
of Modern Britain

 Fontana/Collins

First published in Fontana 1972
Reprinted 1973
Third impression 1974

Printed in Great Britain
by Richard Clay (The Chaucer Press) Ltd
Bungay, Suffolk

Contents

Introduction

This book of readings is the second in a series on British society. The first, *The Sociology of Modern Britain,* already published, deals with the main elements of the social structure which form the background to the study of social problems. It is not a comprehensive guide to the social problems of modern Britain, since this would require a much larger book, but we try to bring out ways of looking at situations, within a general sociological frame of reference, which will help the reader to make sense of aspects of the society in which he lives.

The organisation of the book is straightforward. Chapter I looks at social problems in general, definitions, perspectives, explanations and the way in which their incidence changes over time. It stresses the importance of an analytical approach to them, and the need to look at social problems in comparative terms. Some suggestions are made for general reading and reference at the end of the chapter as it is not possible, nor desirable, to provide all the relevant factual and theoretical material in this one volume. Each of the following chapters has an introductory section which has two main purposes. The first is to refer to some of the most relevant and useful ways of working at the theme of the chapter, without in any way attempting to provide a detailed consideration of all the concepts and issues, and the second is to introduce the readings which make up the main content of the chapter. At the end of each chapter there is a brief section on Further Reading consisting of books referred to in the readings or books which follow up the most important themes. At the end of the book there is a *Textbook Bibliography* providing cross reference to the textbooks with the widest circulation in this field. It is significant that almost all of them are American, and this emphasises the need to provide a book, with some comparative information and sources built in, geared specifically to the

British situation. The format has been a successful one in *The Sociology of Modern Britain*, and we hope to stimulate discussion of the right questions.

The principles on which the selection of readings is based are similar to those for the earlier companion volume. One of the most important is readability. Given the audience that we had in mind we did not wish to concentrate too much on sociological writing of a theoretical kind. Moreover, we thought that this was best dealt with in the first chapter, which is designed to provide an overview of social problems, the ways in which they are perceived, their characteristics and methods of tackling them. The material presented can thus be used in relation to a whole series of theoretical or practical standpoints.

A second concern was with the accessibility of the reading in its original form. Many of our selections are drawn from journals and sources which are not readily available to the general reader or to the student and which, if recommended on courses of study, may be required by large numbers in a situation where there is only one copy in the library. Some of the most relevant and significant work is to be found in these sources and it needs to be introduced to a wider audience. In some cases we have used work which is more readily accessible but which covers the subjects in more satisfactory and appropriate ways, from our standpoint, than material less readily available which otherwise we might have used.

Having emphasised readability and relevance, some attention must be given to the balance between contributions and between the different parts of the reader. Here we were governed by the need to make links wherever possible between the various areas in which social problems can be placed. These links are an important element in the teaching and under-standing of the subject. We have adopted a topical breakdown of the subject rather than presenting it in terms of deviance, disorganisation and institutionalisation, which we considered, or by a distinction between those problems likely to be relatively less important in the future and others, like pollution and increase in population, whose social consequences could be catastrophic if they are allowed to develop unchecked.

To obtain a balanced view of the social problems in modern

Britain is in any event a difficult undertaking. To achieve it in some measure we have attempted to provide work drawn from a number of perspectives and points of view. Some of the readings are straightforward presentations of factual material. Examples include some material on crime, unemployment and strikes. There are some subjects that lend themselves to this kind of treatment and in these cases such facts are an essential basis for further analysis and discussion. Suggestions are made for following up the most important topics. Where this framework of facts is not provided reference is made to relevant sources of information. In some cases the writing on a particular subject did not lend itself to presentation in a reader and here we have had to refer, in the introductory and further reading sections of the chapters, to other available and relevant sources. Some of the readings are analytical in their approach and introduce theoretical perspectives. Examples are to be found in the chapters on health, especially with regard to mental illness, and on crime. Some of these extracts are from American sources because it is impossible to look at British society in isolation from other advanced industrial societies, with which it shares some common problems.

The comparative dimension, however, is given limited space in the reader as a deliberate policy, since it is assumed that people begin their study of society and, in this case, social problems, from the analysis of what they know already. There are, however, some contributions about Britain by foreign scholars and observers and others which have general relevance for advanced industrial societies.

Finally, some of the views of those who experience the problems or are involved in them, such as social workers and police, are presented. Some are particularly dramatic, including the contribution by Zeno on what it is like to be given a life sentence in prison and the reading taken from Robert Roberts' *Imprisoned Tongues* about the prison officer's role. The immediacy of the impact of these is considerable. None of these personal comments are dispassionate attempts to look at all the issues that arise but they embody a critique designed to question the system of provision and its inadequacies. Questions about the priorities of social policy are outside the scope of this book.

We are most grateful to all those authors who have allowed their work to be used in this reader. We would like to point out that in some cases only small parts have been quoted from the relevant books and articles and it is not to be assumed that what the author takes to be the main argument of his writing is necessarily to be found in this. There is no substitute for going to the original works and we hope that all the readers of this book will want to refer to the longer versions from which we have taken our extracts. In addition, because of the purposes of the book and the limitations on space, the footnotes from the readings have been omitted although the more important ones are referred to in Further Reading at the end of each section. The whole work is an attempt to provide a framework within which social problems can be viewed as a prelude to expanding that interest and analysis by moving on to far more varied and more detailed sources. The field is quite strong on monographs on specific themes and there is a growing body of relevant research, but the coverage is patchy and few attempts have been made to provide any kind of coherent overview of the situation. If the book that we have prepared helps to do this then we shall feel that we have succeeded.

The audience we have aimed at is a wide one. It includes, as we stated in *The Sociology of Modern Britain*, 'Members of the general public whose interest in the nature of their society may have been stimulated by television programmes, colour supplements and the like. These may or may not move on to adult classes, or courses of study, such as those provided by the Open University, Extra-Mural Departments, by the W.E.A. and by local authorities. Many students at Colleges of Education, Technical Colleges and Colleges of Further Education undertake general introductory courses in Sociology, much of the content of which relates to Britain, and this is beginning to develop in the sixth forms of some schools. Professional or pre-professional courses of training, in-service and refresher courses for such groups as hospital administrators, nurses and social workers, are more and more common.'

Acknowledgements to authors and copyright holders are included in the headings to the readings. We should also like to thank the colleagues, friends and students with whom we discussed the content of the book. We have used a large number of the readings for teaching purposes in the past. In particular we would like to thank Barbara Kindness and Noreen Davey, who undertook most of the secretarial and administrative duties to prepare the book for publication, and Joan Harris, who helped with this during the later stages. Barbara Holmes provided much relevant information which helped us in the selection of the readings. We owe an especial debt to our wives. Not least our thanks are due to Francis Bennett and Lydia Greeves, of Fontana Books, for their courtesy, kindness and restraint in the dealings they had with us.

Eric Butterworth and David Weir

May, 1972

Chapter One   The Study of Social Problems

1. *Starting Points*

When we ask groups of people in society about the main social
problems that face Britain, or any other country in the world,
we get an enormous range of answers. There may be some
agreement about various categories into which we could put
these problems, but there will be conflict about their
importance, how they arose and what can be done about them.
The source of much of our information about social problems
is the mass media, particularly the press, and a large amount
of coverage is given to them. Our perceptions of social
problems are influenced by the information we are given in
the mass media, and here the conflicts, the sensational elements
or the human interest, are stressed. These accounts of social
problems help to condition the climate of public opinion.

  Most 'campaigns' about particular problems, in the mass
circulation parts of the media at least, are sensational and
short term. They simplify as a matter of course, and present
as self-evident matters which are exceedingly complex and
have developed in response to a multiplicity of factors. Studies
of the British press have indicated how lacking in stamina
most campaigns of this kind are—there is a great outcry
for a few days, followed by silence. Our emotions are caught
more than our reason, and a consequence is that those issues
which engage us have an immediate impact and are likely
perhaps to involve situations we do not expect to face ourselves.

  Thus the plight of the patient whose life depends on a
kidney or heart machine engages our undivided, and perhaps
sentimentalised, sympathy, if only for a while. Our attitudes
towards the poor, or one of the groups of deprived or
unfortunate, may be influenced more by our perceptions of
our own experience and opportunities as compared with theirs.
A corollary of the fact that 'we made it' may be a certain

satisfaction that others did not. We are concerned with cherished illusions which sharpen points of conflict and bitterness, and which link them with attitudes and opinions characteristic of the past.

The consequences of social problems are seen in different ways by the groups who have opinions about them. If one takes the example of the assumed increase in violence, from assaults to sex crimes, one could make the main priority an increase in the size of the police force. This would find favour with many responsible for policing. Refinements of the proposal might specify, on the basis of available evidence, that certain areas (down town) were more likely to have outbreaks of violence than others, or that certain times ('when the pubs, or the dance halls, turn out') are more likely to lead to dangerous situations than others. How the police deal with an outbreak of violence where there are many possible approaches, is a crucial question. They could attempt to de-fuse the situation by a reassuring and humorous manner; or they could single out the main trouble-makers, isolate and remove them; or deal by violent and positive action with those involved. There are certain phases in crowd situations where changes in the pace of the action are most meaningful. The presence of the police can act as a challenge and an incitement, and it could be that more police may mean more violence in very different ways from the expectations of those whose faith in repression or containment is expressed in the desire for more police. The consequences, manifest and latent, the functions and dysfunctions, are extremely complex—more so than we may imagine.

For the person who is relatively affluent and is secure, with a stake in society, the problems may well be those of preserving that kind of stability which has provided him with his standard of living and way of life: he may be preoccupied with questions about law and order to the exclusion of issues which affect other people. Anyone who is suffering from poverty or deprivation of any kind will see that problem as a priority because it concerns him directly. This makes the point that our perceptions are related to our own position, in many respects.

What are social problems? In response to this question J. B. Mays asks another. 'Who defines them and in relation to what norms?' He goes on to say: 'I find these difficult questions to answer. Nor does the literature help us very much. If we assume that the social services are brought into being to cope with social problems, one would expect that textbooks on the organisation and origin of social services would indicate how these problems are defined in the first place. In fact, one finds that the authors *assume* that social problems do exist, that they have been defined, and then proceed from there.'

The problems that interest the sociologist are not necessarily those which other people may call 'problems'. It is common to speak about something in society that does not work the way it is supposed to according to official interpretations as a 'social problem'. So there is a distinction to be made between the way in which public opinion, and the official views of 'the *status quo*', look at problems and the way in which these would be regarded by sociologists who are likely to want to study them.

Unfortunately many discussions on social problems start from the premise that it is fairly clear what needs to be done. Often the problem will be defined before research is requested on it, and research may then be seen as justifying the standpoint which was originally taken up.

The sociological problem, as Peter Rose states: 'is always the understanding of what goes on here, in terms of social integration. Thus the sociological problem is not so much why some things "go wrong" from the viewpoint of the authorities and the management of the social scene, but how the whole system works in the first place, what are its preconceptions and by what means it is held together.' He goes on to suggest that the fundamental sociological problem 'is not crime but the law, not divorce but marriage, not racial discrimination but racially defined stratification, not revolution but government'.

What all this means in terms of the approach that we must adopt is that it is not enough to accept the definition of social problems, whether in the fields we have mentioned or of teenagers, juvenile gangs and so on, as these may be defined by those with a vested interest in particular views and by what, in effect, is the world of dominant, respectable, publicly approved values.

The first important point to be clear about, then, is the difference between social problems as they are perceived and social problems as they exist and require attention. We move back more and more, in our effort to understand them, from the ways in which they have been presented, once they have developed, to the aspects of our society that help to bring them into being.

2. *Orientations*

Within the framework of any society are the seeds of particular social problems. As Warner Bloomberg comments: 'Problems are creatures of our discontent, of our negative evaluation of some existing condition.' They have a close connection with moral values and social institutions. All problems have certain elements in common, as Nisbet points out. There is some *obstacle* to action or understanding, there is a perceived *difficulty* not readily resolved in a normal way and there is an *interpretation* of the normal or conventional run of things. Each approach to or perspective on social problems is in its way a kind of searchlight, elucidating some of the facts but leaving others unclear.

Our basic aim must be to show the ways in which the arrangements and values which prevail in society can produce socially condemned results, and how social problems can be 'unwilled, largely indirect, and often unanticipated consequences of patterns of behaviour'. Instead of looking at social problems as a series of discrete and often unrelated, though interesting, topics we need to study them against the background of the whole social framework. This will help us to understand the disorganisation and also to understand that each social and cultural structure has its distinctive kinds and degrees of social problems. There are different pressures on those living in different parts of society. These are pressures which arise through class membership, economic position, age, work, the area in which a person lives, as well as through personality factors.

Despite the fact people tend to be very clear about what needs to be done, it is exceptional to find a general agreement about this. The 'solutions' that are offered to problems are often deceptively simple.

To assume that the ideal society is one without social problems, which is almost a corollary of the way social problems are sometimes discussed, is completely mistaken. If we contrast the problems of advanced industrialised societies such as Britain, with the stability, and the apparent lack of social problems, of earlier, rural societies, then we have to be aware on the one hand that the problems are not usually made the subject of widespread discussion in the latter type of society. Although discussions of social problems may allow deviance and disorganisation to be publicised (consequently leading to the dissemination of models of deviance, taken up by other people) it serves as a focus for public opinion on these subjects. It is also arguable that the price of having a society in which a great number of benefits are offered to its members is, as a necessary corollary, an inevitable level of deviance and disorganisation. At least, as Saul Alinsky, the American community organiser, said: 'A problem is something you can do something about', and he went on to add, with reference to the work of all the organisers in cities: 'This has always been the prime task of the organiser —the transformation of the plight into the problem.'

Any attempt to do away with one social problem may well introduce others. As some of the problems associated with poverty have been dealt with so other problems have arisen. Several histories of social policy point to the change from the preoccupation with basic living conditions, poverty, housing and the environment in urban settings, to a series of others concerned with personal relationships, involving, for example, the family and work.

Protesters may be seen, leaving aside the strength or otherwise of their occasion for protesting, as people who are concerned about the preservation of values, and concerned with liberty and self-expression, which British society has underwritten. From this point of view they are upholders of important and relevant traditions. They may also be seen as people who feel the need to protest because of their place in society, such as, for instance, their relationship to the structure of authority, or their status anxieties which are reflected in extreme political standpoints, and as people who are concerned only to break down what exists rather than build something worthwhile out of the movements of social change.

The 'received ideas' of the past still circulate in some school text books, while where they do not, many people remember the conditioning that they received at school or early in life on these subjects and carry basic sets of attitudes with them throughout their lives. There are many ways in which these opinions may be moderated but it is these preconceptions which are often crucial in efforts to bring about, or prevent, changes. Many people have fairly simple views, for example, of the kinds of personality which are likely to commit crimes and the whole method of thinking about crimes of a large section of the population has little bearing on the realities. If you think that the criminal is a criminal because of his innate biological inheritance this will affect your views about reform and the relative importance of deterrence, punishment and rehabilitation. You can conclude that, to inhibit violence of the kind we are discussing in society, we need a much stronger police force, possibly equipped with heavier weapons, better trained and more mobile than our present one. Or you can argue at the other extreme that what is needed is a different climate of opinion in society which allows for the expression of dissent, and takes it into account, in ways that do not exist in the normal course of events at the present time.

What we try to undertake in this reader is a view of social problems which will relate to the opinions and the attitudes of many people who have not studied these subjects as academic disciplines but who have formed, through their experience as members of society, and the influences to which they have been subject, definite views about them.

When we ask: 'What should be done about social problems?' the answers must have some relation to the resources we can command. In Britain to concentrate upon the problems of one group to the exclusion of another would create many difficulties. Those staffing public services might wish for a more favourable ratio between the clients and themselves. In emphasising the threat that more crime and the more sophisticated methods used by criminals pose for the police, as presented in the Annual Reports of many Chief Constables or newspaper reports, the greater skills (and by implication higher levels of ability and rewards) and resources that are needed to keep the law effectively are also stressed. From the point of view of the organisation there are few limits to these kinds of expenditure. But questions arise here about the consequences that would arise from an enormous input of resources, and the extent to which, for example, much larger numbers of certain professional or quasi-professional groups might affect the character of British life and institutions.

There appear to be, within each group of experts or professionals, tendencies towards making their own contributions appear more important, emphasising the need for greater resources and maximising the sophistication and expertise that the practitioners require. It is worth remarking upon the alternatives that exist for us in the use of resources: for example, in the field of social welfare we can opt for either more money to clients to give them better standards of living, or more trained social workers to help them to adjust to their continuing lack of resources, or a combination of both. Opinions on the situation differ. Another example of a different view of a situation is to be found in the categorisation of certain people as 'scroungers', living—it is said—off the Welfare State and not taking jobs available to them. The political remedy was to appoint officials to investigate these scroungers and make sure they were not earning any money. The consequence may be that millions of pounds are spent on this, which may be greater than the 'cost' of the scroungers, or the costs which might subsequently be recouped. Thus, public attitudes (and the assumed disgust at scrounging) can help to determine the policies pursued, and also bring the resolution of what might seem to be a social problem no nearer, and indeed by heightening public feelings of hostility, make the situation of those who experience the problem worse than it is.

The danger of accepting the verdict of society, as expressed, about social problems is that there may be stigmatisation, or lack of knowledge, which create problems for the groups and oversimplify the issues. The interests of the members of the group have to be borne in mind, and defended, against any attempt to deal with them as objects or as morally inferior. Consensus of the many against the few, or of the powerful against the weak, may mean no more than that certain values are being challenged because they are vulnerable to attack, not that they are irrelevant. The changing structure of authority within the family, and the lessening of the father's importance from this point of view, can be viewed as a loosening of bonds which need to be preserved for the health of society, or as a welcome extension of autonomy and freedom for other members of the family.

3. Social Problems and Social Change

Before discussing social problems it is important to set them
against a background of the kind of society in which people in
Western Europe and other advanced countries of the world
are likely to live. The same social structure and culture, though
differential experience may be involved, provides both the basis
for conforming behaviour, which underwrites in a general way
the implicit purposes of society, and also deviant behaviour,
which threatens those purposes at different levels. As Merton
and Nisbet point out, 'The problems current in society reflect
the social costs of a particular organisation of social life.' The
interpretation that arises from this is that, as we indicated
earlier and must stress again, however society is organised,
patterns of deviance will arise within it.

In a society where there is rapid social change the problems
are likely to arise from this as much as from anything else. One
can distinguish between the problems of minimum provision, in
areas such as poverty and housing, and the problems of
behaviour, which arise from the pressures of our highly-
developed technology or from rejecting the values which appear
to underwrite it. Deviance may result from a whole complex of
experiences, but the forms it takes will reflect the structure of
society and its institutions more than anything else. The idea
that social problems can be regarded with reference to whether
people are 'good' or 'bad' is something that cannot be accepted.
Another range of social problems arise because the institutional
settings in which people live, whether at work or in their home
neighbourhoods, cannot provide a satisfactory way of life. In
particular the problems that arise from people living or being
held in organisations have to be seen against a broad canvas of
change and, in particular, against an awareness of the
differences which exist between the goals of the organisation
and how it in fact operates.

In prisons, hospitals, schools, factories and many other
places, organisational arrangements create tensions and
frustration which, even if they do not result in deviance, are
very much related to attitudes of mind which are negative and
frustrated.

First of all, social problems are primarily problems in
relationships between people. The problems that arise from a

sudden disaster, such as an earthquake or a fire, are not of themselves social problems, though they affect the community. In response to such an event, questions about the way in which help should be provided, and the shared feelings between all those involved, may make it a question of social relationships that can be harnessed to an amelioration or resolution of a problem that has thus become a social one.

The problem of slavery was not seen as a social one, although it could be regarded as a moral one. What turned it into a social problem was the desire for freedom for slaves which became a social movement. Was the social problem created out of the awareness of the slaves or out of the awareness of those others who wanted to do something about the position of slaves by securing their emancipation? We have examples of both responses in the approach to, and attack on, social problems. Where the recognition of the problem comes from a body of people other than those experiencing the problem, then the efforts to solve it can become an exercise in *paternalism*, by which the decisions about the campaign are all made with little reference to the group itself and how it sees the problems. Many groups of this kind are unable to create a feeling of group identity that would allow them to act on their own behalf. This was true of the slaves who lived in the old British colonies, including the United States, although examples of joint action and revolt can be found in other societies. However, many of the groups who suffered deprivation in the past were not organised to resolve their own problems. It was done for them, by philanthropists, who created a movement and an organisational structure, and gave it financial support.

One significant change in recent years, is the extent to which groups suffering from social deprivation, handicap or an adverse institutional structure, are prepared on a *self-help* basis to tackle their own problems. Of course, they may well still need help, and get it, from others, and the extent to which those who suffer from the incidence of social problems have come together to organise themselves, on anything other than a limited, crisis-oriented basis, is still limited. But this is the time of the self-help group in the social problem field: claimants and other welfare recipients, mothers' alone (widowed, divorced, unmarried mothers), squatters and many more.

It follows from what has been written that there is no once-for-all definition of a social problem. It is possible to make some distinctions; the social problems which arise from the way society is organised and the response made to that organisation include both those like poverty and unemployment, which are general in their incidence in particular groups, and those which, like crime and alcoholism, result in individual deviance. However, the distinctions may not be as clear as they seem : poverty may result from the way the money is spent more than from the amounts that are available.

There is another group of social problems which emerge from a highly-developed technology and which are likely to raise fundamental questions about the organisation, not only of our society, but also, eventually, of the use of world resources. These are the problems, such as pollution, of air, water and land, that could lead to the end of the world as we know it.

The decisions which bring about these problems, which initially may be technological or economic, but which need to be examined for their social consequences, are taken in large-scale organisations of one kind or another. The problem of radiation in the atmosphere arose largely from the decisions made by governments to test nuclear weapons. To find ways of influencing these decisions was difficult : the competition of consumer with consumer at the individual level, had its parallel in the competition of nations, concerned with their standing in the world, their self-interest and the requirements of national security.

Pollution was more acceptable in the past. The enormous amount of air pollution was more localised and therefore not apparent to many because it was concentrated in certain areas and because Britain had a much smaller and less mobile population. That problem was aggravated by a number of factors : in the first place, it was not possible to do anything about this level of pollution, except in minor ways. There was not the technology available to tackle it. The alternatives would have been either to carry on as they did, ignoring everything apart from the need to produce, or to stop these methods of production. Later, when some control and improvement became possible, the economic aspect prevented the implementation of these improvements : they were considered to be 'too expensive' for the producer. The social costs of pollution, the effects on plants and trees and the environment, on health and expectation of life, on levels of amenity and the dislocations and annoyances caused by fog and filth, were not adequately assessed. A passive 'always-was-always-will-be' attitude is often adopted by those causing the pollution, and it is reinforced very often by the government and other decision-making bodies who are influenced by the power or the economic importance of the polluters.

At every stage it is necessary to qualify the view that if the problems are made plain, then action on them will follow. The motives to act will be less strong if the problems concern the decision-makers in only a limited way. There are levels of self-interest which are always involved: the pollution of the air by industrial firms was paralleled by pollution from the smoke of coal-burning domestic heating systems, retained for reasons to do with sentiment and cost but not efficiency in heating or for that matter any abstract view of 'the common good'.

4. Stages

There are several stages in the process by which a plight becomes an issue and a problem, and attempts at solving it (or containing it) are made. All problems involve both personal, organisational and societal attitudes and values. Their consequences are far-reaching and cumulative. The man who is unemployed faces all kinds of difficulties because he has less money, not only on the level of personal or family consumption, but in his relationships within his own family and circle of acquaintances. He will feel less secure, and his role may have to be redefined if other members of his family continue to work.

There are economic difficulties if the man has hire-purchase commitments, and he may have to change his style of life quite dramatically, or, if he cannot, be involved with the law or constant bickerings with those who own what he was buying. The effects on his family will also be considerable. He may have been used to security. An increasing number of managers and administrators and professionals have become unemployed, and the adjustment required will be even greater than with workers more used to the experience.

Every social problem moves through a series of stages which will vary considerably in length and intensity. There are several ways of classifying these stages—a rather different one is suggested in Chapter 12—but all contain basically similar elements, and the reader is referred to suggestions for further reading for a wider range of views.

Firstly, there is the *awareness* of the problem. There is a growing consciousness on the part of some members of society, that a particular system of operating, or the plight of a certain group of people, is wrong, and that something can be done about it. The awareness of poverty as an evil that could be attacked, followed on from periods when it was assumed that poverty was an inevitable part of life and that, with the exception of the amelioration that could result from charity, it was to be accepted.

Often a small group of people come together and begin to plan for, say, a better distribution of resources to reduce the number of people living in poverty. Or it may be an individual who crusades for a particular group or cause. In starting out in these ways, those involved are doing no more and no less than questioning the moral fabric of society, often in ways which have approaches in common with those of the agitator. There is likely to be a perhaps unconscious awareness of the need for change in the approach which will lead to the identification of a social problem. Attitudes towards it will be governed in part by views on how far anything can be done about it.

What happens in the next stage is that there is a sharpening of objectives and the beginnings of *organising*. More people are involved in not only identifying the social problems, but also in thinking of ways in which they may be alleviated. This stage will involve, in an ideal-type way, a creation of a structure and supports for the embryonic organisation and the consideration of different kinds of strategies. From this group morale improves and is directed towards the objectives that the group sets itself in the stage of *policy making*.

From the morale and the character of the objectives their grows up a unity of purpose and an *ideology*, at the fourth stage, which consists of statements about what is necessary, and the assumptions from which the group moves, and, developing gradually, a body of writing or speaking or action which condemns the existing state of affairs which the group wishes to replace. It may have a doctrine to protect itself and to justify itself, and a body of belief which deals with the policies that ought to be pursued and possibly also with the kind of tactics which should be adopted and the practical organisation of the movement.

Although many social problems develop at very different rates the stages through which they go will tend to have these elements present. Although some groups and movements will remain extremely small, for reasons which have to do with the problems that they are involved with or very limited resources, others are capable of much greater expansion and may become social movements. It could be argued, for example, that the campaign for nuclear disarmament is a good example of what was basically a social movement which came into being to oppose nuclear warfare because of the complex of social and other problems that could arise.

To define a social problem, then, is to see it in its particular context, to be aware that it will pass through various stages in coming to the attention of those who can do something about it, and to recognise that it is social in its origins, social in its definitions and social in its treatment. It has been defined by Horton and Leslie as 'a condition affecting a significant number of people in ways considered undesirable, and about which it is felt something can be done through collective social action'.

What is a social problem in one society may not be so in another. Religious intolerance may be unacceptable in an advanced industrial society as a basis for either government or social arrangements, although it is to be found in Northern Ireland—and elsewhere—but in the sixteenth century, when prevailing values required not the desire for tolerance but the suppression of dissent, it was not a problem. There are many problems for which combined action will have little relevance, since they are outside the scope of human organisation, but there are many others in which the recognition that something can be done is more important than the identification of the facts.

There is some general agreement, as we noted at the beginning of this chapter, about what social problems are, although judgements may be made according to one's predispositions. Poverty may be taken to be good for the soul by those who are never likely to be poor. A good dose of unemployment is sometimes taken to be good for people in the sense that it encourages those whose jobs might be in danger to work that much harder. There are areas like, for example, cigarette smoking, or the smoking of soft drugs, in which there is no clear indication of whether these are social problems or not, although they are the subject, in some cases, either of restrictions on sale or of legal provisions. The agreement on social problems is never complete and there are enormous differences in the priority that people give to them.

Those who view social problems in an historical way may assume that they are caused by immutable 'natural laws' which invariably apply to society. In fact they argue that with certain social arrangements, certain outcomes are likely and this is largely under human control. This complacent assumption is often the product of *a priori* reasoning rather than of objective enquiry. Social problems are certainly not to be viewed as abnormal. It is misleading to discuss, for example, mental illness or alcoholism or drug addiction without reference to the kind of society in which it takes place. Social problems are not concerned with making moral judgements about the behaviour of people. For example, there are different ways of looking at high divorce rates. Usually they are described as a symptom of social breakdown whereas they may be more accurately seen, at least in part, as an expression of the high value which is placed on happiness within marriage by those involved in the 'problem behaviour'.

It has been said that the average person's study of social problems is a search for the villain, who may be identified and then (in theory) overcome. Whether people are viewed as autonomous and capable of making decisions about their own lives, in which case it is assumed that they make deliberate choices to be bad, or whether their lives are so circumscribed by the conditions in which they live that their conduct is a creation of these conditions, and viewed, therefore, more as a symptom rather than a cause of social problems, is a matter of considerable importance.

The habit of talking about social problems in simple terms and assuming that they always affect *other* people is a characteristic of some groups in society. If we talk about these problems then we may be held responsible for creating them because, for example, the ignorant or the irresponsible may be impelled to act because of the information we give them. Several years ago this was a fairly common way of looking at the problems of race and community relations in Britain. It was assumed that if nothing much was said or done about them then eventually they would sort themselves out. This may in fact apply in some cases, and it is an open question how far an intensive discussion of, say, drug-taking is likely to resolve problems about it or bring it to the attention of a wider group of people. In all these problems there may be present a kind of self-fulfilling prophecy, which, in talking about them, draws lines of battle and causes people to commit themselves to one side or the other. How far a strong public opinion is really going to affect the way in which a social problem is tackled is problematical. There is strong public opinion about some kinds of crime, particularly crimes of violence, but if the solutions which that group proposed were implemented it is unlikely that they would have very much effect on the pattern of violent crime either now or in the future. If tension arises within the field of race relations then it may provide the occasion for outbursts and potential confrontation in conditions where this might not otherwise have happened. At the same time more and more people are becoming aware of the ways in which minority groups are living and the issues that relate to them and this, too, may well be the occasion of action by them.

It is difficult to disentangle all these elements in any given social problem. But we must try to be clear about the extent of the problem and the issues which arise from it. Just as there are no 'goodies' and 'baddies' in all this so it is illusory to believe that everyone would necessarily like to see the problem solved. There are enormous investments in slum housing and it is only when these can be realised with an even higher rate of return that many of those who own these properties are prepared to have them knocked down and replaced by other housing or office development. In Britain, there was nothing like the enormous growth in criminal involvement in gambling, drinking and vice which arose in the United States largely in consequence of prohibition from 1919–33, but at the same time vested interests exist which cater for these matters. Others would argue that gambling in moderation is an acceptable human activity which adds interest and excitement and provides just as great a return as many other forms of expenditure. All is not morally clear and self-evident by any means and social problems range from those which by the values of society are morally neutral to those which are morally undesirable. To say this is not to assume that all are agreed on how these should be judged. Indeed it is no part of the task of the sociologist to make these judgements but only to look at them in relation to values held in society.

The rate of change in views on social problems may be extremely rapid. Just over ten years ago the agitation for the reform of the laws relating to homosexuality brought about great controversies about whether homosexuality between consenting adults in private should be legalised. Now, with this having been achieved, the Gay Liberation Front appears to be suggesting that homosexual activity is as natural as heterosexual activity. To accept this has at the least enormous implications for family life and behaviour in the future.

Again many would argue that violence has increased alarmingly in recent years. Some suggest that it is only a matter of time before the present level in America is reached here. In the United States one American is murdered every 39 minutes; one forcibly raped every 17 minutes; one subject to aggravated assault every 2 minutes and one robbed every 2 minutes. So far in Britain the rate, as recorded, is much lower even when allowance is made for the smaller size of our population, at about a quarter of that of the United States.

If we add to the daily violence those which arise from group conflicts the picture worsens substantially. The levels of violence in Ulster are high at the moment and could get higher; the end result of such escalation can always be the destruction of the existing way in which society is organised.

5. Perspectives

Even though this reader does not contain examples of all the possible sociological perspectives on social problems, which is in part a consequence of the relative lack of interest that has been shown in Britain to many of them, it is appropriate to provide a brief note of what they are. Reference has already been made to the relevance of social change to them.

Social Disorganisation starts from the assumption that a society is more than a mere aggregate of relationships; indeed, the way in which these relationships between individuals and groups is ordered is a key to the functioning of that society. When the accepted relationships break down, or where there is growing conflict between these relationships and expectations arising from them, we have a situation of social disorganisation. If the social system is assumed to be in a state of dynamic equilibrium then the changes which upset this equilibrium, economic, cultural, demographic or whatever, are responsible.

Actual social problems, for example family disorganisation or crime, contain components relevant to a social disorganisation perspective but others relevant, for example, to deviant behaviour (which is discussed later). Any perspective abstracts elements in the social problem relevant to it but leaves others out of account.

A useful definition of social disorganisation is provided by Merton: social disorganisation 'refers to inadequacies or failures in a social system of interrelated statuses and roles such that the collective purposes and individual objectives of its members are less fully realised than they could be in an alternative workable system.' This amounts to a technical judgement of the workings of the social system. The perspective is a particularly relevant one when considering what are conventional standards and expectations. Although sociologists use the perspective widely, there is a dearth of rigorous and valid measures of social disorganisation. The kinds of themes that are covered under this heading in books on social problems include: race and minority group relations, family disorganisation, community disorganisation, work and in particular changes in the pattern of work, poverty and political unrest.

Social pathology has some links with ideas involved in *social disorganisation*. It depends broadly on the application of an organic concept to social problems; that is, looking at society in a biological sense and likening social processes to bodily functioning. Thus, concepts of health and sickness could be applied, in this approach, to societies as much as to people. The categorisation of individuals as defective or delinquent gives a strong moralistic and judgemental flavour to the writings of some of the exponents of the perspective. In the end it seems, as Rubington and Weinberg point out, that 'a social problem for social pathologists is a violation of *moral* expectations'.

It was assumed that individual defects were likely to be transmitted by inheritance, although some writers saw the relevance and importance of the social environment in which the individual was brought up. The school of thought within the perspective which stressed the part played by heredity in the causation of social problems looked to the development of policies to make sure, through eugenics, that the weak and the genetically inferior did not perpetuate themselves. Another school of thought, generally writing more recently, has a markedly different emphasis. These have taken the view that individuals are born good but are corrupted by society and its institutions in a way that recalls some of the philosophers of the Enlightenment in the Eighteenth Century.

The approach to social problems from this perspective is to attempt to change the individuals so that these in turn can change the institutions over time. The model of society which is implicit is one which looks at small integrated groups and communities with favour and finds the sources of many present discontents in the assumed anonymity, the heterogeneity, mobility and other characteristics of big city life.

The perspective which looks at social problems as arising from *value conflicts* is an important one with a strongly developed tradition of writers, including Marx, who share the general standpoint that conflicts of different kinds stimulate social change and the reorganisation or reformulation of the social structure. Conflict in values and roles are seen, for example, when groups are campaigning for changes in laws which disadvantage them or in the methods by which the law is administered.

Fuller and Myers, two American sociologists writing a generation ago (whose work is also referred to on page 419), put forward the view that conflicts of values were a part of all social problems. Groups are in opposition to each other in society, and this occurs because of the different systems of value to which they subscribe. These are three kinds of problems discussed by these authors in one of their most important articles. The first, the *physical* problem, is a condition seen as a threat, as in their most dramatic manifestations in earthquakes and hurricanes. It is not of itself a social problem, though its effects will involve social consequences and value conflicts about the policies to be pursued.

The second problem, the *ameliorative* one, is truly 'social' in the sense that it is a man-made condition: 'By this we mean that value-judgements not only help to create the condition, but to prevent its solution. In the case of crime, certain moral judgements of our culture are to a large extent responsible for the criminal act in the first place. To the degree that our mores of conspicuous consumption enter into the motivation of crimes for pecuniary gain, there is a cultural responsibility for such criminal acts. Or again, traditional prison policies based on our belief in severity of punishment may become part of the causal pattern of further criminal behaviour in the prisoner after his liberation. These same cherished notions of retribution in punishment of criminals operate to dissuade legislatures from adequately financing probation and parole systems, juvenile delinquency clinics, and the schools for problem children.'

The third problem is the *moral* one where there is no consensus that the condition is undesirable. This represents a confusion in values and a consequent moral conflict. It can be the conflict between the values to which people subscribe and their self-interest. 'Hence, though all "right-thinking" people regard such conditions as crime, insanity, and disease as bad, there are interest groups openly defending and perpetuating the conditions classified as moral problems.'

The final perspective is that of *deviant behaviour*. The cause of deviant behaviour is the learning of models for it where the conventional moral order (the fabric of beliefs and values subscribed to by the society as a whole) is less relevant and where the opportunities for learning about it are more limited. Children brought up in 'delinquent neighbourhoods' tend therefore to be delinquent because of the character of the sub-culture to which they belong. The extent of deviant behaviour has a considerable bearing, according to this perspective, on the structure of opportunity within society, and where opportunity is limited. In Merton's words: 'Social structures exert a definite pressure upon certain persons in the society to engage in nonconforming rather than conforming conduct'. He sought to explain crime, delinquency, alcoholism, drug addiction and many other social problems in these terms. Far from the individual being 'sick' he sought to show that forms of deviant behaviour, from a psychological point of view, were as normal as conformist behaviour.

Recently another orientation to deviant behaviour has emerged which is generally known as *labelling theory*. The assumption here is well expressed by Howard Becker when he writes 'Social groups create deviance by making the rules whose infraction constitutes deviance, and by applying those rules to particular people and labelling them as outsiders. From this point of view, deviance is *not* a quality of the act the person commits, but rather a consequence of the application by others of rules and sanctions to an offender. The deviant is one to whom that label has successfully been applied; deviant behaviour is behaviour that people so label.'

The position of the labeller is that his negative label must be accepted by others. Stigmatisation as deviant, with the range of stereotyped attributes and rigid expectations about behaviour that go along with it, assists the labeller in his handling of those he labels and limits the life chances of the 'deviant' which are controlled by those who know about his 'misdeeds'. Lemert deals with the question of secondary deviation in a reading in Chapter 12. It can be profitable at times for the individual to label himself and thus gain some control over his relationship with others. With more knowledge and tolerance there is less likely to be labelling: so the labelling theorists believe.

As a fitting preamble to the specific material on social problems we offer, at the end of this chapter, a reading, trenchant and compelling, which links the study of social problems as we conceive them with the exercise of what Wright Mills calls 'the sociological imagination' and a long and honourable tradition of the study of society.

The Sociological Imagination
C. Wright Mills

Perhaps the most fruitful distinction with which the sociological imagination works is between 'the personal troubles of milieu' and 'the public issues of social structure'. This distinction is an essential tool of the sociological imagination and a feature of all classic work in social science.

Troubles occur within the character of the individual and within the range of his immediate relations with others; they have to do with his self and with those limited areas of social life of which he is directly and personally aware. Accordingly, the statement and the resolution of troubles properly lie within the individual as a biographical entity and within the scope of his immediate milieu—the social setting that is directly open to his personal experience and to some extent his willful activity. A trouble is a private matter: values cherished by an individual are felt by him to be threatened.

Issues have to do with matters that transcend these local environments of the individual and the range of his inner life. They have to do with the organization of many such milieux into the institutions of an historical society as a whole, with the ways in which various milieux overlap and interpenetrate to form the larger structure of social and historical life. An issue is a public matter: some value cherished by the public is felt to be threatened. Often there is a debate about what that value really is and about what it is that really threatens it. This debate is often without focus if only because it is the very nature of an issue, unlike even widespread trouble, that it cannot very well be defined in terms of the immediate and everyday environments of ordinary men. An issue, in fact, often involves a crisis in institutional arrangements, and often too it involves what Marxists call 'contradictions' or 'antagonisms'.

In these terms, consider unemployment. When, in a city of 100,000, only one man is unemployed, that is his personal trouble, and for its relief we properly look to the character of the man, his skills, and his immediate opportunities. But when in a nation of 50 million employees, 15 million men are unemployed, that is an issue, and we may not hope to find its solution within the range of opportunities open to any one individual. The very structure of opportunities has collapsed. Both the correct statement of the problem and the range of possible solutions require us to consider the economic and political institutions of the society, and not merely the personal situation and character of a scatter of individuals.

Consider war. The personal problem of war, when it occurs, may be how to survive it or how to die in it with honour; how to make money out of it; how to climb into the higher safety of the military apparatus; or how to contribute to the war's termination. In short, according to one's values, to find a set of milieux and within it to survive the war or make one's death in it meaningful. But the structural issues of war have to do with its causes; with what types of men it throws up into command; with its effects upon economic and political, family and religious institutions, with the unorganized irresponsibility of a world of nation-states.

Consider marriage. Inside a marriage a man and a woman may experience personal troubles, but when the divorce rate during the first four years of marriage is 250 out of every 1,000 attempts, this is an indication of a structural issue having to do with the institutions of marriage and the family and other institutions that bear upon them.

Or consider the metropolis—the horrible, beautiful, ugly, magnificent sprawl of the great city. For many upper-class people, the personal solution to 'the problem of the city' is to have an apartment with private garage under it in the heart of the city, and forty miles out, a house by Henry Hill, garden by Garrett Eckbo, on a hundred acres of private land. In these two controlled environments—with a small staff at each end and a private helicopter connection—most people could solve many of the problems of personal milieux caused by the facts of the city. But all this, however splendid, does not solve the public issues that the structural fact of the city poses. What should be done with this wonderful monstrosity? Break it all up into scattered units, combining residence and work? Refurbish it as it stands? Or, after evacuation, dynamite it and build new cities according to new plans in new places? What should those plans be? And who is to decide and to accomplish whatever choice is made? These are structural issues; to confront them and to solve them requires us to consider political and economic issues that affect innumerable milieux.

In so far as an economy is so arranged that slumps occur, the problem of unemployment becomes incapable of personal solution. In so far as war is inherent in the nation-state system and in the uneven industrialization of the world, the ordinary individual in his restricted milieu will be powerless—with or without psychiatric aid—to solve the troubles this system or lack of system imposes upon him. In so far as the family as an institution turns women into darling little slaves and men into their chief providers and unweaned dependents, the problem of a satisfactory marriage remains incapable of purely private solution. In so far as the overdeveloped megalopolis and the overdeveloped automobile are built-in features of the overdeveloped society, the issues of urban living will not be solved by personal ingenuity and private wealth.

What we experience in various and specific milieux, I have noted, is often caused by structural changes. Accordingly, to understand the changes of many personal milieux we are required to look beyond them. And the number and variety of such structural changes increase as the institutions within which we live become more embracing and more intricately connected with one another. To be aware of the idea of social structure and to use it with sensibility is to be capable of tracing such linkages among a great variety of milieux. To be able to do that is to possess the sociological imagination.

Further Reading: **The Study of Social Problems**

H. S. BECKER, *Outsiders: Studies in the Sociology of Deviance*, New York, Free Press of Glencoe, 1963.

R. C. FULLER and R. R. MYERS, *Some aspects of a theory of Social Problems*, American Sociological Review. February, 1941.

R. C. FULLER and R. R. MYERS, *The Natural History of a Social Problem*, American Sociological Review, June, 1941.

H. D. GRAHAM and T. D. GURR, Eds., *The History of Violence in America*, A Report, New York, Bantam Books, 1969.

C. F. G. MASTERMAN, *The Condition of England*, London, Methuen, 1909.

J. B. MAYS, *Sociology and Social Problems*, in J. D. HALLORAN and Joan BROTHERS, Eds., *Uses of Sociology*, London, Sheed and Ward, 1968.

PETER I. ROSE, *The Study of Society: An Integrated Anthology*, quoted in Peter BERGER, *Invitation to Sociology*, London, Penguin Books, 1967.

NEIL J. SMELSER, Ed., *Sociology: An Introduction*, New York, Wiley & Sons, 1967.

Chapter Two
Population and the Environment

While you read the last page the population of the world grew by twenty people. Is this a problem? It depends of course, not only on how many people, but on where they are located and what kind of people they are. Whether population growth itself constitutes a problem depends on something else as well—how many resources there are to feed them, to clothe them, to house them, to provide jobs for them. Malthus, the eighteenth-century demographer, posed the problem thus: he argued that population tended to increase in geometric terms, while the supply of food increased in an additive way. Each increase of population then provided a basis for a further multiplicative increase, whereas each increase of the food supply only added in a limited way to the existing situation. At any given time, argued Malthus, the total size of the world population is limited ultimately by the total food supply though the food supply of course is only *one* of the limiting factors which constrain the rate of growth of the population. When the population increases too fast for the supply of food two types of restraint come into operation. The first is the positive checks. These are war, disease and famine. These positive checks operate to reduce the population through the taking of human life. Throughout history these in fact have been the principal factors that have kept the rate of population increase down. The preventive checks operate by reducing the birth rate rather than by removing individuals from the population equation. Preventive checks are a matter of individual decision, positive checks are a matter of social decisions as result from a natural disaster. Malthus argued that the preventive check that was most likely to be efficacious would be to delay marriage.

While the Malthusian theory has come to be somewhat discredited over the last hundred years on the ground that the experience of the developed countries of Western Europe and the United States has invalidated Malthus' prediction, his thesis seems to have a great deal more plausibility when applied to the world at large. For in much of the world the population exists at a minimum level, barely staying alive and subject to a large number of possible positive checks. The recent tragedies of Bangladesh, Biafra and the Amazonian Indians indicate that it is simply not possible to argue that there is some inevitable law of nature which prevents whole societies being wiped out. Whole societies *can* be wiped out and have been during recent history.

But, it may be argued, if the population crisis represents a problem for the world as a whole, what relevance does this have for us in Britain? The experience of the recent past indicates that the relation between population size and the supply of food has been and remains a favourable one. There appears no limit to the rate at which the natural resources in which Britain apparently abounds may be exploited. Do we not inhabit an island in the middle of a sea teeming with life, teeming with food, teeming even with oil and gas-rich shale? If it is the case that the south and east of Britain are relatively over-populated, is there not the whole of the rest of the British Isles, and in particular the highlands and islands of Scotland, where overpopulation is very far from being a problem?

However, a problem there is and it is a problem not simply of the relation of population growth to changes in supply of food; the problem is a multi-variate one. We have to consider, not merely the absolute size of a population at a particular point in time, but its rate of increase or decrease, the natural and technological and cognitive resources that are available to that population, the standard of living that members of that society wish to attain and the possibility of operating on the natural environment in order to produce a desired state of affairs. Over the past hundred years, Britain's role in the world has changed and with it her position in the kind of equation we are considering. Where formerly the Commonwealth and Empire provided an apparently limitless granary, orchard and stock-range from which to fill Britain's domestic larder, the prospect for the next few decades is one of reliance more or less upon the quantity and kind of food which can be produced by ourselves or by countries like us. To the extent to which countries which are currently underdeveloped increase their productive capacity, so their standard of living will increase and so will their demand to retain a greater share of the surplus food which is currently exported to countries like ourselves. But it is to be anticipated that the standard of living in this country will rise as well. The net result—unless more and more intensive methods of cropping the earth's surface without reducing natural resources in any absolute sense are discovered —is one of an increasing pressure on world food supplies.

Let us take the British ocean teeming with British fish as an example. Already we are engaged in serious and protracted disputes with some of our neighbours over the rights to fish certain areas of ocean. Already there are serious doubts about the capacity of oceanic fish stocks to survive the consistent over-fishing and extraction of young fish and fish in the crucial stages of the reproductive cycle by some nations.

The 'Blueprint for Survival' represents not so much an analysis but rather a justification for a particular type of political programme. It is therefore on a somewhat different plane from some of the other readings in this volume. None the less, it constitutes a radical and coherent critique of many assumptions, which are commonly taken for granted, not merely or perhaps not especially by sociologists, but which according to the authors of the Blueprint constitute in themselves the origins of some of the most profound problems facing British society. The authors identify as chief sources of the problems facing western society the growth of consumption coupled with the increase in the size of the population. These have in the past been regarded as the essential bases of prosperity itself. While natural resources in the earth are in finite supply they cannot adjust to an indefinite increase in demand such as is implied by the simultaneous uncontrolled expansion and economic growth of developed and underdeveloped nations. Moreover, uncontrolled growth and, in particular, growth which is managed in the interests of only one species—man—may threaten the very viability of the complex web of inter-dependencies between many species and the environment on which all life depends. The social implications of this analysis are considerable, but some sociologists will disagree with the rather simplistic accounts of the origin of crime, urban pollution and the decline of community that are implied in this account.

Ehrlich and Freedman examine the suggestion that population density has a direct effect in creating social problem conditions. Their conclusions are moderately positive. They argue that cities serve some functions extremely well and that there is no simple answer to the question of whether density on its own is a good or bad influence on social behaviour. This kind of agnosticism about specific consequences of what we can in general terms call 'environmental pollution' is a useful antidote to some of the more scarifying literature.

Aldous examines the problem of industrial pollution in Britain. The increase in the scale of this problem in recent years is not commonly recognised, but such is the power of modern technological innovation to outstrip the capacity of basic scientific knowledge to control it, that it is now possible for an accidental discharge of a few milligrams of a chemical compound to put the whole of a vast sewage plant out of action for days. And what is at stake in the field of water pollution is not the accidental contamination of some isolated pond or lake, but the possibility that all the surface and underground sources of water in a region may be rendered sterile. The 'death of life' on this scale is almost incomprehensible to the layman and no one seems to have evolved a coherent strategy for presenting in a meaningful fashion to the public the appropriate choices which society must make.

Even if Malthus' equation is the wrong one, it is indisputably true that *some* equation links population, the state of technology, natural resources and societal expectations together. The limiting factor is the level of resources. If resources are consumed at a level which precludes their replacement, the standard of living of the population in question cannot continue to rise. It may be argued that human technology has always in the past apparently risen to meet the challenge but this is not so. History is full of instances of population explosions being followed by population implosions —a catastrophic fall in population due to natural disaster or more commonly to war, starvation or pestilence. Moreover, western society has introduced a new dynamic element into the equation. This is the expectation that things *must* inevitably continue to improve. At its crudest this is summed up in the nostrum beloved of both major political parties in Britain that the 'real' solution of our political problems and our economic problems is economic growth. But growth, as we have seen, has problems of its own.

There seems no doubt that the *technical* problems of preventing a population implosion are not insoluble. A society which is capable of putting men on the moon or transplanting hearts from one individual to another, or keeping people alive for twenty years on a kidney machine, need not be terrified by the technical problems involved. The problems of practical action and decision are far greater. The story is told of a

Calvinist Scots minister who addressed his flock one Sunday
morning in the following terms: 'I see you all, sinners, thieves,
fornicators, adulterers. But God is not mocked. And when the
great day of judgement comes and He sits upon his throne you
will get down on your knees before Him and you will cry "Oh,
Lord, forgive us, forgive us for our sins for we did no' ken,
we did no' ken." And the Lord will look down upon you,
and the light of His countenance will shine down on you and
out of His infinite wisdom and His infinite mercy He will smile
upon you and He will say "Ah weel, ye ken noo'"'.'

As Malthus gave a warning in the early years of the
nineteenth century, it might seem to future generations a little
implausible to claim that 'we did no' ken'.

We have not attempted in this chapter to provide basic
information about the size of the population, birth and death
rates, in/out migration of the regional distribution of
population. Such information is readily available in other
books, of which perhaps the clearest for the student is *Britain
in Figures* by Alan Sillitoe, published by Penguin. *Social
Trends*, published by HMSO, is also useful.

Blueprint for Survival

Reprinted with permission from *The Ecologist*, Vol. 2, No. 1, January 1972, pp. 2–6.

The need for change

The principal defect of the industrial way of life with its ethos of expansion is that it is not sustainable. Its termination within the lifetime of someone born today is inevitable—unless it continues to be sustained for a while longer by an entrenched minority at the cost of imposing great suffering on the rest of mankind. We can be certain, however, that sooner or later it will end (only the precise time and circumstances are in doubt), and that it will do so in one of two ways: either against our will, in a succession of famines, epidemics, social crises and wars; or because we want it to—because we wish to create a society which will not impose hardship and cruelty upon our children—in a succession of thoughtful, humane and measured changes.

Radical change is both necessary and inevitable because the present increases in human numbers and *per capita* consumption, by disrupting ecosystems and depleting resources, are undermining the very foundations of survival. At present the world population of 3,600 million is increasing by 2 per cent per year (72 million), but this overall figure conceals crucially important differences between countries. The industrialised countries with one-third of the world population have annual growth rates of between 0.5 and 1.0 per cent; the undeveloped countries on the other hand, with two-thirds of the world population, have annual growth rates of between 2 and 3 per cent, and from 40 to 45 per cent of their populations is under 15. It is commonly overlooked that in countries with an unbalanced age structure of this kind the population will continue to increase for many years even after fertility has fallen to the replacement level. As the Population Council has pointed out: 'If replacement is achieved in the developed world by 2000 and in the developing world by 2040, then the world's population will stabilise at nearly 15.5 billion (15,500 million) about a century hence, or well over four times the present size.'

The *per capita* use of energy and raw materials also shows a sharp division between the developed and the undeveloped parts of the world. Both are increasing their use of these commodities, but consumption in the developed countries is so much higher that, even with their smaller share of the population, their consumption may well represent over 80 per cent of the world total. For the same reason, similar percentage increases are far more significant in the developed countries; to take one example, between 1957 and 1967 *per capita* steel consumption rose by 12 per cent in the US and by 41 per cent in India, but the actual increases (in kg per year) were from 568 to 634 and from 9.2 to 13 respectively. Nor is there any sign that an eventual end to economic growth is envisaged, and indeed industrial economies appear to break down if growth ceases or even slows, however high the absolute level of consumption. Even the US still aims at an annual growth of GNP of 4 per cent or more. Within this overall figure much higher growth rates occur for the use of particular resources, such as oil.

The combination of human numbers and *per capita* consumption has a considerable impact on the environment, in terms of both the resources we take from it and the pollutants we impose on it. A distinguished group of scientists, who came together for a 'Study of Critical Environmental Problems' (SCEP) under the auspices of the Massachusetts Institute of Technology, state in their report the clear need for a means of measuring this impact, and have coined the term 'ecological demand', which they define as 'a summation of all man's demands on the environment, such as the extraction of resources and the return of wastes'. Gross Domestic Product (GDP), which is population multiplied by material standard of living appears to provide the most convenient measure of ecological demand, and according to the UN *Statistical Yearbook* this is increasing annually by 5 to 6 per cent, or doubling every 13.5 years. If this trend should continue, then in the time taken for world population to double (which is estimated to be by just after the year 2000), total ecological demand will have increased by a factor of six. SCEP estimate that 'such demand-producing activities as agriculture, mining and industry have global annual rates of increase of 3.5 per cent and 7 per cent respectively. An integrated rate of increase is estimated to be between 5 and 6 per cent per year, in comparison with an annual rate of population increase of only 2 per cent.'

It should go without saying that the world cannot accom-moderate this continued increase in ecological demand. *In-definite* growth of whatever type cannot be sustained by *finite* resources. This is the nub of the environmental predicament. It is still less possible to maintain indefinite *exponential* growth— and unfortunately the growth of ecological demand is proceed-ing exponentially (i.e. it is increasing geometrically, by com-pound interest).

The implications of exponential growth are not generally appreciated and are well worth considering. As Professor For-rester explains it, '... pure exponential growth possesses the characteristic of behaving according to a "doubling time". Each fixed time interval shows a doubling of the relevant system variable. Exponential growth is treacherous and mis-leading. A system variable can continue through many doub-ling intervals without seeming to reach significant size. But then in one or two more doubling periods, still following the same law of exponential growth, it suddenly seems to become overwhelming.'

Thus, supposing world petroleum reserves stood at 2,100 billion barrels, and supposing our rate of consumption was increasing by 6.9 per cent per year, then demand will exceed supply by the end of the century. What is significant, however, is not the speed at which such vast reserves can be depleted, but that as late as 1975 there will appear to be reserves fully ample enough to last for considerably longer. Such a situation can easily lull one into a false sense of security and the belief that a given growth rate can be sustained, if not indefinitely, at least for a good deal longer than is actually the case. The same basic logic applies to the availability of any resources including land, and it is largely because of this particular dynamic of exponential growth that the environmental predicament has come upon us so suddenly, and why its solution requires urgent and radical measures, many of which run counter to values which, in our industrial society we have been taught to regard as fundamental.

If we allow the present growth rate to persist, total ecologi-cal demand will increase by a factor of 32 over the next 66 years—and there can be no serious person today willing to concede the possibility, or indeed the desirability, of our accommodating the pressures arising from such growth. For this can be done only at the cost of disrupting ecosystems and exhausting resources, which must lead to the failure of food supplies and the collapse of society. It is worth briefly considering each in turn.

We depend for our survival on the predictability of ecological processes. If they were at all arbitrary, we would not know when to reap or sow, and we would be at the mercy of environmental whim. We could learn nothing about the rest of nature, advance no hypotheses, suggest no 'laws'. Fortunately, ecological processes *are* predictable, and although theirs is a relatively young discipline, ecologists have been able to formulate a number of important 'laws', one of which in particular relates to environmental predictability: namely, that all ecosystems tend towards stability, and further that the more diverse and complex the ecosystem the more stable it is; that is, the more species there are, and the more they interrelate, the more stable is their environment. By stability is meant the ability to return to the original position after any change, instead of being forced into a totally different pattern—and hence predictability.

Unfortunately, we behave as if we knew nothing of the environment and had no conception of its predictability, treating it instead with scant and brutal regard as if it were an idiosyncratic and extremely stupid slave. We seem never to have reflected on the fact that a tropical rain forest supports innumerable insect species and yet is never devastated by them; that its rampant luxuriance is not contingent on our overflying it once a month and bombarding it with insecticides, herbicides, fungicides and what-have-you. And yet we tremble over our wheatfields and cabbage patches with a desperate battery of synthetic chemicals, in an absurd attempt to impede the operation of the immutable 'law' we have just mentioned—that all ecosystems tend towards stability, therefore diversity and complexity, therefore a growing number of different plant and animal species until a climax or optimal condition is achieved. If we were clever, we would recognise that successful long-term agriculture demands the achievement of an artificial climax, an imitation of the pre-existing ecosystem, so that the level of unwanted species could be controlled by those that did no harm to the crop-plants.

Instead we have put our money on pesticides, which although they have been effective, have been so only to a limited and now diminishing extent: according to SCEP, the 34 per cent increase in world food production from 1951 to 1966 required increased investments in nitrogenous fertilisers of 146 per cent and in pesticides of 300 per cent. At the same time they have created a number of serious problems, notably resistance—some 250 pest species are resistant to one group of pesticides or another, while many others require increased applications to keep their populations within manageable proportions—and the promotion of formerly innocuous species to pest proportions, because the predators that formerly kept them down have been destroyed. The spread of DDT and other organochlorines in the environment has resulted in alarming population declines among woodcock, grebes, various birds of prey and seabirds, and in a number of fish species, principally the sea trout. SCEP comments: 'the oceans are an ultimate accumulation site of DDT and its residues. As much as 25 per cent of the DDT compounds produced to date may have been transferred to the sea. The amount in the marine biota is estimated to be in the order of less than 0.1 per cent of total production and has already produced a demonstrable impact upon the marine environment ... The decline in productivity of marine food fish and the accumulation of levels of DDT in their tissues which are unacceptable to man can only be accelerated by DDT's continued release to the environment...'

There are half a million man-made chemicals in use today, yet we cannot predict the behaviour or properties of the greater part of them (either singly or in combination) once they are released into the environment. We know, however, that the combined effects of pollution and habitat destruction menace the survival of no less than 280 mammal, 350 bird, and 20,000 plant species. To those who regret these losses but greet them with the comment that the survival of *Homo sapiens* is surely more important than that of an eagle or a primrose, we repeat that *Homo sapiens* himself depends on the continued resilience of those ecological networks of which eagles and primroses are integral parts. We do not need to utterly destroy the ecosphere to bring catastrophe upon ourselves: all we have to do is to carry on as we are, clearing forests, 'reclaiming' wetlands and imposing sufficient quantities of pesticides, radioactive materials, plastics, sewage, and industrial wastes upon our air, water and land systems to make them inhospitable to the species on which their continued stability and integrity depend. Industrial man in the world today is like a bull in a china shop, with the single difference that a bull with half the information about the properties of china as we have about those of ecosystems would probably try and adapt its behaviour to its environment rather than the reverse. By contrast, *Homo sapiens industrialis* is determined that the china shop should adapt to him, and has therefore set himself the goal of reducing it to rubble in the shortest possible time.

Failure of food supplies

Increases in food production in the undeveloped world have barely kept abreast of population growth. Such increases as there have been are due not to higher productivity but to the opening up of new land for cultivation. Unfortunately this will not be possible for much longer: all the good land in the world is now being farmed, and according to the FAO, at present rates of expansion none of the marginal land that is left will be unfarmed by 1985—indeed some of the land now under cultivation has been so exhausted that it will have to be returned to permanent pasture.

For this reason, FAO's programme to feed the world depends on a programme of intensification, at the heart of which are the new high-yield varieties of wheat and rice. These are highly responsive to inorganic fertilisers and quick-maturing, so that up to ten times present yields can be obtained from them. Unfortunately they are highly vulnerable to disease, and therefore require increased protection by pesticides, and of course they demand massive inputs of fertilisers (up to 27 times present ones). Not only will these disrupt local ecosystems, thereby jeopardising long-term productivity, but they force hard-pressed undeveloped nations to rely on the agrochemical industries of the developed world.

Whatever their virtues and faults, the new genetic hybrids are not intended to solve the world food problem, but only to give us time to devise more permanent and realistic solutions. It is our view, however, that these hybrids are not the best means of doing this, since their use is likely to bring about a reduction in overall diversity, when the clear need is to develop an agriculture diverse enough to have long-term potential. We must beware of those 'experts' who appear to advocate the transformation of the ecosphere into nothing more than a food-factory for man. The concept of a world consisting solely of man and a few favoured food plants is so ludicrously impracticable as to be seriously contemplated only by those who find solace in their own wilful ignorance of the real world of biological diversity.

We in Britain must bear in mind that we depend on imports for half our food, and that we are unlikely to improve on this situation. The 150,000 acres which are lost from agriculture each year are about 70 per cent more productive than the average for all enclosed land, while we are already beginning to experience diminishing returns from the use of inorganic fertilisers. In the period 1964–9, applications of phosphates have gone up by 2 per cent, potash by 7 per cent, and nitrogen by 40 per cent, yet yields per acre of wheat, barley, lucerne and temporary grass have levelled off and are beginning to decline, while that of permanent grass has risen only slightly and may be levelling off. As *per capita* food availability declines throughout the rest of the world, and it appears inevitable it will, we will find it progressively more difficult and expensive to meet our food requirements from abroad. The prospect of severe food shortages within the next thirty years is not so much a fantasy as that of the continued abundance promised us by so many of our politicians.

As we have seen, continued exponential growth of consumption of materials and energy is impossible. Present reserves of all but a few metals will be exhausted within fifty years, if consumption rates continue to grow as they are. Obviously there will be new discoveries and advances in mining technology, but these are likely to provide us with only a limited stay of execution. Synthetics and substitutes are likely to be of little help, since they must be made from materials which themselves are in short supply; while the hoped-for availability of unlimited energy would not be the answer, since the problem is the ratio of useful metal to waste matter (which would have to be disposed of without disrupting ecosystems), not the need for cheap power. Indeed, the availability of unlimited power holds more of a threat than a promise, since energy use is inevitably polluting, and in addition we would ultimately have to face the problem of disposing of an intractable amount of waste heat.

The developed nations consume such disproportionate amounts of protein, raw material, and fuels that unless they considerably reduce their consumption there is no hope of the undeveloped nations markedly improving their standards of living. This vast differential is a cause of much and growing discontent, made worse by our attempts at cultural uniformity on behalf of an expanding market economy. In the end, we are altering people's aspirations without providing the means for them to be satisfied. In the rush to industrialise we break up communities, so that the controls which formerly regulated behaviour are destroyed before alternatives can be provided. Urban drift is one result of this process, with a consequent rise in anti-social practices, crime, delinquency, and so on, which are so costly for society in terms both of money and of well-being.

At the same time, we are sowing the seeds of massive unemployment by increasing the ratio of capital to labour so that the provision of each job becomes ever more expensive. In a world of fast diminishing resources, we shall quickly come to the point when very great numbers of people will be thrown out of work, when the material compensations of urban life are either no longer available or prohibitively expensive, and consequently when whole sections of society will find good cause to express their considerable discontent in ways likely to be anything but pleasant for their fellows.

It is worth bearing in mind that the barriers between us and epidemics are not so strong as is commonly supposed. Not only is it increasingly difficult to control the vectors of disease, but it is more than probable that urban populations are being insidiously weakened by overall pollution levels, even when they are not high enough to be incriminated in any one illness. At the same time international mobility speeds the spread of disease. With this background, and at a time of widespread public demoralisation, the collapse of vital social services such as power and sanitation, could easily provoke a series of epidemics—and we cannot say with confidence that we would be able to cope with them.

At times of great distress and social chaos, it is more than probable that governments will fall into the hands of reckless and unscrupulous elements, who will not hesitate to threaten neighbouring governments with attack, if they feel that they can wrest from them a larger share of the world's vanishing resources. Since a growing number of countries (an estimated 36 by 1980) will have nuclear power stations, and therefore sources of plutonium for nuclear warheads, the likelihood of a whole series of local (if not global) nuclear engagements is greatly increased.

There will be those who regard accounts of the consequences of trying to accommodate present growth rates as fanciful. But the imaginative leap from the available scientific information to such predictions is negligible, compared with that required for those alternative predictions, laughably considered 'optimistic', of a world of 10,000 to 15,000 million people, all with the same material standard of living as the US, on a concrete replica of this planet, the only moving parts being their machines and possibly themselves. Faced with inevitable change, we have to make decisions, and we must make these decisions *soberly* in the light of the best information.

By now it should be clear that the main problems of the environment do not arise from temporary and accidental malfunctions of existing economic and social systems. On the contrary, they are the warning signs of a profound incompatibility between deeply rooted beliefs in continuous growth and the dawning recognition of the earth as a space ship, limited in its resources and vulnerable to thoughtless mishandling. The nature of our response to these symptoms is crucial. If we refuse to recognise the cause of our trouble the result can only be increasing disillusion and growing strain upon the fragile institutions that maintain external peace and internal social cohesion. If, on the other hand, we can respond to this unprecedented challenge with informed and constructive action the rewards will be as great as the penalties for failure.

We are sufficiently aware of 'political reality' to appreciate that many of the proposals we will make will be considered impracticable. However, we believe that if a strategy for survival is to have any chance of success, the solutions must be formulated in the light of the problems and not from a timorous and superficial understanding of what may or may not be immediately feasible. If we plan remedial action with our eyes on political rather than ecological reality, then very reasonably, very practicably, and very surely, we will muddle our way to extinction.

A measure of political reality is that government has yet to acknowledge the impending crisis. This is to some extent because it has given itself no machinery for looking at energy, resources, food, environment disruption and social disruption as a whole, as part of a general, global pattern, preferring instead to deal with its many aspects as if they were self-contained analytical units. Lord Rothschild's Central Policy Review Staff in the Cabinet Office, which is the only body in government which might remedy the situation, appears not to think it worthwhile: at the moment at least, they are undertaking 'no specific studies on the environment that would require an environmentalist or ecologist'. There is a strong element of positive feedback here, in that there can be no appreciation of our predicament unless we view it in totality, and yet government can see no cause to do so unless it can be shown that such a predicament exists.

Possibly because government sees the world in fragments and not as a totality, it is difficult to detect in its actions or words any coherent general policy, although both major political parties appear to be mesmerised by two dominating notions: that economic expansion is essential for survival and is the best possible index of progress and well-being; and that unless solutions can be devised that do not threaten this notion, then the problems should not be regarded as existing. Unfortunately, government has an increasingly powerful incentive for continued expansion in the tendency for economic growth to create the need for more economic growth. This it does in six ways:

Firstly, the introduction of technological devices, i.e. the growth of the technosphere, can only occur to the detriment of the ecosphere, which means that it leads to the destruction of natural controls which must then be replaced by further technological ones. It is in this way that pesticides and artificial fertilisers create the need for yet more pesticides and artificial fertilisers.

Secondly, for various reasons, industrial growth, particularly in its earlier phases, promotes population growth. Even in its later phases, this can still occur at a high rate (0.5 per cent in the UK). Jobs must constantly be created for the additional people—not just any job, but those that are judged acceptable in terms of current values. This basically means that the capital outlay per person employed must be maintained, otherwise the level of 'productivity' per man will fall, which is a determinant of both the 'viability' of economic enterprise and of the 'standard of living'.

Thirdly, no government can hope to survive widespread and protracted unemployment, and without changing the basis of our industrial society, the only way government can prevent it is by stimulating economic growth.

Fourthly, business enterprises, whether state-owned or privately owned, tend to become self-perpetuating, which means that they require surpluses for further investment. This favours continued growth.

Fifthly, the success of a government and its ability to obtain support is to a large extent assessed in terms of its ability to increase the 'standard of living' as measured by *per capita* gross national product (GNP).

Finally, confidence in the economy, which is basically a function of its ability to grow, must be maintained to ensure a healthy state of the stock market. Were confidence to fall, stock values would crash, drastically reducing the availability of capital for investment and hence further growth, which would lead to further unemployment. This would result in a further fall in stock-market values and hence give rise to a positive-feedback chain-reaction, which under the existing order might well lead to social collapse.

For all these reasons, we can expect our government (whether Conservative or Labour) to encourage further increases in GNP regardless of the consequences, which in any case tame 'experts' can be found to play down. It will curb growth only when public opinion demands such a move, in which case it will be politically expedient, and when a method is found for doing so without creating unemployment or excessive pressure on capital. We believe this is possible only within the framework of a fully integrated plan.

The emphasis must be on integration. If we develop relatively clean technologies but do not end economic growth then sooner or later we will find ourselves with as great a pollution problem as before but without the means of tackling it. If we stabilise our economies and husband our non-renewable resources without stabilising our populations we will find we are no longer able to feed ourselves. As Forrester and Meadows convincingly make clear, daunting though an integrated programme may be, a piecemeal approach will cause more problems than it solves.

Our task is to create a society which is sustainable and which will give the fullest possible satisfaction to its members. Such a society by definition would depend not on expansion but on stability. This does not mean to say that it would be stagnant—indeed it could well afford more variety than does the state of uniformity at present being imposed by the pursuit of technological efficiency. We believe that the stable society, as well as removing the sword of Damocles which hangs over the heads of future generations, is much more likely than the present one to bring the peace and fulfilment which hitherto have been regarded, sadly, as utopian.

Population, Crowding and Human Behaviour
P. Ehrlich and J. Freedman

Reprinted with permission from *New Scientist and Science Journal*, 1 April 1971, pp. 10–15.

How does population density, or crowding as it is usually referred to, affect human beings? Few questions of such importance are so little understood. Interest in the broader problem of overpopulation has fortunately blossomed over the past few years. By now all reasonable people appreciate the threat that the world's increasing population presents. But the consequences of overpopulation must be distinguished from the effects of population density *per se*.

This distinction is clearest and most important in our great urban centres. Certainly the cities have monumental problems. They are centres of crime, drug abuse, poverty, welfare cases, unemployment, riots. Some authors have suggested, indeed have unhesitatingly assumed, that many of these ills are inevitable consequences of the high population density prevailing in the cities. They claim that crowding *causes* mental, physical and social breakdown. If this were true, we would obviously be in serious trouble even if we could reduce our total population because people have always concentrated in the cities. If it were true, we would be forced to abandon the cities, or at least greatly reduce their size. But is it true? Does high population density produce bad effects by itself?

It is important that the effects of crowding itself, not crowding in conjunction with poverty, malnutrition, noise and filth, be clearly understood. Crowded slums should be eliminated even if crowding by itself is of positive benefit to human beings. But as the world becomes more and more packed with people it is critical that we be able to predict how human performance and interpersonal relationships will change even if crowding is not accompanied by other deterioration of the environment. For instance, the soundest ecological strategy may well be to encourage tall, high density dwelling units in cities instead of suburban sprawl. Farmland will be at a premium as the world food problem worsens, and suburbs are all too often built on farmland. In addition, resources (including energy) can be conserved by housing people more efficiently and closer to their jobs. Obviously we would hesitate to take that course if crowding *per se* were in some sense 'bad'; if, for instance, it led to antisocial behaviour or to mental or physical deterioration.

There are a number of studies that demonstrate disruptions produced by overcrowding in rats, mice and other animals. John Calhoun and his associates have observed rat colonies in enclosed areas that were provided with sufficient food and water and allowed to grow. Rats are very good at reproducing and quite soon these colonies were teeming with animals. When the number of rats became quite large, social and physical pathologies began to appear. Males became either overly aggressive or unnaturally passive; they became homosexual; they invaded the nests of pregnant females; and some became cannibals. Females no longer built adequate nests, nor cared for their young sufficiently, and as a consequence infant mortality soared. And so on. Whereas with fewer animals, the colony functioned well, all animals had separate nests and raised their young successfully, with the larger population the social structure broke down and eventually the colony's continued existence was in doubt. Similar observations have been made of a wide variety of animals ranging from mice, rats and voles to deer and even monkeys. There is little question that, as population increases, at some point it begins to have extremely negative effects on the animals involved.

One group finds solace in the results. They look to natural controls on the size of the human population. When we get 'too crowded', population growth will cease: people will lose interest in sex or die of stress, or women will resorb foetuses, or Jonathan Swift's 'modest proposal' will be instituted and parents will eat their young. It is difficult for us to view such a 'solution' with equanimity, but it will never be the 'solution', in any case. It is clear that many other limiting factors (food, raw materials, capacity of environmental systems to handle wastes) will come into play long before the human population reaches a size at which density itself will pose a limit. People living in Manhattan, Tokyo and other extremely crowded areas today do not show such behavioural pathologies to a significant degree. But if only 25 per cent of the land surface earth were populated to the density of Tokyo, the world population would be some 600 billion people. This is perhaps 500–1000 times more than the planet can support in reasonable comfort on a permanent basis.

*   *   *

We conclude from statistics on crime and war that aggression seems much less likely to be the result of density alone than of many other factors. Perhaps density has other negative effects. It has been loosely suggested that high density produces mental illness, physical deterioration, depression and other kinds of mental, physical or social breakdown. Analyses of statistics relevant to these possibilities produce much the same result as for crimes. There is a strong tendency for high population density to be associated with higher rates of mental illness, suicide, infant mortality and so on. But, as before, when other factors such as income and educational level are equated, the effect of density disappears. Areas of high density have no more mental or physical illness than equivalent areas of lower density.

Several years ago it became apparent to us that questions of the effects of crowding on the behaviour of people would be unlikely to be resolved without some experimental work on human subjects.

* * *

We conducted a series of studies on the effects of density on various behaviours and reactions. All of the studies followed the same basic model. Groups of people spent four hours in rooms that were either very crowded or not at all crowded. The 'crowded' rooms were designed so that every person had a seat, but there was no space for anyone else to fit in the room. In other words, there were as many people as there possibly could be without them actually sitting on or physically interfering with one another. For example, in one study the room was 35 square feet and held 9 people, thus allowing less than 4 square feet per person. In contrast, the less-crowded rooms allowed 15–20 square feet per person. Keep in mind that we were not interested in the effects of density when it became so great that people were actually physically uncomfortable, or when odours or temperature became unpleasant. We wanted to know if crowding itself, apart from these other conditions, produces negative effects.

Skills in a crowd

This experimental method obviously is limited in many important respects. The most critical is that the time span is relatively brief compared to many real life situations, although quite long compared to most laboratory experiments. The crowding is very intense, more than ordinarily occurs in natural settings (except the New York subways) for this length of time. But four hours is still only four hours. And since the subjects know that the time is limited, they know that they will eventually get out of the crowded environment. How the effects of this intense, short-term crowding compare to less intense, long-term crowding is unknown, but ordinarily we would expect the direction of the effects to be similar even if their magnitude is different.

Our first series of studies focused on the effect of density on performance of a variety of tasks. We discovered that there was no effect. The individuals dutifully and competently crossed out sevens on a sheet of random numbers, memorised words, counted erratic clicks coming over a loudspeaker, solved anagram puzzles, formed words from scrambled letters and made up original and ingenious uses for a variety of common objects such as a brick. They did all of these tasks equally well regardless of the size of the room. The degree of crowding had no noticeable effect on any of the tasks, nor did any effect show up over time.

In contrast, our second series of studies revealed that more complex forms of behaviour and emotional reactions are influenced by population density. We now have evidence that the degree of crowding has some effect on competitiveness, vindictiveness and liking for others. But the effects are not simple. The fascinating aspect of this work is that men and women appear to respond in opposite ways to the level of crowding we have used.

Males compete

Our first study consisted of putting high school students in either small or large rooms, letting them get to know one another, discuss various topics and play a mechanical game requiring a high level of coordination between partners. The groups were either all boys or all girls. During the last hour of the study the groups engaged in a game that allowed each person to choose either a cooperative or competitive play. The game is called the prisoner's dilemma, because it is based on the classic problem of two men (Jack and Bob, say) accused of a crime who, questioned separately, are given the opportunity of either confessing and incriminating his partner, or else not confessing and trusting his partner not to do so.

In our study, we did not threaten the students with sentences—instead we offered them money. If they all choose blue, they would each get five cents (not much money for affluent suburbanites, but there were many trials and it could add up). If, however, three chose blue and one chose red, the one choosing the red would hit the jackpot and get 30 cents while the others would lose 20 cents a piece. But if more than one chose red, they also lost. Thus, the cooperative play is to choose blue, hope everyone else chooses blue and take a sure five cents a trial. But by competing and choosing red, each individual might gain a lot more at the cost of a loss to the others and the risk of losing himself. A dilemma, though not as serious as that facing Jack and Bob.

Under these circumstances, a clear pattern emerged—the boys played more competitively in the small room while the girls played somewhat more competitively in the larger room. That is, crowding increased competitiveness among boys and slightly decreased it for girls.

A second experiment used a different setting, different subject population and different measures. Men and women over 18 were recruited by classified ads in newspapers. The subjects ranged in age from 18 to 80, and represented a wide variety of ethnic groups and educational and income levels. Once again they were placed in either a large or small room for approximately four hours. During that time, they first engaged in informal discussion and then listened to a series of taped courtroom cases for which they served as the jury. The group discussed some cases openly and did not discuss others, but for all cases each individual indicated his own decision separately and privately. In addition, the subjects responded to a questionnaire on which they were asked how much they liked the other members of the group, how much they enjoyed the session and other similar questions designed to measure their subjective reactions to the experience.

Females cooperate

The pattern of results is similar to that of the previous experiment, but differs somewhat in emphasis. Just as before, the men respond more negatively to the small room while the women show the opposite tendency. The men give somewhat more severe sentences in the smaller room than they do in the larger room; while the women are lenient in the smaller room. Unlike the previous results, however, this difference between rooms is much stronger for the women than for the men. Crowding has an even stronger effect on the individual's subjective reactions. The men in the small room find the experience less pleasant, like the other members less, consider them less friendly and think they would make a less good jury than the men in the large room; whereas every difference is reversed for women who rate the experience more pleasant, the other members more likeable, friendlier and a better jury in the small than in the large room.

Thus the results of the two studies are quite consistent. Apparently under these circumstances, men respond negatively to crowded conditions—they become more competitive; somewhat more severe and they like each other less; whereas women respond positively, become more cooperative, more lenient and like each other more. Interestingly enough, when mixed groups took part in this last study, no effects of crowding were observed either for the group as a whole or the men and women separately.

This dramatic difference between the sexes is intriguing and difficult to explain. Some might be tempted to interpret it as evidence for innate feelings of territoriality among males that are not present in females. Despite the simplicity of this explanation, it seems highly implausible. It is true that defending their territory from encroachment is seen primarily among males of other species, but the people in our room are hardly protecting territory in the usual sense, nor is there any evidence that women are generally any less protective of their home than are men. Although it is obviously silly to deny certain innate differences between human males and females this does not seem to be one of them.

A more likely explanation is that in our society men and women learn slightly different reactions to social situations and close physical contact in particular. There is evidence, for example, that two men who are talking stand farther apart than do two women, suggesting that men are less accepting of physical contact with other men than women are of contact with other women. Men are also probably somewhat more prone to be suspicious of other men than women are of other women. However, the exact form that these hypothesised differences take is sheer speculation. The main point is that our findings are probably due to learned rather than to innate differences, and are affected by the specific situation (as evidenced by the disappearance of the effect with mixed groups).

How should we interpret this and the previous research on density? The first answer is 'with great caution'. The studies of the cities are still very rough. Any work with massive amounts of data collected under uncontrolled conditions must be considered only suggestive. Our experimental work suffers from the opposite problems—it was well controlled, but produced relatively little data, on very few people, and under special conditions. With that important disclaimer, we must note that this is all we have to go on at the moment and some tentative conclusions can be drawn.

Getting along in crowds

There is little evidence that population density *per se* produces dramatic effects (negative or positive) among human beings. Those who predict loss of efficiency or total breakdown of productive activity as population density grows will find no support in the available data. Density had no effect on performance. At first thought this might be surprising, but a similar lack of effect has been found for other factors such as exceedingly loud noises. Man is remarkably good at ignoring distracting stimulation so even if crowding were unpleasant (which is not at all certain), it might not affect performance.

The evidence from the cities and from our studies also showed no dramatic effect on anti-social behaviour. There was no relationship between a city's population density and crime or other such behaviour. Our last two studies did indicate that all-male groups were somewhat more competitive and severe under crowded conditions, but the effects were not large, were balanced by opposite effects for all-female groups and disappeared entirely in the more natural mixed-sex groups. This is not to deny the effects, but to put them in perspective. Nothing we or others have found indicates that density is a major (or for that matter even substantial) factor in causing mental or social breakdown.

We should therefore not be surprised that the cities, despite their monumental problems, continue to function, and that the people on the underground do not suddenly turn into a brawling mob. The problems of the cities have increased enormously over the past 10 years, a period in which their population density has remained static or even declined in most instances.

The problems are not caused by density *per se*, and will not be eliminated merely by reducing density.

This is of the utmost importance. Critics of the cities have correctly cited overcrowding as a major problem but in their zeal some critics have confused the logistic and economic problems caused by the concentration of population with supposed negative effects of crowding *per se*. It is certain that Manhattan's 75,000 people per square mile present difficulties in transportation, providing enough jobs and houses and schools, keeping the parks green, disposing of waste, eliminating pollution and on and on. But there is no reason to believe that this great concentration of population has negative effects on people. The difference between these two statements is crucial. If we view the problems as primarily logistic and economic, we can fight them and get something done. If we decide that crime is inevitably higher in the cities because crowding causes crime, the only answer would be to disband the cities—and this would be a bad mistake even if it were possible. We happen to disagree in our feelings about cities (Ehrlich hates them, Freedman likes them), but we agree that cities serve some functions extremely well. Overpopulation is a problem that must be solved, but high concentrations of people may well turn out to be desirable as long as we deal with the technical problems.

The second conclusion from this research is that whatever effects density does have are complicated. They depend largely on who is being crowded and the situation in which the crowding occurs. We did find that there are times when crowding has negative effects on at least some people; there are other times when it has positive effects. We cannot specify details, but the general point is clear. The few instances we can cite are provocative. All-male juries or cabinets or international conferences should probably be avoided, or at least be given spacious quarters. Better still, women should be included, not only to give them equal representation, but because apparently any negative effects of crowding disappear when the sexes are mixed. There is thus strong argument to eliminate the secretive meetings of men in back rooms deciding our fates—and bring them out into the open where their decisions are less likely to be aggressive.

More generally, the question of whether or not high concentrations of people are desirable depends on the particular situations and the types of behaviour involved. It seems likely that no simple answers will emerge—that for some people and for

some purposes, high density is a bad idea, while for other
people and for other purposes, it is fine.

Pollution by Industry
T. Aldous

Reprinted by permission from T. Aldous, *Battle for the Environment*,
Fontana, 1972, pp. 207-16 and 220.

The subject of this chapter of course itself merits a whole book
—or even a series of books. The present examination can be no
more than an attempt to analyse the size and nature of the
broad problem and illustrate it by one or two examples.

Pollution by industry is of several kinds: pollution of the air
by harmful or unpleasant gases; and pollution of water,
whether salt or fresh, and whether by land-based industry or by
ships; pollution of the land, whether by the products of industry or by dereliction. These three—pollution by air, water and
land, are perhaps the types of pollution most commonly associated with industry. But I would like also to mention two
others: noise pollution; and—a cross category—what I will
call visual pollution.

None of these is new. Ecologically speaking, as Sir Frank
Fraser Darling pointed out in his 1969 Reith Lectures, Bronze-
Age man had begun to pollute his environment and raid his
stock of unrenewable resources when he burned wood to smelt
copper and tin. In Britain the first really big impact came with
the Industrial Revolution, and the growth of the nineteenth-
century *laisser-faire* industrialism saw also a single-minded exploitation of technology with little regard for environmental
considerations. Today in Britain, though we still—particularly
in the north—suffer the legacy of industrial dereliction, firms
know that both planning law and public opinion will continue
to impose ever more exacting standards—at least on air, water,
land and visual pollution. And yet ... And yet pollution is
today out of all proportion a more serious problem than it was
in the nineteenth century. Why? There are, I think, three
fundamental reasons: scale of operation, complexity of the
processes involved, and pace of change.

Let me give examples of change in scale. First, steel production. In the immediate post-war period, Britain's largest steel-works produced about 700,000 tons a year. The largest operational British steel-works today is at Port Talbot with an annual output of $3\frac{1}{4}$ million tons; but the Japanese and the Russians have units capable of producing 8 to 10 million tons with expansion plans which will bring them up to 20 million tons by the early eighties. In Britain British Steel Corporation plan two works of 10 million tons. Modern steel-works both use less land and have more efficient anti-pollution devices for both air and water. But, despite the improvements made possible by the change from 'open hearth' to 'basic oxygen' production, control methods are far from perfect; and the increase in scale itself (though concentration of production makes cleaning up easier) means that there is more in the way of fumes and effluent to clean up.

Another example of increase in scale. When Bankside power station in the centre of London was built in the late forties despite much opposition, it was the biggest and most modern power station Britain had ever had. It had an initial capacity of 180 MW. Now there are several coal-fired stations of 2,000 MW and a 3,300 MW oil-fired power station is being built at the Isle of Grain on the Thames estuary. Chimneys are taller, the smoke that comes out of them looks cleaner (they contain even more efficient 'washing' devices). But fumes do blow away into the atmosphere, and more and more of them. We have only a very imperfect idea of where they go and in practice industry is less interested in their destination and effect when they cease to be traceable. That, however, does not mean they do no harm. National boundaries rarely look more out of date than in the context of atmospheric pollution. The Swedes complain convincingly that their atmosphere is polluted by both the Norwegians and the Germans. The only answer at present is international agreement on control at source, and that was one reason for calling the 1972 Stockholm Conference. But multi-national agreements are even more difficult and slower to achieve than domestic legislation with an over-crowded parliamentary timetable. And if enforcement remains with the different national authorities, international control may well turn out to be only as effective as its weakest link.

Water pollution illustrates the linked factors of complexity of industrial process and rate of technological change. A Confederation of British Industry pollution expert cited to me recently the case of a north London factory which accidentally let a minute trace of the chemical pentachlorphenol go down the drain into the local sewer. It was present in the waste, the Water Pollution Research Establishment later concluded, only in the proportion of around 0.00001 parts per million. Yet because of the nature of modern biological sewage treatment processes, that chemical put a whole large sewage works out of action for several days.

Though the CBI man was no doubt right when he said: 'I don't think anyone could have expected that result,' concentration of production does make monitoring, control and tracing after the event easier. In Britain we have the contrast in the field of water pollution between a Thames cleaner now than it has been for a century, and rivers like the Mersey and the Tame, which are used as a drain by scores of firms large and small for the discharge of their industrial effluents. In the Mersey, the quality of river water is now such, incidentally, that not only is swimming very definitely not recommended, but victims of involuntary immersion are routinely given injections against tetanus and a number of other infections (producing that ecological sick joke, 'The quality of Mersey is not strained'). It has not yet reached the plight of the River Cuyahoga in Cleveland, which is so full of chemical effluents that it is classified a fire risk. Nonetheless the Mersey in its present state is a standing affront to a supposedly civilised society, and an indictment of the price we have been prepared unthinkingly to pay for the conveniences of industrial and economic growth.

In the longer term, the answer may lie in concentrating new chemical and other effluent-producing industry where its waste products can be dealt with in bulk. This solution has been adopted in one instance in Germany where a 'sealed stream' collects liquid wastes from a number of Rhineland industrial plants and carries them to a single treatment works.

Existing industry is the problem. Some experts say the powers are adequate, but their application is a delicate balancing act with economic and public opinion. Suppose the Mersey and Weaver River Authority suddenly got tough with half the works discharging waste into the Mersey, instead of applying pressure where it seemed realistic to demand improvement. What would happen? Some of the firms would either instal better anti-pollution equipment or move. Some would go out of business, either because they could not pay the cost of improvement or because in practical terms improvement was not feasible on that site. Others would judge that their competitiveness—especially international competitiveness —would not survive the expense, and choose to go out of production. Result: loss of jobs and local prosperity, and—in a region where there is considerable unemployment still—very possibly a hostile reaction from public opinion and politically to anti-pollution measures generally.

So this aspect of any campaign against pollution falls down because of lack of public comprehension. People understand what lost jobs mean: that is 'for real'. So, in a minor way, is 5p on the price of a packet of detergent. The possible 'death' of a river or lake is not. Yet it has happened. Incidentally, one misconception which colours talk of water pollution is the notion of 'dirtiness'. Dirt is not the same thing as pollution. A river can be very dirty after heavy rain without being seriously polluted. Conversely, a river can look very clean and yet be quite seriously polluted. The measure generally adopted is 'B O D'—biological or biochemical oxygen demand. This is what makes a river live. When the B O D falls too low eutrophication follows, and a river or lake 'dies' as Lake Erie in North America has done. It is choked with algae, the only plant life it can support. No fish, no insects, no other plants. It is a blank, dead space in the complex of ecological cycles which keep our world alive, productive and habitable—and as such a frightening warning of what might happen on a wider scale.

The field of marine pollution presents an even more worrying example of public mis-assumptions. People are of course worried about oil tankers breaking up at sea. They know oil is nasty messy stuff because little Sarah sat in some on the beach last summer, and then trod another lump into the car seat. They have also been told that it can do serious damage to marine life. But what they usually do not appreciate is how vulnerable marine life is. They think of the oceans as limitless, and assume that what lives in it is somehow inexhaustible. The truth is, marine biologists tell us, that some 90 per cent of that richness is concentrated in something like 1 per cent of ocean areas—those nearest our coasts. And those are the areas most vulnerable to oil spillage, partly because those are the likeliest collision areas, partly because floating oil tends to end up there. Because of the relative tidelessness of the Mediterranean, and the recklessness with which some nations tip all manner of waste and untreated effluent into it, the Mediterranean has suffered worst from this. There are signs that its coastal strip, once so rich in marine life, is already dying, and it may already be too late to save large parts of the Mediterranean from becoming literally a 'dead sea'.

The only really safe solution to the problem of oil pollution is not to ship oil on—or for that matter under—the sea. Until we have developed a fuel as convenient and cheap however, that is in practical terms no solution. We have instead to look for palliatives: safer sea lanes and shipping practices, better salvage arrangements when accidents do occur, and better techniques for dealing with oil as floating slicks and, in the last resort, on the beaches. Britain is a lot better prepared now than at the time of the *Torrey Canyon* affair, but technically we are still by no means well prepared. Many scientists doubt, for instance, whether we should go on using detergents (products, incidentally, of the same industry which spills the oil) rather than mechanical means to clear up the mess. In 1969 a Swansea shipping consultant Michael Spencer-Davies developed a craft called the Sea Mantis, a catamaran towing dracones (or huge floating sacks) of 1,000 tons each and with long booms which would be linked to tugs. The Sea Mantis has a fair turn of speed, and its strategy is to get to the slick fast, contain it with the booms, and suck the oil into the dracones. Government scientists dubbed it 'the best oil clearing system we have yet seen'. Oil company experts have examined Sea Mantis but at the time of writing nothing seems to have come of it, though the principle is undoubtedly sound. It is difficult to believe that if the international oil world faced the option of either developing an effective means of coping with slicks or closing down, it would not have leapt on this and any other promising solution and poured money and effort into developing it.

The truth is that industry needs generally to be pushed into expensive action either by governments or exceptionally strong public opinion; governments and administrators also need to feel the spur of public opinion; and public opinion has to be made aware of the true costs and dangers of pollution, either by a slow and steady process of education or by the salutary lesson of catastrophe. All one can hope is that catastrophes when they come will be just big enough to drive home the lesson, and no bigger. Here again concentration of resources and the modern law of economy of scale both allow better control and reduction of pollution risks, yet at the same time offer the bleak prospect that when, inevitably, an accident occurs, the mess will be bigger and its possible ecological chain reaction that much more serious.

Natural gas has, rightly, been heralded as environmentally the most acceptable fuel we have. Its only snag from that point of view seems to be the network of masts necessary for tele-metered remote control of flows. The same will not necessarily be so if North Sea oil is brought ashore by pipeline. The pollu-tion caused by oil escape off the California coast at Santa Barbara in 1969 was the writing on the wall for that kind of exercise. The North Sea bed is not geologically so stable nor its waters so free of storms that we can afford to take such a warning lightly. There is, of course, an element of risk in any technological advance, and decisions whether to go ahead or not will usually depend on the best assessment possible of that risk. But when the environmental penalty of things going wrong is huge and the risk assessment a shaky process involv-ing many unknowns, then arguments about the need for eco-nomic growth should not be allowed to weigh too heavily.

What I find most worrying in all the detailed arguments about pollution dangers and control is the frequency with which, if you really press the point, the experts will admit: 'We do not know for certain what the effect of this will be. No one knows. We are only making the best assessment we can of what we think its effects will be.' Thus some scientists predict that general adoption by the world's airlines of supersonic air-craft would result in damage to the earth's atmosphere which could quite possibly be fatal to life on earth. Others say this is unlikely. Their arguments are respectable, but no one knows. In the Cleveland Potash mining affair, the company said they were sure that a mile-long pipeline out to sea would ensure harmless dispersal of powdery waste solids from the potash production process; the minister said he thought it would, but wanted the option of stopping production if it were shown to be otherwise; and marine biologists from the nearby Wellcome Laboratory at Robin Hood's Bay said there was just a chance that the waste, if it were carried back in sufficiently heavy con-centrations towards the shore, might clog and suffocate marine life of certain kinds and seriously damage the ecological balance. But no one really knew. They were only beginning to understand the factors involved.

This sense of the smallness of scientific knowledge of areas into which technology is single-mindedly breaking is, to me, frightening. Of course science works on the basis of probabilities, but science works in limited, controlled situations. Technology moves in on a mass-production scale, with big money involved and prosperity mortgaged to its success. In his 1969 Reith Lectures, Sir Frank Fraser Darling warned against the danger of technology's working up an irresistible momentum—and indeed this almost happened, and may still happen, with the supersonic airliner. The danger is that so many jobs, so many people's prosperity may come to depend upon a project that it is its own justification. Perhaps you point out that the SST gets a few thousand people across the Atlantic an hour or two quicker while making life unpleasant for hundreds of thousands who live near airports or on flight paths (leaving aside the possible bashing it gives to the earth's atmosphere) and that this is too high a price to pay. 'Ah!' say the technologists, 'but you cannot stand in the way of "progress".' This is akin to the argument that men must risk climbing mountains because they're there. Fair enough. But when the costs to the community of rescue operations grows too high, steps may have to be taken to limit the numbers licensed to risk their own and others' safety.

What I am arguing, I think, is this. That politically and socially we need to fit better brakes to the powerful sports car of technology; we need to spend much more on the scientific research which enables its driver to see where he is really going; and we need to take the environmental corners rather more slowly and carefully than we do at present. Thalidomide was a warning of this which has to some extent been heeded. I am rather concerned about 'engineers' tunnel vision'—their tendency to solve the practical problem in hand without too much thought for environmental niceties. Commercial technology tends to suffer from a similar failing. The community as a whole needs to put very much more money and skilled resources into a wide variety of research which can alert it if technology seems to be taking a dangerous road, and can warn convincingly from really detailed, thorough knowledge.

After the frightening imponderables of murdered marine life and damaged atmosphere, 'visual pollution' appears as a relatively simple problem. It has basically two varieties: one is the wanton creation of industrial dereliction such as colliery spoil heaps or abandoned works—largely the product of the single-minded industrialism of the past. The other is the more conscious and calculated variety which says: 'We accept that this installation spoils your view, but the gains to the community or the nation outweigh the loss, which we will try to keep to the minimum.'

The assault on derelict land has at last, in recent years, really begun to make some impact. There are, I think, three reasons for this. One is a more critical, impatient public, placing a higher value on 'good environment' and affronted by the needless squalor of messes not even justified by continuing industrial activity. Second is the means—great new earth-moving machines doing in days what would previously have taken months, and in months what would before have seemed impossible. And here the Coal Board, through its Opencast Executive, is atoning to some extent for the past sins of its industry. Third is Aberfan—again tragedy as a catalyst to action. Wales needed Aberfan to concentrate its mind on what was possible and desirable.

In recent years the Welsh Office's Derelict Land Unit, a similarly expert unit set up by district councils in Monmouthshire, and individual local authorities, have been transforming in a positive way the environment of numerous communities in the mining valleys of South Wales. This has not just been a matter of removing dangerous or oppressive slag heaps towering over people's homes. It has created, in narrow valley bottoms where space has always been short, new flat areas both for housing and recreation, and for building factories to provide jobs to replace those lost in colliery closures. Government grants provide 85 per cent of the net cost of approved schemes in a development area, and rate equalisation grants often take the true proportion higher. Even so, it is argued, a small local authority with a low rateable value may find it difficult to meet even that proportion. That may be so. One or two small urban councils, however, have actually managed after selling land to industry to make a profit on derelict land clearance.

In England an outstanding example of what can be done is provided by the city of Stoke-on-Trent—winner in 1971 of *The Times*/Royal Institution of Chartered Surveyors Awards for land reclamation. The award-winning project was a 128-acre site containing the long-standing dereliction of huge, unsightly colliery spoil heaps and pottery marl holes. This has now been transformed into a natural-seeming, hilly and wooded landscape with special paths and trails for walkers, cyclists and horse-riders, football pitches, a pitch-and-putt course, and a lake for boating.

Almost the sole reminder of its past is the retention of the colliery pit-head gear, both as a dramatic piece of industrial archæology and as a viewing platform looking over the city. Central Forest Park is being linked to other reclamation areas in Stoke-on-Trent by a system of 'greenways' landscaped out of the disused railway lines of which the city has a profusion, which used to link them as live industrial sites, and which lost their viability at the time of the colliery closures of the late 1950s and early 1960s.

The project was conceived in 1967 by a London firm of landscape architects, Land Use Consultants, and in particular by its partner Clifford Tandy, later president of the Institute of Landscape Architects. It has been very much a joint endeavour by them, the National Coal Board's Opencast Executive and Stoke's planning and parks departments—though *The Times*/ R I C S judges criticised the Coal Board for the high price it charged for land sold to the city.

The attitudes of mind which create dereliction almost unthinkingly still, however, persist. British Rail is one of the worst offenders. I travelled recently on a branch line where colour light signalling had some time ago been installed. The signal columns were neat enough in themselves, but British Rail's method of dealing with the redundant signal boxes had been to immobilise them. There they stood, every mile or two, smashed up and derelict. Whether British Rail did most of the smashing, or vandals is not the point. It should be axiomatic, and enforceable at law, that if any industrial or commercial concern no longer uses a building or structure, it must either keep it in good order or demolish it and remove the debris. Just as the law provides ways of dealing with an unsafe structure, or a 'nuisance' which affronts the nose or ears, so it should provide remedies for 'visual nuisance'.

* * *

The right 'long-term', ecological answer is, of course, recycling: using industry's waste products—liquid, solid and gaseous—to create new products or useful energy. Industry has done it again and again in two sets of circumstances—when it perceived an unfilled commercial market for a potential product of recycling: and when the discharge of a product in the ordinary way became too difficult or unpopular. We need to reinforce both these motives: not only by pointing the way through research to what is technically possible, but by favouring those who recycle and progressively more stringently penalising those who do not. What is needed is a fiscal policy which will make it worthwhile for industry to search out every opportunity for recycling. The negative system of penalising the polluter is not enough. Public opinion disapproving of the apparent and visible manifestations of pollution is not enough. We need to translate into cash terms the black and red of the ecological balance sheet. And this must somehow be achieved on an international basis (the Common Market should be a helpmate not a hindrance) and quickly: for the long term is now not so long. Serious ecological damage on a scale that will make us rue our technological recklessness may well be just round the corner.

Further Reading : **Population and the Environment**

* 'Blueprint for Survival', *The Ecologist*, London, 1971.
* J. K. BRIERLEY, *Biology and the Social Crisis*, London, Heinemann, 1969.
* R. CARSON, *Silent Spring*, Harmondsworth, Pelican, 1965.
* DEPARTMENT OF THE ENVIRONMENT, *Nuisance or Nemesis?* London, HMSO, 1972.
  J. FORRESTER, *World Dynamics*, Cambridge, Mass., Wright Allen Press, 1970.
HMSO, *Social Trends*.
  T. MALTHUS, *Essay on Population*, 1782.
  J. E. MEADE and A. S. PARKES, *Biological Aspects of Social Problems*, London, Oliver and Boyd, 1965.
  D. MEADOWS et al., *The Limits of Growth*, M.I.T. Press, 1972.
  J. PEEL and M. POTTS, *Population and Pollution*, London Academic Press, 1972.
* A. F. SILLITOE, *Britain in Figures*, Pelican, 1971.

* Available in paperback

Chapter Three   The Family

Most discussions on the family in recent years have been filled
with predictions of gloom. A strong body of orthodox opinion
has suggested that the changes in the functions of the family,
and what appear to be the spread of values inimical to family
solidarity, are indicative of the decline of western civilisation.
Everyone considers himself an expert on the family and its
problems.

Looking at the family many of these interpretations are
obviously far-fetched. The disorganisation seen by some is, in
fact, a reorganisation which results from adaptation to social
change. It has been suggested that in place of a rigid and
authoritarian pattern of family relationships a new entity can
be created based on the intimate associations, the affections and
loyalties that the family can provide. Perhaps theological
expectations demand the decline of the family as a cause
around which to unite 'right-thinking' people. The idea of
marriage as a sacred institution is much less acceptable in this
secular society than it was in the past. Today marriage is often
seen as a convenient arrangement which may turn out for a
growing minority to end in divorce.

The basic changes in the functions of the family, seen over
time, are from an institution which impressed every aspect of
life to one which has possibly greater relevance than ever
before in more limited areas of life. Although the family in
the past may have been inter-dependent, possibly an economic
unit, certainly a social one, and one which gave great support to
its members and extended outside the nuclear family to the
wider kinship network, it was also full of constraints. Today,
smaller families, with the growth in leisure and rising
opportunities and expectations, whatever the dangers and
difficulties these can create, appear to provide more opportunities for social interchange between their members without
the stress that arose from material deprivation and was the
experience of so many families even in the recent past.

The stress and tensions are now of a different kind. From a

family structure which was static, in which roles and expectations were geared to what parents had done, we have moved to one in which levels of aspiration and awareness of opportunities are high; so much so that there is a great danger that these become unrealistic or that parents, conscious of their own more limited opportunities, try to gain their satisfactions through the achievements of their children.

There is also the question of the isolation of the nuclear family which can mean that the husband and wife and children are thrown together more frequently in what can become an emotional hot-house atmosphere. This is different from the old traditional situation when many kinsfolk lived nearby and the emotional demands on much larger numbers of children were likely to be less. Essentially the family today is a mobile unit centred on the town. It still retains its enormously important function in socialising children in their early years. The environment in which it is placed has a great bearing on how that process proceeds, and links up with the section on education, and particularly the reading taken from the Plowden Report.

The changing expectations within the family reflect all kinds of changes in the wider society. The present discussion about women's rights is in part focused on the issue of different pay for the same work, different opportunities, the triviality of domestic work as opposed to the importance of work (for which one also gets paid), and, at the extreme, about the predatory way in which men exploit women. Without going into the details of these controversies it is self-evident that roles of men and women within marriage and the family are susceptible to many changes. The whole basis of work for women has changed dramatically within the past hundred years from a situation in which the main sources of employment were as domestic workers, washerwomen and mill operatives to one which, despite the large inequalities that exist, now spans much more of the spectrum of all available work.

All these issues are sources of discussion and potential bases for change. The same applies within the family situation in the relationships which develop between parents and children. Often if we consider the possibilities of family breakdown mention is made of the enormous damage that this can do to the development of children, but the ability to cope with stress and tension on the part of children may well be necessary within the family situation, and it could be argued that it is desirable in view of the tension that modern life is likely to create for them in the future. The traditional way of looking at the social problems that concern the family is to identify them as firstly, marital breakdown, sometimes ending in divorce, with particular reference to the divorce rate. High divorce rates mean more disorganisation and it is assumed that this is more unsatisfactory. Delinquency is also mentioned in these traditional discussions of family problems and the whole issue of mental health, in particular the extent to which certain family structures help to create certain forms of mental illness.

To categorise in these ways is inadequate as a basis for analysis. It is quite possible to argue that divorce is a healthy symptom of the desire of individuals to obtain happiness in marriage, and their unwillingness to forego this in a situation in which they are more conscious of the disadvantages than the advantages. One of the best justifications for the continuing relevance of marriage is that most people who are divorced will re-marry. Moreover, marriage is subject to more stress because people marry younger and will generally live longer. Thus, whereas in the past the achievement of a Golden Wedding was exceptional, it could well become the norm in the future. It has been suggested that we may well have to be concerned, in the way the family is organised in the future, not so much with the problem of looking after aged parents but, if the low age of marriage continues, with the problem of looking after aged grandparents.

The relevance of the study of abnormal family situations to more normal ones is brought out in the reading by Gillian Parker. She considers categories into which family structures can be grouped and goes on to aspects of family cooperation necessary to reasonably integrated functioning, involving respect for individuality, mutually congruous images of its members, security and the ability to deal with tensions between the sexes, age groups and with people outside. Experience and events such as the birth of a child, not usually considered to be a threat to family stability, can present many difficulties. The reading as a whole gives some idea of the enormous range of situations and issues with which any family has to deal.

The conflict between parents and children may be heightened by the extent to which the peer group, the friends and associates of the children who are of the same age, provide models of behaviour and attitudes which are at variance with those to be found in the home. Some of the most significant of crises within the family are to be found within the range of influences from outside; they include the consequences of accidents, death and other factors outside the control of the family and its members. Internal catastrophies are another area which create individual and personal problems. If these extend to significant numbers within the population they may be a social problem. Included among these are disabilities, whether mental or physical, of some members of the family, severe mental retardation and chronic or incurable physical conditions.

The contact between members of the family and those in official positions is the subject of the next reading. Geoffrey Parkinson looks at some of the problems that arise when matrimonial issues are dealt with by the Probation Officer. The whole question of the role of the social worker in relation to family stress is discussed thoroughly and in the article a practising social worker looks at the ways in which the service may be improved. The basic point that Parkinson is making is that the provision of resources and a role that is not necessarily dispassionate is more use to the Probation Officer and his clients than the neutrality of the more conventional social worker. The reading by Maureen Cain takes the situation of the policeman's family and the kinds of stresses that arise because of his duties, the hours he works and the way in which his role is viewed in the community as a whole.

Certain occupations, like this one, provide more inbuilt tensions for the family, either because of the character of the jobs of the head of the family or because the jobs involve a good deal of mobility. The author compares and contrasts the different kinds of pressures on the police in town and country areas. What emerges has relevance for the high rate of turnover in the police. Great tensions build up with the inevitable moves from place to place of those in country forces and these are felt particularly by children and wives, having to find new friends and make new contacts.

These are some of the consequences of the overall policy both of recruitment and career patterns, and questions about the ambiguities of the role of the policeman as seen by superior officers on the one hand and members of the public on the other are posed.

Although the problems which arise from socialisation within the family are considerable, there are many more for those who are brought up or confined to institutions. Maureen

Oswin's reading takes the case of two handicapped children, one of whom is living in a hospital and the other of whom is living in a residential school. Both types of institution, in fact, care for similarly handicapped children but the difference between the experiences of the two children in this study is most marked. This is an example of material drawn from the direct observation and experience of the writer and it shows the extent to which children in institutions may be deprived. It also poses questions which can be followed up about similarly handicapped groups, whether of the blind, the deaf or the mentally ill, who may be confined to institutions or who may be enabled to live a more satisfying life within the community, given imaginative policies of provision and support for their families.

The reading from Dorothy Wedderburn provides much information about old people and their situation in British society. It pursues questions about the policies which are being followed and in particular the adequacy of provision, problems of coordination, conflicts of interest between administrators, professionals and beneficiaries (and how these are to be reconciled), and the philosophy of the provision of public services in an affluent society. The author makes the point that 'need is dynamic'. This must be borne in mind by all those formulating or administering social policy and setting targets for the future. The question of the aged playing an active part in the shaping and running of the services is raised, and this is an important matter. The desire to be not merely recipients of what is provided for them but actively involved is being expressed by more and more groups in society. It is probably much more important therefore to look at ageing today as a phase in the total life cycle rather than as a social problem group. The problems discussed are best seen as being in no way unique to the aged: they are shared with other disadvantaged groups and are particular illustrations of general problems facing the welfare state and society generally.

Family Patterns of Stress and Distress
Gillian Parker

Reprinted with permission from Gillian Parker, *Family Patterns of Stress and Distress* in J. Gould (ed.) *The Prevention of Damaging Stress in Children*, J. and A. Churchill, London, 1968, pp. 103–11.

The well functioning family is characterized by its ability to undergo the commonly encountered stresses and distresses of living in such a fashion that no undue or irreparable damage occurs to its children. Such protection of the children stems from the family's capacity for foresight, self-healing, and making use of available cultural patterns appropriate to crises. These families, which must form the major part of any stable community, are not the topic of our immediate concern. Nor does this chapter dwell on those factors in a child which allow him to triumph (as many do) over damaging experiences, for example, 'bad' parents; broken homes; unstable environment; uprooting from a motherland.

Any attempt to prevent damaging stress to a child, or to uncover the causes thereof, demands a close investigation into the whole family environment. This chapter sets out to examine the main emotional problems of families in order to assess the attendant risks to the children involved. The first section deals with the problem of becoming a family, and the meaning of children to various families. The second section draws attention to overstimulation, in various forms, of both children and family, and how children's adaptive capacities may be seriously affected by oft-repeated interruptions of ordinary experiences. Usually this is associated with situations of over-crowding and under-privilege. There can be, however, conditions amounting to an emotional slum in situations of prestige and/ or material plenty. These families fail to shelter the children from undue stimulation and disturbance by the continual unpredictable changes in the family's life. The third section deals with the plight of sick families. Here the very nature of the illness of the parents, whether physical or psychological, results in unstable emotions and prevents the parents from protecting the children from the disturbed family climate. The last section deals with researches into prevention of the risk to children, and the treatment of families in situations of stress and distress.

At times of crisis a child looks naturally for comfort and support to those persons from whom it is accustomed to receive help in resolving problems—especially such as arise from doubt and fear. Usually the child turns to one or both parents. In any case, the ordinary loving family gives the required help, but also maintains reasonable balance between the needs of the individual and the demands of the family.

Investigations into patterns of stress and distress in various types of families shows that at one pole lie well functioning families, which may be stricken by a series of unpredictable disasters. At the other pole are very sick families, ill-equipped from the outset to withstand strain. For these the original marriage may well have been contracted largely as a defence against fears of inner personal disaster—futility, emptiness or fears of sheer madness. In between these extremes lie, realized or not, various patterns of reaction to stress and distress, which carry, in differing measure, pressures of an urgent external reality and anxieties associated with inner turmoil. The child enmeshed in any such situation is in serious danger, but the age at which this occurs is important in influencing the nature and gravity of the risk.

Furthermore, any important experience may have several 'dimensions', the balance of which needs to be determined. First the family may allow a greater or lesser degree of personal identity to each member. This will affect the 'meaning' ascribed to the experiences by the family. Secondly, some experiences penetrate deeply, wherefore their intensity and duration is important, while other experiences involve many areas of family functioning and here it is the amplitude which must be assessed. Finally, arising out of these 'dimensions' come the questions of how the experience may have affected the integrity of the family and of the individual members. The reaction of a family to an overwhelming experience may well be toned by shame, guilt and anger. This can affect the capability of the individual to become reconciled to the inevitable changes in family circumstances. All this may apply to the family as a whole and to any member of it.

Research into neurotic breakdown and rehabilitation suggests that all families possessing family structure can, broadly speaking, be grouped into three categories:

1. The family that can permit the individuality of its members, and meet the needs of young and old, healthy or infirm, has commonly been a family which has held its own for several generations in the community, facing reality. It exemplifies a good degree of internal security in relation to stress.

2. The family that recognizes its members' feelings and needs, but can offer security over a reduced range of circumstances, and is more vulnerable to stress. It may well be a family which has been dislocated from its historical or cultural heritage. It exemplifies a significant but lesser degree of internal security than Category 1.

3. In contrast to the foregoing there are families which operate by means of an unwholesome 'family myth'. Such families require the members to enact certain fixed roles or to hold certain outlooks on life. In this way such families are able to function coherently but with a very limited relationship to reality. Individuality in these families is likely to be crushed and the cost of the security offered therefore is high.

Families, if they are to become reasonably integrated, need to develop five aspects of family co-operation. Firstly they have to establish a pattern whereby the individuality of each member is respected as well as the unity of family functioning. Secondly, alongside this, the members of the family must develop a set of mutually congruous images of themselves and of each other. Thirdly, the family thereby evolves modes of mutual interaction regarding general family concerns and themes. Fourthly, the family must establish a boundary to its own 'world of experience', which gives security, but can also expand with the developing needs of family members. Fifthly, it has to find a way of dealing with the significant bio-social issues of family life, for example, the tensions between the sexes, between the generations, between kith and people outside the family relationships.

Only artificially can these aspects of co-operation be separated in this manner. In reality they are all interwoven and dependent on the developing maturity of the key family members—usually the parents. The family in which the key members have behind them a history of fairly successful social relationships will evolve, during the first several years of married life, these five aspects of co-operation. This in itself is a stressful process, made more so by inevitable changes in the image each had of himself and of the other and magnified at times by changes in the circumstances in which they live, and their inescapable involvement in the critical issues of their day.

A domestic event able greatly to change the circumstances in which a family lives is the birth of a child. During the first years of married life several children may be added to the family. Each child in turn becomes, for a while, the prime responsibility of the parents and will cause further change in family circumstances. As each child reaches a stage of development where he should not only cease to depend so much on the parents, but also begin, consciously and unconsciously, to affect and to be affected by his brothers and sisters, his own sense of personal identity will begin to unfold. The parents' responsibilities will thereby change and differentiate. From the time the first child is born, certain 'foci of anxiety' beset the parents, whose attitude towards these depends upon their *own* feelings and phantasies about sex, power and responsibility. In many marriages in which there has been a disturbance of the initial phases of the process of becoming a family, there is often an important but unclear element in the original mutual attraction and complementation in the parents. At its best, mutual attraction encompasses loving kindness and can give both partners something neither can find in his own self. At its worst, it is a compelling bond making for unresolvable conflict between husband and wife. In this case, children may be needed by the parents to accept roles which tend to balance the disequilibrium of the marriage. In such circumstances the parents, influenced by their own personalities and problems, select, usually unconsciously, the roles they need their children to play. The same parental factors also determine how insistently the parents impose these roles upon the children.

Families differ very much in the way the parents interact with the children, some desirably amending or reshaping their own aims as their children grow and develop. But where the parents expect the children to do all the adapting, there is little room for growth and the process of self and mutual discovery is unwholesomely limited. Families differ also as to how parents help their children through childhood; whether they push, encourage, restrain or disregard them. The nature of parental stimulation, its intensity, frequency and diversity, expresses much of the parents' attitude towards the instinctual life and the values placed on personal relationships. Winnicott, in his papers on transitional objects, touches on the important parental problem, namely, how much of a child's world rightly belongs to himself, and not by right to the parents and further, the child's freedom to play happily alone in the presence of the mother in the room, to explore its own feelings and ideas in relation to the objects and pets within its reach, without too quickly having to refer the matter back to mother. Lowenfeld has suggested that much of a child's feeling of love is thus temporarily transferred from mother to the objects in his little world, about which he thus becomes intensely and manipulatively interested.

Some of the child's activities will give greater pleasure to his mother than will others, in harmony with the mother's predilections and experience of life. An example drawn from a young woman in analysis whose child's development had been closely observed by the therapist can illustrate this. 'I think he is going to be an architect', said the ecstatic mother, watching her firstborn toddler display a certain aptitude for piling bricks one upon another. There was evidence that this remark betrayed her loving admiration for her own father, her regret that she had not been the son the father had wanted, the exciting thought that *her* son might one day be the equal of his grandfather, together with her natural maternal delight in her child enjoying himself. This mother will be likely to provide her little boy with play material which allows him to put things together, and will let him get on with it, using his own ideas as to what he wants to do—an excellent state of affairs!

Some mothers, however, cannot help invading the private play space of their child. If a mother does not recognize her baby's right to his own identity and does not feel sufficiently separate from her child, she will impute to him her own ideas and views of the world. She does not allow him to experience his separateness nor to feel differently from her. He is thus severely handicapped in developing his own perceptions. A child so treated is likely to become frustrated and angry, even without knowing why, because he has no sanction to recognize his own sensations for what they are. Longing to remain in touch with his mother—and what young child will readily accept the alternative—he is compelled to develop a 'false' self; his 'true' self remaining potential, with the conscious recognition of certain only nascent feelings, indescribable but disturbing. An example from a young man in analytic treatment shows this. His over-possessive mother could not accept that part of his play in his childhood associated with his incipient masculinity. The cumulative affect of this upon him, as he expressed it while in treatment, was 'I have a blank in my middle, not quite like having to wear a fig leaf, but just nothing there.' The play his mother liked when he was little was 'cuddly play'. In other words as this was as much as she had been able to enjoy, it became the growing child's own picture of his acceptable self. As a young man this patient had developed a marked capacity for being kind, courteous and very understanding with girls, but believed that any masculine assertiveness would prove quite unacceptable to them.

The meaning the child has to his parents. The sense of identity and the sense of belonging begin and develop during childhood. These are derived from the meaning and significance mutually accorded by members of the family to the child and each other. Recent research into family functioning demonstrates that particular personal bonds, based on special images—both benign and damaging—evolve from the personalities and the life experience of the family at any salient point of experience in the family history. Thus a child whose birth is accompanied by more than usual risks will be precious to the family but may also be regarded as the cause of a later ailment of the mother. Whenever this child takes a new step, such as going to school or puberty, the family may well react with anxiety which on analysis may prove to be a re-enactment of the birth anxiety. This has been noticed particularly in the study of premature infants and Rhesus babies.

To understand the full implications of damaging stress on certain children it is not enough to study the environmental pressures of relationships in the family, but the whole family entity with its corporate powers of formation, restriction and even partial self-destruction. The first task for the observer is to erect a framework, within which can be undertaken a meaningful investigation of the family as a whole. Such a conceptual framework includes an appreciation of the social pressures on the family; the family's system of values interacting with these social pressures and the parents' tendency to invest the child with parts of themselves which are commonly derived initially from their own unfulfilments. Such parental projections then serve as a pathway of communication between parents and child which also permits discrepancies between the real personality of the child and the parents' picture of him to become clearer. In the family dealing with stress, or acting in a fashion less mature, the pathway of communication will be formed by unacceptable and unrecognized projections, while in extreme distress messages unwelcome to the parents about the real nature of the child's personality will not be received or will be misinterpreted. This process will be reduced in measure as each key member of the family can deal with his own conflicts and values so that the child can be experienced as an individual in his or her own right.

Nevertheless even in the evolution of the most normal families, there may be experiences which seriously disturb the parents' ability to operate in this way. For instance, the parents may so greatly value the child, long waited for as the embodiment of their own creative ability, that to discover him to be markedly less competent than they had hoped and expected may be a serious blow. As illustration, consider a middle-aged couple who, after a series of miscarriages, produced one child. They came for advice because of their awareness of difficulties with their child. They were highly intellectual, successful, kindly, professional people, but their child had great difficulty in learning. This increased in proportion to his fear of proving to be a disappointment to the parents. In the end, the boy effaced himself in all social relations. The parents were distracted; all they seemed to be able to do was to highlight the child's deficiency and their own oppressive sense of failure at not being more successful parents.

To give another clinical example: the wife loved and admired her husband as a very clever and creative man. He was delighted when at last they had a small daughter who was not only clever but also very pretty. When about three years old the little girl was badly burnt about the face and shoulders, the mother having put no guard in front of the fire before she went out into the garden. Severe facial scarring destroyed the child's beauty. Later when the little girl began to mix with other children, the mother was no longer able to defend herself from her own sense of guilt. She felt acutely threatened by the child's disfigurement, and therefore reacted to the child as if the child were aggressive and hostile to her. In self-defence against this, the child adopted a masculine attitude, identified herself with her father and, as a child, only enjoyed being with him. Mother seemed to develop two images, one when the daughter was absent, of the beautiful child she should have been; and the other when the daughter was present, that of an attacking and accusing child. Later, the child became very aggressive towards her mother and, for a time, 'uncontrollable'.

The emotional equilibrium of the family. A family may react in different ways to the death of a relative, should this occur about the time of the birth of a child. A mother lost her brother at the time of her daughter's birth. Such was the grief, that try as she might, she could not involve herself deeply with the baby. Without maternal warmth, and despite the father's best loving efforts, the baby became over anxious, precociously alert, seeming to look to herself for help. This child developed a pseudo-independence, a great sense of responsibility and an outward concern at being exploited.

Another variation of the above situation is for the mother to see in the little girl the qualities of the dead brother. This would be a way of dealing with the grief, namely, minimizing or denying the loss, by means of substituting, in the mother's mental economy, the new arrival for the departed one. Sometimes this device serves the *family* purpose of keeping mother from being too depressed, but if, in the process, it forces the child to enact the role of a personality not his own, it gives the child little chance of developing his real self.

A family may not need to hold a particular child in a fixed role all the while. So long as someone in the family accepts the role when this is necessary, the family purpose—to maintain a system of equilibrium—is served. For instance when parents, with two or more children, are dealing with disruptive, contradictory feelings in themselves about each other, they may need to regard one of their children as 'the good child' and another as 'the naughty child', with all the implicit repercussions this would have upon the children.

Here is an example of a couple who had two little girls separated by four years. The family underwent two separate crises, also separated by four years. When the first baby was born the parents were in difficulties with their own two mothers and with their roles as husband and wife. 'There was not a single night', so the couple alleged, 'that Mary didn't cry when we went up to bed together.' The husband was very unsure of his masculinity as something loveable. He needed to feel that his wife fully accepted his virility in the marriage not only as natural but also in order to give him self-assurance, following his own mother's disappointment that he had not been a girl. The wife, prudish about sexual matters by reason of her mother's fear for her as the only girl in a large family of boys, felt dirty and devalued by sexual relations and guilty about being pregnant. She loved her little daughter dearly, but she experienced her own sexual guilt and distress by believing the child to be unable to tolerate the parents sleeping together. At the same time her own tensions, affecting the child, made the latter disturbed at bed time, thus completing the pathological emotional cycle between mother and child.

When the couple had become more emancipated and experienced, following treatment, the second child was born and was seen as happy and contented. Later, when the second child was four years old, there came in the family's history a further period of distress. This was due to the illness of the paternal grandmother, together with depression in the wife, all of which made the husband very anxious. He had to go away on business. The elder girl now aged eight, hitherto regarded as 'the naughty one' took over the role of the good and comforting child while the younger became 'bad' and attacking.

Two factors have to be appreciated here, the one that at certain ages the children of a family will react more openly to a distress in their parents by non-conforming and difficult behaviour; and the other that certain parents at certain times find such non-conforming behaviour convenient to their emotional needs and so a collusive situation occurs. Children of certain age groups are more likely to find themselves in self-damaging role-playing by reason of some developmental crisis through which they are passing. Such states also can be unconsciously exploited by the family. Research into families in considerable socio-emotional distress suggests that the 2–4 year olds and the adolescents were especially vulnerable in these respects. Furthermore these children are ill-fitted to tolerate being regarded as 'bad' because they secretly fear that there might be in fact something 'bad' about their inner feelings.

Marriages on Probation
G. Parkinson

Reprinted with permission from G. Parkinson, 'Marriages on Probation', *New Society*, 22 May 1969.

Most probation officers feel uneasy about their work with matrimonial cases. Such recent and reasonable studies as have been made suggest that we are not very good at it and are left to do the work mainly because no other professional body is willing or in a position to take over the responsibility. 'Mats' are in many respects regarded as an irritating duty added uneasily to a probation officer's caseload.

At first glance this may seem curious since, unlike most of our clients, 'Mats' come willingly, they seek help, they have generally recognisable problems and they are thus eligible for 'casework'. Quite a few probation officers in training get excited at the prospect of treating damaged marriages; the idea of learning about other people's sex lives, of hearing men and women squabbling is not without its attractions, especially when, after treatment, emotional wounds may be healed, sexuality enriched and the probation officer gratefully recognised as the doer of good. Yet, once in the field, the young probation officer's enthusiasm is all too often blighted. He may even join the growing ranks of colleagues who feel 'this is not really our work'.

Why should this be? Dr H. V. Dicks, the doyen of professional matrimonial workers, held generations of probation officer trainees enthralled by his brilliant case studies of broken and unhappy marriages. We sought to imitate his ways, which to my memory involved assisting husbands and wives to see the errors and inaccuracies of their Oedipal ways by methods so subtle and sensitive that even the most painful of insights came as creative experiences.

Once in the courts we were to learn a hard lesson. 'Mats' were no more open to traditional casework than were delinquents even though they entered our offices voluntarily. 'Mats' proved stubborn. They did not want to look at the personality of their marriage or their own personalities. They didn't want to see any of the complications or subtleties of their own reactions or the reactions of their spouses. They seemed generally to be fixated to the present; the only feelings that had any meaning for them were the feelings they felt at that moment and these were usually as blind as they were overwhelming.

We tried to give interviews a sense of depth but in the end all they wanted was a summons or a letter ticking their husbands off. They ran to us as children run to teachers in a playground to settle some dispute, swiftly and with authority, and we for the most part sat benign and neutral, fiddling around with our insights. We soon came to feel, certainly I felt, that our role for these clients was closely prescribed and that to break out of the set limits was not only difficult but probably quite pointless.

For a while I joined the ranks of those who believed we should get rid of the work.

The dilemma of 'Mats' in the probation setting is either assisted or handicapped by the situation in which the work is obtained, according to one's viewpoint. Magistrates' courts in London usually carry out their matrimonial duties by a routine which involves directing applicants in the first instance to the scrutiny of a probation officer. The aggrieved wife—and it usually seems to be only the wife we see—can't get a summons against her husband for persistent cruelty, desertion or any other matrimonial offence, without a *prima facie* case; and this often becomes the officer's major quasi-legal function. He usually assesses the situation and may apply to the court on her behalf.

The yardstick for matrimonial offences is rather crude to middle class eyes and was at one time, in my opinion, unpleasantly rigid. Persistent cruelty, for example, had in practice to be three blows to the body during the previous six months, in the presence, if possible, of a witness, and I can never remember making an application on the grounds of mental cruelty. If only two punches were readily recalled, the officer might scratch around his client's uneasy memory, even asking such curious questions as 'Do you mean to say that when your husband got drunk at Christmas he didn't come home and punch you?'

Frequently applicants do not pursue their original intention of summonsing because, after a chat, they decide they want to 'make another go of it'—and leave after requesting the officer to write a letter to the husband telling him to behave himself. From this sort of situation an axiom arises: many clients think they want to end their marriages but unconsciously they wish to make a go of things and this is their way of seeking help. On such a cunning psychological principle I often used to send a wife back to the slaughter of her marriage, taking with her one or two unhappy children. She believed I was helping; that adds to the irony of the situation. I think the essence of the matter is in many respects the reverse of this axiom: many women want to end their marriages on a conscious level but are unconsciously committed to a sado-masochistic drama.

Our case files show the same monotonous repetition of detail. Sometimes one feels the unhappy histories follow a few stereotyped lines and only the clients' names and faces are different. Mrs A with three children has a husband who drinks heavily at the weekends, takes most of the housekeeping money and punches her when she protests. Mrs B who loved her naughty husband until she produced naughty children whom she preferred and thereafter thought her husband should be good. Mrs C who sits up into the early hours of the morning fascinated and fearful while her workshy, drunken husband goes into rages about her imagined infidelities.

One knows the stories behind such marriages are complex and their drama serves perverse needs for both husband and wife. One is, for example, familiar with the unconscious problems existing in a drunkard's wife and one knows that individuals may often avoid disturbance in themselves by living in a disturbed marriage. Many traditional casework methods would attempt to reveal such truths to these unhappy women. They would theoretically be expected to understand their choice of partner, their need for a depriving angry male, part child, part monster. All this might be fine except that it doesn't often work. Insights are largely useless except to the worker who may use them as psychological amphetamines, keeping him interested and alert during depressing sessions.

A large percentage of the women visiting us are highly masochistic. Most of them have never reflected upon themselves or the nature of their behaviour and they are thus both the innocents and slaves of their unconscious conflicts. The men they married may have once delighted them with their heavy drinking, their half-playful anger, their irresponsibility in work, their abuse of feminine qualities and their aggressive, though not always effective, sexuality. When the marriage reaches our office all this has crumbled into moans, violence, economic deprivation, partial desertion and meaningless intercourse, with the husband finding such satisfactions as he may in light ales, and the wife such pleasures as she can from her small, uncontrolled and anxious children. If the officer is aware of anything from these situations, it is that the clients need action not insight.

The psychoanalytic morality and motives of some caseworkers, however stimulating, are useless unless they can be blended with traditional methods of mending marriages in a neighbourhood. In the East End, and the body of my experience is in that area, the probation officer has now to some extent to fulfil the role previously played by fathers and brothers. Thirty years ago a daughter would ultimately have gone back to dad with her complaints about her husband and dad would have either made it clear that she had 'made her bed and must lie on it,' or, if the complaints were persistent and her parents sympathetic, possibly send one or two of the men in her family to see the defaulting husband and show him the error of his ways, if necessary by a swift punch-up.

This happens less and less frequently as the function of the family in the East End diminishes and the environment becomes more complex and generally less threatening. Thus now, instead of dad, the court and the probation officer are expected to deal with things. A gently phrased letter inviting the husband to discuss his difficulties may be all therapy and light to the officer who sends it. The husband, however, when he notices the printed notepaper 'Probation Service' knows his wife is putting the pressure on; he is going to be ticked off at the best and dragged into court at the worst. Invariably he feels he does not want to answer questions put to him by some clever middle class official and, partly from a sense of guilt, he probably believes that only his wife's side will be believed. The letter is usually torn up and the husband either proceeds to fortify the wife's *prima facie* case or for a time gives up his bad habits and promises to be better.

My present approach to 'Mats' is based upon solving one central problem, the apparent lack of sincerity of clients in their search for help. By lack of sincerity I mean their inability to decide between contradicting forces both within themselves and within the marriage. Though matrimonial clients rarely admit to faults, all agree that they vacillate insofar as they find it difficult to take appropriate steps in dealing with their marriage problems.

It is of this that I most regularly and persistently accuse them: 'Well maybe your husband does hit you, but why are you there to be hit?' or, 'Why shouldn't your husband think you like being kicked around? You have never done anything about it until now. You may not do anything about it even now.' I have often elaborated on this more extensively and personally: 'You are young and attractive and you can still make a go of life. If you let things drift, in ten years time you will have four or five kids and you will be stuck and nobody will want to help you very much.' All the time I repeat my central theme: 'You must make him realise you are serious about this. Things must either get better or you must end it.' I am often accused in my approach of being biased on the wife's side. In a sense this is true. The wife, not the husband, is usually the client and the wife rather than the husband suffers most physically and financially.

Our clients lack beautiful middle class egos and come from depressed uncreative backgrounds. Frequently if the husband is a drunk so was the father; if the client is knocked around so also was her mother. And if I am 'on the wife's side' it is not through a failure to grasp the husband's position or any lack of sympathy for his viewpoint; my approach often implies a considerable understanding of his aggressive feelings since I deal with aggressive feelings the wife provokes in me by making comments and requests containing a high content of anger—like 'You must...' or 'It is no good your...' For me the sure guide to a masochistic wife is my desire after ten minutes to get up and hit her.

My methods, by making me happy, make me more useful to the client, and the client feels this. In earlier days she liked the irresponsible brashness of her husband, now she can enjoy the more responsible brashness of the caseworker. Since I am seen as being on her side, I can say things to her which she would not accept from someone more 'impartial'.

I frequently use the court, or the threat of the court, as a technique. Husbands must see the limits, and the law is often the best way of achieving this. For years Mr X has hit Mrs X in front of the kids; now suddenly this is challenged by the disappearance of Mrs X and the kids, and the appearance of a summons to explain to a judge why he, Mr X, is behaving like this. His wife now becomes a person with ideas and an identity of her own. He now, summons in hand, knows he loves her.

Whether at this point the wife continues to proceed against her husband or returns to him must depend on a whole variety of factors, but provided she is clear in her own mind that the situation must never be allowed to deteriorate in the same way again then all may be well. In her intention to establish a different type of relationship she must know that the probation officer will play the role of her supporter expecting her to report at the earliest point any signs of deterioration. By a different relationship incidentally, I mean only one thing: no more extreme violence or financial deprivation or whatever the offences may be. Just as with delinquents, the central focus must be around acts of crime, so with matrimonials the central focus must be around the ending of specific acts of cruelty. To be sidetracked in any way from this is exceedingly dangerous. Husbands may give subtle reasons for hitting their wives, but in the end they hear from me that they must either put up with their wives more or less as they are or they must get out. They can't have it both ways. Incidentally, I now always make a point of regularly sending reminding letters to wives offering them further appointments, and these are used by wives to show their husbands when things get a little difficult. They are quite effective.

The probation officer is probably wise to seek very limited objectives and abandon any attempt at an extensive 'cure'. If punching is the complaint then the cessation of punching is probably the aim. In seeking this the officer will indirectly alter many aspects of the marriage, some in a positive, others inevitably in a negative way. The central problem posed by most matrimonials is their inability to act effectively and in this they are ably assisted by the housing shortage and poor economic conditions; therefore the officer should probably spend a great deal more time than he has in the past helping complainants to find places of refuge from violent and defaulting husbands.

The probation officer has an important role to play with matrimonial clients, utilising and transcending the quasi-legal function given to him by the courts. The starting point must be the abandonment of therapeutic methods and goals so persuasively argued by those whose matrimonial work is effected in a more genteel sociological and casework atmosphere.

The Life of a Policeman and his Family
Maureen Cain

Reprinted with permission from Maureen Cain, 'The Life of a Policeman and his Family' in Ben Whittaker, *The Police*, Eyre and Spottiswoode and Penguin, 1964, pp. 123–33.

Tensions rooted in the interrelationships between the policeman, his family, the community in which he lives, and his colleagues and superiors affect the town and country forces differently. A study carried out in 1962 and early 1963 showed that tension between the husband and wife was very slightly greater in the county force, as were tensions generated by the relationship between the policeman and the local community. Similar conflicts between the men and their colleagues or superiors were far more frequent in the county. In one experimental situation 73·4 per cent of the men said they would experience these, compared with 54·5 per cent of those in the city.

Family tensions are perhaps the most important factor in wastage, though their overall incidence was lower than that for conflicts arising from the other sources.

> A Police Constable does not merely take a job; he embarks on a new way of life ... the first claim on him must be made by his duty and the convenience of his wife and family must be a secondary consideration.

This applies not only to constables. One superintendent told how his annual leave had been postponed by the chief constable just as he and his wife had their bags packed and were on the point of leaving the house. Such incidents occur more frequently in county forces, where the hierarchy of authority remains more autocratic. Yet despite this, country policemen's wives frequently say, 'Oh, one gets to accept it. It's all part of the job.' Because of this attitude many of the potential conflicts inherent in their situation never became actual: 59 per cent of the country policemen said they were satisfied with the effects of the job on their private life, compared with 51 per cent of the city men.

These proportions are, however, low even in the county force. The hours and the inability to make arrangements are the main causes of dissatisfaction, but there are others as well. In the county the greatest inconvenience to the family, is caused by frequency of transfer. In one force the men's average length of stay in a post was 2·7 years—just sufficient time for the whole family to form roots so that the next move would again entail an emotional as well as a physical upheaval. Adults can adapt themselves to this situation—at least they are able to choose; children cannot. Eldest children of the county men averaged four schools each; over a quarter of the children had already attended five schools or more. Here are some of the men's own comments about this: 'The elder girl suffered from this last move. She had to give up taking one or two subjects which weren't taught at the new school.'

'All this changing schools is the trouble with a county force. There was my girl of eight, she could hardly read. And when this business of the eleven plus came along for the elder one I realized for the first time what I'd been doing to my children.'

Another man told of how he had been obliged to move on the day before his daughter sat for her eleven plus, and others of how their children had been emotionally disturbed for months after a particularly inopportune move. In the county 69 per cent of the children were said to have an unfavourable opinion of their father's job, compared with 35 per cent in the city. 18 per cent of policemen who were interviewed in one force said that they would not wish any eligible son of theirs to join the police.

Only a few of the parents said that their children met with antagonism because of their fathers' work, but there were rather more in the country than in the towns, where school-fellows do not necessarily know his occupation. Again, in the country, more men said that their children suffered because teachers and others in authority expected a higher standard or 'example' from them.

From the wife's point of view the moves entail far more than the loss of friends. There is the additional work and expense of refitting curtains and carpets every three years, and the redecoration of the new house. The maximum allowance of £30 goes only a small way towards meeting these expenses. There is therefore no incentive to plant the garden or decorate the house, though in fairness it must be said that most stations are very well kept. On average the wives had each lived in four police houses. In some forces, bad administration causes families to be given only a fortnight's notice or less before a move.

A higher standard is expected of the policeman's family in many matters, and they are all very much aware of this. Physically isolated and lacking the support of his colleagues, known personally to all the local inhabitants, the country policeman is highly vulnerable to criticism from his neighbours. For this reason he attempts to conform to their expectations of him, and he experiences conflict when he is unable to do so. The city man can get encouragement from his colleagues should such a situation arise. He is also in a stronger position in that he is often uncertain of what the general public really expect him to do, and if he does know he may be indifferent since he need not come into contact with those who disagree. Avoidance is the simplest way of resolving such a potential conflict. Speaking of a minor motoring offence which might occur at an inconvenient time, one country beat man said, 'If it were on my own patch I'd have to do something, because people would see and wonder if I let him off; you can't afford to do that. But if it happened somewhere else, well, then that would be different.' Another remarked, 'I always try to look as a policeman should be dressed ... In a little town like this it would be very difficult for anyone who liked to dress casually. One thing, you see, everyone knows you....'

A myth has grown up among city folk that the country policeman has an idyllic life as the hub and centre of his own little world, a man treated with respect and courtesy by the local people, and whose judgement is relied upon implicitly in a wide variety of matters. Much of this is true, but there are other equally important factors left out of the description. The life of a country policeman in a rural area can be a very lonely one. It is true that he is treated with respect, but this by definition implies a certain amount of social distance. All too often he is regarded as someone 'different', with whom it would therefore be impossible to make friends on equal terms, and his wife and family also will be treated with a not unkindly meant wariness. 'I think they like me all right but they're not friendly,' said one country policeman's wife. Isolation based on respect is as painful as isolation based on mistrust. Another rural wife spoke of her embarrassment when the local shop-keeper regularly insisted on serving her first, regardless of how many other customers were already waiting, while many more said that conversation tended to stop when they approached.

How far in fact are policemen a race apart? And how far does such separateness as does exist result from their own choosing? Broadly speaking, city police either do not come into contact with civilians to any great extent because they live in a group of police houses, or because they have chosen to be isolated. In the country the contact is there. More often than not the isolation is forced on the policeman's family by the local population, though here too there are those who choose it. 'If you get too friendly and they do something wrong they expect you either not to report them or to cover it up in such a way that they're not prosecuted.' This is not always the case. In an organically solid village community the consensus of values is high. One constable spoke of an occasion when a personal friend continued to infringe the Diseases of Animals Regulations, after repeated warnings. With apologies the constable explained that he would now have to report him, but that he hoped their relationship would remain friendly. Apparently it did. A policeman is expected to do his job. But the fact that this compromise solution worked in this case does not mean that the conflict the constable experienced was any the less, and it is understandable that many men choose instead to avoid friendship and therefore potential conflict. As the Federation representatives have said, a policeman 'cannot expect to enjoy full social freedom in the police district where he serves', and if a man happens to live in the district where he serves, that is a misfortune. His behaviour must always be exemplary, as must that of his family, and his duty as a policeman must always be uppermost in his mind, for those with whom he comes into contact will regard him primarily as a policeman and will force professional considerations upon him although technically he may be off duty and more anxious to turn his mind to leisure pursuits. Such is the strain under which the rural constable often lives, not from choice and not because his senior officers demand it from him, but because the people on his beat expect it of him. He must conform because both he and his family are dependent upon their goodwill and cooperation.

The expectations of the community will vary from place to place, and they will certainly differ at many points from the expectations of the higher ranks of the force. The community will have its own ideas as to which offences should be dealt with severely and which should not, how often a policeman should visit and how he should behave when he does. City-born men working country beats often spoke of the length of time it took them to settle down, in particular to adjust their pace of working to that of the people they were dealing with. These community opinions carry heavy sanctions, and strong conflicts can arise for the man whose family or superiors have a different set of expectations about his behaviour.

Just how much contact do the policeman and his family have with the wider community? Despite difficulties of transport and physical isolation the men in the county force met more civilians socially on more occasions than did the city men. The total scaled score for social contact with the community was 3·3 on average for the county men, and 2·4 for those in the city. This bears out the hypothesis of the county man being more dependent on the local civilian population. But his desire to be accepted by this civilian community is also stronger on account of this greater dependence, and 74 per cent of the county men compared with 44 per cent of the city men thought that they would have more friends if they had a different job. (The Royal Commission Survey found that 66·8 per cent of policemen said that the job adversely affected their outside friendships.) City men tended to show a cheerful confidence about their social relationships with the community at large, since these relationships were less important for them, and they claimed to have more friends locally than did the men from the rural areas. Yet only 40 per cent of the city men had been born in the same town or county, compared with 64 per cent of the men from the county force.

For the wives the relationship between the two forces was rather different. 59 per cent of the county wives and 55 per cent of the city wives had been born locally. The county wives met fewer people socially than did their husbands, but they tended to see these few people more frequently. Wives in the city met more people socially than did their husbands, as well as seeing them more often, and they also scored much more than the country wives on both these counts. It is understandable that the wife of a country policeman becomes dissatisfied when her social life is so much restricted. Physical distance and the demands of the job mean that she can leave home less often, so she even tends to see her relatives less often than her husband or the city women did. At the same time she lacks her husband's opportunity of meeting many people each day on a professional level. County wives were also more isolated than their equivalents in the city in their contacts with the families of other policemen. One reason for this is that 17 per cent of the county wives compared with 25 per cent of the city wives lived in groups of six or more police houses. Moreover, there were fewer organized social activities for wives and families in the county, as well as the ever-present problem of poor public transport and physical distance.

For the men in rural areas it would seem that transport is not a worry. Just as they had a greater number of social contacts with civilians than did their city counterparts, so too they had on average social contacts with more fellow policemen. These contacts were mainly at sporting activities organized by the force, whereas in the city they tended to be less formal. For the city men too their work each day involved contact with their colleagues. This accounts for the fact that the county men claimed far more often than city men that their colleagues or superiors would disagree with an action they intended to take. In a conflict situation it is far more important to them that they should conform to the expectations of their family, or the local community, than with their colleagues or

superiors whom they see far less frequently and who are unlikely to watch what they do.

For the city man the situation is quite different. Often he
will work some distance from home so his family and neighbours need not know of his actions at work, whereas he is in
frequent contact with his fellow policemen, and dependent on
their backing. He must therefore conform to their expectations
and not forfeit their goodwill. Thus the city man will tend to
solve his conflicts or conflicting expectations in accordance
with the requirements of his fellow policemen.

Although there are no corresponding figures for the total
community with which to compare them, the available data
suggest that the relative isolation of both the men and their
wives that policemen often talk of is not in many cases fact,
although it is both perceived and experienced. This perception
and the tensions resulting from the conflict experiences which
have been described (especially in the country where the man's
actions are visible to at least two of the groups concerned) and
the strain of being constantly in the public gaze are all factors
in wastage. The fact is that quite apart from professional
work, a large number of actions which would normally be
private are controlled to some extent by the expectations of
workmates, superiors, and the public at large.

Relationships inside the force varied again between the city
and the county. The city men claimed to have more friends on
the job—statistically, 5·3 as against 3·1 in the county. County
men said that those friends they had were men with whom
they had joined. It was not always wise to get too friendly with
men working neighbouring beats: they were suspicious of their
colleagues because of the promotion struggle and because of
the fear that if a mistake is made and discovered a sudden
transfer could result. In any case, the men say that firm friendships are impossible when one is constantly being moved. In the
city the picture is different. Friendships tend to develop in
working together on the beat or mobile patrol, in sharing difficulties over some disruly members of the public or over a
senior officer. The backing of colleagues is essential in a tight
corner and strong ties of loyalty develop. This loyalty is the
prime virtue, together with the other 'heroic' attitude that the
weak must be protected; wives and such women as could be
regarded as potential wives are treated with exaggerated re-
pect (which involves leaving them in considerable ignorance of
many of their menfolk's activities). This last attitude also en-

ables them to avoid conflict between some of the demands of their job and their family's expectations for them. It was significant that on an inter-dependence scale the city men scored much higher than those in the county (4·7 compared with 2·6). They perceived both themselves to be far more dependent on the force, and the force to be far more dependent on them, than did the county men.

There are some points at which the relationships with other members of the force can lead to wastage. In city forces much of the formality has been dropped from these relationships between ranks, but in the county the hierarchic structure is rigidly adhered to. A county inspector would never call one of his constables by his christian name while on duty, and it is unlikely that he would do so off duty either. The relationship with senior officers in the county remains to some extent paternalistic. Thus fewer men said they were dissatisfied with the amount of interest their superiors took in them than of the city men. Yet senior officers in the county are more feared, for they have correspondingly more autocratic powers. Their authority under the Discipline and other regulations is the same in both forces, but in the county infringements tend to be arbitrarily 'punished' by a transfer, without formal examination. If a query should arise the move can always be justified on other grounds. So a county man is anxious always to 'keep in step' with his superiors, because otherwise his whole family will suffer. In the city discipline matters are dealt with more openly, and generally the Federation is strong enough to see fair play.

The rationalization of discipline in the larger forces, whether city or county, is a further example of that process of increasing bureaucratization which is itself causing tensions of a different kind at other points. One is that the beat men feel that their individual responsibility is being sapped away and that their job is therefore a less interesting one, and this is true in many cases. Further tensions of bureaucratization arise where the structure is not yet completely rational. Men in specialist departments, such as dog handlers and mobile patrols, often claim that they are the victims of divided authorities which on occasion can give conflicting orders. They are responsible both to their specialist superiors and to the senior officers of the divisions where they work. 'You've always got one of them on your back, and it makes things very difficult. You can't please everyone.' Although legally he alone is responsible for his actions and must bear the consequences of them, the constable is in the anomalous position that he also has the opinions of his senior officers to bear in mind. He has to satisfy their requirements, those of the people with whom he is dealing, and the law. In the city these responsibilities will be considered in that order; in the country the first two may well be reversed.

As members of what is by definition a minority group, the police are continuously in a defensive position. Their uniform is a visible cue for prejudice against them, and they become sensitive and unable to concede the need for any internal change as a result. Some of them lessen the tension produced by this situation by attempting to disown the job, and conform as far as possible to more general standards. 'I always go home in civvies; you don't want to advertise the fact that you're a copper, do you?' 72 per cent of men interviewed said they did not like to be recognized as policemen while on holiday. Others attempt to exclude themselves from what they perceive to be a general public attitude of antagonism by saying that the force has changed since they joined, that young men joining today are of a lower standard, and that the job is not the same any more. (Even some young men do this.) Those who have done National Service say that the trouble lies with those who haven't; those who enter direct say that the trouble lies with the increased numbers of cadets. Much of this dissatisfaction results from a feeling of low status, which in turn sometimes gives rise to violence, verbal or physical, against prisoners as an outlet, which gives further backing to the negative stereotype. In parts this accounts for the greater incidence of violence in city areas, where the public expectations are less favourable. The realization of this is one of the causes of early leaving, though it is unlikely to appear in statistics of reasons for leaving, since the men concerned are scarcely aware of it on a conscious level.

Accommodation in 'police colonies' can serve only to enhance this feeling of separateness. In the main the men do not want to admit that they are different (though in fact they are more conscious of the difference than most members of the public), and housing of this type is never popular. The wives as well object to living in too close proximity with other police wives. There are problems of rank, embarrassments when friends get promoted, which the wives feel more keenly than the men since they have no accepted pattern of behaviour to follow in this situation. There are problems too of lack of privacy: the feeling of being constantly under the gaze of neighbours leads to friction. The men bring their work problems home, and the atmosphere can deteriorate into one of unkind gossip and antagonisms. Another problem arises between women whose husbands work different hours. One may be in the C.I.D., and another on shift work. Each will regard the lot of the other as the more favourable, probably because the one does not have to work night duties, while the other can always plan his free time in advance.

Significantly only 18 per cent of the men in one force stated categorically that they would prefer to live with other policemen, and most of these objected to the large colonies. Yet though large police colonies are unpopular, the men do not want to live with the general public indiscriminately. There are frequent complaints about police houses or flats in 'bad areas', about the schools in these areas which the children have to attend, and the lack of 'suitable' playmates for them. This applies to the adults too. One wife remarked, 'I mean, you couldn't make friends with the people round here, could you?' and another, for the same reason, 'I don't see many civvies really; you wouldn't make friends in an area like this anyway.' Yet local authorities cannot give their police preference in the siting of houses: their situation is a matter of expediency, rather than a result of any established policy that the men should 'mix'. The colonies are, too, the result of purely practical considerations. In the past it was cheaper and easier to build large numbers of houses together, but the dangers of this practice in minority group feelings and tensions inside the force have now been recognized, and very few police authorities would now build more than ten houses in a cluster. But it will be many years before this particular source of wastage can be removed.

These then are the main reasons for early leaving. Many of them, as has been seen, stem from the fact that the tasks determined for the policeman by society do not conform to either his own or the public's conception of his role, and they also impinge on his role in family life. Yet none of these factors independently is sufficient cause for a man to leave; their effect is cumulative. Again it must be emphasized that the 'pull' factor, the external circumstance which seems so much better than one's own, must be present before a man will leave. This accounts for the much greater loss of manpower in the urban

areas, although the tensions produced by the job in a rural area
are equally great. Many of them are everywhere unavoidable;
others could be reduced if some senior officers had a greater
insight into the nature of the problems with which their men
have to cope. A long look at their own relationships both with
colleagues and the men under their command might help.
Police training should now be geared to the reduction of the
service's most pressing problem: both senior officers and men
should be shown how to make an objective appraisal of their
position in society, and thus helped to adjust to it and to each
other.

Two Deprived Boys
Maureen Oswin

Reprinted with permission from Maureen Oswin, *Two Deprived Boys, Our
Children*, Council for Children's Welfare, Autumn 1968, pp. 9–17.

I have noticed disquieting deficiencies in the patterns of child-
care in hospitals where handicapped children live and sometimes spend their entire childhood. These deficiencies in child-
care are not found in the residential schools for handicapped
children. I therefore carried out the study of which this article
is an extract.

The hospital in the study was not chosen because it had
unusually poor standards of child-care; nor was the school
chosen because it had unusually good standards. But they support the disturbing observation that there are characteristic
differences in patterns of child-care according to the type of
institution; the widely different patterns of child-care found in
these two places described below were typical of their particular establishment. Yet, both types of institution care for
similarly handicapped children.

Jimmy lived in a residential school. He was aged six, a lively
boy, cerebral palsied, mentally retarded and unable to walk or
stand unaided. He could crawl, and could ride a tricycle with
his feet fastened in pedal-straps and use a wheel-chair. He
needed help with toilet, dressing and bathing.

At 8.15 am on a cold Sunday in February, Jimmy was playing quietly on his bed with his teddy bear. Six children slept in

this bedroom, which was furnished with carpets, curtains, wardrobes and wooden lockers. Three little wash-basins were in one corner. The low divan beds were arranged at angles. Toys were dotted round the room. Pictures were on the walls and there was gay contemporary wallpaper. The children were being given a lie-in, because the clocks had been put forward the night before and they had lost an hour.

At 8.30 am Jimmy's housemother went in and drew the curtains and Jimmy was first up. He washed himself at one of the basins and then dressed as much as possible without help: he could not manage his trousers. He was taken along to the toilet by his housemother. While dressing he played with his locker door and chatted about a framed picture of an elephant which hung on the wall opposite his bed. His housemother moved round the room helping the children and chatting.

At 9.30 am Jimmy was taken down in the lift to breakfast. The twelve separate tables in the large bright dining-room had been laid with utensils, sideplates, bread and butter and fruit. Big curtained windows looked down the drive. Jimmy had breakfast at a table with four other children. He fed himself, poured out drinks for himself and the other children and handed round the bread and butter. Two of the other children needed feeding and one housemother sat at the table to feed them. There was a lot of talking from all the children in the room, and the staff spent a long time trying to explain about the clocks going forward.

At 10.10 am Jimmy finished breakfast. Everybody started moving out of the dining-room. Jimmy said, 'Take me to the playroom' (lounge). When he got there the curtains were still drawn and the room in darkness. He said, 'Draw the curtains, they have a string, pull the string.' This lounge was furnished with armchairs, carpets, piano, record-player and table. The windows looked onto the gardens.

At 10.25 am Jimmy's housemother came to him and told him that she was going off for a while. He said, 'No, don't go yet.' She sat down in the hall armchair and took him on her lap. He cuddled her and said again 'Don't go.' She stayed in the armchair with him for a quarter of an hour. Then she went off, making sure that she handed him over to another house-mother, who immediately suggested that Jimmy helped to light the coal-fire in the lounge. This was a thrilling job to help with and he eagerly hurried off with her. They swept and cleaned the grate and put paper in the fireplace. Jimmy talked about the blackness of the coal and the sticks which he had helped to collect from the woods. Jimmy put lots of wood on the fire and then they lit it and sat back for a few moments, watching it burn. Then they put the fender and guard up.

At 12.00 Jimmy washed his hands at a hand-basin in one of the several toilet rooms on the ground floor. Then he began helping the same housemother to do the laundry. They put sheets and pillowcases into a small truck and wheeled it round the house, leaving clean laundry at each bedroom. On the way they stopped and chatted to other housemothers and children, who were playing and talking in groups around the large old house. In one bedroom two children were unwell and were sitting with the school-matron and playing with toys and books. When the truck was empty Jimmy was lifted inside for a ride and wheeled away, laughing and calling out. He then went to the toilet and washed his hands ready for lunch.

From 3.45 until 4.35 Jimmy played in the garden with his tricycle. For a little while he rode up and down the paths. Then he got off and played garages for a long time; he crouched by a rose-bed and pretended to fill the tricycle with petrol. Earth was 'petrol' and Jimmy poured handfuls of it over the back of his tricycle.

At 4.35 pm Jimmy was called in to be cleaned up ready for supper. He was covered in earth, and mud was down his rubber boots and in his clothes. The staff laughed at his incredible grubbiness and the amount of earth in his rubber boots.

At 4.55 pm supper was ready. Jimmy was pushed through to the dining-room. He helped himself to bread and butter and cake, and poured tea for himself and the other children at his table. He was then taken up to his bedroom, where he played on the floor, crawling around, and teasing other children about who were to have a bath.

There was much laughter and giggling and romping around on the floor. Amidst romping, the children started to get themselves ready for bed, some beginning to wash at their washbasins and others undressing as well as they physically could. The housemother was in the bathroom. Jimmy played with some toys and continued to romp about.

Tony lived in a hospital. He was aged eight, handicapped by spina-bifida. He had loss of use of his lower limbs and was unable to walk. He had a wheel-chair and could manoeuvre it competently. He had been in the hospital for about two years. He appeared dull, possibly being educationally subnormal.

At 6 am on a cold, dark February morning, a group of six children were sitting round a table in the upstairs ward, looking at scrap-books and large old bumper annuals. Two night nurses had just finished getting them out of bed. There were 13 children in the ward that Sunday, some children being away for the week-end. Four of the 13 had to stay in bed to be attended to by the day staff, so the two night nurses had nine children to get out of bed. They did not have to wash them, nor do their hair, nor toilet them unless necessary, nor did they have to fully dress them. But at 6 am the nine children were up, either sitting at the table waiting for breakfast (which would be served at 7.15 am) or wheeling themselves up and down the ward.

The ward was long, holding about 18 beds and having swing doors at both ends. There were no curtains or carpets. The walls were distempered or emulsion painted. A metal locker was beside each bed. A walled balcony was outside.

Tony was sitting in his wheel-chair dressed in shirt, jumper, nappie-square and slippers. He did not have his trousers on.

At my appearance in the ward the children set up a clamour of 'Lady, lady, lady, come here, come here and talk to us.'

From 6 am until 7.15 am Tony alternately pushed himself up and down the ward between the beds, or just sat doing nothing. The night nurses busied themselves with the beds and tidying up the ward, and did not talk to the children. At 7 am the Light Programme was put on very loudly.

At 7.15 am the night nurses served the cold part of breakfast from a trolley which they pushed into the ward from the adjoining kitchen. Tony ate his cereals in his chair, nesting the plate on his bare thighs, his nappie showing below his jumper.

At 7.30 am the day staff arrived. The hot part of breakfast also arrived, this came from the central kitchen: only cold food was prepared in the ward kitchen.

The night nurses stopped serving breakfast and moved away to finish the beds. The day shift took over the breakfast trolley, but none of the children seemed very interested in the hot breakfast as they had already filled up with cereals and bread and butter. As the children in wheel-chairs ate their breakfasts they constantly moved around the ward between the beds, the plates held on their laps.

At 7.50 am Tony's plate was put on the trolley. He then went into sister's office, which adjoined the ward. He stayed there for a few moments and watched nurses reading the duty lists which told them which children they had to 'do' that day and what ward duties.

At 8.05 am Tony was put on a bed-pan on his bed, on a rubber sheet. No screen was put around him. He sat there, not saying anything. The staff busied themselves getting children toileted, washed and bathed and fully dressed. The toilet/bathroom accommodation was accessible through the swing-doors and off the landing at one end of the ward. The accommodation was cramped and small, having one bath and three washbasins for eighteen children.

At 8.45 am Tony was taken off the bedpan, having sat there for 40 minutes.

From 8.45 am until 9.15 am Tony was helped to dress as he sat on his bed, and was then taken to the bathroom to have his face washed. The senior nurse tried to encourage him to do his button on his shirt-sleeves. This was the only training in dressing that was observed during the week-end on this ward.

At 9.15 am Tony was dressed, washed and in his wheel-chair again. He sat at the end of the ward by the piano, staring into the sister's office.

From 9.15 until 10.05 am Tony remained either staring into the office or pushing up and down the ward with nothing to do. Then he was arranged in a circle with other children who were in wheel-chairs or ordinary chairs.

From 10.05 until 10.30 am the children sat quietly in a circle, waiting for the arrival of the vicar to take Sunday school. Then the vicar arrived, in a rush, with jolly cries of 'Hello, children, hello!' The children had been sitting silently waiting for him for 20 minutes, so they greeted him thankfully and with some noisy excitement. While the children had waited at one end of the ward, the nurses had tidied the other end. They swept the floor, sorted linen and clothes, and pushed beds onto the balcony to air in the sun. Sunday school lasted 15 minutes; the vicar talked, and played the piano, and they all sang 'Glad that I live am I' and 'All things bright and beautiful.'

At 10.45 am the service finished and the vicar departed through the other end of the ward, with a cheery wave of his hand. The children dispersed from the circle and roamed listlessly up and down the ward. Tony wandered out to the balcony, which was crammed with beds being aired. There was not much room and it was difficult to see over the wall.

Tony came in from the balcony and said loudly, 'It would be

nice to go out.' There was no answer from anyone. The sun was shining and the sky was blue. He said again: 'I wish we could go out.' One or two other children set up cries of 'Are we going out?' 'Oh, will sister let us go out?' 'Will we be able to go downstairs and outside?' The nurses did not answer. The children kept looking unsuccessfully for paper and pencils, trying to open their stiff metal locker drawers and arguing with each other fretfully. No attempt was made to give the children an occupation.

Some of the children sat and quietly watched the nurses working. One backward boy asked for a broom and after he had pleaded incessantly for some time, the nurses let him sweep the floor at one end of the ward. The children were given drinks. Some had their hair washed.

From 11 until 11.45 am Tony moved up and down on the balcony between the empty beds. Other children sat still in their chairs in the ward, or moved around the ward looking for something to do. At one time Tony found a toy policeman's helmet and put it on.

At 11.45 am the children were got ready for lunch. Some sat in the wheel-chairs and some round the table. The table was not laid with plates, mats or utensils. Lunch arrived from the central kitchen and was served from the trolley at the end of the ward. Tony sat in his wheel-chair and had his plate on his lap. He did not help himself to vegetables, and his utensils were given out at the same time as he received his plate of food.

At 1.20 Tony went into the lobby room (a small room adjoining the ward and used for school during the week). He looked at a book for a moment.

The nurses brought the beds in from the balcony. They put them in straight rows and turned down the covers neatly, all ready for bedtime. Then they tidied up the tops of the lockers again and dusted.

From 1.35 until 2.15 pm Tony sat still, or again just pushed himself around the ward. He didn't say anything, but once called over to me and said, 'Shall we talk, can we talk?'

Some of the children asked me to find pencils and paper, but only blue pencils and torn scraps of paper were found jammed in the drawers of the scratched metal lockers.

At 2.15 pm a visitor arrived. Tony sat and stared solemnly at her. She sat by the television, having tea and biscuits as she talked to her little girl. Tony, staring at the visitor, was joined by other children in wheel-chairs who gradually gathered round. These children formed a small circle a short distance away from the visitor and her child and stared silently at them.

From 2.15 until 2.45 pm the encircled children continued to stare at the visitor. Then the hospital-shop trolley arrived. Pocket-money was kept in individual purses in a large biscuit tin in the office. The sister brought out the tin and handed round the purses. The lady who brought the shop was a former nurse and the children called her 'sister' although she was not in uniform. Two voluntary workers helped her. The children enjoyed choosing their purchases.

At 3.30 pm the television was switched on. Tony and another child again sat and watched the visitor. The nurses continued to clean the lockers and sorted out clothes. Tony sat quite still in one spot, just staring.

At 4.30 pm the nurses started getting the children ready for bed, undressing, washing and toileting them. (The day before, this preparation for bed had started even earlier with one deaf spastic boy being put into his pyjamas at 1.30.)

Until 6 pm Tony continued to half watch television and push himself up and down the ward between the beds. Some children were already in bed. Many children were crying and squabbling.

At 6.45 pm Tony was taken to be undressed, toileted and washed. Just before he was put into bed, Tony had a drink. He was the last child to be 'done'. The first child had been 'done' just after tea at 4.30.

At 7 pm the radio was turned off. The senior nurse gave the children a quick 'good-night' cuddle before she put the lights out.

The contrast between Tony's day in the hospital and Jimmy's day in the school gives a glaring example of the different patterns of child-care in the two establishments.

These extracts are brief; evidence throughout the complete report showed that the children in the hospital were severely deprived on five main counts:

1. *Culturally deprived*, through the poor environmental conditions and pattern of life.

2. *Maternally deprived*, through not having a mother-substitute provided for them.

3. *Linguistically deprived*, through little verbal contact with the staff.

4. *Recreationally deprived*, through not having play facilities.

5. *Depersonalised*, through being treated as one group, one crowd, having numbers, being segregated by age, having few personal possessions, and undergoing mass routines.

These aspects of deprivation *may add additional handicaps* to children who already suffer physical and mental handicaps —those additional handicaps could be the ones of emotional insecurity, further intellectual retardation, and social incompetence.

Imagine, if a children's officer found a foster home where the children were got out of bed at 5.30 am, made to sit in their nightwear and wait for breakfast until 7.15 am, given no privacy at toilet or bath, were sometimes left sitting on pots for an hour or longer, were sometimes put into pyjamas at 1.30 on a fine Sunday afternoon, and were confined to one room! Imagine a foster mother who ignored children's pleas to be played with or talked to because she was too busy tidying up, or who kept handing the children over to strangers to look after! Such a foster home or foster mother would be considered as totally unfit to have charge of children. Yet, *unheeded*, this goes on daily in our children's hospitals.

Old People in Britain
Dorothy Wedderburn

'Old People in Britain' is reprinted from *American Behavioural Scientist*, Vol. 14, No. 1 pp. 97–109, by permission of the publisher, Sage Publications.

A review of the situation of old people in Britain today raises most of the issues being debated in relation to the welfare state as a whole. The main ones are (1) the adequacy of public provisions in relation to need; (2) the problems of coordination of services designed to meet different, but essentially interrelated, needs; (3) the reconciliation of conflicts of interest between administrators, professionals, and beneficiaries; and (4) the philosophy of public services in an affluent society—or the principle of universal as against selective provision.

At the same time a study of old people raises a number of problems of more general theoretical interest to behavioural scientists. For example, the contemporary concern with the role of women and of the nuclear family in modern society, although mainly focused upon the young, can be illuminated by a study of the aged. Old age is very much a woman's problem. The greater longevity of the sex means that three or four out of every ten people over 65 is a single or widowed woman.

Another theoretical issue of considerable interest at the moment is alienation. Discussions about a related issue, the theory of disengagement, have occupied a great deal of the time of sociologists working in the gerontological field. It now appears that it is more fruitful to view the changes which take place in the patterning of old people's social relationships as a major restructuring in response to objective events such as retirement or the death of close kin rather than as disengagement. But a study of this restructuring process may itself be useful in increasing our understanding of the way in which the individual is integrated into the wider society.

In this paper I shall touch on some of these issues by first discussing the nature of the welfare state provision for the aged in Britain, with some general comments upon its strengths and weaknesses. I will then turn to consider in more detail the areas of work and retirement, income maintenance, and integration and participation as they relate both to the development of policy as well as to some more general theoretical problems.

The idea that there was something unique to Britain in the provision of a body of social services which came to be called the welfare state has been challenged. Neither the level nor the redistributive nature of postwar provisions could be regarded as pioneering nor as specifically socialist. (The one exception might be the National Health Service.) A framework where the central government guarantees some minimum level of income security together with social services in kind is common to most European countries. If any qualitative difference between countries is to be found, it is between the European experience on the one hand and the American on the other. In the United States both the system of income maintenance and of services in kind is much less extensive than in Europe. But despite a certain common pattern, each European country has its own variation of welfare services influenced both by local needs, by historical development, and by ideology.

What are the main services publicly provided for old people in Britain? Income maintenance is the responsibility of central government in a two-tier system. Social insurance provides a retirement pension, still basically flat rate with a benefit level below what is officially regarded as subsistence. Old people whose total resources are below the subsistence level may obtain a supplementary pension after investigation of their means. In 1967–68 total expenditure on retirement and supplementary pensions was £1,610m or 4.5 per cent of the gross domestic product. The National Health Service, available to all age groups, is mainly financed by the central government out of general taxation. The services of doctors, hospitals, and drugs are available free of charge to all retired people (retirement age is 65 for men and 60 for women). Total expenditure on the health service in 1967–68 was £1,490m or 4.1 per cent of the gross domestic product. On a *pro rata per capita* basis this would mean that 0.6 per cent was attributable to the elderly. We know, however, that this is an underestimate since the elderly are heavier users of medical services than some other age groups, although unfortunately no very reliable estimates exist to show just how much heavier their use is.

Other services for the elderly are mainly supplied by local government, sometimes, however, with financial assistance, or encouragement and guidance from the central government. There is considerable variation from area to area and a recent review said 'the local authority personal services for old people in many areas remain underdeveloped, limited and patchy'. Recent legislation may help to improve the situation by extending the powers of local authorities.

At the moment, local authorities may build special housing, usually with subsidized rents, and they own some 400,000 one-bedroom dwelling units suitable for the elderly, most of them built since the Second World War. They are also empowered to provide residential accommodation for people who, because of age, infirmity, or other circumstances, are in need of care and attention. There has been much discussion about the role which such residential accommodation should play in the care of the elderly. There is great variation between local authorities in the amount of such accommodation available, as well as in the type. It is generally agreed that far too many old people are housed in unsuitable and frequently appallingly low-standard buildings dating from the era of the Poor Law. On the other hand, considerable progress has been made in the design and building of new types of accommodations.

Local government is also responsible for the supply of many personal services to the elderly: health visitors, home nursing, and home helps. They may also supply prepared, delivered meals—'meals on wheels'—and give support for the provision of recreational activities for the aged. Altogether, the total expenditure on these personal services used by the aged in 1968 amounted to about £72m or another 0.2 per cent of the gross domestic product. Other services for the elderly are provided by voluntary effort. In general, cooperation between public and private providers is good. Sometimes a voluntary organization will experiment and pioneer a service which is then taken over and run on a larger scale by the local authority. But there are some problems. On the one hand, the voluntary effort may be cast in the 'Lady Bountiful' or 'do good' tradition. On the other hand, public provision may lack flexibility and imagination. Problems of coordination between the various bodies can also arise. But the case for voluntary effort to provide opportunities for citizen participation, to reveal new needs and to expose shortcomings in existing services, has been strongly made by the official committee established to review the structure of welfare services provided by local authorities.

Against this background of public provision, how does the position of the elderly in Britain compare with other countries? Some data is available from the cross-national study carried out in Britain, Denmark, and the United States in 1962. From this, it appears that the elderly in Denmark were better off in relation to needs than the elderly in Britain, who, in turn, were better off than those in the United States. This is an extremely bold and somewhat subjective generalization. It is difficult to combine evidence about financial position (which was objectively measurable) with evidence about the satisfaction of health needs or feelings of loneliness which could only be indirectly assessed. But even if this ordering of the three countries is disputed, it remains the case that the cross-national study provided little basis for complacency about the position of the old in Britain.

Debate about the adequacy of provision for the elderly has been almost continuous in Britain in the post-war period. At first there was considerable alarm about the prospective increase in the proportion of the population over retirement age and many references to the 'burden' of the aged. There was extensive pressure, at one time, for raising the official age for the receipt of the government retirement pension from 65 to 67. Gradually, however, the demographic problems assumed a new and less alarming perspective. It is now anticipated that the proportion over retirement age will fall from 15.9 per cent in 1970 to 13.6 per cent by the year 2000, although, of course, the absolute numbers will increase. There was also a shift toward the view that economic growth would automatically provide more resources which could be devoted, among other things, to the care of the elderly, thus raising standards without necessarily the need to forego other things.

This provided only a short-lived period of optimism. It seems impossible to meet the developing needs without some major reallocation of resources. The cross-national survey is not without some relevance here. It is important to note that the United States with a gross national product per capita some 50 per cent higher than that of Britain and Denmark nevertheless had some more serious problems among its elderly. This suggests that economic growth alone is no cure-all but only a politician's panacea. The issue of redistribution cannot be evaded.

What is becoming painfully clear is that need is dynamic. Over the post-war period in Britain, standards of provision for the elderly have undoubtedly improved, albeit slowly. For instance, the retirement pension for a married couple as a percentage of average male earnings had risen from 30.9 per cent in 1948 to 34.2 per cent in 1967. The continuing sense of inadequacy arises because notions of what is a reasonable standard themselves change. Much of the effort of administrators and academics in Britain is currently concerned with ways of measuring need. The problem has three aspects. The first revolves around ways of devising minimum standards of service which can change with rising expectations as society becomes more affluent. The second attempts to obtain reliable global estimates of demand for services at those standards. From these, the overall allocation of resources required at both national and local levels can be determined. A large measure of agreement has been reached about the size of the required expansion in the supply of a wide range of services from home helps and housing to income supplementation by studies using quite different approaches. The third, and in many ways the most difficult step is the actual identification of and contact with the individual old person in need of the service.

Public opinion generally seems favourably disposed toward a greater allocation of resources to meeting old people's needs dynamically. A recent survey of attitudes to the social services in Britain concluded:

'there was no doubt that it was the pensioners who commanded most sympathy. Over a half of all respondents thought that there were some social services on which the government should be spending more money and among these a large number wanted to see more money spent on widows or retirement pensioners in one form or another.'

The old themselves also feel they have a claim to better services although their expectations have been described as remarkably modest. How then is it possible for provision for the aged in Britain to lag behind public opinion? In the welter of competing claims for scarce resources, the social services generally—and those of the aged are no exception—suffer because they are not seen as themselves contributing to the overall goal of economic growth, the primary objective of both political parties. The old also lack any effective political power. This statement requires qualification because by comparison, say, with the United States, the commitment by both the Labour Party and the Trade Union movement to the principle of public provision of welfare services has been extremely important for the aged. The problem is that the preoccupation with economic growth as an end itself overshadows the question of what economic growth is for.

In the remainder of this paper I would like to examine in detail three major problems of the elderly in Britain. The first is work and retirement, the second is financial provision, and the third is the issue of integration and participation. All three are closely interrelated.

Despite a large body of literature and some official studies, no consistent policy toward retirement has been developed in Britain. The main government emphasis has been upon the desirability of older people remaining in the labour force because the total population of working age is expected to grow very slowly. If people remain at work after the official retirement age and continue to pay insurance contributions, they can earn small increments to their pension. On the other hand, the pension is a retirement pension, and subject to a rising rate of deduction if people drawing it between the ages of 65 and 70 are also earning. Another factor influencing patterns of retirement is undoubtedly the considerable increase in the prevalence of private occupational pension schemes. It is estimated that some 65 per cent of the male occupied population is now covered by such schemes. Not all those covered will eventually qualify for a pension, but in 1962 more than a quarter of all income units aged 65 and over were in receipt of an occupational pension. Most of these schemes require retirement at age 65, or earlier.

The proportion of people taking their government pension at the earliest age of 65 has been rising steadily in the last ten years. It has been argued that this reflects employment opportunities for older workers as a result of technical change. On the other hand, it could well be the result of the undoubted rise in the real standard of living of the aged. Other evidence which must also be considered suggests that the proportion of long-term sick in the age groups approaching retirement age may be rising and that some people find that their health improves when they retire. Nonetheless, there are still groups of workers who find themselves forced out of the labour force against their wishes by arbitrary age limits or because of arbitrary management assumptions that they cannot be retrained.

The most desirable official policy would be one which tried to provide genuine freedom of choice. This view has been well summarized by Gordon.

'Freedom of choice between work and retirement is not meaningful if prospective retirement income is seriously inadequate. As old-age benefits increase, the proportions of elderly pensioners who choose to retire will no doubt gradually increase over the long run, but there will be a residue of persons strongly motivated to continue at work particularly in those occupations in which intrinsic interest in work is high. Making it possible for such persons to continue work is an important social goal.'

The reference to intrinsic interest in work is important. Some attention is now being paid to the need for a more sophisticated study of adjustment to retirement by different occupational groups. Differences in the experience of retirement between white-collar and blue-collar workers was suggested by the cross-national study. Evidence is now accumulating, however, which suggests that different groups of blue-collar workers both seek and obtain different rewards from work. This would suggest, *a priori*, that they might experience retirement differently. Nor has much consideration been given in Britain to the possibility of distributing increasing leisure in a different pattern over the life cycle. We seem to be following the American example of extending the period of dependency of the young at one end of the life cycle and of the old at the other. The logical policy might, however, be to enter the work force earlier, to leave it later, but to have 'sabbatical' periods for retraining in between. Such a policy might run into greater difficulties of financing than would an old age pension programme. It would require financial assistance to able-bodied people at levels which would be reasonably comparable to their current earnings. But much radical rethinking is urgently required.

The problem of finance for the aged is intimately linked to the whole problem of work and retirement. Although older people at work tend to have lower earned incomes than younger age groups, the gap in income levels between those over retirement age still at work and those who have ceased work is much larger. Other sources of income—e.g., from assets, from private occupational pension schemes—are available to some old people, but, nevertheless, well over a half of the old people in Britain are virtually entirely dependent upon their retirement or supplementary pensions, and another 15 per cent are very largely so.

Despite the addition of a small element of wage relation in 1959, the British pension system remains basically flat rate, not wage-related, with supplementation after examination of means. When in opposition the Labour Party introduced, as long ago as 1957, proposals for a major overhaul of the pension system and for the adoption of a basically wage-related system geared to increases in the average standard of living. Since then there has been much discussion and controversy. Now the Labour Government has committed itself to a fully worked out wage-related scheme which is likely to become law in the near future. The proposals follow a familiar basic pattern. They are that pensions should be financed by wage-related contributions from employers and employees with a contribution from the general exchequer. The formula is, however, redistributive. The individual contributor's earnings for each year after the scheme commences are expressed as a percentage of average male industrial earnings in that year. The pension earned by the contributor is than calculated on two bands. Up to half of the national average earnings, it is calculated at the rate of 60 per cent. Between one-half and the upper limit of one and a half times the national average earnings, it is calculated at the rate of 25 per cent. National average earnings will be the level prevailing at the time of retirement—

i.e., the pension earned will be increased during working life for any increase in real earnings. Once in, payment pensions will be reviewed every two years and as a minimum will be increased to keep pace with any increase in prices. There is no guaranteed real increase, however, after payment has commenced although discretionary increases are not ruled out. One important aspect of the scheme is that it has a new conception of the importance of pension provision for women. When combined with the Labour Government's move toward equal pay for women, the proposals may eventually go a long way to dealing with the hitherto apparently intractable problem of the poverty of widows in old age.

The widespread existence of private occupational pension schemes has presented the government with a serious problem. Some commentators, although not, of course, the insurance companies, feel that too many concessions have been made to these special schemes in the new proposals.

Two other major objections may be made to the new pension proposals as they now stand. The first is the time to be taken for the scheme to reach full maturity. If the legislation becomes effective in 1972 the scheme will be fully mature only after twenty years. The second is that apart from linking pensions in payment to changes in the cost of living through a two-yearly review, the scheme provides nothing for existing pensioners. Thus, for a number of years, the majority of pensioners will either receive no or little benefit from the scheme, and the problems of the adequacy of pension levels will remain acute. Moreover, as has been powerfully argued, on the assumption that the public conception of what is an acceptable minimum income will rise as general living standards rise, if the fully matured pensions are not increased in real value once in payment, a need for supplementation will again emerge.

The new pension proposals have many virtues. Official estimates suggest that the share of pensioners in total personal consumption should rise from the present 10 per cent to 12 per cent at the turn of the century. But the criticisms which have been raised are major ones reflecting the fundamental philosophical dilemma of public provision in the affluent society. The principle of social insurance is a useful one for providing pensions universally, as of right, to achieve what has been called 'equality of status' rather than economic equality. To attempt to provide adequate pensions on this basis, particularly when facing competition from private schemes, leads ultimately to the adoption of wage-relation and an effort to beat the market at its own game. The price paid, however, by adopting this method is to deal less efficiently with the problem of need among the poorest. On the other hand, the logic of concentrating resources where they are most needed implies the use of an extensive means test which runs into opposition from the beneficiaries as well as into the danger of creating a group of second-class citizens.

Work and the income which work produces are still probably the most important integrators in capitalist society. In the concern with family relationships in old age there may have been a tendency to overlook this fact. But it is now well established that where there are children, contact with them in old age is close. Children are major sources of help in sickness and infirmity. When children are not available, the elderly seek substitutes by developing close relationships with other kin. In this respect Britain is no exception.

It is, however, special in one respect. No less than 42 per cent of the old people with children are keeping house with at least one of them. Economic factors do not appear to be the main reason. Some have suggested that there may be particularly close kinship ties, others that external constraints, like housing, are the important factors. Whatever the reason, these joint households undoubtedly facilitate the helping relationship of children and their aged parents.

But there is now increasing evidence that the family may not be an adequate mechanism for integration. Many old people describe themselves as lonely even when they are keeping house with their children. About another one in four have no children. In seeking alternatives it has been suggested that the social services should be viewed not only as a means of meeting specific needs, but also as a way of developing a network of viable and functional social relationships around the old person. Two illustrations can be given from housing and health.

Debate continues about the most suitable forms of housing for the elderly. There are advocates of flats versus bungalows, of special areas of housing for the elderly versus housing for mixed age groups, of private housing versus residential accommodation. Experiments will continue. Some local authorities in Britain are now building 'plus granny annexes' to their council houses. At the moment, however, there is insufficient evidence available to judge what type of housing is most needed because hitherto few realistic choices have been available.

This is particularly true in the area of residential versus private accommodation. The idea that old people prefer to live in their own homes has acquired something of the quality of a myth. What we do not know is how far the opposition to residential accommodation stems from the often bad and inhuman standards which prevail. At the moment, less than 5 in every 100 people over 65 are in institutions in Britain. But among those over 75, this proportion rises to 8 in every 100. While the numbers in the age group 65 to 74 are expected to increase by 7 per cent by the end of the century, those over 75 are expected to increase by 35 per cent. These demographic changes alone are likely to require a reassessment of the role of institutional care. But it is interesting that at the other end of the age scale, the possibilities of communal living in units larger than the nuclear family are now tentatively, and voluntarily, being explored. These explorations could provide some experience of significance for the aged.

The second illustration comes from the area of medical care. Within the framework of the National Health Service, Britain has developed a remarkable specialist geriatric hospital service. But medical care for the aged suffers from three defects. The first is the general one of inadequate resources, common to the health service for all age groups. The second is the relatively low status of geriatric care which lacks the glamour of, say, heart transplants. Finally, it suffers from difficulties arising from the need to coordinate a number of different authorities concerned with the provision of medical care for the aged.

Two aspects, in particular, of the medical care for the elderly call for emphasis upon coordination. First, it is generally agreed that more attention needs to be given to prevention. This in itself would make a major contribution to the integration of the elderly. To the extent that they are enabled to remain more active and mobile, the more able they are to engage in this normal range of activities. But second, coordination is needed in a situation where typically the presentation of health problems is one of multiple disorders.

Fundamental proposals for the reorganization of the health and welfare services, not only for the aged, but for the whole community, are now under discussion. At a time when some trends in health care indicate the need for more and more specialization, the needs of the elderly may point in the other direction. Undoubtedly the general practitioner could become a vital link between the old and society, particularly if, with the aid of ancillary workers, he were enabled to keep regularly in touch with those among the old who were known to be especially at risk, for instance those recently bereaved.

So far this discussion has stressed only the passive links between the aged and the social services. Where the welfare services are dominated by a mixture of the Lady Bountiful and Horatio Alger traditions little more is to be expected. Another way of achieving integration, however, is by greater participation of the beneficiaries themselves in the provision of these services. This issue was raised tentatively in an official report referred to earlier: 'In the provision of social services the users are seldom consulted nor as things are at present does the retired person often enough play a significant part in the management of any scheme designed to help him.' Participation can be interpreted in many ways and is difficult to realize. However, integration becomes more realistic if it is seen not as the rest of society providing and administering services for the old, but as the aged themselves playing an active part in the shaping and running of those services. But here we touch on an issue in no way unique to the elderly, but one shared by all groups disadvantaged by being excluded from or with only marginal access to the market of capitalist society.

In this survey of the position of the old in Britain I have tried to describe the main problems. In the post-war period great progress has been made in both the recognition of and the meeting of the needs of the old. What seems to emerge is that the present problems can be seen, not so much as special to the elderly, but as particular illustrations of general problems facing the welfare state and society generally. This may hold an important lesson for future research, for instead of studying the elderly as an identifiable subgroup of the population we may need, more than ever before, to study ageing as but a particular phase in the total life cycle.

Further Reading:　**The Family**

* H. GAVRON, *The Captive Wife. Conflicts of Housebound Mothers*, Harmondsworth, Penguin, 1966.

M. GORDON, *Income Security Programs and the Propensity to Retire*, in R. Williams et al., *Processes of Aging*, New York, Atherton Press, 1963.

J. and E. NEWSON, *Infant Care in an Urban Community*, London, Allen and Unwin, 1963.

C. ROSSER, and C. C. HARRIS, *The Family and Social Change*, London, Routledge and Kegan Paul, 1965.

W. G. RUNCIMAN, *Relative Deprivation and Social Justice*, London, Routledge and Kegan Paul, 1966.

* M. SCHOFIELD, *The Sexual Behaviour of Young People*, Harmondsworth, Penguin, 1968.

E. SHANAS et al., *Old Age in Three Industrial Societies*, London, Routledge and Kegan Paul, 1970.

P. TOWNSEND, *The Last Refuge*, London, Routledge and Kegan Paul, 1962.

P. TOWNSEND and D. WEDDERBURN, *The Aged in the Welfare State*, London, Bell, 1965.

* Available in paperback

Chapter Four Poverty

Until a decade or so ago statistics were difficult to interpret in ways which threw much light on the problem of poverty. The assumptions made were that as society became more affluent poverty would diminish and eventually disappear. These were strongly challenged in the wake of research and information which suggested that there were certain categories of people within the country who were losing ground in the move towards affluence. What happened in Britain was also happening elsewhere, notably in the United States where Michael Harrington, for example, in his book *The Other America* suggested that about a quarter of Americans were living in poverty.

The first point to make in the definition of poverty is that it is a relative concept. By the standards of less affluent societies, the poor in Britain would be judged to be well off, while conversely, many who do not consider themselves poor, nor are poor according to criteria worked out about income and so on, would be so in a society such as the United States where the standard of living is higher.

Basic needs and how they are seen relate to the general standard of living in the community in question. Norms such as 'subsistence level' or a 'decent standard of living' are thus established. The income enjoyed by the most numerous group (the median) tends to set minimum standards of expectation. Many fall short of this and are becoming increasingly aware of it. As Professor Galbraith has noted: 'People are poverty-striken when their incomes, even if adequate for survival, falls markedly below that of the community. Then they cannot have what the larger community regards as the necessary minimum for decency, and they cannot wholly escape, therefore, the judgement of the larger community that they are indecent. They are degraded for, in the literal sense, they live outside the grades or categories which the community regards as acceptable.'

The second point to make about poverty is that it is

concerned with both objective and subjective elements. The objective ones are those which are measurable, such as income in relation to needs, and the subjective ones are those which involve the state of mind of the individual. It is possible to feel that you are poor when the income you have is higher than that of many others.

If we consider the elements that would form a part of a definition of poverty we have to include 'conventional necessities'. There are good historical expositions of this. For example, Adam Smith in *The Wealth of Nations* says 'A linen shirt . . . is, strictly speaking, not a necessity of life. . . . But in the present times, through the greater part of Europe a creditable day-labourer would be ashamed to appear in public without a linen shirt, the want of which would be supposed to denote that disgraceful degree of poverty which, it is presumed, nobody can well fall into without extreme bad conduct.'

Alfred Marshall, the economist, also spoke of defining poverty in a way that would take into account '. . . some consumption of alcohol and tobacco and some indulgence in fashionable dress which are in many places so habitual that they may be said to be conventionally necessary, so that in order to obtain them the average man and woman would sacrifice some things which are necessary for efficiency'. Equivalent standards would have to include, in our society, provision for television and other entertainments and recreations.

Having established that more than mere physical standards are involved, it would be useful to look at what these standards are. Objectively, income must provide for a sufficient degree of physical efficiency. It must take into account social factors which involve the conventional necessities of which Adam Smith and Marshall wrote. Thirdly, it must provide an income which is necessary for economic efficiency. Any standard set by the Government in determining benefit is not able to take into account the physical and social standards which affect workers in different occupations. The manual worker in primary industry will need far more food to preserve and maintain economic efficiency than the clerical worker. The occupational necessities that vary considerably include the provision of tools or some services after the work has been completed, the costs of transport, or the maintenance of vehicles and other forms of capital expenditure. However, it is possible, when trying to equalise out these factors to come to some conclusions about the amounts of money required for individuals and also families of particular sizes, but there are enormous problems. The escalation of house prices and rents and the particularly high rates that prevail in South-East England, mean that there are great differences between the money that has to be paid for similar accommodation in different parts of the country. The individual's dietary needs vary a lot. It is not always the case that the poor can buy in the cheapest market: indeed, the evidence of commodity prices in poorer areas suggests it is more difficult for them, particularly as the cost of small amounts of commodities, which groups such as elderly, often living on their own, of necessity buy, is higher than for larger quantities. All this means problems in attempting to be clear about the incidence of poverty in any society and to discover, in fact, whether the proportion in poverty is increasing or decreasing.

The main groups living in poverty at the moment are the old, a substantial proportion of whom have been in this position over a long period of time, the sick and chronically handicapped, the unemployed and those living on low pay. In all the discussions about poverty the relevance of low paid work now looms large. From assumptions that it was relatively unimportant, opinion is moving towards recognising its significance. Professor Atkinson discusses what is low pay, relating it to scales of benefit, and then goes on to enquire who the low paid are. He considers questions about how far low earnings are temporary, how far attributable to ill health or disability and how far concentrated in particular industries or regions.

The reading from Nicholas Bosanquet's article is a valuable complement to the one before. The point is made that those who act as advocates for the poor have tended to be shut off in a special and restricted lobby concerned only with social security, whereas the issue needs to be contested on questions of general economic policy. Secondly, the need to raise the pay where it is too low has been looked at without reference to wider issues in society which have a strong bearing on what is believed to be provided. Once full employment was assumed to be a basic principle of government policy, following on from the reports by Beveridge and others during the last war, but in recent years there has been a significant move away from this aim. Not only do low paid workers have to contend with too narrow a view of their needs but also with changes in the pattern of employment which affect them more than other workers. These are structural shifts of the kind where some industries are in decline; notable examples of these are in textiles and manufacturing industry generally. Moreover, the existence of vacancies does not mean that those who are unemployed are able to fill these particular jobs. There have been increases in the numbers of long-term unemployed and the author suggests that the whole 'problem' of the so-called 'work-shy' ought to be looked at again.

Hilary Land raises questions about the extent to which the income provided for large families, for example in the shape of family allowances, is sufficient for their needs. She points out the kinds of restrictions on some of these families which are felt in many aspects of their lives. Even if there is not poverty there is likely to be a problem of pressure on space because of the number of children, and because of outgoings, less likelihood of being able to buy their own home. Debt is something which is a common experience for those families living on incomes below basic subsistence level. Problems of keeping in touch with relatives, to maintain what may be mutually helpful relationships, are much greater for such families, given the costs of transport.

A further important theme, on which evidence is presented, is the way in which social services are administered. There are numerous implications for the working of the statutory services involved and there is evidence of a lack of flexibility in the response. There is widespread misunderstanding about entitlement to benefit and a consequent lack of take-up of these. Not only do the families themselves know little about their rights but the evidence suggests that sometimes social workers and teachers do not know enough either to help the family to receive its entitlement. The ambivalent attitudes towards those who need financial support from the State are given sharp focus. The material in this reading could be looked at along with those from Holman, later in this chapter, and Parkinson, in Chapter 3. Moreover, the extract has implications for the way in which poor people are viewed and also the extent to which services should be 'universalist', i.e. available to all, or 'selective', i.e. restricted to groups in the population considered not to have sufficient resources to cover their needs.

The need for money for those who are poor as opposed to considerations of the 'culture of poverty', now fashionable, and 'problem families' is the theme of the article by Professor

Schorr, an American scholar with experience both of conditions in Britain and the United States and an earlier career as an administrator. He makes a strong case for the need for a 'ground strategy' for poverty and this is relevant both for Britain and the United States, and the article may be seen against the continuing discussion about the priorities of social welfare. We need to be aware of how great the problem of poverty is and Schorr quotes with approval the opinion of Octavia Hill in the nineteenth century when she pointed out that despite the reputation that charitable Trusts concerned with housing had in London in the middle of the nineteenth century all their work over thirty years was sufficient to house only six months of the population increase. In the days of community development projects and the concentration of not particularly great resources on small areas, the need to bear in mind the size of the whole problem, and not to assume that because something is being done the problem is being adequately tackled, is vitally important.

In recent years there has been a great development in organisations, among them claimants and squatters, which have been created to help their own members. Dr. Holman discusses such groups and considers how they operate. Taking Birmingham as an example he points to administrative inflexibility including 'policy not to inform', and suggests not only that there need to be changes in administrative procedures and the extension of rights but that the political system at the local level is not now capable of dealing with many of the problems that those who are deprived and powerless face.

Poverty in Britain and the Reform of Social Security
A. B. Atkinson

Reprinted from A. B. Atkinson, *Poverty in Britain and the Reform of Social Security*, Cambridge University Press, 1970, pp. 87–93, with the permission of the Department of Applied Economics, University of Cambridge, and the author.

Low earnings

The analysis of the previous section suggested that low earnings are a more important problem than is commonly believed. In this section I examine the incidence of low earnings in more detail in preparation for the discussion of measures to help the low paid.

The questions with which I shall be primarily concerned are:

(1) To what extent are low earnings a temporary phenomenon for a particular worker? Do they simply reflect a short working week?

(2) How far can low earnings be attributed to ill-health or other disabilities?

(3) Are low earnings concentrated in particular industries or regions? Are they associated with workers of a particular age?

(*a*) *Temporarily low earnings and short hours.* Firstly, it may be the case that low earnings are essentially a temporary phenomenon for any particular worker—representing a bad week when, for example, bonuses fell below normal. If this is so, the evidence discussed in section 1 is less disturbing than at first sight, since it is with a person's normal earnings that we are really concerned.

In the case of their 1966 enquiry, the Ministry of Social Security estimated that about 1 in 5 of the low income families where the father was in full-time work had normal earnings which were higher than those in the week of the enquiry. It does not follow, however, that they would have been sufficiently higher to raise them above the National Assistance scale, and there were undoubtedly some families above the poverty line in the week of the enquiry who would normally have fallen below. In the case of the Department of Employment and Productivity 1968 earnings survey, the figures quoted were adjusted to include average amounts of bonuses etc. over a representative period (where these differed from the actual amount received) and people paid for less than their normal hours were excluded. Much of the temporary fluctuation in earnings had therefore already been eliminated from these figures. On this basis, it appears that people with temporarily low earnings account for only a small proportion of the total low paid. This is supported by the results of the 1966 Family Expenditure Survey, which collected information about both 'last week' earnings and 'usual' earnings. This showed relatively little difference between the two; for example, 9.2 per cent had last week earnings below £13, compared with 8.0 per cent who had usual earnings below this level.

It might be argued that rather than just averaging over a period of a few months, we should take account of cyclical fluctuations in the level of activity in the economy, and consider whether it is possible that low earnings can be explained as a cyclical phenomenon. As far as the Ministry of Social Security enquiry is concerned, however, this explanation is not very plausible, since the enquiry was carried out in mid-1966, when unemployment was 1.1 per cent and average weekly earnings had risen by some 8 per cent in the previous year.

It is of course possible that low weekly earnings reflect short working hours rather than a low hourly rate of earnings. In the case of the Ministry of Social Security enquiry, the fathers of the families with incomes below the assistance scale worked an average of 42 hours a week, and although this is less than the average for fathers above the scale (47 hours), it does not indicate widespread short-time as a cause of low earnings. The 1968 earnings enquiry provided details of the distribution of hourly as well as weekly earnings. If we take a weekly level of £15 as our criterion for low earnings and assume that this applies to a standard week of 40 hours, then a person can be said to have low hourly earnings if they fall below 7s 6d. From the results of the enquiry, we can estimate that 14.4 per cent of adult men working full-time had hourly earnings below this level (compared with 7.9 per cent with weekly earnings below £15). An estimated 3.3 per cent had hourly earnings below 6s 3d (which would give £12 10s for a 40 hour week). On this basis, there appear to be a substantial number of people with low hourly earnings, and the problem cannot simply be put down to short hours.

(b) *Ill-health as a cause of low earnings.* In recent years there has been increasing interest in the extent to which low earnings are a reflection of ill-health or some degree of mental or physical disability. There is, however, at present only very limited information about this aspect.

In the Ministry of Social Security enquiry in 1966, each father in work was asked whether his health was normally good. Where the answer was no, he was then asked whether he felt that his earning power was limited by ill-health. In the case of families with incomes below the National Assistance scale, 14 per cent said that their earnings were in fact limited by ill-health, compared with only 4 per cent in the whole sample. Not too much weight can, however, be attached to these answers since, as the report emphasises, people vary considerably in their awareness of ill-health and in their willingness to reveal it (particularly in the case of mental illness). It may be noted, however, that 51 per cent of the fathers of low income households had been absent from work during the preceding year as a result of sickness or injury, compared with 32 per cent for the whole sample. Moreover, of the wage-stopped families visited by the Supplementary Benefit Commission when it reviewed the operation of the wage-stop in 1967, only a third said that they were in good health and it was clear that in a good many cases ill-health was an important cause of their low earning capacity.

In the course of the 1968 earnings enquiry by the Department of Employment and Productivity, employers were asked whether the employee concerned suffered from a mental or physical handicap, and when the results from this are available, they should throw further light on the extent to which low earnings can be attributed to disabilities of this kind.

(c) *The industrial and regional distribution of low earnings.* As a basis for examining the industrial and regional distribution, I have adopted two definitions of 'low earnings'. The first is based on the level of gross weekly earnings required to bring a family with one child to the Supplementary Benefit scale (I.A.R.). This gives a figure for September 1968 of around £12 10s. (The reasons why this level is of interest should be apparent from the discussion of the previous section.) As a basis for the second definition of low earnings I take the rather higher figure of £15 a week which has been put forward by a number of the proponents of a national minimum wage.

From the recent Department of Employment and Productivity survey, we can find the proportion of workers in different industries whose earnings were below these two levels in September 1968. The results are set out in Table 1, which relates to all adult employees (both manual and non-manual) working full-time. In interpreting these figures, it should be borne in mind that:

(i) earnings include a 'normal' level of shift-payments, commission and bonuses,

(ii) any income in kind and in gratuities is excluded (which may be important in the case of such industries as agriculture and catering).

As we should expect, the overall figures conceal wide variation between industries. The first striking difference is that between manufacturing and non-manufacturing industries: whichever of the two definitions of low earnings that we adopt, the proportion falling below was over twice as high in non-manufacturing as in manufacturing. There are, however, wide variations within non-manufacturing itself, and we can distinguish certain industries where low earnings are particularly widespread: agriculture, distribution, professional and scientific services, miscellaneous services (including catering and garages) and government service. Others (such as transport and construction) do not differ very much from manufacturing. Also, of course, there are industries within manufacturing that have a high proportion of low paid workers, although this does not show up very clearly with the rather broad industrial groupings at present available.

These results suggest, as we should expect, that there are certain industries where low pay is prevalent. However, it should not be assumed that these industries necessarily account for most of the low paid workers in the country. The five non-manufacturing industries singled out above account for only slightly over half of those earning less than £15 a week, and in fact nearly a quarter of those below this level are in manufacturing. It does in fact appear that low paid workers are spread quite widely over a range of industries and that there are not just a few 'sweated trades'.

The results so far available from the 1968 earnings survey are based on rather broad industrial groupings, and in order to obtain information at a finer level of detail we have to go back to the enquiry into earnings carried out in 1960. This is rather unsatisfactory, not only because it is now out of date but also because the coverage of the enquiry was incomplete. It covered only manual workers and excluded a number of major industries outside manufacturing. Using the results of this enquiry, Mrs. Judith Marquand has, however, made a number of

Table 1.   Industrial distribution of low earnings—1968

	Proportion of men (21 and over) working full-time earning less than	
	£12 10s a week %	£15 a week %
All industries	2·1	7·9
All manufacturing industries	1·3	4·1
All non-manufacturing industries	3·5	10·7
Agriculture	14·5	36·6
Mining and quarrying	1·5	9·7
Construction	1·3	4·6
Gas, electricity and water	0·8	3·7
Transport and communication	1·4	4·7
Distributive trades	4·2	13·9
Insurance, banking and finance	3·4	9·3
Professional and scientific services	4·4	13·6
Miscellaneous services	9·2	18·2
Public administration	3·2	14·3

Source: derived from 'Results of a new survey of earnings in September 1968', Tables 15 and 16.
Note: The figures for earnings below £12 10s are obtained by linear interpolation, and for this reason may not be so accurate as those for the £15 level.

interesting points about the characteristics of low paid industries. She defines as 'low paid industries' those that fall in the bottom quarter when industries are ranked according to the earnings received by the worker at the lowest decile (industries are defined in terms of minimum list headings, which are very much narrower than those shown in Table 1). On this basis she concluded that:

(i) the industries right at the bottom were mostly ones where Wages Councils were in operation,

(ii) there was a strong tendency for the manufacturing

industries with widespread low pay to be ones which were contracting or expanding less rapidly than the average.

The results of the 1960 enquiry also support the earlier conclusion that low earnings are not concentrated in a few low paying industries. If we take all the industries which Mar-

Table 2.   Regional distribution of low earnings—1968

Region	Proportion of men (over 21) working full-time with weekly earnings below	
	£12 10s %	£15 %
South East	2·0	5·6
East Anglia	4·0	12·0
South Western	3·5	10·9
West Midlands	2·1	6·3
East Midlands	2·0	7·2
Yorkshire and Humberside	2·8	9·6
North Western	2·4	7·8
Northern	2·6	9·4
Wales	3·2	11·1
Scotland	3·4	11·0
Great Britain	2·1	7·9

Source: 'Results of a new survey of earnings in September 1968', Table 10. See note to Table 1.

quand considered to be low paid, then they accounted for under half of all the workers whose earnings in 1960 were less than £10 a week (which was roughly the same proportion of national average earnings as £15 a week in 1968). The Wages Councils industries just referred to accounted for less than 5 per cent.

Turning to the question of the regional distribution of those with low earnings, I have shown in Table 2 the proportions in different regions earning less than £12 10s and £15 as derived from the 1968 earnings enquiry. As might be expected, a number of regions had a much higher than average proportion of low paid workers. These included East Anglia, the South West, Wales and Scotland, which had around twice the proportion in the South East and the Midlands (although the South East still accounted for nearly a quarter of all those earning less than

£15). The enquiry did not cover Northern Ireland; the results of the 1967 Family Expenditure, however, showed that 31 per cent of full-time adult male employees earned less than £15 in Northern Ireland, compared with 14 per cent for the United Kingdom as a whole.

Table 3. Distribution of low earnings by age—1968

Age	Proportion of men working full-time with weekly earnings below £12 10s %	£15 %
21–4	5·2	14·9
25–9	1·9	5·6
30–9	1·3	3·9
40–9	1·4	5·1
50–9	2·3	8·6
60–4	4·3	15·2

Source: 'Results of a new survey of earnings in September 1968', Table 8. See note to Table 1.

It seems reasonable to expect that those with low earnings would be more heavily concentrated in the youngest and oldest age groups—reflecting the tendency for earnings to rise with age in the twenties and to decline after reaching a peak in the late forties. This expectation is borne out by the evidence from the earnings survey as shown in Table 3. Low earnings were more common for those in the youngest age group (21–4) and for those aged over 50. In fact about half (47 per cent) of all workers earning less than £15 a week were over 50.

Summary

It may be helpful to summarise the conclusions of this section:

(a) Low pay cannot be explained as purely a temporary phenomenon for a particular worker or purely as a result of short hours.

(b) It is difficult to assess the effect of ill-health until further information is available, although it is undoubtedly important in a number of cases.

(*c*) There are a number of industries with above average proportions of low paid workers, but low paid workers are spread fairly widely over the range of industries.

(*d*) There is a tendency for the industries with low pay to be ones where Wages Councils operate, and where employment is contracting.

(*e*) There are definite regional differences in the importance of low earnings.

(*f*) Nearly half of the workers with low earnings are over 50.

Finally, it should be stressed that this section has been concerned only with those in employment and not with the self-employed. From the Ministry of Social Security enquiry, it can be seen that the self-employed account for about 1 in 5 of the 70,000 families which fell below the National Assistance scale even though the father was in full-time work. However, as the report emphasises, information obtained about income from self-employment may not be very accurate.

Jobs and the Low-paid Worker
Nicholas Bosanquet

Reprinted with permission from N. Bosanquet, 'Jobs and the Low-paid Worker', *Poverty*, No. 18, Spring 1971, pp. 2–6.

Endless and repetitive discussion of special 'plans' for low pay —under successive Governments—has tended to obscure one cardinal fact. The low-paid are much like the rest of us. Their economic prospects depend on general economic policies rather than on specific and (usually chimerical) policies for dealing with low pay. The rate of growth of their real earnings depends primarily on real rates of growth in the economy. An extra one per cent on real GNP might be a better tonic for the low-paid than the FIS bill.

The pattern of debate has had clear political consequences— in two main ways. First, the advocates of the poor have let themselves be shut off into a special lobby in which they appeared only to be concerned with policies for social security. No challenge has been made on the central ground of general economic policy—and its effects on the low-paid. Secondly, the debate on low pay in employment has concentrated on methods of raising pay—as if employment could be left to take care of itself.

But plans for a minimum wage—or even strong trade union pressure in favour of the lower paid—are likely to achieve little in a slack labour market. A minimum wage is bound to have some employment effects—falling particularly hard on marginal workers whose work rate is not high because of personal disabilities. Trade union pressure for differential increases will have some of the same employment effects—and neither government nor trade union policies will help workers who do not have jobs at all—whether they are registered unemployed or people who have left the labour force altogether.

The most serious present threat to the interests of the low-paid is not the absence of a minimum wage, but the extent to which we have slipped away—eerily, almost without noticing it—from the post-war targets of 'full-employment'. It is of little use to a low-paid worker to be told that society has guaranteed his earnings levels in employment—if he cannot get a job at all.

The importance of expanding employment opportunities to the low-paid becomes clear once we take a sensible view of the causes of low pay. Basically there are two main lines of thought. The first—which would be favoured by economists whatever their political persuasion—stresses economic determinism as a cause of low pay. The low-paid are such because their productivity is low. Low-paid workers would tend to have one or more of a number of handicaps: lack of skill, mental or physical handicap, age, or lack of information about job opportunities.

The second approach—favoured by non-economists—tends to put weight on what might be called the 'David Copperfield' theory of low pay. This is that the low-paid are such because of their own lack of bargaining power. The first priority then becomes for the organised labour movement to 'shame' employers into paying better wages.

Certainly there are numerous cases of exploitation—not least in the public sector where 58.3 per cent of the lowest paid male manual workers (on 1968 data) are concentrated. There is a great deal of room for trade union pressure on bad employers—and for stricter enforcement by government of Wages Council Orders. But the 'David Copperfield' theory lacks plausibility as a general theory of low pay.

In terms of the 'bargaining power' theory of low pay, expanding job opportunities become a matter of secondary importance. Large differential increases will not have much effect in reducing employment. But in terms of the 'economic' theory, job opportunities become a matter of prime importance, and it is in this context that we need to look at recent events in the labour market.

Accumulating evidence of a number of different kinds now suggests that the labour market has become terribly bleak for workers who are not young, highly skilled or mentally and physically capable of maintaining a fast work rate—the kinds of workers who make up the bulk of the low-paid. Their problem is now not one of earnings levels—but the starker and more anguished one of how to find a job at all. The labour market is becoming bleaker, too, for a second group—those who are not necessarily handicapped, but who were working in contracting and low-paid industries. Finally, all problems of personal handicap and industrial location have become much worse for people in development areas—and worst of all for people in isolated communities within development areas.

Conventionally the unemployment figures—in conjunction with the vacancy figures—are taken as the measure of pressure on the labour market. But we know that many people on losing their jobs do not register as unemployed and leave the labour force altogether. Thus married women and workers past retirement age would tend to join the 'labour reserve'—the group who are not registered as unemployed but would be interested in a job if there seemed any chance of landing one. Many people disappear into the night without stopping off at the labour exchange.

Thus in addition to looking at the unemployment figures, we need to look at the figures for *employment*. These show a most troubling picture. While *unemployment* has shown a rise over the past year from 2.3 per cent in November 1969 to 2.5 per cent (seasonably adjusted) in November 1970, employment has shown a sickening fall. Recent figures are not available for the whole economy. But employment in the aggregate in manufacturing, agriculture, mining, construction and public utilities —which account for about half of total employment—had shown by October 1970 a 2.6 per cent fall on the level in August 1969. In practical terms this means about 250,000 fewer jobs in this part of the economy alone—over a period of twelve months. Part of this fall reflects the rapid rundown of the mining industry—and the contraction of agricultural employment—but there has still been a fall of 1.84 per cent of employment in manufacturing.

Movements in employment of course reflect other factors than the strength of the demand for labour. Demographic factors—or the greater availability of full-time education—may reduce the working population. But over a period of twelve months these factors cannot explain such a significant fall. It reflects a genuine decline in job opportunities.

This decline, in its scale and pattern, is fraught with particular peril for the low-paid for two main reasons. First it reflects a decline in the *general* level of activity of the economy in relation to productive potential. The demand for labour has turned down in all except a handful of export-orientated industries. In these circumstances workers whose personal productivity is low, in whom firms have invested little in terms of training and who are in the latter and most inactive part of their working lives—in short, the low-paid—will tend to be laid off first. At the same time firms will hold on to highly skilled and/or young workers when short-term considerations would suggest laying them off.

Secondly, the fall in the general level of employment has been in part brought about by specific structural shifts which have hit particularly hard those industries within manufacturing which employ large numbers of low-paid manual workers. Thus while employment in mechanical engineering—a highly paid industry—only fell by 0.7 per cent from October 1969 to October 1970, employment in the textile industry fell by 6.58 per cent—and in clothing and footwear by 4.04 per cent over the same period. Thus structural shifts have tended to reinforce the serious effects of the general down-turn in the demand for labour on the fortunes of the low-paid.

Many of the low-paid are employed in the public sector and in the service industries, and not in manufacturing. For these sectors the employment figures are not as fresh—but just as ominous. Between June 1968 and June 1969 employment in the distributive trades fell by 2.16 per cent—and in public administration by 1.53 per cent. The fall in public sector employment comes after a number of years in which it had been increasing rapidly. The only parts of the economy to show real growth in employment were the white collar and professional sectors—insurance and banking and professional services. But it is of little comfort to the lower-paid that the demand for computer programmers is rising rapidly.

The employment figures over the past two years are not the only cause for disquiet. A further worrying piece of evidence is to be found in changes in the official figures for the working population—the total of those economically active—over a longer period. A recent issue of the DEP Gazette attempted to explain a notable mystery: that the working population fell by 350,000 between 1966 and 1968—and by 440,000 between 1966 and 1969. The effect of policies of successive governments has been to shrink the size of the British economy and of the British labour force year by year. In relation to the DEP's earlier forecasts of working population, the fall—comparing the actual figures with the forecast figure for 1969—is more than a million: 1,062,000. The forecast was made on the assumption that the pressure of demand for labour would remain at its 1966 level.

With full employment now a legend fading into an Arthurian twilight, the most important short-fall is between actual working population in 1966 and actual in 1968–69, rather than between actual and forecast working population. Part of the fall can be explained in terms of increased educational opportunities—people in full-time studies do not count as economically active. Part too can be explained by reducing economic activity by the over sixty-fives reflecting better pension arrangements. But alarmingly there has been a significant fall of 120,000 in the numbers of men of prime working age—25–64—in employment. The DEP attempts to explain this fall. It thinks that there have been 15,000 additional classifications as long-term sick. But for the remaining 105,000, it is left groping for an explanation. They have vanished into the night.

The third piece of evidence of the slackness of the labour market lies in the unemployment figures. These are usually quoted in terms of the overall rate—currently 2.6 per cent of the labour force. But five-sixths of the unemployed are men. The rate for men is 3.5 per cent. The labour market for women is in many ways separate from that for men. Thus the overall unemployed rate understates the slackness of the market in which the low-paid male worker is attempting to find a job. In the same way unemployment rates in the most hard hit parts of the development areas understate the slackness of the labour market—thus in Sunderland in September 1970 the overall unemployment rate given in the DEP Gazette was 6 per cent. But the rate for male workers would be close to 8 per cent. In

Pontypool the overall rate was 8.4 per cent—but the male rate
would have been nearer 10.5 per cent. The chances of a young
fit worker getting a job in the face of such heavy unemployment are poor enough. But an unskilled worker aged fifty and
in poor health faces, in such places, the certain prospect of
fifteen years of rotting in idleness before he can even draw his
old-age pension.

It is not only by their general policies for demand management that governments have added to the plight of the lower
paid. One of the main fiscal policies of the Labour Government—the Selective Employment Tax—has had exactly the
same effect. Whatever its merits in stimulating productivity in
the service industries, SET is undeniably a swingeing tax on
the lower paid. The method by which it is currently levied—as
a *per capita* tax rather than as a percentage of payroll, twists
the knife even further into the low-paid—if we are right in our
basic assumption that low pay is related to low performance.
This is a flat rate tax which falls equally on workers whatever
their levels of efficiency. As a matter of logic, it can be predicted that firms would lay-off—in the face of such a tax—
workers with the lowest efficiency levels. They would tend to
substitute skilled workers for unskilled workers and women for
men—as the tax falls more heavily on men than on women.

Recent research—that of Professor Reddaway—has shown
that the tax has had some of the predicted effects. One quarter
of retailers who took part in the enquiry had concentrated on
skilled rather than on unskilled staff. One-eighth reported the
dismissal of staff beyond retiring age. One trade association
commented:

> 'In the large businesses there are frequently long-service em-
> ployees whose standard of efficiency is below normal, and
> who are retained for sentimental reasons or out of a sense of
> responsibility. The imposition of SET has forced a number
> of firms to review their policy towards these people.'

The overall effect on employment has not been large—but it
has been on workers who would find it very difficult to get
another job.

Firstly, recent events in the labour market suggest that full-
employment is under threat. We are not yet back to the 1930s,
but in some parts of the country we are half-way there. Lack
of job opportunities hits many—but it hits the low-paid most of
all, because they have the least to offer in the labour market.

Thus there is need for all those interested in poverty to press as a matter for first priority for general reflation of the economy. The best immediate help to the low-paid would be a growing economy with abundant job opportunities. Schemes for minimum wages have a place in such a context of growth—but until we have such a context they are of secondary importance.

Secondly, recent events suggest the need to arrange tax policies so that they do not fall crushingly on handicapped workers. Removal of disincentives to the employment of low-paid workers needs to be accompanied by policies for increasing their skill and the information about jobs available to them.

Thirdly, the evidence—together with other pieces of evidence—suggests the need for a reassessment of the 'problem' of the work-shy. The number of long-term unemployed, those who have been out of work more than six months, has more than doubled—to 172,000. About one in three of all unemployed have been out of work more than six months—and one in five for more than a year. It could well be that many of the work-shy appear such because they cannot find work. The reason they cannot work is that there is none to find.

Large Families in London
Hilary Land

Reprinted with permission from Hilary Land, 'Large Families in London', *Occasional Papers in Social Administration*, No. 32, pp. 142–8 (Codicote Press), 1970.

The majority of the families have several sources of income. Their standard of living is determined not only by the total amount of income they receive but also by the reliability of each source of income. The level below which the family's income cannot fall depends on the father's basic wage or salary together with family allowances. However basic wages are low for the majority of these fathers. Children's tax allowances adjust family income to family size to a limited extent and affect the rich families more than the poorer ones. Family allowances, although they have doubled in size since this study was carried out, are still too small to cover the subsistence cost of a child as William Beveridge originally intended, so although important to a large family, they do not ensure that the family income is adequate. In these circumstances overtime earnings together with mother's earnings become the major methods by which the family's income is brought up to an adequate level. Other research has shown that fathers of large families work longer hours on average and that the lower his earnings the more likely the mother has paid employment. However it is also found that these methods of supplementing the family's income are likely to be unreliable, especially for the large family. The fathers as well as the mothers experience more interruptions in work. The father's ill health is the main cause for these interruptions. In addition there are times when the father's ill health, while not preventing work altogether reduces his capacity to work long hours. In the twelve months prior to the survey illness had affected the earning capacity of one in four of the fathers. Seven of these fathers were chronically ill and were unlikely to work again and eight had illnesses of a recurrent nature. By the time that family building has been completed the parents tend to be in their forties, and at the stage when the needs of the family may be greatest, when the children are aged from, say, five to fifteen years, the father may be in his fifties. By this time most men have passed the peak in their earnings and are more prone to illness.

The amount of money some families receive from the Supplementary Benefits Commission (the National Assistance Board at the time of the study) to supplement unemployment or sickness benefit is limited by the operation of the 'wage-stop'. 'Normal earnings are hard to assess when a man's earnings fluctuate, so they are likely to be assessed on the stable element of a man's earnings—basic wages. These together with family allowances determine the maximum amount of money the family receives from the state in the form of National Assistance. Thus although, in theory, state benefits take family size into account by giving an allowance for each child in the family, the extent to which these allowances in practice adjust the income of the low wage earner with several children during periods of sickness or unemployment is limited. Ten of the fourteen families in this study who were dependent on state benefits did not receive the National Assistance scale allowances in full because of the operation of the 'wage stop'.

A low income places severe restrictions on the lives of some of these families. These restrictions are felt in many aspects of their lives. Choice of accommodation is restricted because these families need more rooms than the average house or flat. The richest families in the study had been able to buy large enough houses with all the amenities they needed. As their families grew in size they had been able either to build extensions to the house in which they were living or to move to a bigger one. The families with less money to spend on their accommodation and no security on which to raise a mortgage had to rent their accommodation. The fact that a significantly higher proportion (three-quarters) of large families than households in general are living in rented accommodation at the time of the survey suggests that large families have less chance of buying their own homes than smaller families. This would not matter if they could find adequate rented accommodation, but the experiences of these families indicate that in London at least, rented accommodation which is suitable to the needs of these families is in limited supply. This is true of the private market and of local authority housing. As a result the majority of large families have no choice but to live in overcrowded flats or houses, many of which lack the basic amenities.

A low family income places restrictions on all members of the family but in many ways it is the mother who feels them most. Firstly, the mothers economize most severely on expenditure on themselves. Although the diets of all members of the poorer families are restricted compared with the higher income families, it is the mother who is the most likely to go without cooked meals completely. All members of the poorer families rely to some extent on secondhand clothing, but the mothers are often dressed entirely in secondhand clothing. Eleven of the poorer mothers had not bought a new coat or dress since their marriage. In the winter when fuel is precious these mothers work in a cold home all day, saving the fuel for the evenings when all the family is at home. Secondly, the mothers in the low income families almost invariably have complete charge of the family's finances, because their housekeeping is done on a day to day basis. The mothers in these families are dependent on other sources of income besides the father's earnings. These essential supplements to the housekeeping money—family allowances, their own earnings and working children's contributions, are given directly to her and so are under her control. As the housekeeper she, more than any other member of the family, is responsible for keeping a tight control over the family budget at all times. The poorer mother has no alternative but to buy 'little and often' or resort to buying on credit. They know these are expensive methods of buying, but they have insufficient money to practise economies of scale. Even daily budgeting does not enable some families to stretch their income over a full week so they have to borrow money regularly. Three quarters of the families below basic National Assistance scales were in debt at the time of the survey. In contrast, the rich parents are able to share their responsibilities for managing and running the home more than the poorer parents. They are able to budget over a longer period of time and while the mothers are responsible for daily or weekly payments, the fathers are responsible for making long-term payments. Over half those with incomes over 40 per cent above this level had savings.

In one respect, however, the responsibilities of the poorer parents are shared to a greater extent than among richer families, because there are more occasions when their roles are interchanged. The mother sometimes has to act as partial breadwinner by taking paid employment when the father's earning capacity is reduced and the father has to take over the role of housekeeper when other members of the family are ill. Not only are these occasions more likely to occur in the poorer families but they have little outside help to call upon at these times. Lack of time and money make it more difficult to maintain contacts with relatives from whom they are physically isolated. (Three quarters of the parents in this survey were no longer living in the same London borough or town in which they were born, a third came from outside London.) Only the richer families can afford to take advantage of improvements in communications and so maintain mutually helpful relationships with relatives who live elsewhere. The poorer families are also more reluctant to call upon the help of neighbours, partly because they do not want to accept help they feel unable to return and partly because relationships with neighbours are sometimes strained. These families therefore have little choice but to see themselves as a self-sufficient unit, seeking support from each other but not from 'outsiders'.

Where the father of a large family has a high and reliable income, the lives of both parents and children reflect few of the restrictions felt by the poorer families. However, family size imposes certain patterns of organization on the family, irrespective of income. Cramped accommodation lacking in amenities add considerably to the amount of energy needed to run a large household while washing machines, automatic dish washers and other labour saving devices remove much of the drudgery from the housework of those families able to afford them. However there is a limit to the amount of time even the richest families can save because the amount of time and attention the children seek from their parents is difficult to reduce. The richer parents felt restricted compared with their friends who have fewer children, because their continual involvement with the children leaves them little time to have their leisure activities together. On the other hand they want more time to spend with each of their children individually. In some families the responsibilities are divided between the mother and the father, the mother being more concerned with the younger children and the father with the older ones. Nevertheless the amount of attention each child receives from its parents is limited because of the demands of the siblings. The organization of a large family is therefore likely to have considerable implications for the patterns of socialization of children brought up in a large family, particularly if lack of parental attention is compensated for by attention of older siblings rather than other adults. Many of the parents in this study stressed the value of learning to share and co-operate with other members of the family. Others were aware that there was less opportunity for the children to develop their own interests. We need to know far more about these aspects of large family life and at the same time we need to know to what extent the socialization processes that occur in large families in all income groups determine these children's intellectual development. The material collected in this study only allows us to suggest that given the nature and structure of the education system, children from large families are likely to be at a disadvantage compared with children from smaller families and although material deprivation magnifies these disadvantages it is not their sole cause. Many teachers while recognizing these children, particularly from the poorer large family, are likely to be at a disadvantage compared with children from smaller families, lack the time and resources to fully understand and deal with these problems.

The results of this study demonstrate that the methods of adjusting family money income to family size are unsatisfactory, particularly for the poorer families. Methods of supplementing low wages are either inadequate like family allowances, or unreliable like overtime earnings. When the father is out of work, the inadequacies of low basic wages and family allowances are perpetuated by means of the 'wage stop'. These inadequacies are likely to remain as long as family allowances fail to be seen as an integral part of any incomes policy and as long as they are considered apart from the regular reviews of dependancy allowances in social insurance, social assistance and income tax.

A family's low income can also be supplemented by welfare benefits in cash and kind. These too fall short of meeting the needs of the poorer families. One reason for this is that the benefits are basically too low. For example, there are rent rebate and differential rent schemes which take no account of household size and are based solely on total household income. Consequently in this study the majority of the low income families were found to be in rent arrears.

A second and more important reason lies in their administration. The experiences of the families in this study illustrate the importance of ensuring that the methods by which welfare benefits are administered are known and understood by those who need them. Misunderstandings about the conditions of entitlement to assistance can result in families making the wrong decision which could have a long-term effect on their future welfare. For example, in this study there was a mother with eight children who had been deserted by her husband. Mistakenly she had the impression that she would be entitled to receive help from the National Assistance Board only if she took out a court order against her husband. This action not only probably diminished the chances of a reconciliation but also reduced the amount of financial support the father was prepared to give. Families who are not told of benefits to which they may be entitled conclude, often wrongly, that assistance is not available to them. Those who are well-informed and persistent are more likely to receive the benefits to which they are entitled but they run the risk of being labelled 'scroungers'. The support of a social worker or teacher often increases a family's chance of receiving benefits because it re-assures the family that they are entitled to assistance and because it helps to convince officials that the family 'deserves' it. The families who receive all the benefits to which they are entitled are not necessarily the poorest. Other families are ignorant of the availability of the assistance they clearly need. They are not in contact with anyone able to dispel their ignorance. The experiences of the families in this study show that sometimes social workers and teachers have insufficient information about the family's financial circumstances as well as about the conditions of entitlement, to enable them to help a family receive as much assistance as existing provisions allow.

The third reason is a more fundamental one. Society has ambivalent attitudes towards those who need support, particularly financial support from the State. On the one hand we believe everybody has a right to financial security in times of adversity and dependency in childhood, sickness and old age. People have a right to work and those who are unable to do so should be given financial assistance. The State therefore makes provisions to assist people during these periods. On the other hand we still place a high value on independence. Success is measured by a man's ability to support himself and his family by his own efforts. Financial security is a reward for hard work and so must be earned. Those who have to ask for assistance in feeding and clothing their families feel a loss of self-respect and status because it means admitting to themselves as well as to others that they have failed. The methods by which some of the benefits are administered: the means test procedures and the distinction made between the recipients of these benefits and those who can afford to pay (as for example, children receiving free school meals were identified by the other children in their class) reinforce these feelings and make the families concerned feel that perhaps they do not deserve such help. Vouchers instead of money to buy a school uniform for example, carry the implication that unlike the majority of people the families cannot be trusted to spend money wisely. These methods of administration are the consequence of selective services argues Richard Titmuss: 'Universality in welfare is needed to resolve and remove barriers of social and economic discrimination. Separate services for second class citizens invariably become second class services whether they are organized for 10 per cent or 50 per cent of the population. Moreover, those who staff the services may come to believe that they themselves are second class workers. Hence when exercising discretionary powers in giving or withholding benefits and services they may adopt a more punishing attitude to those whom they may disapprove of.'

The further we move away from universal services available as of right to everyone by virtue of citizenship, towards selective services concentrating on 'the poor' the greater the sense of stigma attached to using the services. 'Those who use the minority public services come to feel that they represent a "public burden"; they cannot respect themselves nor do they respect others for using a public service. The implication then is that they can only achieve self-respect (and avoid shame) by not using a public service, by going without, by living in poverty, by not bothering anyone, by retaining their independence or by attempting to buy in the private market.' It is therefore, the implicit values society places on 'work', 'success' and 'independence' which effectively restrict demands on the social services. The families in this study shared these values and therefore restrained their claims for welfare benefits just as much as those who administered them. As a result the inadequate incomes of some families are not supplemented although the State has made provision to do so.

The lives of the parents and children of large families are affected by their status within the community. Society tends to disapprove of those who fail to, or choose not to, limit their fertility unless they are prosperous. The richer families therefore suffer no loss of status because their several children are not seen to increase their dependence on the State. The poorer families do feel a loss in status, especially if the father is sick or unemployed. A low income clearly reduces the level of material comfort of a large family to that well below the standards set by the rest of the community. Their low status magnifies their feelings of deprivation and serves to increase their isolation from relatives and neighbours as well as from the social services. Ironically, inability to control their family size, whether for religious reasons, ignorance or failure of techniques, perpetuates and increases the lack of control and choice in all other aspects of their lives. It is essential, therefore, that parents rich or poor should be given adequate help to limit their fertility if they want to do so. The Family Planning advice and assistance some of them, particularly the poorer parents, had received had not been sufficient or of the right kind to enable half of those parents who had attempted to limit their fertility to do so successfully. This is not to suggest that the problems of the poor large family could, or should be solved by ensuring that low paid workers only have one or two children but that the ability to chose the number of children they have should be as great for poorer parents as for richer parents. This choice will not be a real one if children from poor large families continue to experience the deprivations and the restricted opportunities of many of the poorer children in this study. Over twenty-five years ago Eleanor Rathbone, one of the chief advocates of family allowances for *all* children, irrespective of the father's income, said: 'Children should receive a little share of the national income given to them not in respect of their father's service in industry but *in respect of their own value to the community as its future citizens and workers*' (author's italics). The responsibility is ours if we allow large families such a small share of the community's resources that their children can only become second-class citizens and workers.

Poverty and Money
A. L. Schorr

Reprinted with permission from A. L. Schorr, 'Poverty and Money', *New Society*, 17 August 1967, pp. 219–21.

It was bound to come to this. With wonted malice and without elaboration, the *New Yorker* has quoted an American government official explaining 'that the basic problem with the poor is an economic one'. Although literary types may think the proposition self-evident, today's administrators and sophisticated social scientists come to it with a sense of discovery, if at all. Public discussion of poverty is filled with terms such as 'culture of poverty' and 'problem family'. Countless doctoral dissertations testify to the inadequate personalities of those who are now poor or long out of work. If vulgar money occupies the minds of those who lack it, students of the lack are clearly more civilised.

With reasonable pains and scholarships, it would be possible to demonstrate that lack of money—or its equivalent in elementary human requirements—is the most powerful force that prevents the majority of poor families from improving their situations. Of the despair and apathy that are currently being documented, and of the alcoholism and crime that were fashionably documented the last time around, a large share is a response to the accurate perception that without money or the influence that accompanies money there is no way out. Here I should like to argue a narrower point: even if one is persuaded that personal or cultural qualities are a key to poverty, the simple monetary definition is worth keeping firmly in focus. For a monetary definition supports sound public policies which are otherwise likely to be altered or attenuated.

To begin with, the monetary definition permits poverty to be counted in a stable fashion for the first time in the history of the United States or, probably, of any country. The basis for counting—a projection of other needs from the cost of food for families of specified size—can be criticised on various grounds: (*a*) the definition of poverty is niggardly; (*b*) account is not taken of assets, of income in goods and services, or of access to public services; (*c*) the definition is absolute, over-looking the fact that one's perception of poverty tends to ex-pand with a nation's rising standard of living. Despite these limitations, the definition is agreed upon in advance and can readily be established. It is possible to observe whether the number of poor people has increased, or declined, or declined rapidly. With this simple technical achievement, poverty acquires a tool of some political potency.

National policies tend to be dominated by countable qualities —gross national product, unemployment rate, cost of living. It is not difficult to develop technical criticisms of the method of determining unemployment rate, but a change in the rate of three tenths of a per cent stirs a government to pride or frenzied activity. Because quantitative measurements play so powerful a role in public policy, the American government and the Russell Sage Foundation are involved in a considerable effort to develop *social* indicators. With quantification, the quality of life (health, a sense of community, clean air) might gain parity in national debate with the purely economic measures that now loom so large.

In the same sense, the measurement of poverty is an official social indicator. It may no longer suffice that the gross national product rises if poverty fails to fall. Between 1963 and 1966, the number of poor people in the United States declined from 35 to 31 million. But it now becomes clear that in some earlier years poverty did not decline and, indeed, increased. Between 1953 and 1954, for example, when the Korean war ended and many lost their jobs, the number of poor people increased by three million. If we come upon such a year again *and know it*, the fact will unquestionably be regarded as a shortcoming of national policy. A government will call this criticism on itself only with the greatest reluctance.

Another effect of the monetary definition of poverty lies in the grand strategy for a campaign against poverty to which it leads. When one focuses on money, it is difficult to avoid examining what sort of jobs are available and how those who are unemployed might find work. As for those for whom work is not suitable, it is difficult to avoid the sort of debate to which Britain has lately found itself pressed. How does one get money to the aged? Why have the programmes that were forged after Beveridge failed to prevent poverty among children? The solutions to which such debate leads are rarely cheap but commonly effective.

In contrast, discussions that focus on the exotic attitudes of poor people are likely to move in a different direction. People then want to confront the problems of problem families directly, with family counselling, psychiatric treatment, or advice on home management. They conceive a series of programmes that essentially intend the alteration or improvement of those who are poor in order that they may earn their own way. (J. E. MacColl told the story some years ago of two old East End ladies watching a worthy female pass by. Said one to the other, 'Well, you know I'm not a difficult person, but I do so 'ate bein' worked amongst.') It is a case service approach. The weakness is not that the service is not needed; probably the service is widely needed by those with plenty of money as well as those who do without. But in practice personal services do not provide sufficient leverage to alter the external circumstances of very many people.

One dare not overlook the rejoinder that the attitudes and behaviour patterns of poor people may be the very root of their problem. That is, one must observe clinically (not morally, certainly) that the jobs and money provided may be forfeited and squandered. But I am not arguing against the provision of case services. The development of programmes for jobs or income doesn't preclude the development of personal services. But it is readily supposed—or at least has been many times supposed—that programmes for problem families dispose of their problem and of poverty in general.

One of the reasons for this supposition is that personal services have a quality of visibility compared with the provision of money that permits a nation that is doing little to believe it is doing much. Octavia Hill pointed to a similar case in criticising the charitable trusts of the mid-nineteenth century. Even now, one may pardonably hold the impression that the trusts made a phenomenal effort to improve the housing of poor people. Yet she pointed out that all their work in London from 1845 to 1875 was sufficient to house only six months of London's population increase. Services such as the family service units and reestablishment centres can all too easily be similar cases. Because they do good work, it may be difficult to bear in mind that they deal in hundreds and poverty—for that is the target—deals in millions.

Because of this quality of visibility, national policy based on personal services tends to be inexpensive. This is not because such services are themselves inexpensive; they are frequently more costly per person than the annual income they are meant to produce. But if they reach comparatively few people their overall cost is, of course, small. The choice that is made to develop an expensive service which is inexpensive overall is not necessarily deliberate or thoroughly understood—particularly on the part of the electorate. We may intend more, but unfortunately our understanding of how to engineer and deliver personal services is as yet primitive.

We may set out to deliver a service to everyone. We rapidly discover that we do not have enough properly trained personnel; the time for their development is five to eight years. It seems reasonable to build an expanded service on already existing organisations. Existing organisations might fight and destroy a modern service if they did not possess it but, possessing, they subvert it. We may understand how to organise a service in a comparatively small city. However, some cities are too big for the same pattern to work. As for small towns and the country, they do not have related facilities for the proposed service to rely on and the personnel, once they are trained, cannot be induced to move there.

The point may be clear, but let me put it briefly thus: a grand strategy derived from musing on a cultural or attitudinal view of poverty tends to be organised about social services that we may be just beginning to learn how to deliver and, therefore, the strategy turns out to be comparatively inexpensive. Such a policy has both intellectual and fiscal appeal. Its only shortcoming, when compared with the expensive measures that derive from a monetary view of poverty, may be that it is not effective.

The final effect of the monetary definition of poverty is its tendency to direct attention to what might be called the functional uses (as opposed to the subsistence uses) of money. That is, if one defines poverty culturally, monetary needs enter into policy mainly in the terms with which we have long been familiar—'a decent level of living', 'an income sufficient for subsistence'. These terms, whatever they explicitly mean, go to sustaining people at the level that for the moment seems to be minimally acceptable, while another therapy is applied to improve them. When one *focuses* on money, however, it is necessary to ask how money affects self-improvement. It is odd that we rarely ask this question in relation to poor people, for it is well understood that the operative reason that the rich get richer is money.

The distinction I am describing is analogous to that between the lay and professional views of assisting developing countries. The layman may carry an image of technical assistance, consenting without much thought to direct aid that enables a population to survive while it is developing the necessary skills. The professional perceives that the development of skills waits on the factories, schools and transport system to which to apply them. These in turn require that a country have surplus money to deploy after food and other basic needs have been provided. In the words of W. W. Rostow, 'Take-off awaits the build-up of social overhead capital...'

One need not be fanciful to recognise that take-off for families may depend on enough money to establish oneself in another town where jobs are plentiful, or enough money to be able to spare the earning power of a youth who wants to continue in school, or enough savings to give up a poor job for work that will pay better but is in some fashion risky. Research also suggests that income above a certain threshold establishes sufficient confidence about the future so that advanced training or education are preferred to early marriage and child bearing (of course, the latter are, in turn, further impediments to any escape from poverty).

Thus, addressing the functional financial issue in poverty raises a new set of questions: how much money is needed not for adequacy but for take-off? At what periods in a lifetime or in family development is take-off possible? How much money is really needed then? Currently, public policy appears to answer these questions perversely in both the United States and Britain, concentrating money that is more nearly adequate among the old rather than the young and among the young only after their slide into poverty has advanced to a point where it is difficult to reverse. Insufficient attention is apparently being paid to money itself as a resource in family improvement. It is more difficult to commit such an oversight when one takes a monetary view of poverty.

In sum, setting aside the historic question of the character of poor people, I think that a sound public policy is more likely to flow from keeping money in focus. The monetary definition provides a stable measure that feeds back figures year after year. The figures, if they are vexing, provide a handy tool for any opposition party. The monetary definition makes it difficult to overlook employment and income maintenance. No combination of programmes that omits these two can be of more than token service. And the monetary definition makes us attend to money's developmental function for the family as well as its better understood function in expressing the nation's sense of community or solidarity. For such reasons, if not for more basic ones, poverty-wise, money is in.

A Voice for the Voiceless
Robert Holman

Reprinted with permission from Robert Holman, 'A Voice for the Voiceless,' *British Hospital Journal and Social Service Review*, 16 January 1970, p. 118.

Grass-root organisations have employed four main strategies. They operate as *normal pressure groups* to improve national policies relating to their members, and members are informed of their legal rights and helped to obtain them. For instance, claimants have been told of their right to appeal against official decisions and helped to take their case to the Appeals Tribunal. In addition, group activities *support the members* who are often ostracised by society. Most controversially, they have used *conflict strategy*. Thus the Claimants Union threatened to expose unhelpful officials by sending members to interviews with hidden tape recorders. Their news-sheet is full of terminology about 'fighting' the Ministry. The Balsall Heath tenants have begun a rent strike against the council in protest at the conditions of their dwellings, the lack of repairs, and the failure of some tenants to get rehoused.

It is impossible to explain exactly what caused the rise of such organisations, but clearly the extent of their deprived position and the virtual impossibility of improvement were important aspects. Claimants, and they include unsupported mothers, deserted wives and the disabled, as well as the unemployed, are very poor. A mother might receive £5 11s (plus rent) for herself and her child per week. Research, as reported in *Mothers Alone*, shows that normal living cannot be attained from this amount. They may not starve, but there is no provision for the usual extras of life like holidays or outings which a child needs, and no continual provision for extra demands such as new clothes or repairs to domestic appliances. Housing conditions in Balsall Heath include damp in all rooms, holes in the ceiling, overcrowding, outside wcs, repairs not done, dysentery and rats. And it must be remembered that Balsall Heath is by no means the most deprived ward in Birmingham. These environmental conditions shape not only the high infant mortality rates but also the attitudes, opportunities and behaviour patterns of the inhabitants.

Deprived conditions are one thing, the prospect of change another; *it is the absence of hope that drives people to drastic action*. There are four serious reasons for despair in Birmingham:

First, tenants and claimants complained that approaches to officials were *dead-end roads*. A common story was (and is) that of the tenant of a council slum dwelling who asked for repairs and the matter was recorded on a slip at the housing department. After weeks of non-action, the tenant again made the journey—probably a long one by bus and laden with children—to the housing department. The form was completed again, and assurance given. The tenant later tried to get through by telephone, all to no avail. It is not known how general this treatment has been, but it certainly existed. I know several cases, including one woman who waited months for repair to her outside wc which had holes in the roof so large that her family could not use it during wet weather. If the non-service is combined with official attitudes of unhelpfulness and condemnation, as the Claimants Union says, these recipients are just ground into the dust.

Secondly, at times it seemed *policy not to inform* (or to misinform) people about the social services. Claimants were not necessarily told about the discretionary payments and exceptional needs grant which could be made. Tenants claimed that they were given dates for repairs or rehousing which were not fulfilled.

Thirdly, their powerlessness is related also to their *lack of legal rights.* The Department of Social Security legally refuses to allow the public to see the A code which regulates benefit allocations. Tenants have no legal powers to enforce the council to improve their dwellings, although the council itself can compel private landlords to do certain repairs and install essential amenities.

Fourthly, *faith in many politicians has been lost.* One councillor, who is also an MP, after hearing tenants and their student supporters speak at a meeting, openly declared his support for them. A few days later he joined other councillors in stating that he did not recognise the rent strike and would not meet the tenants because they were led by dangerous elements. These complaints, as expressed by tenants and claimants, may be exaggerated, and no doubt some councillors and officials are humane and helpful. But the people described were (and are) in a circle of hopelessness from which there seemed no escape. They were told to use the normal channels to get redress, but they found them blocked. They tried departments, councillors, MPs. Nobody needed to heed them because they can be regarded as unimportant, powerless groups. They were told to be patient, yet continuously their young were exposed to an environment which not only kills infants but can harm the social development of those who live. Therefore, they turned to militant action.

Further Reading :   **Poverty**

* B. ABEL-SMITH and P. TOWNSEND, *The Poor and the Poorest*, London, Bell, 1965.

* P. ANDERSON and R. BLACKBURN (Eds.), *Towards Socialism*, London, Fontana, 1965.

* DAVID BULL, (Ed.), *Family Poverty. Programme for the Seventies*, London, Duckworth, 1971.

* K. COATES and R. SILBURN, *Poverty. The Forgotten Englishmen*, Harmondsworth, Penguin, 1970.

* R. HOLMAN (Ed.), *Socially Deprived Families in Britain*, London, Bedford Square Press, 1970.

D. MARSDEN, *Mothers Alone. Poverty and the Fatherless Family*, Harmondsworth, Penguin, 1969.

A. SHONFIELD and S. SHAW, *Social Indicators and Social Policy*, SSRC, 1972.

P. TOWNSEND (Ed.), *The Concept of Poverty*, London, Heinemann, 1970.

* Available in paperback

Chapter Five   Urban Problems

Britain was the first country in the world to experience
large-scale urbanisation as a result of industrial development.
The community that was then created, and the physical
equipment which serviced it, remain as the focus of many social
problems today. Their characteristics within Britain
are governed by historical developments, including the
concentration of housing around factories, the pollution of
the atmosphere by industrial processes and the general blight
on the environment which affects not only the levels of
amenity but also the health, opportunities and aspirations of
the population.

The movement of population to the South East, which
has been a feature of British society for hundreds of years, has
had all kinds of consequences. The demand for accommodation
has led to enormous increases in house prices, favourable
to those who bought homes before the prices rose but posing
enormous problems for families with few assets who need a
home. Access to different kinds of housing is affected by such
factors as overall demand, availability of resources and the
provision of new building. Where housing is scarce and prices
rising there is a tendency for overcrowding and other features
associated with massive and varied social problems to develop.

The urban community may be viewed as a concentration of
all the really basic social problems which are to be found
in society. The loneliness that comes from being present in
large aggregates of people without having any effective contact
with them, may seem to be an argument in favour of much
smaller groupings, possibly in rural areas. But this could be
impossible to achieve in practice, giving the many significant
advantages which urban life possesses, for, from a different
point of view, it can be argued that the city is the centre of
all the most constructive forces within society, the source of
social mobility, of opportunity, of social change, of which
social problems are relatively minor though not unimportant
side-effects.

We must also consider the effects of the attraction of the city and the large concentration of people in urban areas—in Britain four out of five people live in towns—which affect the quality of life and the opportunities which exist outside in the country. In recent years, there has been a movement from the city to areas which are relatively easy of access. This is not a realistic alternative on any sigfinificant scale, however, for people who live in large metropolitan areas. The affluent may be able to get out at the weekends but the poor are condemned to live within a relatively small physical area near the centre of the city.

There are many differences between towns in terms of the industries and activities on which they are dependent, the range of those industries and the extent to which industries are either expanding or declining. In some areas the large industries are in decline and others must take their place unless the population, or a substantial proportion of it is to move elsewhere. The dilemma of allowing workers to go where work is or creating work where there are workers unemployed is particularly acute where the basic industry, and possibly the only one, is in almost complete eclipse In Durham there are mining villages where only elderly people are left because the only work is in the towns and cities.

The separation of the city into different areas with particular characteristics is a useful preliminary to looking at ways of life there. In particular the inner city areas, or zones of transition, present a range of issues. To understand the ecology of the city one must have an idea of areas having different kinds of uses over time. The most obvious example of the 'zone of transition' is the former middle-class area near the centre which is used both by poorer income groups, once the middle classes have left for the suburbs, and by various commercial and administrative undertakings. The processes of change are at work all the time but it is easy to assume that they are caused, particularly where areas decline in status, by the groups which are entering them. This idea that problems adhere to areas irrespective of the changing population within them is vital for the understanding of social problems.

The first reading, from the Shelter Report, exposes the ways in which insecurity is created or intensified. The examples given speak for themselves. They are only one side of the question, but they illustrate far more effectively than figures or academic discussions what the reality of life in such housing conditions is like.

Concern about overcrowding in homes has strong historical roots going back to the public health movement of the nineteenth century. The second reading documents progress since then and points out that in Hong Kong today in housing designed to alleviate overcrowding, the density is several times that regarded as acceptable in Britain. It is shown how the relation between the amount of housing and the rate of household formation needs to be borne in mind, particularly since the latter has increased with the larger number of elderly people in the population. The authors look at the extent of overcrowding and ways of tackling it and suggest that now it is not so much overcrowding which is an indication of the worst housing conditions but multi-occupation involving shared basic amenities in inadequately converted houses.

In the brief extract from his study of Sunderland Norman Dennis poses the key questions which arise in deciding between the replacement or retention of existing dwellings.

The study by Roy Haddon is important both from the point of view of considering the distribution of West Indians in a particular part of London and also for the way in which poor housing conditions are viewed as an aspect of social deprivation which the members of the minority experience as an integral part of urban poverty. The position of a minority has to be examined not only in relation to work but also in relation to what the author calls 'the apparatus of social policy' and its rules of eligibility. The kind of housing that people live in, and in particular the tenure, indicates many things about their position in society and the decline in the kinds of housing which the members of minority groups are most likely to require, above all in the private rented sector, is examined.

The aspect of individual choice is seen in the problems caused by traffic congestion in the city. This has implications for the quality of public transport, and the planning of traffic systems and the provision of parking facilities to cope with the influx of workers and others. The problems posed by the car have grown enormously in the last 25 years.

The construction of motorways poses serious questions about the use of land, as features of the present situation are the enormous increase in the value of land, and the pressure of demand for alternative uses, which have no strong economic support for them, such as recreation. If the car is allowed to

dominate the provision of transport in the city then a very
large proportion of the area near the centre will be taken up
with roads or parking. The crisis that is discussed by George
Clarke in connection with Acklam Road and the building of
the motorway, will be a much more common occurrence. He
raises questions about what happens to people in this situation
and in particular what kinds of sanctions are available to them
in order to prevent undesirable consequences or at least to see
that, instead of having to accept them, something is done to
change their situation for the better. The most important point
concerns the response of the inhabitants who, dissatisfied
with what they had to endure, organised themselves in order
to effect some satisfactory change on their own behalf. Clark
suggests that unless people make their voices heard they are
likely to get little satisfaction from the system, and the lesson
is that people can be powerful when they combine.

The case study of families threatened with eviction is the
theme of the contribution by Margaret Jones. What emerges
of particular interest is the view of social attitudes in a
relatively isolated community, the extent to which various
groups using a range of approaches were involved in attempting
to resolve the issue, and the final question about the part that
social workers and others should play in similar situations.
Social workers have been chary as a group of becoming
involved in situations where they appear to be opposing the
authorities that employ them or their colleagues. At the same
time, professionalism ought to mean that there are decisions
which are made by the individual on grounds not of expediency
or departmental convenience but of values in society to
which the professional subscribes. The questions are posed
for further discussion.

Peter Gregory's subject is polluted homes in an area which
has experienced pollution for a long time at a high level.
Conflicts of interest are identified, in particular as to whether
there should be a move from the area to better accommodation
or an attempt to improve the existing environment and the
'image' of the people living there. The problems for the local
authority are highlighted in the discussion on policy, which
shows how difficult it is to give weight to all the factors
involved where there are differing views among the inhabitants
about leaving or staying.

Eviction and Insecurity

Reprinted with permission from *Notice to Quit*, a Shelter Report, 1968, pp. 2–27.

Our research has uncovered 13 main areas where insecurity is created or feelings of insecurity are intensified.

1. *Furnished tenancies.* Although it takes time, it is a relatively simple process to evict any tenant from furnished accommodation. The postponements that are possible within the law (to enable the tenant to find new accommodation) may be ample for most of the country, but the time allowed is often inadequate in areas of housing stress.

2. *Ignorance of the Law.* Housing legislation is highly complex and the low-wage tenant is usually ignorant of his rights. Initiative and a reasonable knowledge of legal provision are needed by the tenant at some stage and, in many cases as a result of economic or social oppression, he lacks both.

3. *Harassment.* Harassment of tenants continues. Even where the tenant knows his rights, his case is difficult to prove; and even if he wins, he still has to live with the insecurity created by the growing hostility of the landlord.

4. *Illegal eviction.* Families are still being illegally forced to leave their accommodation. Others are being tricked into going. Word of illegal evictions spreads quickly through overcrowded districts, intensifying the feelings of insecurity of other families as well.

5. *Tied accommodation.* The tenant of a house that is tied to a job is again only partially protected and his problem is intensified by the fact that he loses home and job at the same time.

6. *Slum clearance victims.* The important slum clearance or demolition projects of local authorities create insecurity for tenants of furnished accommodation who often are in doubt as to whether they are going to be rehoused, encourage landlords to try to achieve vacant possession by evicting tenants, and can lead to homelessness for those families who unknowingly moved into the houses after the compulsory order was served.

7. *Rent arrears.* Not all families evicted for rent arrears are guilty of negligence. There are those who must struggle with large families, low incomes and high rents. There are those

who suddenly suffer setbacks, and there are the sad cases of women and children who are abandoned with rent arrears about which they knew nothing or are left with a mass of debts they must pay.

8. *Backlash from the rent tribunal.* For many families, a visit to the rent tribunal has been the first step towards homelessness. Landlords don't like being taken to rent tribunals, don't like rents being reduced, and many make their subsequent dislike of the tenants quite clear. Often the result is harassment and legal or illegal eviction.

9. *Competition with landlord.* Where the landlord suddenly decides he wants more space, or wants to sell, the tenant finds himself in difficulty and occasionally in the position of being the certain loser in a vicious competition. This kind of insecurity can strike a tenant without warning, and in the case of a furnished tenant his protection is severely limited.

10. *Illegal tenants.* Many desperate families move into accommodation when they know their presence is illegal. This creates nagging insecurity. But many others do not know they are illegal tenants. In some cases a landlord has a mortage which does not allow him to sub-let; often this comes to light when the landlord defaults on his mortgage and loses the house. The tenants all have to leave.

11. *Overcrowding.* If the laws on overcrowding were enforced, hundreds of thousands of people would be on the streets overnight. Because of this, authorities do not enforce the regulations on a large scale. But the fact that they are illegally overcrowded means that many families constantly fear discovery.

12. *Unfit housing.* All families, and there are thousands of them, living in houses that are structurally unsound, unhealthy, or insecure against entry by unauthorised persons, are living with insecurity every day of their lives.

13. *Children.* Children are often the cause of their family's housing problem. The birth of children leads to many legal and illegal evictions. Many private landlords are unwilling to take children, and the feeling of insecurity among many families with children in privately rented accommodation is intense.

Some cases

'One Saturday last year (1967), the landlord decided he wanted to get rid of the family for good. He switched off their gas, electricity and water, all in rapid succession, and refused to put them on again when asked. The family called the police and when they arrived the landlord said he was going to switch off the gas, electricity and water every Saturday. The police warned him he would be asking for trouble. Soon after this, while Mrs. G. was in the kitchen, and her husband elsewhere in the flat, the landlord burst into the kitchen and began to attack Mrs. G., hitting her in the stomach (remember, she was pregnant) with his stick (he was semi-crippled). Her husband heard her screams and raced in, throwing the landlord out of the room so that he fell and broke his ankle. Mrs. G. was rushed to hospital for examination and later went to stay temporarily with her mother. They were terrified to go back to the place. Her husband went to stay in a hotel at considerable expense. The Town Clerk's department was prepared to prosecute the landlord and Mrs. G., in fact, took out a summons against him for assault. Shortly afterwards, with the protection of the police and some friends, they went back to the flat and collected their belongings. Finally, two days before the baby was born, they were rescued by a housing association and dropped the summons for assault which was due to be heard the same day as the baby was born.'

SHELTER Researcher talking about a case in East London:

A number of factors contribute to the continued harassment of tenants. One is the ignorance, common to so many families living in privately-rented accommodation, of their rights under the law. Another is fear of the landlord — fear so deeply rooted that families will not exercise their rights. Another is the difficulty of getting witnesses to private acts of harassment. Even if the tenant has the courage to take his landlord to court, the burden of proof is often too great. Finally, there are many and varied ways in which a landlord can make life rough or unpleasant for his tenant without actually doing something that could be proved in court to be a criminal attempt to deprive the tenant of his accommodation.

In considering the plight of the harassed tenant, we should not overlook the fact that even if a case against the landlord is not only taken to court but won, continued existence in the landlord's house and his continued hostility create an insecurity of their own.

Some landlords are even prepared to risk prosecution and a fine for harassment in the knowledge that whether the tenant wins or loses his case, he will probably go in the end, and the average fine for harassment is laughable when compared with the additional income obtainable when the tenant is out. (One landlord got an additional £1,500 for a house because he could sell it with vacant possession. When this is compared with the average fine for harassment, is it possible to see why some landlords are prepared to regard prosecution for harassment as merely part of the cost of operating a profitable enterprise.) Between 8 December 1965, and 31 March 1968, there were 714 summonses for such offences. Only 60 of the 408 fines exceeded £50, and only four offenders were sent to prison. The maximum fine for a first offence is £100.

A Paddington family of father, mother, two-year-old and baby, lived in two rooms on the first floor of a house and paid £6 a week rent. The landlord wanted vacant possession, so they went to the Rent Tribunal who gave them six months security in their furnished flat, with a later extension of three months. The landlord, not prepared to wait, struck the father with a hammer so that he had to have stitches. While the father was at work, the landlord threatened his wife, creating a nerve-wracking situation in which wife lived at home in fear while husband went worried to work. Then the Rent Tribunal, having visited the home, reduced the rent by £2 and, since the landlord was not observing fixed rents, they ordered him to pay the arrears. This considerably annoyed him and he took the father to court for being drunk. The case was dismissed by the courts as being 'completely unfounded', but the publicity caused the family much distress.

A London couple with one child were living in furnished property. The landlord had not even given them a rent book. He decided he wanted more space for himself, and told the couple to move. He cut off the electricity as an added inducement. The husband had to give up work to help find a new home and the family, father unemployed, is at present staying with a former neighbour.

Mr. N. went to live in a furnished room on the ground floor of a London House. When Mr. N. married, his wife came to live in the room with him. They were allowed to share the kitchen and the bathroom with the landlord's family. The room was damp but the best they could get. The landlord began to impose one restriction after another and use any small incident for an argument. There were arguments over cleaning the stove. When the tenant accidentally broke a window, the landlord called the police. By now, Mrs. N. was pregnant and when she went to the council to see if they could get on the council waiting list, the landlord, who they believed had a G.L.C. mortgage and did not want it known that he was sub-letting, gave them notice to quit. The nagging got worse. The landlord's wife would walk into their room without knocking and turn off the radio. The children were being encouraged to get on the young wife's nerves by chanting insults. Finally, the landlord's wife pulled Mrs. N's. hair and pushed her downstairs. Fortunately, the promise of a housing association flat induced the couple to move into temporary accommodation, and later they were rehoused.

One family in North Kensington was told by the landlord to 'Forget about the rent for a few weeks'. Because they were going through a rough time, they, rather naïvely, accepted his offer with gratitude. Then suddenly, he demanded his rent for the previous six weeks. Of course, they had not got it, having spent the money on essentials like clothing for the children. He promptly took them to court for non-payment of the rent. The landlord's version prevailed.

Another family, this time living in North London, had great difficulty in establishing exactly who their landlord was, and to whom they should pay the rent. They were never given a rent book. Given a situation like this, few poor families could save money, and in this case gradually rent arrears grew until the landlord's solicitor, without warning, brought a court action against them. They lost and were ordered to leave. So far the landlord's representatives have not come to turn them out and they are desperately searching for another home. There is little hope of finding one and their insecurity is considerable.

Overcrowding
Vere Hole and M. T. Pountney

Reprinted with permission from Vere Hole and M. T. Pountney, *Trends in Population, Housing and Occupancy Rates 1861–1961*, HMSO, 1971, pp. 5–8.

Overcrowding is usually defined as a person/room ratio in excess of a certain arbitrary limit. More than 2 persons per room has in Britain been traditionally regarded as an indication of overcrowding. For this reason successive censuses have recorded densities of 2 or more persons per room; in the 1961 census the highest density recorded was $1\frac{1}{2}$ persons per room. When it is remembered that the Hong Kong Housing Authority, operating in a different social and economic climate, builds on the basis of 4 to 8 persons per room in new housing which is intended to relieve overcrowding, the arbitrary nature of definitions of this sort is even more apparent.

In this country concern about overcrowding in houses was closely related to the emergence of the public health movement. The inquiries conducted in the 1830s and 1840s had demonstrated that the highest incidence of disease and mortality occurred in the most densely populated areas of towns, where insanitary conditions were at their worst. It was recognised, however, particularly by Chadwick in his report on the *Sanitary Condition of the Labouring Population of Great Britain*, that the high rates of disease and mortality were the product of a whole syndrome: of insanitary conditions; of poverty of those who were overcrowded; and personal habits and a way of life which increased susceptibility to disease. This sophisticated understanding was often lost in later discussions of the evils of overcrowding, when a simple cause-and-effect relationship between crowding and disease was often assumed.

The toll of diseases such as typhus, cholera and tuberculosis in the town centres was so great in the mid-nineteenth century that it is not surprising that some of the earliest attempts to define acceptable minimum living space utilised criteria for physical health: the volume of space per person which would be required to ensure an adequate supply of fresh air, calculated on the basis of the oxygen consumption rate of an individual, and the rate of air change in a room. In practice, however, the space allowance per person in poor law establishments, army barracks, accommodation for police constables and common lodging houses varied from 8m to 14m. On this criterion of space per person (by which occupancy of lodging houses in England and small dwellings in Glasgow was placed under police control) the permitted occupancy worked out at about 2 or slightly more persons per room. It is from this experience that the traditional association between 2 persons per room and the concept of overcrowding emerged. However, even in these first definitions of space standards, other social criteria were introduced: the Act of 1851 that regulated Common Lodging Houses established the principle of sex separation for sleeping for persons other than married couples.

Later standards, such as that adopted by the Manchester Public Health Committee, added the refinement of age: sex separation only applied to individuals over the age of 10 years. Children under 10 were counted as half a unit and up to the age of 1 year were omitted altogether from a count of number of persons in the household. In the national survey carried out under the Housing Act in 1935, the variable of floor area of rooms was added to those of age and sex as the measure of overcrowding. A further refinement has been to distinguish the function of a room, for example for living or sleeping, and, in families over a certain size a living room has been allowed for as well as bedrooms. This was utilised in a special analysis of part of the data from the 1931 census, and in national surveys of housing in 1960 and 1964. However, the current statutory definition of overcrowding lays down a permitted number of occupants in relation to total number and size of rooms in a house, irrespective of whether these rooms are bedrooms or living rooms, and adopts the same requirements for sex separation and counting those aged under 10 as half a unit, as did the Manchester Health Committee. It is perhaps worth noting that the far cruder measure of over 2 persons per room has been found to correlate quite highly, at least in urban areas of high density, with a measure of overcrowding based on the sex separation of persons over 10 and the counting of children under 10 as the equivalent of half a unit.

The extent of overcrowding

The earliest indication of the extent of overcrowding in the population as a whole came with the census of 1891, which revealed that at least 11 per cent of the population, over

3,000,000 people, were housed at densities of over 2 persons per room. Since the analysis was confined to dwellings of up to 4 rooms only, it would underestimate crowded conditions since multi-occupancy in large dwellings can cause overcrowding. Booth's survey of London at this period showed that the areas where overcrowding occurred tended to be those inhabited by the very poor. This and other evidence suggests that the measure of over 2 persons per room gave a reasonable if crude indication of the magnitude of bad housing conditions in the country at that time. The inquiries into the living conditions of the working classes 50 years earlier had cited many particular instances where from 8 to 12 persons inhabited a single room, but there is little to indicate the number of families affected by these acute conditions or of those subjected to lesser degrees of overcrowding. The only statistic available before 1891 is the wholly inadequate one of persons per house. In view of the steady decline throughout the century in the average number of persons per house, and in the ratio of households to dwellings, it is reasonable to assume that, over-all, overcrowding had also decreased. Nevertheless, in 1885, the Royal Commission on Housing of the Working Classes was convinced that overcrowding had increased in certain areas of London, following the demolition of houses to make way for commercial expansion and street improvements in some of the inner areas. This would seem likely since, between 1851 and 1881, the average number of persons per dwelling had increased from 9·5 to 9·7 in inner areas such as Holborn and the City, and from 7·2 to 7·9 in the East End, whereas over the country as a whole, it had declined from 5·11 to 4·98. What this implied may be better understood from details of the area of St Georges in the East, where the average was 7·6 persons per house. In dwellings with 2 or 3 rooms of about 9·3 each, from 4 to 6 persons were living in each room in the most crowded dwellings. The incidence of overcrowding varied greatly from one part of the country to another, and was related to the number of small dwellings in the local housing stock. At the turn of the century, 16 per cent of London's population was living at densities of over 2 persons per room, and in the Tyneside area the proportion was about 33 per cent.

Figure 1 summarises the changes that have occurred in room densities over the last 50 years, the main feature being a steady decline, from one census to the next, of persons living at the higher room densities. It will be noticed in Figure 1 that

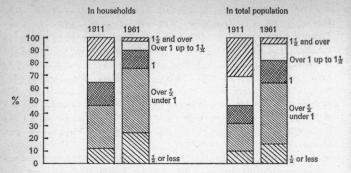

Figure 1 Persons per room, England and Wales, 1911 and 1961
Sources: R G Census of England and Wales 1931, Housing, Table VIII.
R G Census of England and Wales 1951, Housing Report,
Table 8A
R G Census of England and Wales 1961, Housing Tables,
part 1, Table 13.

a smaller proportion of households than of population were
living at high person/room ratios: this is because, as will be
demonstrated later, large households tend to live at higher
room densities, and, obviously enough, include more people,
although they represent a comparatively small proportion of
total households. However, although the overall trend towards
lower room densities has been continuous, the proportion of
persons who were living at a density of 2 or more persons per
room, and so were overcrowded, actually increased up to 1931.
The fall in housebuilding which had occurred before the First
World War, together with its almost total disruption during
the war, created a severe housing shortage by the early 1920s.
Although the housebuilding in the decade did something to
ease the situation, the more extreme degrees of overcrowding
(over 4 persons per room) persisted and, in absolute number,
increased from 253,000 persons in 1911 to 331,000 by 1931.

The role of public housing in reducing overcrowding

Since the aims of public housing included the relief of overcrowding, it is of interest at this point to examine the available
evidence on the subject. Because public housing was a comparative novelty in 1931, the census made a special extraction
of data about room densities on the LCC's Becontree Estate,

and the public housing estates in Liverpool, Manchester and Birmingham. This revealed the now familiar picture of a greater preponderance of 4- and 5-person families, and fewer small households than in the national distribution of household sizes. It also showed that, while a proportion of households ranging from 3 per cent to 16 per cent on the 4 estates were living at densities of less than 0·5 persons per room, there were a number of larger families who were overcrowded, at densities of 2 and sometimes 3 persons per room. The range of house sizes clearly did not correspond with the range of family sizes, although, unfortunately, it is not known whether there was a greater degree of correspondence at the date of rehousing. The census revealed that over 10 per cent of families in each area contained lodgers or other persons who were not part of the elementary family (parents and children) and these in part accounted for the overcrowding.

A national survey undertaken under the Housing Act of 1935 used a more elaborate definition of overcrowding, in which sex and relationship of household members were included, so that the appraisal of conditions was made in terms of sex separation for sleeping. In assessing sleeping accommodation, however, it was assumed that living rooms would also be used for this purpose. It was intended that this survey should cover all housing inhabited by persons of the working class, but the definition of working class was left open, and all property below a rateable value of £20 was often included. Overcrowding amounted to only 3·8 per cent in all property examined, a percentage very similar to that produced for all houses in the 1931 census. Some underoccupation in council property, due to changes in family composition, was revealed. But the survey also showed that, in London, large towns and rural areas, public housing contained slightly more overcrowded families, on the survey definition, than other property thought to be occupied by working class persons. The survey recognised that local authorities had fulfilled their duty by giving preference to large families whose original housing was unsuitable, but that the houses which the authorities built were mostly designed for the average, and not the large family. The Registrar General had commented earlier that by concentrating on building the 4- and 5-room house, a housing stock was being produced that was at variance with trends in household size. Despite these earlier warnings, this practice of local authorities was not changed until recently.

Although it was the stated intention of official housing policy, embodied in the Act of 1935, to eliminate overcrowding, only 23,915 houses had been built for that specific purpose by 1939, as against 341,000 houses which the survey had found to be overcrowded. An additional but unknown number of overcrowded families were rehoused as part of the more extensive slum clearance programme which went on at the same period. Building within the public sector was clearly insufficient to bring about the rapid solution to the overcrowding problem which was desired. Nevertheless, the peak output of housing in the private sector during the 1930s, the rise in real wages and marked fall in the birth rate all contributed to an easing of the housing situation in general, and so indirectly to the reduction of overcrowding. The 1930s would appear to mark a turning point in relation to the highest room densities. Even with the virtual cessation of housebuilding, and the destruction of houses during the Second World War, a sample survey in 1947 showed a decline since 1931 in persons living at densities of 2 or more persons per room. By the 1960s the high room densities had been reduced still further, and it might be said that overcrowding had ceased to be a national problem.

Nevertheless, as noted earlier, the persistence of a small proportion of cases at the extreme end of the scale is not incompatible with an overall reduction in room densities. The Milner Holland investigation of housing conditions in London in 1965 was able to cite instances of large families with children living in a single room. Although overcrowding in the contemporary situation is still linked with poverty, two recent studies of inner metropolitan areas, namely Notting Hill Gate and Camden reveal a different set of circumstances which give rise to overcrowding. In these areas the demand for accommodation is high. There is restricted access to certain parts of the local housing stock, such as council housing and controlled tenancies, and newcomers to the area are forced into furnished accommodation which has been subdivided into bedsitter-type and other small lettings. The high room densities which occur in this situation are not necessarily associated with the poorest families in the area.

The most important points to emerge from this consideration of overcrowding in long-term perspective are: firstly, the reduction in high room densities to such a degree that, on a national scale, this is now a negligible problem; secondly, while overcrowding is still associated with poverty and housing shortage, the grossly insanitary conditions that first focused attention on the problem have now disappeared, so that its implications in the contemporary situation are quite different. Further, overcrowding is no longer an indicator of the worst housing conditions which today are associated with sharing basic amenities in houses which have been inadequately converted for multi-occupancy.

Dwellings: Replacement or Retention?
Norman Dennis

Reprinted with permission from Norman Dennis, *People and Planning*, London, Faber and Faber, 1970, pp. 125–7.

The choice between the replacement or retention of an existing dwelling depends upon an assessment of expected benefits. In any particular case the essential questions to be answered are:

1. What weight should be given to the various advantages and disadvantages, the specification array, of living in a particular house in a particular area—the effectiveness of the dwelling as a protection from the weather, how much fresh air and sunlight it admits, how easy it is to keep it clean, how private it is, how costly, the accessibility of friends and relatives and so forth?

2. What weight should be given to the interests of the different groups involved in a replacement programme? How may one rate the welfare of the children in the family against the selfish or merely mistaken desires of their parents? What weight should be given to the interests of the landlord as against those of the tenant, to the interests of the owner-occupier, the interests of the family whose home will be demolished as against the interests of others who may benefit from the demolition, the interests of the building industry, the interests of housing officials, and in general the interests of those who gain from demolition as against those who lose?

3. Who should weigh these various losses and gains, the beneficiaries and victims, one against the other? How much power should lie with the private landlord, with the tenant, with the local authority, with the councillors, with technical officers, with any particular government department? When a man has a choice between on the one hand making an autono-

mous decision and yet risking material hardship for himself and his children, and on the other hand of having a better chance of material prosperity by allowing someone else to decide for him, under what circumstances should he choose the one or the other? How much improvement in public health may be regarded as adequate compensation for how much distress on the part of how many families rehoused against their will?

A set of data on the structural condition of given dwellings, on infant mortality rates, rates of morbid conditions among children and adults, road accidents to young and old, rents, tenure, expressed preferences and so forth, may be regarded by all as fully validated by the evidence. But depending on the society's culture or his membership of a sub-group within the society, one person's answer will be to demolish, another person's answer will be to preserve, while a third person will say, 'I haven't the right to wield any power one way or the other, it is for each family to make the best or the worst of its chances.'

The number of new houses to meet Sunderland's replacement needs cannot be given, therefore, by applying any set of technical criteria or by following blindfold the confident step of a particular profession. What is the minimum standard of housing that must be insisted upon by public authorities? An answer to that deceptively simple request can be found only when its meaning is fully understood. As recently as 1966 the Ministry of Housing clearly recognised the severe problems connected with this issue. Its sub-committee on standards of housing fitness was asked to consider 'the *practicability* of specifying objective criteria for the purposes of slum-clearance, rectification of disrepair and other minimum tolerable standards of housing accommodation'. The sub-committee was asked 'to go ahead with devising new standards without undertaking major research projects'. Even if full research had been recommended and carried out, the search for standards would have been fruitless so long as it continued to be misconceived as a question of technology. In Weber's terms, the crucial issues are those which are primarily oriented to the ends to which replacement decision must refer.

The task of analysis is to clarify the elements in the present and possible future situation upon which the ultimate judgments of value depend. Such a clarification will be aided by knowledge of past replacement decisions.

A Minority in a Welfare State Society
Roy Haddon

Reprinted with permission from Roy Haddon, 'A Minority in a Welfare State Society. The Location of West Indians in the London Housing Market', *New Atlantis*, Vol. 1, No. 2, 1970, pp. 88–95.

The position of West Indians in British society is only partly covered by describing their spatial distribution. Historically there are undoubted associations between the social differentiation and spatial segregation of the urban population in Britain, but these ecological correlations probably depended for their sharpness and clarity upon the conditions under which British industrial urbanisation proceeded. Robson has pointed out that the assumptions underlying the simple ecological models were more appropriate to towns developing in the context of the private market, with minimal public intervention in the form of municipal housing and planning controls, than they are to contemporary British towns. He demonstrates in his study of Sunderland, for example, that simple indices of socioeconomic differentiation are useful at only a very crude level within the private housing areas of the town, and he is able to demonstrate that rather different results are obtained if simple ecological associations are calculated for the private housing areas on the one hand, or for the whole town (including the areas of municipal housing) on the other.

The absence of the black ghettos may give rise to qualified optimism, but it should not be allowed to obscure the possibility that West Indians, residentially clustered or not, occupy a definable and, generally speaking, socially deprived position within British urban society. This possibility will be examined in relation to housing conditions, but it could equally well be tested in the fields of employment and income, education, access to social services and environmental amenities. The emphasis will be shifted from concern with *spatial* distribution and the spatial structure of urban areas by themselves, to include consideration of *social* conditions, institutions and structures; in particular to a concern with the location of the West Indian in the housing market. This involves treating poor housing conditions as part of the social deprivation that is an integral component of urban poverty. We should not lose sight of the relationship between social and spatial structure in the modern city, however. The relevance of this relationship will be taken up below when the zone of transition as a typical area of West Indian settlement is considered; and in any case the housing market is a major determinant of place of residence and as such is to be regarded as a key element in the urban social structure.

It should however be noted that West Indians share many of their socially deprived circumstances with an even larger number of the British population in the inner parts of the city. Colour is an issue in its own right in British society and this should not be obscured by pretending that the more universal problems of housing and poverty can be substituted for it. In this respect Graham's charge that the American War of Poverty was an establishment attempt to redefine the racial issue in such a way as to enable the white elite to seize the initiative and wrest control of the civil rights movement from black leaders is a relevant warning. The critical question is not so much whether ghettos are in formation, but whether the black population is being recruited *en masse* into the ranks of the contemporary urban poor, and contributing significantly to the growth in the numbers of the urban poor.

More importantly, since poor housing conditions are a component of social deprivation, the existence of an urban poor has to be related to the consequences of public housing policy. This means that in examining the position of West Indians, or any other group of the population, in British society, we have to consider not merely position in relation to the productive system (though this remains important), but also position in relation to the apparatus of social policy and its rules of eligibility. Housing has been effectively a matter for public social policy since the First World War and, as with a considerable part of social policy provision, it carries within it the seeds of an implicit, if not an effective, challenge to the play of pure market forces. Housing policy has been at the centre of this debate about priorities and values, which, in essence, revolves around the question of whether social policy can be effectively committed to securing decent housing conditions for the whole population, whilst the labour market does not provide a reward system that enables the whole population to purchase housing space and amenity commensurate with its housing needs. The result of the imbalances between housing needs, housing costs and people's ability to pay is seen in the displacement of costs onto local authorities' housing revenue accounts, where the burden has become particularly acute in inner London. The confusion in the British 'system' of housing subsidies is to be seen to a considerable extent as the result of the underlying ambivalence of values and not only as a result of piecemeal and unco-ordinated increments to housing and financial legislation.

There is a further reason for dealing with the position of West Indians in British society in the context of housing in the city. Whereas immigration into Britain was stimulated by economic pressures (shortage of manpower), it is argued that restrictions of the rates of immigration were largely precipitated by social pressures deriving from housing shortages.

The housing market

The ability of West Indians to find housing accommodation will be considerably determined by the prevailing conditions in the housing market. The major trends in the housing market are a decline (both absolutely and proportionally) in the privately-rented sector, and increases (absolutely and proportionately) in both owner-occupation and local authority accommodation. Table 1 sets out the proportion of all households in different types of tenure in 1961 and 1966.

There are wide variations in this pattern, however, between one borough and another in Greater London, though there are relatively few exceptions to the direction of the trends. Although, for example, the proportion of households living in privately-rented unfurnished accommodation varied between 47.2 per cent (Islington, and Hammersmith) and 6.7 per cent (Barking) in 1966, there was no London Borough which did not experience both an absolute and proportionate decline in the number of households in privately-rented unfurnished accommodation between 1961 and 1966. The rate of this decline however, varied from 32 per cent in Barking to only 7.2 per cent in Redbridge. The proportion of households living in local authority accommodation in 1966 showed an even wider variation, from 66.8 per cent in Barking, (and 51.7 per cent in Tower Hamlets) to 7.6 per cent in Kensington and Chelsea (and 8.6 per cent in Brent). Again the trend of an increase in local authority accommodation in both absolute and proportional terms was reflected in every London Borough, although there were again variations in the rate of this increase between 1961 and 1966, from 77.8 per cent in Westminster to only 1.7 per cent in Harrow. Only one borough (Tower Hamlets) showed both an absolute and proportionate decline in the number of households who were owner-occupiers between

Table 1.   Tenure pattern 1961 and 1966

| Tenure | England and Wales | | Greater London | |
	1961 %	1966 %	1961 %	1966 %
Owner-occupiers	42·3	46·7	36·3	38·5
Local authority	23·7	25·7	18·2	21·6
Privately-rented furnished	4·0	3·4	8·9	8·6
Privately-rented unfurnished	23·9	19·1	33·5	28·5
Other	6·1	5·1	3·0	2·8

Source: 1961 and 1966 Censuses.

1961 and 1966, and two other boroughs (Hackney and Hammersmith) showed a decline in the absolute numbers but not in the proportion. Leaving aside these boroughs with an absolute decline, the rate of increase in the other boroughs varied from 1.6 per cent in Brent to 15.1 per cent in Kensington and Chelsea.

The most inconsistent trend is found in the privately-rented furnished sector. In Greater London as a whole there was a decline in furnished accommodation between 1961 and 1966 of 5.1 per cent, but this varied between an increase of 11.6 per cent in Haringey, and a decline of 39.1 per cent in Waltham Forest. Seven boroughs in all showed an absolute increase (Haringey 11.6 per cent, Richmond 8.6 per cent, Kensington and Chelsea 7.3 per cent, Brent 6.3 per cent, Hammersmith 4.8 per cent, Barnet 4.2 per cent, and Hounslow 2.8 per cent). In addition, Islington showed an absolute decline, but a proportionate increase. Of equal significance was the fact that in 1966 a small number of boroughs had very high proportions of their households living in furnished accommodation (Kensington and Chelsea 34.9 per cent, Westminster 24.5 per cent, Camden 22.4 per cent, Hammersmith 17.4 per cent, Islington 16.1 per cent).

These broad trends in Greater London are made up from a series of more specific currents of change, which stem from economic, legal and demographic conditions which affect different tenures and different localities in various ways. Furthermore, because of the spatial distribution of different tenures, reflecting the historical development of Greater London, and the demographic composition of the different migration streams, some of these currents of change will be focused on specific types of area within London.

There is, firstly, little new building for private renting, for as Nevitt has pointed out the cost of land and the taxation provisions relating to rental income inhibit private landlords from getting sufficient returns from their present properties to cover replacement costs. New building is concentrated in the local authority and owner-occupier sectors, therefore, and this by itself means that privately-rented accommodation will form a decreasing *proportion* of the total housing stock, and that owner-occupied and local authority housing will increase both absolutely and proportionately.

Owner-occupation has increased at the expense of privately-rented accommodation for a second reason—the conversion of formerly privately-rented houses to owner-occupation. The reasons for this are to be found, in part, in the relative tax positions of the owner-occupier and the landlord, and in the effects of rent control and decontrol. Sales of privately rented houses to owner-occupiers have involved at least two distinct processes—(a) sales to an existing tenant, and (b) sales to higher status groups who can afford to spend considerable sums on improving the property. In the second case, conversion to owner-occupation has been seen as a means of promoting the improvement of existing houses, but it has had the result in a number of areas of changing the nature and population of the area, upgrading it and pricing it out of the reach of working-class households. Thus, this loss to the privately-rented sector has also involved a serious depletion of the stock of low-rented accommodation in central city areas. It is also an indication that the 'suburban ideal' is not universal amongst all of the comfortably off.

Further loss to the privately-rented sector has been occasioned by the fact that, since much of it is old and of a low standard, it has been the most affected by slum clearance and redevelopment schemes. This loss through demolition has a double impact on the proportions of houses in different tenure categories, since a large part of what is built to replace the demolished properties is local authority housing. In so doing, too, this process of urban renewal has begun to affect the relationship between the age and tenure of dwellings and nearness to city centre, so that large areas of inner London are now occupied by modern purpose-built local authority flats. Because of land prices in central areas, however, the rents prior to rebates and subsidies to tenants and sometimes after as well, are likely to be high. This process of urban renewal is also likely to eliminate some of the older owner-occupied houses (especially houses that have been converted from private renting but not substantially improved) and this is probably the reason for the loss of owner-occupied housing in Tower Hamlets, where there has been large scale redevelopment.

Prior to demolition, some privately-rented accommodation will be acquired by local authorities and 'patched' for temporary use, or in some cases rehabilitated for rather longer use. This means that the local authority sector grows and the privately-rented sector declines by conversion from private renting to local authority. An example of large scale acquisition for rehabilitation is the Walterton Road Estate in the London Borough of Westminster. The London Borough of Camden has acquired a considerable stock of formerly privately-rented housing too, as has Birmingham Corporation; and there is a case study of the acquisition of heavily multi-occupied houses by the London Borough of Lambeth. The Lambeth and Westminster cases both relate to streets of houses in which there were large numbers of West Indians living at the time of acquisition.

An analogous process to this acquisition by local authorities is the practice of charitable housing trusts purchasing older properties with the explicit intention of improving them, bringing them under good management, and letting to working-class families. They are agents of improvement therefore, but frequently attempt to retain the housing for people who cannot afford high rents. They are able to do this to a degree because of the injection of charitable gift capital, loans and subsidies from the Exchequer and local housing authorities, and the availability of improvement and conversion grants. Nevertheless, they have to buy the properties on the market and pay interest on the money they do borrow, so that the larger their scale of operation, the more difficult it may be for them to keep rents as low as they may wish, particularly in inner city areas. In some areas, for example in Kensington and Chelsea, the housing trusts work in close cooperation with the local housing authority, and bear the burden of much of the improvement policies in the area. For census purposes, the housing trusts are classified as private landlords, so that the movement of property from the private landlord to the housing trusts is not reflected in any additional decline in the privately-rented sector, except that, since housing trusts rarely let their accommodation furnished, and insofar as the houses they acquire formerly contained furnished lettings, this conversion is likely to lead to a small net movement from the furnished to the unfurnished sector.

One final major trend has been, particularly, but not only since 1965, a conversion from unfurnished to furnished accommodation within the privately-rented sector. This is a process which has been accelerated by the inadequate provisions for rent regulation and security of tenure in furnished lettings as compared with unfurnished decontrolled lettings, since the 1965 Rent Act. It should be pointed out, however, that some of the difficulty here stems from the fact that a considerable amount of furnished accommodation represents part of owner-occupied dwellings sublet by their owners. Related to this, is the fact that in some areas the increase of furnished accommodation may be related to the purchase of old houses by owner-occupiers who then let off, say, the basement in order to help meet the repayment, repair and improvement costs. In one or two local authority areas, this practice is actively encouraged as a means of retaining small units of accommodation for small households. In addition to the impact of the 1965 Rent Act, however, the increase of furnished accommodation in certain areas seems likely to be partly the result of demand brought about by the composition of the inward migration stream to central London—young, small households seeking employment or studying in central London. The gross rent-paying capacity of this group of the population may be considerably higher than the low-paid worker and his family who are often in competition with them for the use of the same dwellings. It is likely therefore that private landlords will be selective in which demand they choose to cater for.

Since the financial advantages to householders living in the owner-occupied and local authority sectors, in terms of the housing they can get for an equivalent amount of money, are one of the most important sets of underlying factors affecting the changes in the tenure pattern, we would expect to find some association between this latter and the movement of households between tenure types. Clearly other factors such as employment, family life cycle, household type, and social class will affect these streams of movement. The major movements between sectors revealed by the Rowntree Housing Survey in England and Wales were (a) from the privately rented sector as a whole, to the owner-occupied sector; (b) from unfurnished privately-rented accommodation to local authority accommodation; (c) from furnished to unfurnished within the privately rented sector; and (d) considerable movement *within* tenure types. There was, however, very little movement in reverse directions.

Because of the concentration of housing types and tenures in particular localities, reflecting both contemporary changes and the fact that changes in the provision of housing over time are given a spatial dimension by the historical development of urban growth, these movements between tenure types will also tend to have a spatial expression. In its crudest form this has usually been expressed in terms of 'upward and outward' movement. That is to say, social mobility as expressed by movement into the better housing conditions of the owner-occupied sector has a spatial dimension in the movement from city centre to the suburbs, where the newer and generally cheaper owner-occupied dwellings are built. Similarly, a large proportion of the movement into local authority accommodation has had its spatial counterpart in the process of rehousing from the inner city slums to the out-county council estates—what Rex and Moore referred to as the working-class version of the 'suburban ideal'. Some of the currents in the housing market that have been noted above, however, require that this crude generalisation be modified. For some people, the desire for owner-occupation can be met in conjunction with a central location. For others, central location can be achieved in furnished privately-rented accommodation; and increasingly, a considerable amount of local authority accommodation is more centrally situated as redevelopment and slum clearance proceeds, and people are rehoused from the demolished houses.

The Lesson of Acklam Road
George Clark

Reprinted with permission from George Clark, 'The Lesson of Acklam Road', *New Statesman*, 7 August 1970, pp. 139–40.

The Greater London Council's decision to start now with the rehousing of those North Kensington residents who are suffering most from Section Five of London's new elevated urban highway, known as Westway, is a triumph for a new kind of community action. The road cuts through an area which contains some of the most overcrowded housing conditions in the whole country. There is no open space for a population of about 10,000 who live in the 68 acres of North Kensington known as Golborne. To add to their misery the residents in one street, Acklam Road, are now suffering from noise twice as loud as the maximum laid down by the Wilson Committee. But it is now clear that the authorities, in their disregard for a community they believed unable to protect itself, can no longer have it all their own way. Through the Golborne Social Rights Committee, which started barely twelve months ago, there is a chance that community power can begin to turn the scales of social justice.

Few experiences are more sickening than the official occasion designed to celebrate so-called progress. The opening ceremony of the Western Avenue Elevated Highway was typical: except that the residents of Acklam Road exposed the humbug, when they demanded: 'Get us out of this hell, rehouse us now.' Whether we like it or not, the road is there. The important question was whether the Social Rights Committee could proceed from its success in the publicity battle to the achievement of the basic demand that these people be rehoused by Christmas at latest. It has now been answered. The GLC, while taking a side-swipe at the Ministry of Housing, and saying this could not be regarded as a precedent, has effectively crumbled.

Work in Acklam Road began in 1965. Late in 1963 people on the south side heard through rumour and gossip that their houses were to be pulled down, and the tenants rehoused. In the words of one, now living in High Wycombe: 'We heard about it through the council workmen and then, when nothing happened for months, we thought nothing was going to come of it. I heard in September 1964 from the council that we were going to be rehoused, and by Christmas of that year we were out. They were very good. We managed to get where we wanted to go and they paid our removal expenses.' Not all the tenants living in the direct line of the road were so fortunate. A number could not stand the uncertainty, and in the face of total silence from the authorities, moved on. Others living in furnished accommodation were sometimes treated as lodgers: some of these tenants have said to us that they moved because they were told they were ineligible for rehousing. They did not question this information; they had no idea what their rights were.

After the houses on the north side had been demolished, the hazardous space was taken over, in the summers of 1965 and 1966, by local children as play space. It was the first piece of direct action by residents and they got away with it: no prosecutions, no trouble from the police. But on the south side, 34 houses were left standing.

These houses were built 105 years ago: three stories and a basement, intended for artisans and labourers. They had a useful economic life of 80–90 years, but lacked the investment necessary to keep them in reasonable condition beyond that time. More than a third of the houses have not been painted, repaired or renovated for at least twenty years. Twelve of them have no bathroom; fourteen have outside lavatories. In one, the original gas fittings are still there: it has never had electricity. Even if the motorway had not been built, something would have had to be done about these houses within the next five years, and preferably sooner.

But the residents—some 404 persons in 117 households, which is three or four households to each building—resigned themselves at first to nothing being done. 'We were left to rot and make the best of it,' says one woman, who has lived in the road most of her life. Official information was hard to obtain, but we have various indications of official thinking. For instance, the local borough council moved a family into the block of flats they own there only two and a half years ago. The Kensington Housing Trust refurbished No 39 at a cost of well over £1,000, and moved a family into the basement and three old-age pensioners into the other floors, only four years ago. The Notting Hill Housing Trust made one of its rare mistakes in acquiring No 41, and has been trying to get rid of it: nonetheless, they put tenants in.

One might ask what the local authority was doing during this period. The Leader of the Council, Sir Malby Crofton, has written to *The Times* (3 August 1970) claiming a high degree of cooperation between the GLC, Kensington and the local Housing Trusts. But the GLC *knew* that the noise from the motorway would be unacceptable in houses within 50 feet. The block of borough council flats is within 23 feet, and the houses belonging to the trusts are within 35 feet. Was this just bureaucratic incompetence? Or is it evidence of official indifference to the suffering caused to the people living so close to the new road?

In 1967, the pile-drivers began laying the foundations for the road. The contractors, Messrs Laing, claim that more than 200,000 letters of explanation were sent out to householders. They apparently did not know that in houses in multiple occupation letters addressed to the landlord (or occupier) do not reach the tenants. Left in ignorance, the people of Acklam Road could only stare in awe at the massive machinery which moved into their road, closed it to traffic, ripped up the road surface and pavements and generally made life intolerable. Constant pleas and entreaties were made to the rent collectors coming round from the council, to the gas and electricity men, to the public health officials. But either the messages were not passed on or they were ignored by all the authorities.

One of the streets which the Notting Hill Summer Project covered in a house-to-house survey was Acklam Road. Our interviewers reported the difficulty they were finding in getting a response from the residents. There was more hostility than elsewhere. At the time, we were heavily involved in a project which included more than 8,000 units of accommodation in more than 60 roads. We were not equipped to deal with a particular local grievance. But, retrospectively, I think this was a mistake. If we had moved to get a street organisation going here in 1967, we might well have succeeded in getting these houses demolished, and the people rehoused, before the motorway opened. This may sound arrogant, but is not unreasonable in the light of the successes our community organisations have achieved in the past three years. Whatever the final verdict, it is true that at that time we were not prepared to be diverted from our set goals. There is an important lesson here; as there is in the length of time a local community group needs to force policy changes on the authorities.

When the discoveries of the housing survey emerged, we decided to mount a Housing Rights Campaign in the Golborne Area to see whether the residents could be persuaded to join in a massive rent registration drive. (We had found, for example, that a family of three or four living in two rooms paid a median rent of £4 14s 6d.) It was at this point that we got our first real response from the Acklam residents.

In 1968 we formed the Notting Hill Housing Service. This is quite separate from the trusts, and has no connection with, and little cooperation from, the local authority. The service provides legal and social advice on all aspects of housing problems. It represents tenants at rent tribunals and in the courts; it negotiates rehousing with the local authority. In the spring of 1969 the London Cooperative Society loaned us their van equipped with loudspeaker apparatus. It made an admirable mobile office, and we parked it on the corner of Acklam Road.

High rents were not, it turned out, the main source of discontent. The failure by owners to carry out repairs, and by the local authority to bring pressure on them to do so, was the most frequent complaint. Three months later, at a street meeting attended by more than 300 locals, we drew up a petition to the borough council and formed ourselves into the Social Rights Committee, electing 14 of our number by a straight show of hands. More than 900 people signed, and the petition was presented to the council in September 1969. There followed two months' silence. Then, late in October, news filtered down that the council would purchase the houses. It looked as though the battle had been won without a shot being fired. Tension in the neighbourhood mounted during the dustmen's strike: the dustbins in this part of London were not cleared for 22 days after the strike ended. We decided to remind the council of our existence. Two streets were chosen, Acklam Road and Bevington Road, and one Sunday in January this year all the dustbins were emptied into the roadway. The council reacted swiftly: the rubbish was gone by Monday night. Another lesson in community action had been learned, and the newly-formed Social Rights Committee asked for a meeting with the leader of the council and the town clerk. They got it.

Solemn promises were made about rubbish disposal, and somewhat lighter undertakings about the situation in Acklam Road. We were told that the council were seeking authorisation to acquire the houses, and that a resolution would be passed at the next meeting. A week later, 600 people turned up to a public meeting at which we decided to give the council every opportunity to fulfil the promises they had made. The chairman of the local Conservative association remarked that more people had attended that meeting than vote in the ward at local elections.

In March, we learned that the local council were claiming that responsibility lay with the GLC. The resolution Kensington had passed was only a 'contingency resolution'. We sent a duplicated letter to the borough, the GLC, the Ministry of Housing, the Ministry of Transport, and the Prime Minister, setting out the story in detail, and asking for action.

In their replies, Kensington, the GLC and the Ministry of Housing blamed each other. We asked for a deputation to be received at County Hall. The Committee put together at weekly meetings what became known as the Golborne Declaration, saying bluntly that it no longer believed the council's promises. We demanded that the people living in Acklam Road be rehoused before the motorway opened. More than 1,500 people signed, and we marched to the town hall.

Against this background, discussions began with the Greater London Council. Mr Robert Vigars steadfastly maintained that the GLC had no powers, but finally agreed to formulate a resolution which would be put before the council in July. It was obvious we could not get the families out before the motorway opened, so we tried a conciliatory approach. The Housing Service drew up, within 10 days, a register of housing need which we passed on to the GLC: their officials admitted it was a job which would have taken *them* three or four months. We agreed to a programme of rehousing the people before the end of the year.

But the position then seemed as unsatisfactory as it was at the beginning of the year. We have a letter from the Minister of Housing, dated 10 June 1970, which states:

'Within the terms of Section 28 (Town and Country Planning Act 1968) it is open to either the GLC or the Royal Borough to negotiate purchase of the properties or make a CPO (Compulsory Purchase Order). If it were necessary the ministry would consider a loan sanction.'

Nevertheless, the delay continued. We knew the Royal Borough could rehouse their own tenants, who live at No. 19,

There was no valid reason why the Housing Trusts should not rehouse the tenants living at Nos 37 and 41. The GLC have authorisation from the Ministry of Housing to proceed with negotiations for purchase, and have passed a resolution (on 21 July) authorising this. The truth was that the hold-up was not about powers at all: it was about money in the form of grants payable by central government. Of course there are 'wider issues involved' which affect the whole of the compensation aspect of London's road policy. But, in my view, the treatment the people of Acklam Road were given, until they made their voices heard, was a telling example of the way our welfare state uses devices of exclusion against its most unfortunate citizens.

In the emergency which was created by this particular disaster, some essential lessons have been learned. Not least important, for the residents of Acklam Road and people like them elsewhere, is the power they have when they come together. They are now learning how to use this power. Perhaps the Golborne Social Rights Committee can help to provide a model of the form of local community organisation which will emerge in the future. We can now regard ourselves as part of a new social and political force at the local level. In time, it will have national significance.

Eviction Threat
Margaret E. Jones

Reprinted with permission from Margaret E. Jones, 'Eviction Threat', *Social Work Today*, 10 February 1972, Vol. 2, No. 21, pp. 9–11.

On 16 July 1971 three neighbouring families on a housing estate were given notice to quit. Despite strong protests from social workers and voluntary pressure groups, the notices were reluctantly upheld by a magistrates' court on 26 October and confirmed a few days later at a full meeting of the Urban District Council. Yet, on the 23 November, only 15 hours before the families were to be ejected, the council reversed its decision by an astonishing majority of nine votes to two. The way this reversal of a manifestly unjust decision was achieved makes a fascinating study and raised a number of interesting questions for social workers.

None of the three families could be called a 'problem family' and none was in arrears of rent. The eviction order was served under an outdated law known as The Small Tenement Recovery Act of 1838, the terms of which do not require the council to give reasons for eviction, and a magistrate's court has no option but to rubber-stamp the council's decision. On being pressed, the council stated that the families' standards were low and there had been complaints from neighbours about noise.

In the case of one family, who I will call the Wilsons, the problem was a simple one of overcrowding. This family of father, mother, and six children under six, live in a two-bedroom, first-floor flat. The father, a long-distance lorry driver, is out of work. The council has long promised them re-housing in a four-bedroom house. The Wilsons are co-habiting, pending Mrs Wilson's divorce, and she felt sure that this fact added to local prejudice against them. The flat was always tidy when visited and social workers were unanimous in their agreement that she coped extremely well in these cramped conditions.

Their close neighbours, the Richards, have four children aged 14, 12, 8 and 2. Before being allotted their three-bedroomed house the whole family lived in one room. At first their standards were extremely low but after warnings from the housing department they decorated the house throughout and maintained the improvement thereafter. This father also was unemployed, having lost his job at a local factory through ill-health, and, in a town with 10 per cent unemployment, was unable to find another. Though living in some degree of poverty, this is an affectionate and united family and the children are well-cared for.

The third family, the Stubbs, are a young couple with two children aged three years and fifteen months. The father had been in prison and the marriage was currently in jeopardy. This was the most disturbed family of the three.

The setting for these events is a picturesque fishing centre, often cut off by bad weather. This isolation has led to outdated social attitudes and some councillors are reactionary to the point where they have almost a Poor Law approach to their less fortunate citizens. From the social work point of view, the town is poorly served, with the neighbouring town providing the necessary services, usually on a weekly basis.

The probation officer was the first to hear of the eviction orders and immediately alerted the director of social services in the county and also the local area office. Letters of protest were sent by the area children's officer, the probation department and my own society, urging the council to reconsider is decision, and offering the families casework and material support in this event, Our letters were read at the next housing committee meeting, as were reports from the health inspector and the housing officer, stating that in all three homes standards had improved immeasurably. The committee remained quite unyielding and to the fear expressed in our letters that the 12 children involved might have to be taken into care, a councillor remarked that this might well be the best thing that could happen to them.

While social workers on the spot were wondering what action to take next, the matter was mentioned at a BASW* branch meeting. It was immediately taken up by a member who is on the national executive of the CPAG.† He alerted the press and later in the week reports appeared in local and national newspapers. The local MP also made a strong protest, and the director of social services had a meeting with the housing committee urging them once again to reconsider and pointing out the damage which would inevitably result for these 12 children if they were made homeless. The CPAG threatened direct action if the evictions took place.

Despite these representations, at the ensuing meeting of the full council, the eviction orders were confirmed by a majority of eight votes to six. No substantial reason had yet been given for the eviction, but the families found it significant that the brother of the chairman of the housing committee lived next door to the Richards. The chairman was later to deny in a newspaper interview that this fact affected his judgment.

On 26 October, the case came before the local magistrates. The press by this time was beginning to lose interest, and social workers to lose heart, since the outcome of the court hearing was known to be a foregone conclusion. However, a local solicitor had undertaken to defend the families and, on his own initiative, contacted *Shelter*, who agreed to pay for a barrister. This ensured that the council had to take the court

* British Association of Social Workers
† Child Poverty Action Group

case seriously, and that it would receive press coverage. Neighbours were called as witnesses, alleging noise, fighting between two of the couples, and nuisance caused by children and dogs. All the complaints were very unspecific and the barrister had no difficulty in demolishing them. The chairman of the housing committee was called. He maintained that his duty was to all the tenants, and he refused to acknowledge that families with specific needs might need special and sympathetic treatment.

After a two-hour hearing, the chairman of the magistrates said that they must 'reluctantly grant the order' since they had no discretion in the matter, but he hoped the council would give sympathetic consideration to these cases in the next 30 days. Apparently such a rider was most unusual and encouraged the councillors fighting on behalf of the families immediately to arrange a further meeting. The situation looked very hopeful, but at the last moment, a councillor who had been expected to vote against the evictions, was persuaded to change his mind, with the result that the housing committee won by one vote, a majority of eight to seven.

The publicity, and the constant raising and dashing of their hopes, was having a most distressing effect on the three families. The department of social services was in a difficult position because it did not want to produce alternative accommodation too soon and thus let the housing committee 'off the hook'. Sudden homelessness on such a scale in a small place was in any case a tremendous problem since the department had pledged itself to keep the families together. The papers made emotional capital out of the fact that the children might have to go into care, and although the families were assured otherwise, they naturally were influenced by what they read daily in their newspapers. All three families were searching independently for alternative accommodation, but they found prejudice against them in the town, and were precluded from going further afield by lack of funds. Meanwhile the already hard-pressed Wilson family suffered a sad loss. The baby, Paul, who had been born during this period and had attained a healthy five weeks, died quite suddenly of pneumonia and enteritis. The other children were also ill with colds and upset stomachs as were the Stubbs children, thus further hindering them in their search for new homes.

The turning point came during the weekend of 13/14 November, 10 days before the eviction order expired, when two quite separate decisions were made. First, the editorial board of the *Northern Echo* decided to run a vigorous and sustained campaign on behalf of the families and second, two local housewives launched some local action. From 15 November onwards, the *Northern Echo* under the campaign heading 'Let Them Stay' produced a long illustrated feature daily. The two women, relatives of Mr Wilson, organised a local petition. Until this time it had been assumed that local opinion was largely unsympathetic, and one councillor claimed that he had 'visited every tenant in the road and that the majority wanted the evictions to go through'. The two women disproved this by obtaining 17 signatures among the near neighbours of the families. I think it was evidence of this local sympathy in addition to the unnerving publicity which finally caused the council to crumble. Moreover, it was nearing Christmas and this fact, together with an early snowfall, cast the council's intentions in an even more sinister light. The chairman of the housing committee was meanwhile being driven into an extreme and absurd position and in a statement to the press said: 'These sort of families should be put into intensive units, for training and education. When they are ready to come back into society I would be the first to allow them back. This would be best for the children. I treat my cat better than they treat their children.'

Quite fortuitously, the monthly meeting of the full council was scheduled for the evening of the 23 November. By asking leave to waive standing orders, the seven defending councillors raised the matter again, and by a majority of nine votes to two, the decision to evict was reversed. The chairman of the housing committee and two other members of the committee abstained, the two members later resigning.

What results have emerged and what conclusions can be drawn by social workers, especially in the light of topical discussions on social action? Positive benefits, apart from the obvious fact that the families keep their homes, are already apparent. The wide news coverage ensures that housing authorities will think twice before issuing eviction orders, and there is evidence that they are indeed already doing so. The Wilsons are being re-housed and, interestingly, so are the Stubbs' neighbours, who were the chief complainants. Social workers have been alerted in an area where they are thin on the ground, and a monthly meeting for representatives of all social agencies covering the town has been instituted. The repeal of the iniquitous Small Tenement Recovery Act, already promised by the government, may perhaps reach the statute book earlier because a dossier has been prepared by the solicitor who defended the families, for presentation to the minister for the environment.

In retrospect, an interesting pattern of protest appears. As one pressure group failed, another seemed spontaneously to emerge; unfortunately, nobody ever thought of counting heads so that it came as a surprise, eventually, to find how many opponents the housing committee had, particularly among other councillors and local people. Should social workers have done more to mobilise this opposition? As a profession we are reluctant to use the media, and with reason, for in bringing the case to their attention we lose control of the situation and become dependent on editorial policy. Our clients are so vulnerable that we fear to expose them in this way. In the town, one mother refused repeatedly to speak to the press or to allow her children to be photographed, and only succumbed right at the end. The anti-climax when the case abruptly finished and was dropped into oblivion brought its own tensions. There can be no simple happy ending in a crisis of this sort, and, foreseeing this, social workers try to minimise the risks, sometimes proving too timid in the process.

As a BASW branch we wrote to the local housing committee and our letter received as short shrift as the others had done. Should we then, on finding we were not dealing with reasonable people, have adopted a more militant attitude and ourselves organised publicity, despite its dangers, or were we correct in limiting our action to letter writing and pressure by individual departments? How right would we have been to have used more aggressive methods when it was proved that moderate intervention had failed?

Polluted Homes
Peter Gregory

Reprinted with permission from Peter Gregory, 'Polluted Homes', *Occasional Papers in Social Administration*, No. 15, G. Bell and Sons Ltd., 1968, pp. 56–8.

Haverton Hill is very probably the most heavily polluted settlement in this country. This pollution is in the form of dust and gases and affects the appearance of the area. Plant life is stunted and destroyed, metals and fabrics corrode rapidly, and there is usually an unpleasant smell. There is, however, no conclusive evidence of an adverse effect on the health of those who live there, but this may be due simply to the fact that most respiratory ailments are not notifiable. The high rate of turn-over also may damp down respiratory invalidity.

It is probably because of this unpleasant environment that the estates suffer from a high level of population turnover. This appears to result in a community from which those of higher social and economic status have moved.

The sample survey indicated that 56 per cent of the population were ready to move. Many, however, appeared to have strong local ties with the area, which were not apparent from an examination of the crude figures for tenancy turnover. Those with ties were largely made up of the 44 per cent who did not want to move. They were more likely to be I.C.I. than local authority tenants. The population seems to consist of two groups—those with local ties and those without. It is unfortunately impossible to generalise adequately as to who those with ties are—the local authority households, for example, though younger and holding their tenancies for less time, were more likely to have been born in the area and to have relatives there. Neither of these groups is overwhelmingly dominant and the estates are neither like the old-established working-class community of Bethnal Green, portrayed by Peter Willmott and Michael Young, nor are the local ties of residents as slim as those existing on some post-war housing estates. It is, however, possible to say that the Haverton Hill estates are more like the latter than the former type of community.

As a consequence of this, it is likely that the social problems which would arise in adjusting to a new environment would be less for the residents of the Haverton Hill estates than for people re-housed from the slums of our great cities. It would be foolish, however, to think that no social problems would arise, especially since Haverton Hill people seem to be held in low esteem by the inhabitants of Billingham. The higher rents for accommodation in Billingham would also, without doubt, create problems for the large number of people on low weekly incomes.

This study could not provide an answer to the question: 'should the estates be demolished?' Nor was this the intention. The decision is essentially a matter of judgement for the local authority. The study does show, however, that both the retention of the estates and their demolition present problems.

The case for demolishing the estates at first sight appears strong. The environment is extremely unpleasant and causes considerable damage to the houses, fabrics, and, less certainly, health. By stunting plant life and imposing impossible difficulties on housewives trying to keep their houses clean, it encourages a 'couldn't care less' attitude. In consequence the area is regarded in Billingham as not only physically filthy but also an area in which only 'rough' people will live. The residents show their resentment of the physical and social conditions by the fact that over half of them want to leave and under half would wish very much to have their present neighbours near them if they did. Re-housing, then, would give the families a better environment and would end the physical and social isolation of Haverton Hill people from the rest of Billingham (many did not consider themselves to live in Billingham at all).

Demolition would, however, create problems. The purpose here is merely to discuss the nature and severity of these problems. It is hoped that this will provide the basis for a judgement on the desirability or otherwise of demolition.

The crucial factors are the cost and quality of housing. There is no doubt that the Haverton Hill estates provide relatively high-quality housing at low rents. Recent studies have shown that, though post-war council accommodation meets the needs of the poorer sections of the community, its rent demands are still too much for the very poorest members of society, who tend to live in low-grade and low-priced privately rented accommodation—in other words slums. The Haverton Hill houses fill an important need in that they are sufficiently low-priced to be accessible to some people who might otherwise have no alternative to slum accommodation. The size of this group of people is fairly large in Haverton Hill, as the survey showed—a sizeable minority of heads of households are drawing social security benefits, average weekly income is low, families tend to be large with three or more children and over a quarter of the sample anticipated financial problems if they had to move to Billingham. With rent arrears in the district already higher than for Billingham, the prospect of having to pay another 10s or more a week may well prove beyond the means of many.

Even if there were conclusive evidence of medical pathology due to air pollution, that caused by slum housing may often be worse. Thus the argument that the financial problems may outweigh the advantages of movement to a more wholesome environment deserves serious consideration. At the least it points to the necessity for a carefully designed rent policy should it be decided to demolish the estates.

The other main argument for maintaining the estates is that the social costs of movement may be high. People like living with their 'own type' and an enforced move into Billingham new town might create real difficulties of social integration for many.

The basic difficulty in making a policy decision on demolition is to know what weight to give to these different factors. The dislike of a minority of the Haverton Hill population for Billingham should probably not be allowed to determine policy for the majority who would like to move, even though this majority is not a large one. On the other hand, some special provision would have to be made to cater for the people who might find the move difficult for financial and social reasons. It would be ironical if in the interests of improving the housing environment, even a minority were forced back into substandard accommodation because they could not meet the costs—once for all and continuing—of a move to Billingham.

In the last analysis, therefore, the problem facing the local authority—as they clearly recognise—is one of deciding priorities. The economic and social value of basically good housing has to be weighed against the severe environmental deficiencies. The benefits of transferring the families to a more wholesome environment has to be seen in relation to the economic and social problems to which such a transfer would give rise. If it is decided to demolish the estates then the local authority have a clear responsibility for mitigating the hardship which will be caused to a significant proportion of the families. If it is decided that the estates should remain the local authority are faced with an environmental problem for which no easy solution is apparent. And it may well be that the social isolation of the area may increase with a rising standard of general affluence.

Further Reading: **Urban Problems**

* D. V. DONNISON, *The Government of Housing*, Harmondsworth, Penguin, 1967.

J. GREVE, D. PAGE and S. GREVE, *Homelessness in London*, Edinburgh, Scottish Academic Press, 1971.

W. HAMPTON, *Democracy and Community*, London, Oxford University Press, 1970.

* D. M. HILL, *Participating in Local Affairs*, Harmondsworth, Penguin, 1970.

B. JACKSON, *Working Class Community*, London, Routledge and Kegan Paul, 1968.

MINISTRY OF HOUSING AND LOCAL GOVERNMENT, *Housing in Greater London* (Milner Holland Report), London, HMSO, 1966.

* ROYAL COMMISSION ON LOCAL GOVERNMENT IN ENGLAND. Research Studies 9, *Community Attitudes Survey*, London, HMSO, 1969.

P. SAINSBURY, *Suicide in London*, London, Allen and Unwin, 1963.

A. L. SCHORR, *Slums and Social Insecurity*, London, Nelson, 1964.

* Available in paperback

Chapter Six   Health

For many people the major problems and private troubles of their personal lives are centred around health and illness. Everybody is likely to be ill during his life some of the time and some unfortunates may be ill all of the time. What constitutes a private trouble for the individual, even if a temporary one, constitutes a problem of massive scale for society at large. The constitution of the World Health Organisation promulgates the view that health is not merely the absence of disease or infirmity: it is a 'state of complete physical, mental and social well-being'. But even this definition is inadequate for coming to grips with the complexity of the individual and the social problems of health. For we must introduce the concepts of *needs* and of *expectations* before we can completely understand health as more than the mere absence of disease or incapacity. No society is ever perfectly healthy. While there is work to do and rewards are offered for doing it thoroughly there are some at least who cannot afford to be ill. But how much illness can the individual tolerate? How much can society support?

Much research has been undertaken, especially since the inauguration of the National Health Service, into the inequalities which prevail in the field of health. Studies of mortality, morbidity and the growth and development of individuals as members of social groups have demonstrated that there still exist quite profound inequalities in life chances in relation to health, even in relation to the most important life chance of all, that of staying alive. And if there are inequalities in the distribution of health itself, there are likewise inequalities in the distribution of the provision of medical care, society's response to the diffuse problems of sickness. Indeed the structure and organisation of the health service itself embody the attempt to reverse inequalities which had previously existed. But if this was the intention, the practical experience of the health service has produced rather mixed conclusions as to how far these means have been realised in practice. It has been argued that, as in the field of education, it is the middle classes who have benefited most from the provision of a national and universal system of dealing with medical needs. There is, therefore, a problem of access to these institutions. Are the conditions under which they operate such as to preclude those who might benefit most from utilising the service they provide? It could be argued of course that the problems of health illustrate only in an exacerbated form the difficulties of ensuring and maintaining adequate social provision in general. If individuals as members of society prefer to spend almost as much annually on tobacco and on alcohol as they do in supporting the institutions which are designed, in part at least, to cope with the effects of over-indulgence in tobacco, alcohol and other forms of self-destructive conspicuous consumption, is this anybody's business but their own? And this issue becomes even more salient as British society gropes towards a way of coping with such 'crimes without victims' as derive from the existence of addiction to currently outlawed soft and hard drugs.

All these problems are related to the individual and his access to the institutions which embody the system of medical care. But there are infra-structural constraints on the quality of the service which is provided as well. It is possible to raise questions about the rationality of a system of medical provision which (though possibly in response to popular demands) appears to give higher priority to the high prestige activities of organ transplantation and advanced surgery than to the creation of a comprehensive system of occupational and industrial medicine or indeed preventive measures on a large scale. For within the medical profession (as in many others of course) the prestige and the rewards accrue to those who establish a reputation for individual excellence within a specialised and conceivably rare field. The most difficult role to play in the system, and the one demanding the widest range of abilities and capacities, is probably that of the general practitioner, whose status as a 'family doctor' has long since been eroded by the growing pressure on his time and demands, albeit sometimes perceived by him as unreasonable, for his services.

In an insightful analysis of the fate of idealism in the medical school Becker and Geer identify the transformation of the medical student, who enters with an idealist image of the medical profession, into a sceptic who approaches his job as any professional man does, that is with limited ambitions and consequently limited involvement and commitment to medicine or the patient. The clash between the therapeutic and the commercial ethic has not, until recently, been as visible in Britain as in the United States, but several features of the present situation may prove indicative of a coming crisis in this sphere within the medical profession. Firstly, there is the renewal of the recurrent battle over the provision of private beds, supported very largely by various forms of individually or corporately bought health insurance, and serviced by consultants as a means of topping up their emoluments under the National Health Service. Secondly, there is the scare of the mid-sixties about the threatened exodus of home-grown doctors, particularly from within the ranks of junior hospital staff, dissatisfied as much at the prospect of low long-term career earnings as at what they see as being the inequitable distribution of rewards and status between themselves and their seniors in the rigid hospital hierarchy. Perhaps not surprisingly the exodus was mainly not to parts of the world where medical need on some objective interpretation was arguably highest but to the greener grass of more affluent societies. If it be argued that this story indicates that doctors are much as other men, even other professionals; there would seem to be grounds, in accepting this judgement, for concluding that the clash between the ethic of commercialism and individual self-enhancement and that of the idealistic, hard-working group devoted only to the collective good may carry over into the field of medicine also. A short indication that pressures exist to re-examine the orthodox concensus of the most appropriate method of providing medical care is the controversy about the effects of the implementation of the Abortion Act. Almost immediately, specialist clinics offering an intensive and apparently highly efficient service became productive (if that be the right word) and profitable. But such institutions came under heavy fire from within the medical profession.

But the problems of the social organisation of physical health and physical sickness appear trivial by comparison with the morass of uncertainty, inadequate empirical and theoretical knowledge and incipient politicization which beset the topic of mental illness. If everyone suffers physical disorder at some time or another and the language of physical incapacity is commonly used, the mentally ill still suffer from a stigma which is both widespread and universally invidious. Moreover, it is commonly believed, nobody *dies* of mental illness. But disorders of cognitive functioning and interpersonal capacity— if we can side-step with such a re-conceptualisation some of the currently unsolvable problems of causation and etymology —are probably the biggest cripplers in Western society.

At the one extreme of the analysis of what exactly the problem of mental illness is really a problem of, come those who seek a biochemical origin of the functional psychoses. For their physical treatments have a proven capacity, if not to cure, at the least to alleviate the symptoms. At the other come those, like Szasz, who discuss the 'myth' of mental illness as a source of strategies for handling difficult life situations which do not meet with the approval of one's colleagues, family or friends. It is significant, of course, that the public reaction to the symptoms of mental illness is usually quite different from that which is characteristic of physical illness. Significant also no doubt that the mentally-ill individual may appear to be *alienated* in some disturbing or threatening way from the rationality which apparently characterises the cognitive behaviour of his fellow men. For in many ways the person who is mentally ill constitutes a threat to the sanity of the rest of us. His claim that he is the son of God may not be easily tested and his pretentions as a religious teacher laughable, but the threat embodied in giving one's money and even one's clothes to the poor may be a real and provocative one to those imbued with the values of a materialistic culture.

These issues are discussed in specific detail in the readings which constitute this chapter. In their book, suggested for further reading, Coates and Rawstron conclude that regional variations in mortality are significant and that in some instances at least they correspond closely to environmental differences. It is accordingly essential, if the National Health Service is to operate so as to *equalise* the life chances of individuals living in the deprived areas of the United Kingdom, that there should be a deliberate policy decision to counteract the market forces which have operated quite systematically (and possibly to an increased degree over the post-war period) to make London and the South-East of England appear more advantageous a place to live than the rest of the United Kingdom.

Rein's paper discusses the persistence of inequalities in the use of services within the National Health Service. Although Rein finds that the health service operates in an *equitable* manner, he reserves judgement about the extent to which the policy has been equally successful in creating an *adequate* service.

But policy is not easily made and McNerney's paper identifies some of the reasons why. The under-financing and conservatism of the National Health Service are identified as problems now, which are likely to give rise to crises in the near future. The author advances the somewhat heretical idea that, as the concept of social equality has clearly not been met by the experience of the health service to date, an alternative and possibly more positive basis for policy-decision would be the specification of particular outputs in relation to which relevant inputs could be evaluated.

Sainsbury refers to a classical sociological problem, the relation of rates of suicide to social integration. He discusses attempts to test this proposition, originally advanced by Durkheim, by relating suicide rates to indices of social isolation in a city. But his analysis also indicates ways of relating the knowledge accumulated over many years of systematic and accumulative study to methods of diagnosing and dealing with individuals who appear to be especially highly pre-disposed towards suicide. Sainsbury is able to show that some of these methods have been successful.

A more critical and radical position in relation to the impact of sociological knowledge on the problems of health and illness is given by Szasz, who argues that 'mental illness' is commonly used as a name for problems of living. When someone is diagnosed as mentally ill by a psychiatrist, it is commonly the case that the diagnosis is made in terms of an established deviance in behaviour from a certain norm. The danger of illicitly translating the concepts and practices which have a proven relevance in the field of physical disease into the realms of mental illness are clearly outlined by Szasz.

Social Class and the Health Service
M. Rein

Reprinted with permission from *New Society*, 20 November 1969, pp. 807–10.

In his *Commitment to Welfare*, Richard Titmuss wrote: 'We have learnt from 15 years' experience of the Health Service that the higher income groups know how to make better use of the service; they tend to receive more specialist attention; occupy more of the beds in better equipped and staffed hospitals; receive more elective surgery; have better maternal care, and are more likely to get psychiatric help and psychotherapy than low-income groups—particularly the unskilled.'

An unpublished recent attempt by Ian Gough at the University of Manchester to study inequalities in the distribution of medical care services in Britain also concludes 'that inequalities in the *use* of these services persist within the National Health Service'. I wish to review the evidence on the use of general practitioner and hospital services that leads me to the opposite conclusion.

No adequate measure of the distribution of morbidity rates by social class is at hand to permit us to make a summary statement of whether the poor and/or lower skilled occupational groups are sicker. This poses an awkward problem in understanding the findings of high use by lower classes for both general practitioner and hospital services. But these issues of interpretation should not be confused with the findings.

The most comprehensive data on the use of general practitioners' services are in the government's *Survey of Sickness*, based on repeated representative samples of the adult population of England and Wales from 1945 to March 1952. People were asked to report on their use of the services of medical practitioners. The use of services can be measured either in terms of the *number of visits* for all patients who consulted (a monthly or annual consultation rate), or in terms of the *number of patients* who visited as a proportion of a specific age or sex group (a patient consultation rate). For the most part I shall, in the interest of space, rely on annual consultation rates. Somewhat different conclusions are suggested when the proportion of patient visits is used as a measure, but these merely qualify the main findings.

Trend data before and after the introduction of the National Health Service in July 1948 are illuminating. Medical consultation rates for males with income under £3 rose from 1947 to 1949 and then declined in 1951; for females they rose and then remained unchanged. The under £3 per week income is likely to include a large proportion of aged, thus confounding age and income factors. It is, therefore, useful to compare the rates of utilisation for the income grouping above £3 per week separately.

After the introduction of the National Health Service, in 1949, the consultation rate for males in the £3 to £5 10s income group rose from 38 to 48 per hundred persons interviewed, while rates in the highest income group, £10 and above, declined slightly from 38 to 35. The same pattern continued in 1951, yielding slightly higher consultation rates for the lower income and slightly lower rates for the higher income groups.

Consultation rates among females show an even more dramatic shift, because in 1947 the lowest income group (£3 to £5 10s) showed slightly lower rates than the £10 and above income groupings (38 compared to 49), but in 1951 the class gradient ran in the opposite direction, with the lowest income group showing the highest rates and the highest income groups showing the lowest rates (56 compared with 39). Thus the introduction of the National Health Service contributed to an increased use of physician services by the lower income groups.

What of the more recent trends? Ann Cartwright conducted a study in the summer of 1964 on a random sample of 1,400 persons. Consultation rates were developed by asking the patients how often they visited their doctors. Comparisons between the studies are difficult, since one is based on income groups and the other on social class. But some crude comparisons of trend can be made. The findings in Table 1 suggest that in 1964, as in 1952, there is a positive social class gradient, with lower income and lower social class groups being highest users and professional and upper income groups the lowest users.

One cross-national study of medical care offers further evidence of a positive class gradient in utilisation patterns. The English area studied was in and around Chester. A similar pattern emerges, although a different scheme for the classification of occupants was employed.

Annual consultation rates were highest among the semiskilled (6.3) and unskilled (8.1) and declined somewhat among lesser executives and skilled workers (5.6 and 4.3). One unexpected finding was that executives seem to have the highest consultation rates (11.1). Managers and clerical and skilled workers had about the same consultation rates (4.8, 4.4, and

Table 1. Annual consultation rates in the Cartwright (1964) and survey of sickness (1952) studies

| Cartwright study (1964) | | Survey of sickness Feb. and March (1952)* | |
Social class	Estimated annual consultation rate	Estimated annual consultation rate	Weekly income of head of household
1 Professional	3·5	3·1	over £10
2 Intermediate	3·5	4·1	£7 10s to £10
3a Skilled (non-manual)	4·4	4·5	£5 to £7 10s
3b Skilled (manual)	4·6	5·8	£3 to £5
4 Semi-skilled	4·9	7·4	up to £3
5 Unskilled	6·0	—	—

* Based on a survey conducted for the Committee on General Practice and the Survey of Sickness—unpublished.

4.3 respectively). In the urban area, even higher consultation rates were found among the unskilled (9.2 as compared with 8.1).

A major difficulty with these comparisons is the failure to separate out age and class variables. Cartwright's data permit us to do this. In the age group 45 to 74 there are only slight differences between working and middle classes, but those under age 45 in the working class have consulted their doctor more often. In the under-45 age group, 23 per cent of the working class, as compared with 14 per cent middle class, were high users (five or more consultations in the past 12 months). By contrast, 52 per cent of the middle classes in this age range visited the doctor from 1 to 4 times per year as compared with 42 per cent among the working classes. In the 45 to 74 age group there are no differences in frequency of consultation. Only in the above-75 age group do the middle classes tend to be high users (over five per year). When the top and bottom of the social class scale is examined, without taking account of age, we find that 16 per cent of professionals were high users as compared with 33 per cent of unskilled workers.

So far we have looked at studies that have calculated consultation rates by asking directly of patients the frequency of their contacts. To reduce memory error, these studies tend to be based on experience in the two weeks preceding interview and the rates are then projected on an annual basis. We next turn to a study jointly sponsored by the College of General Practitioners and the General Register Office, conducted from May 1955 to April 1956 and published in 1960. In all, records of 76 practices (about 120 practitioners) were processed.

The study confirms the findings of studies based on a random sample of the population. For men aged 15 to 64, there is a clear social gradient going from 2.2 consultations in class 1 to 3.7 in class 5. This reaffirms the pattern seen in studies previously cited. The pattern for children is somewhat different. The highest rates are in class 3 (2.2). Rates increase from class 1 to class 3 and then decline again for classes 4 and 5. Class 5 has about the same rates as class 2 (2.9).

Comparisons between the sexes are available by socioeconomic groups rather than social class. Females have consistently higher rates than males. The highest rates are found among the semi-skilled for both males and females. The same general pattern of higher frequency of use in lower socioeconomic groups persists when sex differences in given age groupings are compared. Cartwright offers the following main conclusions of her inquiry:

'Consultation rates were higher among the working than the middle class and among the unskilled manual workers than among the skilled. The differences were reduced but not eliminated when age was taken in account.'

These general conclusions apply to all other studies of the utilisation of general practitioners' services by social class. But the interpretation of the findings remains obscure because irrelevant factors may be contributing to the pattern of higher use by lower social classes. For example, it is widely believed that, when absent from work, people who hold manual jobs may be required to secure medical certificates more frequently than those in non-manual jobs. Employer expectation and trust may thus affect the social class demand for consultations.

Information on the use of hospitals for children under five years of age is based on the classic Douglas and Blomfield follow-up study of a random national sample of all legitimate births in the first week of March 1946 (*Children Under Five*). Their striking conclusion is that the poorer children, particularly those of the unskilled manual workers, were both rather more likely to be admitted to a hospital and, when admitted, to stay longer.

More recent, unpublished raw data drawn from the continuing longitudinal study of these children suggest that sex differences may be more important than social class differences in accounting for the use of in-hospital services by children. About 51 per cent of male children of lower-class manual workers had never been admitted to a hospital by age 15, as compared with 40 per cent among upper-middle income groups. But there were virtually no differences for female children in any of the social groups studied.

Or consider the use of hospitals for tonsillectomies. Upper middle-class boys are more likely to have their tonsils removed by age eight than male children of lower-class manual workers. But no class differences were found for girl children of the same age.

Although the effort to gather data on the social class of all patients in hospitals in England and Wales was abandoned, Scotland has in fact conducted such inquiries on an annual basis since the early 1960s, basing them on a complete census of the patients in all its hospitals except maternity, mental, and mental deficiency hospitals, also excluding the latter units in general hospitals.

The findings of the 1963 inpatient study in Scotland was subjected to a useful analysis reported by Carstairs and others. The findings are dramatic and surprising. Males and females in class 5 (unskilled occupations) have admission rates of 49 per cent and 56 per cent above average, respectively. For males, a positive class gradient is found between class 2 and class 5, with those in class 1 having a slightly higher rate than those in classes 2 and 3. With the exception of class 1, then, a strong trend in rates of admission by social class for males is apparent. Also, an inverse trend by social class emerges for the mean length of stay for all diagnoses—the lower the class, the longer the stay in the hospital. The mean length of stay in class 5 was 12 per cent above average, while class 1 was 23 per cent below average.

It is interesting to compare the findings of the 1963 study in Scotland, 15 years after the introduction of the National Health Service, with the 1949 study of hospital in-patient services in England and Wales, conducted one year after the new system of health care was introduced. Brian Abel-Smith and Richard Titmuss have analysed the discharges of 1949 from three groups of hospitals for all diagnostic categories for males age 25 to 64, excluding injuries. They conclude: 'As a whole there is not much difference between the hospital proportions and the social class proportions for England and Wales. For the London teaching hospitals, classes 1, 2, and 3 are well represented while the semiskilled and unskilled classes (4 and 5) are slightly under-represented. For the provincial teaching hospitals and regional board hospitals tentative comparisons with the population at risk indicate that, in general, there is little difference in the social class proportions.'

By contrast, Carstairs concludes, 'It is apparent from this analysis that differences between the social classes do exist in the use made of inpatient services ... Generally there is an upward trend from class 1 to class 5 for most diagnostic groups at most ages. Even where this is lacking, class 5 is still higher than the other classes.'

Abel-Smith and Titmuss state that 'semi-skilled and un-skilled groups are making fewer demands than might have been expected from their relatively higher mortality experience'. Carstairs cautiously notes that the reason for the observed class differences 'are not immediately apparent and are likely to be complex'. She suggests that 'differences in admission rates between the classes are not necessarily a reflection of differences in morbidity', although there may be more morbidity and mortality in the lower classes.

Whereas Abel-Smith and Titmuss were concerned with lower-class under-use, Carstairs is concerned with lower-class overuse. She offers several suggestions for possible leads in unravelling this new puzzle. She suggests that overcrowding and lack of amenities may 'make it more difficult to nurse a patient at home' and that 'it is likely that the adequacy of domestic care may influence discharge'. The lower social classes may be more susceptible to diseases causing chronic incapacity and, of course, upper income groups have a greater access to alternative forms of care—i.e. to hospital private beds.

The main themes to account for use rates, then, are either the lack of responsiveness of the medical care system to the higher needs among the lower classes, or the overreadiness of the hospital system to act as a substitute for improved housing and increased availability of domestic care resources. Perhaps the nature of the patient's physical rather than psychological condition (such as greater tendency to chronic illness) offers a more promising arena to probe for explanations for higher use and longer stays by the Scottish lowest classes. But it is evident from the report and from discussions with those responsible

Table 2. Mental hospitals, England and Wales: first, second and subsequent admission rates per million home population of males aged 25–65 and over, by social class and age, 1956

First admissions for all diagnostic groups

	Age at admission				
Social class	25–34	35–44	45–54	55–64	65 and over
1	740	745	1,034	1,084	2,022
2	741	694	873	998	1,330
3	891	973	976	1,396	1,767
4	961	981	998	1,120	1,491
5	2,699	2,201	1,765	1,960	1,735

Per cent with social class not given	4·8	3·8	3·5	5·5	25·8

Second and subsequent admission rates for all diagnostic groups

1	490	433	931	1,004	1,108
2	491	490	535	682	726
3	697	764	702	923	776
4	898	955	829	829	558
5	3,211	2,685	1,699	1,513	789

Per cent with social class not given	7·9	6·9	5·8	6·6	21·1

Source: The Registrar General's Statistical Review for 1955–56, supplement on mental health, HMSO, 1960.

for analysing the data that the findings of a strong positive relationship between social class and the use made of in-patient services was a surprise.

When account is taken of age in the relationship between social classes and use of mental hospital inpatient services, the puzzle becomes more complex. In all diagnoses for inpatients of mental hospitals, there is an inverse relationship between class and age. This produced the following surprising findings: at age 25, the highest rates of use (first admissions and second and subsequent admissions) were in the lowest social class, and the lowest rates were in the highest class. By age 65, the pattern is reversed. Class 5 rates have declined, and class 1 rates not only have increased but they account for the highest rates of use of inpatient services. The data for those 65 and older must be approached with caution because of the large percentage of cases where social class is not reported. But in the 25 to 64 age groupings the trend is very clearly in this direction (see Table 2).

The 1963 study of psychiatric care in Scotland confirms the same general trend that the use of inhospital services for mental illness increased with age for class 1 and declined with age for class 5. But these figures are not as dramatic as the study in England and Wales. The impact of age on the social class utilisation of mental hospital facilities has received almost no attention in the professional literature. If the data can be taken as an index of morbidity rather than use, a doubtful proposition at the least, then it might appear that if stress in the physical environments among younger age groups increases the need for hospital inpatient service for lower classes, increased psychological stress in the environment of the upper class may over time increase their need for mental hospital inpatient services. But this interpretation is speculative. The data do show that the relationship between class and use of inhospital services for the mentally ill is neither simple nor self-evident.

One major difficulty in finding an answer to the question of how healthy are the lowest classes is that we have no adequate conception of physical health. The subject of health is approached in terms of specific disease, illnesses, and other conditions. We cannot simply aggregate these negative conditions to arrive at a positive condition of health. Of course, all of this is widely known. But the ghosts of these unresolved conceptual questions come to haunt us when we seek to discover whether the lower classes are sicker than other groups. Although results of comprehensive medical examinations of a random sample of the population are not at hand, even if such information were available it could not by itself readily resolve the formidable conceptual difficulties.

Perhaps the best way to illustrate this thesis is to treat the analysis of the records of 76 general practitioners (the closest reliable information available on the physical conditions of different social groups secured by direct medical examination) as if these data were secured directly from a random stratified sample of all social classes. But even if we make this heroic assumption and thereby avoid confounding the true incidence of class morbidity with the differential class response to illness, we would still find it extremely difficult to interpret the findings. This difficulty arises from the important work of Jerry N. Morris, showing that there are illnesses of poverty, illnesses of affluence, and illnesses which are not related to social class and income.

If we examine the proportion of patients consulting general practitioners for specific conditions, we find that about two-thirds of the patients appear to follow other than the class-related patterns in Table 3.

Among patients with class-related illness, more than half are concentrated in the lowest class. By itself this is an insufficient criterion for determining which classes are sicker. Presumably, one wants to examine the diseases these patients have (or more accurately the labels used to describe clinical syndromes, which themselves are a crude summary of a complex interplay between medical and environmental conditions) in relation to the severity of these conditions. If we define severity in terms of diseases that are life-threatening and those resistive to therapy, the findings in Table 3 are still more difficult to interpret. Many of the conditions that class 5 have, although they are life-threatening, are also responsive to treatment. On the other hand, psychoneurotic diseases, of which most class 1 patients complain, are not life-threatening but resist treatment. By the criterion of responsiveness to prevention we might conclude that more highly skilled white-collar groups are sicker than unskilled manual groups.

But it is difficult to see how an overall assessment of morbidity by class and income can be secured by simply gathering more data without a framework for their analysis. In the absence of such a framework, we can only conclude that environmental factors appear to generate different diseases and illnesses for different occupational groups. There is no easy way of converting these data into a single measure.

Another attempt to answer the question of whether the lower social classes are sicker approaches the task by examining mortality rates by class. One conclusion reached from this analysis is that since the lower social classes have higher death rates, then they must be both sicker or less likely to secure treatment than other classes. (Death rates among unskilled

Table 3. High and low standardised patient consultation ratios, by diagnoses within social class, for males aged 15–64

100 is the standard consultation ratio in each case; figures above or below 100 show variance of social class groups from that standard

Selected disease or condition	Number of patients consulting for each disease	Social class				
		1	2	3	4	5
All diseases and conditions	40,911	93	96	103	99	99
High in class 1 (over 120)						
Psychoneurotic disorders	2,831	123	113	102	82	90
Migraine	261	130	106	115	115	71
Hypertensive disease	486	120	127	99	70	89
Hemorrhoids	873	125	97	103	88	109
Acute pharyngitis	2,035	126	90	105	97	87
	6,486					
High in class 5 (over 120)						
Otitis media (no mastoiditis)	612	72	80	104	99	122
Pneumonia	324	70	87	90	121	132
Bronchitis	3,932	49	70	99	118	146
Gastritis and duodenitis	1,308	69	60	108	109	129
Fractures	913	68	62	98	136	125
Contusion and crushing with skin surface intact	1,972	45	63	96	151	122
	9,061					

Source: W. P. D. Logan, Studies on Medical and Population Subjects, No. 14, *Morbidity Statistics from General Practice.* HMSO, 1960.

men aged 20 to 65 between 1949–53 have been accepted as higher than for all other groups. Discrepancies have been observed in the information obtained from census data and from death certificates which raise serious problems concerning the classification of some occupational groups. More recent data are not yet available, partly as a result of these difficulties.)

But while death rates are higher on average, it is useful to examine selected diseases in which there is a clear mortality class gradient and then compare these rates with the proportion of patients in each class who consulted their physician for treatment of these diseases. Table 4 shows that for certain illnesses, class 5 has high death rates and low consultation rates. However, the same pattern of high death rates and low consultation rates is also found for class 1. On the other hand, high death rates can also be associated with high consultation rates, a pattern which also holds for both classes. Perhaps a reasonable inference to be drawn from these findings is not that class mortality is an index of class morbidity, but that for certain diseases treatment is unrelated to outcome. Thus both high and low consultation rates can yield high mortality rates for specific diseases. Of course other interpretations are possible. For example, persons in the middle class may be more likely to be treated for ulcers in hospitals rather than by general practitioners. Unless the whole pattern of provision of medical care is brought into focus, the use of consultation rates as a measure of morbidity may be misleading. Still, these data do not appear to lead to the compelling conclusion that mortality rates can be easily used as evidence of class-related morbidity. It is perhaps of interest to note that during the periods 1930–32 and 1945–53, for men aged 20–64 mortality rates increased by 8 per cent for class 1 and 7 per cent for class 5. If mortality was an index of morbidity and if the data are valid, we would need to conclude that both the professionals and the unskilled are getting sicker.

Even if the lowest social classes make greater use of hospital inpatient and general practitioner services than other groups and the determination of whether they are sicker remains inconclusive, we still need to inquire into the quality of the medical care they receive. Do the lowest social classes receive poorer care than other groups? Here we also confront formidable conceptual problems. What measures of quality of care can be used?

I wish to comment briefly on two criteria of quality: measure of inputs and measure of outputs. One approach to quality of care concerns the quality of the input—medical facilities and manpower. One obvious measure is class access

Table 4. Comparison between distribution of standardised patient consulting ratios, males aged 15–64, May 1955–April 1956, and standardised mortality ratios, males aged 20–64, 1949–1953

Selected disease	Standardised patient consulting ratio, males 15–64 social classes 1–5 1955					Standardised mortality ratios, males 20–64 social classes 1–5 1949–53				
	1	2	3	4	5	1	2	3	4	5
All conditions	93	96	103	99	99	98	86	101	94	118
Respiratory tuberculosis	102	85	105	102	91	58	63	102	95	143
Diabetes mellitus	89	123	100	108	74	134	100	99	85	105
Coronary disorders and angina pectoris	89	108	102	89	93	147	110	105	79	89
Hypertensive disease	120	127	99	70	89	123	106	103	83	101
Influenza	83	82	103	113	107	58	70	97	102	139
Pneumonia	70	87	90	121	132	53	64	92	105	150
Bronchitis	49	70	99	118	146	34	53	98	101	171
Ulcer of stomach and duodenum	48	78	99	88	116	68	76	101	99	134

Source: W. P. D. Logan, *Morbidity Statistics.*

to teaching hospitals. They are presumed to offer better care than other hospitals: mortality rates are lower for certain diseases in teaching hospitals than in other hospitals. If we accept this as a measure of care quality, we find from a 1964 analysis of a 10 per cent sample of discharges in St Thomas's, the London teaching hospital, the conclusion that 'there is ... no evidence to suggest that selection is operating against any social class group'. These findings are consistent with the 1949 study of the use of hospital inpatient services, which also showed that the proportions of different classes who used provincial teaching hospitals corresponded to the distribution of social classes in the population. Similarly, Ann Cartwright's study of a random sample of patients who use hospitals in a six-month period in 1960 and 1961 in twelve areas in England and Wales concluded that, 'There is no evidence from this inquiry that middle-class patients were either more or less likely to go to a teaching hospital than working class patients. Whether a patient goes to a teaching or non-teaching hospital seems to be largely determined by the area in which he lives.'

Another measure of quality may be access to specialists in the outpatient departments of hospitals. Unpublished evidence from the study of the St Thomas's out-patient department suggests a slightly higher rate of use by lower social classes. A study by J. W. Palmer of the population in Lambeth shows greater use of outpatient facilities by males in the lower social classes. The measure of use in this study was the mention to interviewers that respondents had contact with an out-patient department (15.2 per cent in classes 4 and 5 mentioned that they had such contact as compared with 12.1 per cent in classes 1 and 2). No class difference was noted for women. The Cartwright study of general practice found that 'there was no difference between middle and working class patients ... in the proportion who had been hospital outpatients in the previous twelve months'. If the measure of quality is taken to be the characteristics of the physician, such as the prestige of the medical school he attended, or his appointment to a hospital or whether he had taken postgraduate courses, then Cartwright found none of these factors seem to be related to social class.

Turning next to measures of quality based upon the outcome of treatment, I was able to locate one unpublished study that followed the history of a specific illness by social class. Among schoolchildren in Kent, Dr Walter Holland attempted to relate the history and treatment of running ear with the findings of drum scarring which remains if the condition is neglected. He found that a condition that used to have a marked social class gradient no longer has one ... and that the care given if one has a running ear is similar whatever the social class. Here is a promising approach. More studies of the history and outcomes of specific diseases for different social classes are urgently needed if we are to understand the complex issues surrounding the quality of medical care.

These scattered findings are inconclusive, but they are suggestive and support the general conclusion of this review that in Britain the lowest social classes make the greatest use of physician and inhospital medical care services and that the care they receive appears to be of as good quality as that secured by other social classes.

The British experience suggests that the availability of universal free-on-demand, comprehensive services is a crucial factor in reducing class inequalities in the use of medical care services. That is to say, user charges for medical services have the effect of inhibiting use among the poor and the unskilled. The self-diagnosis so characteristic of the American specialist-oriented medical care system is replaced in Britain by a system where a patient's access to specialist is screened by the general practitioner. While this limited role of the general practitioner has been a source of some criticism in England, it may contribute to the equalisation of class use of medical services. Perhaps this may occur because the physician, like all professionals, may be eager to dispose of unwanted clients. When this process operates, the physician has in principle two avenues for disposition; upward to a specialist in a hospital outpatient facility, which is also likely to assume clinical responsibility thereafter for the patients' condition; and downward to the nurse and social worker, where the physician remains the accountable agent. There is thus a tendency to refer patients upward to specialist. This hypothesis may help to account for the fact that the unskilled use outpatient, teaching, and inpatient hospital facilities, even more than they do the services of local authority medical and social welfare personnel.

This article argues that the British Health Service is equitable; it is not a review of the adequacy of the system. Indeed there may be a major conflict between equity and adequacy. The challenge in the future is how to advance adequacy without sacrificing equity.

Health Services in Britain
W. J. McNerney

Reprinted with permission from *Problems and Progress in Medical Care*, edited by Gordon McLachlan, Oxford University Press, 1971, pp. 157–63.

The indivisibility of health policy from social policy

Conceptually an integrated system makes it possible to establish *effective tradeoff mechanisms*. For example, priorities of health services, better food, housing, and employment can be identified and debated before policy is finally set. When health welfare and social services are together in one government department, it should become even easier. Subsidies for children and rent and other programmes have been formulated; is it not time for Britain to formalize procedures and to develop more effective social indicators?

No society can hope to solve health problems through health services alone. It is an endless, deplorably expensive task. First, better diet, improved housing, and the morale associated with an intact family and reasonable job are often more important determinants of health than medical care services *per se*. Second, when a problem (whether social, psychological, or physical) falls within the reference framework of health, it may be treated often, and if unresponsive, treated endlessly.

Tradeoff decisions are inevitably difficult. They involve subjective as well as objective factors. There is always the knotty question of the short-run versus the long-run. But, if made with reasonably good humour, they can avoid initially and strategically, grievously expensive and ineffective programmes. Within the orbit of tradeoff, one should include the relative emphasis to be put on school health and occupational health i.e., on prevention as well as cure.

Medical and allied manpower

The national health system made impressive gains in consolidating a front line of primary physicians through which all referrals must be made and in distributing consultants more widely into the provinces. With this system, two pediatricians suffice for Oxford which had a population of 110,000 in 1968, while New Haven, Connecticut, US, with a 1970 population of 133,543 has approximately thirty. Apparently, England is content with fewer neurosurgeons than San Francisco. Nominal needs are spared the costly reflexes of the consultant. However, some operational problems deserve note. Accordingly, to many observers there appear to be, overall, too few consultants. The shortage, if any exists, still varies markedly by area (concentration varies on a scale of 2–1) although the variation has become considerably less in recent years. Attractive, professionally stimulating, areas have little difficulty attracting consultants and, if anything, they experience an excess demand for places.

The supply is artificially depressed by consultants themselves who seem to prefer to work with the subordinate help of a large supply of juniors (registrars, etc.) rather than with equals. Because being a consultant is prestigious and attractive, the numbers aspiring to the posts far exceeds the supply. The consequences are costly. An hour glass configuration develops, inhabited below the neck by many frustrated physicians uncertain about promotion to top status and reluctant to accept 'less' in the form of general practice. Not highly paid, there is always danger they may opt out of the system. The average age at which a man becomes a consultant is 38–9 years, beyond his research and in some cases, his teaching prime. It is bad enough that the average GP does not receive principal status until the age of 30 years. In essence, the problem of geographical maldistribution is compounded by the maldistribution between 'training and established posts' as well as the under-exploitation of organization of practice, mentioned earlier.

A greater supply of consultants (not a major increase) should help the distribution problem; it will not solve it. It is a fact of life that many well-trained men resist living and working in rural or culturally impoverished areas. Foreign doctors who return to their homes after training abroad, compete for posts in urban areas. In the US, over-supply in many skills in 'interesting' environments persists in the face of under-supply in other environments, even when the income to be earned is less. The pressure needed to overcome the inherent resistances involved is so great that its exercise might well jeopardize the system. Other strategies are needed. For example, doctors' assistants (not MDs) can function under radio and television control and periodic contact. Doctors can travel out from the stimulating environment of strategically placed group practices. If there is any doubt about the social and cultural aspects of doctor distribution, consider the fact that in 1967 the per-centages of senior doctors born in Britain showed that 34 per cent were in teaching hospitals and 66 per cent were in non-teaching hospitals, whereas the comparable figures in the case of the foreign born were 12 per cent and 88 per cent. Again, the percentage of foreign-educated doctors is greater among specialities less popular among British doctors. Ways around as well as through a problem of this depth must be found.

Indeed the system is excessively dependent on junior doctors from foreign countries as is the case in the US. One out of five doctors in Britain was born outside Britain. In 1967, the number of immigrant doctors approximately equalled the total output of British medical schools (1900). The US record was even less commendatory. Although some immigrant doctors return to their origins, once trained, too many do not, resulting in a drain on countries that can ill afford it; while in Britain, communications problems arise involving foreign doctors, sometimes disconcerting to patients. Preparation is uneven and not always pre-tested by the country of origin. Importantly, the extensive use of foreign-born physicians must indicate an under-supply in Britain.

If more medical students are to be educated, current schools will have to be enlarged *and* others added. Two new ones under construction (the only two built in this century), even with the expansion of current schools, will not match minimal needs if one accepts the projections of the NHS. Nurses are in short supply with the number at any given time strained by the fact that the nurse is being pulled in two directions at once, i.e., toward more and less professional tasks created by growing gaps in service. Yet, is it impossible to look at the supply of physicians or nurses alone?

Often, the use of medical and allied personnel is taken too much for granted. Previous reference has been made to the fact that new medical schools especially, must explore new ways of organizing doctors and allied skills so that often excessive specialization sought by health personnel (in the laudable name of quality) and the internal needs of various professional domains, can be balanced against cost and consumer satisfaction.

Low pay scales heighten some of the manpower supply and use problems. Not all health workers have been kept up to date. In fact, nurses and allied skills are behind the pace. With a tight supply situation, the work must be paid sufficiently to attract men as well as women and to attract married as well as single persons. Also, the work must be organized so that, for example, primarily nurses do nursing. It is particularly important not to capitalize on dedication to justify lesser payment for services close to the patient. If it were not for the emigration of doctors (300–500 a year), Britain would be less dependent on foreign graduates than the US (the US has little drain). However, a structure that depends to a significant extent on low paid junior staff without full appointments cannot expect to stem the out-flow. What are the relative costs of new medical schools and better pay under better organized medical staffs? Who will decide?

Finance

It is already evident that the NHS is underfinanced if it is to be conceived as a developing utility; and the prospects are that the situation could get worse. There are some symptoms, old physical facilities and gaps in needed physical facilities, long waiting lists, crowding, and some low wage scales. The rate of increase per annum in expenditures on health services in Britain over the past 5 or 6 years had been significantly less than in such countries as the US, Canada, France and Sweden.

The impact of underfinancing is often subtle, because the effect is not immediately evident. Crises can be avoided for several years but the accumulated cost can be serious. In the 1960s the problems of stressful urbanized living, involving several chronic components, moved into the forefront of their dimensions were enlarged by the fact that more people proportionately are living beyond the age of 65. In the decade ahead, there will be greater need created by the demands of middle and advanced age, more complex in nature. In effect, there will be a marked increase in the workload, fed on the one hand by a burgeoning medical science (now traded freely and quickly on an international scale) and on the other by greater demand for service.

Some of the original cost estimates for the system were off the mark, a phenomenon which seems universal. One underlying assumption proved wrong, i.e., that costs would go down as better health services improved the health of the population. Another assumption, more recently set forth, that public expenditures for public services such as health should be in line with the growth of resources as a whole, needs examination. The 5·23 per cent of the national income currently spent on health in 1968, seems low for such a well developed country.

In judging advances, one must take into account that labour intensive fields (in the case of health approximately 65–70 per cent of all expenses are labour expenses) suffer from comparison with growth in national income or the Gross National Product as does, for example, education. Thus, a public policy, already enunciated, that expenditure in public health services be kept in line with the growth of resources as a whole is bound to penalize health. Bringing the expenditure growth lines into *closer* relations is more defensible. Proceeding from a low base, such a public policy puts extraordinary (if not unrealistic) demands on productivity. In this one regard one must take into account that since 1963 the output per man hour in manufacturing industry rose less in England than most industrialized countries. Similarly, wage cost per unit of output has risen more than most industrialized countries. Costs and prices as a result have tended to rise rapidly in general. Some see the remedy primarily as greater capital investment in industry or more rapid installation of labour-saving devices, others call for greater government expenditures. In any event, government expenditures must be evaluated as a contributor to inflation. Thus, health heavily dependent on government spending, suffers a double jeopardy.

The question must be raised as to whether underfinancing is not an inevitable consequence of most (in this case 98 per cent) funds to be spent on health services flowing through a national government channel? As Sir Bruce Fraser, a former Permanent Secretary of the Ministry of Health, put it, 'Political pressures, it seems, must continue to decide the cost of health'.

When set against the problems of inflation, Common Market, general productivity, etc., health can easily be put in the 'let's try harder with what we have' category and usually is. This is usually a safe political bet because most of the population is interested in getting well, and far less in keeping well and largely unconcerned about service until it is needed. Opinion polls in most countries reveal somewhat similar results in seeking out satisfaction. Programmes inevitably get built excessively around what is perceived as available money and much less around goals.

Historically, large systems *per se* become more conservative with time, not less, and, of course, they must start, for better or worse, with what they inherit. If lacking in dynamism, they compete less effectively for scarce public resources. It is hard for the most energetic person in a vast system to break through, if there is no one at the top to make the large decisions and point the way. Some in England feel that the inherent limitations suggested by this theory, which is given added point by the fact that final control is in the hands of top civil servants who are themselves a supportive class in government, outweigh even the impact of the political process. This raises the interesting question of whether the NHS could use more money in several places constructively without a change in the system, in the light of the shortage of professional and particularly management skills.

Sooner or later in the evolution of large centralized health systems, after the glow of well-earned, initial achievement has worn off, one hears the expression, 'health needs are a bottomless pit'. The realization becomes all the more exasperating when underfinancing of reasonable need is at issue. In fact, perceived need is extensive, particularly if a system represents itself as dedicated to the concept of total well-being as well as minimizing physical ailments. The more the system promises, the greater the need becomes. Because of the functional as well as organic components involved and the subjectivity of health demands, a large politically oriented system, without the buffer of individual judgments, predictably turns to 'the budget' as the way out. To complete the circle, the budget must be fair. Thus, the cutting edge of demand gets sacrificed for the good of the whole—a further rounding down process. In Britain and in other countries, the budgeting process has a special twist as has been mentioned. The top civil servants move from one division to another, always upward if they have promise. Mecca is the Treasury. Thus, health budgets are apt to be proposed by men remote from the substantive problems of health services and approved by men still farther remote from the issues involved. It is irrelevant that these men, again, are obviously first-class. The paucity of men of elite stature at the centre who also have first-hand administrative or top clinical experience in health simply underscores the reliance on budget.

Recurrently, private out-of-pocket payments are discussed either as a way of generating more money or 'to share the blame' for difficult, predestined decisions.

Experience bears out the tendencies cited. The Conservative government, as the government before it, recognizes the need for more funds. However, it is focused on other matters of higher priority and is hesitant to complicate matters by reference to a health issue—even if it means improvement of service. Going into the recent election, health was not debated much, if at all, as an issue. The new administration came into office in 1970 without a health policy materially different from the old. This can be construed to mean the ultimate in satisfaction, but also it can connote low priority which is more probably the case. Far better that health financing and services be debated. It is unlikely that many changes will be offered. The balancing act between innovation and equity appears to be too delicate. In the absence of policy, whatever is done is apt to be small in the light of circumstance.

The mixture of low priority, unstated objectives, little policy and the traditional apathy of large populations towards health (historically, people are interested in getting well, far less in keeping well) is something to conjecture about when coupled with a politically rather than administratively oriented implementation system.

Is a strict concept of social equality, even in such an essential service as health, tenable in an economy of scarcity? As laudable as social justice is as an objective, if the same for all becomes an end at the expense of all means—efficiency can be lost, dynamism, unduly compromised and, ironically, the target can become more remote. Is it better, possibly, to agree on outputs (morbidity, mortality, programme accomplishments, etc.) and judge inputs (money, resource allocation, etc.) in terms of their demonstrable relevance?

Suicide and Depression
P. Sainsbury

Reprinted with permission from *British Journal of Psychiatry*, Special Publication No. 2, 1968, pp. 5–13.[1]

The notion that suicide increases when social integration and social regulation are weak was first put forward by Durkheim in 1897. Social integration, according to Durkheim, is manifest as the 'common conscience' of a community: those beliefs, customs and values that members of a society share; and suicide occurs when integration is diminished. Social regula-

1. The reader is advised to refer to the original publication for the specific references and footnotes which have been omitted from this extract

tion, on the other hand, is the control which a society exercises over its members. If this is weak, goals and ambitions are unlimited and the purposes of life become ill-defined. In these circumstances members of a society are also pre-disposed to suicide. I think the concept of social integration, or its converse 'isolation', subsumes both processes. Be that as it may, one way in which Durkheim tested this theory was by relating suicide and integration within the family group; and his observations on marital status are as valid now as they were in his time. Allowing for age, the divorced and separated have the highest rates of suicide, the single and widowed come next and the married have the lowest rate, which is just what his theory required. I attempted to test this further by asking whether suicide was related to social isolation within a city. Various indices of isolation, such as the rates of divorce, of living alone, of living in digs or boarding houses and of foreign born persons were calculated for the 28 London boroughs and correlated with their suicide rates. A very significant association was obtained; but as these statistical relationships might be artefacts, the coroners' records of the suicides were also examined, and I was able to show that the suicides were in fact living alone and were more often foreign born and so on. But living alone is only one measure of social isolation or integration in Durkheim's sense. McCulloch, Philip and Carstairs, in their recent paper, did not find a significant correlation between the suicide rates of the electoral wards in Edinburgh and living alone. However, of their nine measures of the wards' social characteristics that correlated with suicide, five were very good indices of the community's lack of control of its members. Suicide was associated with juvenile delinquency rates, number of children in care, school absences and divorce.

Dr. Barraclough is interested in the problem of suicide in the elderly who migrate to a Sussex seaside resort when they retire, thereby segregating themselves from all that was familiar in their previous social environment. He has so far been able to show that the suicide rate of old women living in resort towns is above that of other towns. Similarly, Dr. Grad and I have found that the referral rate of elderly people with affective disorders is significantly higher for a resort town in our district than for other towns. We hope to go on to show how both suicide and depression relate to the ecology of this retirement area.

To summarize this brief review of the sociological approach

to suicide: social factors clearly relate in a predictable way to the incidence of suicide in a community; though that in itself does not mean that the associations are causal ones. Precisely how this social component should be defined is uncertain; but the concept of social isolation seems to be a useful one, because isolated social groups and socially isolating events are conspicuously associated with a high incidence of suicide.

Such observations also provide a guide to the kind of social action needed to diminish the incidence of suicide. The practical outcome of the epidemiological data has been to indicate that certain groups in the community are more at risk than others, and are therefore the ones to whom it would most repay directing a preventative programme. The risk of suicide increases with age, for example, and the unoccupied man living alone is especially vulnerable; whereas the elderly woman is becoming increasingly so particularly if she is widowed or has moved away from her accustomed social milieu. There is evidence that these social variables also affect the incidence of suicide in people with a depressive illness; but it is not yet possible to say whether they predispose the depressed psychotic to suicide or whether they precipitate the psychosis which culminates in suicide.

To summarize the characteristics of the depressed person who is a bad risk for suicide. He will have an endogenous type of depression and be aged over 40. He will have lost one of his parents in childhood from suicide, and will himself have threatened or attempted suicide. His illness will either have been of short duration or he may recently have been discharged from hospital, and he will now be living alone. He is more likely to harp on his feeling of hopelessness and worthlessness and loss of energy than on his adverse circumstances; though loneliness, recent bereavement or physical illness, in the more elderly depressive, will increase the risk of suicide. He may also be drinking heavily.

The last topic I want to discuss is the more practical aspects of suicide prevention, because I think we have acquired enough facts to provide a basis on which to devise ways of reducing the incidence of suicide. To begin with, most suicides give a clear warning, more often than not to a doctor or psychiatrist. Walk found that 23 per cent of suicides in Chichester and district had had contact with a psychiatrist in the preceding year and 2 per cent had been in-patients. Capstick reported about 78 per cent of suicides had been under medical care in the 'months' preceding death, and 60 per cent had communicated their intentions. Robins' figures were similar, but he adds that the suicidal communications were repeated to many people, and 53 per cent of the important manic-depressive group had received medical or psychiatric care in the four weeks preceding suicide. It therefore seems that psychiatrists, general practitioners and those laymen to whom the community turn in a crisis should be able to evaluate these warnings better and to take more effective action.

First, in my view, more stress should be placed in medical education (a) on the recognition and treatment of depression and other common psychiatric conditions known to have a high risk of suicide, (b) on the systematic examination and assessment of risk in the suicidal patient, and (c) on the importance of discussing frankly with the depressive his attitude to the future, to dying and to suicide.

Next, since affective psychoses so commonly precede suicide, and because they are closely associated with seriousness of intent, the symptoms indicating a risk of suicide should be better known and systematically looked for in doubtful cases.

Thirdly, where the risk is in doubt, admission to hospital for a more detailed evaluation is essential.

Fourthly, treatment must be thorough—half-treated depressives are certain suicides. But, whether treatment is first given in hospital or in the community, a vital rule is that there must be a precise and set procedure for the after-care and follow-up of the patient. The facts show clearly that the most dangerous time is the six months following discharge. The patient needs to know exactly to whom he may turn for advice and support during the hazardous period of recovery. The sentinel may be the psychiatric social worker, psychiatrist, general practitioner or whoever else the patient can trust and confide in.

Lastly, the prevention of suicide in later life depends to a considerable degree on socio-medical measures such as improving the old person's general physical health, correcting apparently minor ailments which limit his well-being and independence, and providing for his social and economic requirements. More serious consideration needs to be given to planning retirement and to determining the real interests and needs of the retired elderly.

If suicide prevention is to be effective and if doctors are to share some of the responsibilities which have fallen to lay bodies such as the Samaritans, we need to plan our services in such a way as to be able to take effective action, and the National Health Service already provides an ideal framework within which to do this. It offers much better opportunities for a more efficient and extensive scheme of suicide prevention than those being set up in the U.S.A. The advantage we have is that everyone is registered with a general practitioner, and he is the obvious figure to whom the suicidal person, his relatives or other lay people such as the police, parson or welfare personnel should be able to turn when confronted with someone threatening suicide. But two requirements must be met if the general practitioner is to be the pivot for the early recognition and management of the suicidal: first his training must equip him for assessing suicidal risk, and secondly he must be provided with effective channels through which to act. These channels would include: an efficiently staffed district emergency centre to deal with the actual suicide attempt; easy access at all times to the local psychiatric services, both community and hospital, to deal with patients needing immediate psychiatric assessment or care; and easy liaison with the social and mental welfare services to whom he can refer the less severe attempts and less seriously ill patients for support or follow-up.

The emergency ward must also be intimately linked with the psychiatric services, and all suicidal attempts routinely referred to them for assessment and treatment. Finally, the psychiatric services would ensure the after-care of all suicidal cases, either through their own clinics and social workers, or through the general practitioner and social welfare services. Lest this sounds too utopian, allow me to end by quoting some experimental evidence that, with improved services, it may be possible to reduce the incidence of suicide in geriatric patients. In 1958 a community psychiatric service was introduced in Chichester in which most patients are treated either at home, as out-patients, or in a day hospital rather than by admission to hospital. An effect of the new service has been to provide treatment for many more elderly people in the district. Walk set out to determine what effects the new service has had on the incidence of suicide. He therefore calculated the proportion of suicides occurring in the district who were known to a psychiatrist some time in the year preceding death. He did this for the five year period before the introduction of the service and again for the five years after. He found the suicide rate in the patients over 65 had decreased significantly, and this had occurred in spite of the number and rate of referrals having increased in the second period.

The Myth of Mental Illness
T. Szasz

Reprinted with permission from *American Psychologist*, Vol. 15 February 1960, pp. 113–18.

My aim in this essay is to raise the question 'Is there such a thing as mental illness?' and to argue that there is not. Since the notion of mental illness is extremely widely used nowadays, inquiry into the ways in which this term is employed would seem to be especially indicated. Mental illness, of course, is not literally a 'thing'—or physical object—and hence it can 'exist' only in the same sort of way in which other theoretical concepts exist. Yet, familiar theories are in the habit of posing, sooner or later—at least to those who come to believe in them—as 'objective truths' (or 'facts'). During certain historical periods, explanatory conceptions such as deities, witches, and microorganisms appeared not only as theories but as self-evident *causes* of a vast number of events. I submit that today mental illness is widely regarded in a somewhat similar fashion, that is, as the cause of innumerable diverse happenings. As an antidote to the complacent use of the notion of mental illness—whether as a self-evident phenomenon, theory, or cause—let us ask this question: What is meant when it is asserted that someone is mentally ill?

In what follows I shall describe briefly the main uses to which the concept of mental illness has been put. I shall argue that this notion has outlived whatever usefulness it might have had and that it now functions merely as a convenient myth.

The notion of mental illness derives its main support from such phenomena as syphilis of the brain or delirious conditions —intoxications, for instance—in which persons are known to manifest various peculiarities or disorders of thinking and behaviour. Correctly speaking, however, these are diseases of the brain, not of the mind. According to one school of thought, *all* so-called mental illness is of this type. The assumption is made that some neurological defect, perhaps a very subtle one, will ultimately be found for all the disorders of thinking and behaviour. Many contemporary psychiatrists, physicians, and other scientists hold this view. This position implies that people *cannot* have troubles—expressed in what are *now called* 'mental illnesses'—because of differences in personal needs, opinions, social aspirations, values, and so on. *All problems in living* are attributed to physicochemical processes which in due time will be discovered by medical research.

'Mental illnesses' are thus regarded as basically no different than all other diseases (that is, of the body). The only difference, in this view, between mental and bodily diseases is that the former, affecting the brain, manifest themselves by means of mental symptoms; whereas the latter, affecting other organ systems (for example, the skin, liver, etc.), manifest themselves by means of symptoms referable in those parts of the body. This view rests on and expresses what are, in my opinion, two fundamental errors.

In the first place, what central nervous system symptoms would correspond to a skin eruption or a fracture? It would *not* be some emotion or complex bit of behaviour. Rather, it would be blindness or a paralysis of some part of the body. The crux of the matter is that a disease of the brain, analogous to a disease of the skin or bone, is a neurological defect, and not a problem in living. For example, a *defect* in a person's visual field may be satisfactorily explained by correlating it with certain definite lesions in the nervous system. On the other hand, a person's *belief*—whether this be a belief in Christianity, in Communism, or in the idea that his internal organs are 'rotting' and that his body is, in fact, already 'dead'—cannot be explained by a defect or disease of the nervous system. Explanations of this sort of occurrence—assuming that one is interested in the belief itself and does not regard it simply as a 'symptom' or expression of something else that is *more interesting*—must be sought along different lines.

The second error in regarding complex psychosocial behaviour, consisting of communications about ourselves and the world about us, as mere symptoms of neurological functioning is *epistemological*. In other words, it is an error pertaining not to any mistakes in observation or reasoning as such, but rather to the way in which we organize and express our knowledge. In the present case, the error lies in making a symmetrical dualism between mental and physical (or bodily) symptoms, a dualism which is merely a habit of speech and to which no known observations can be found to correspond. Let us see if this is so. In medical practice, when we speak of physical disturbances, we mean either signs (for example, a fever) or symptoms (for example, pain). We speak of mental symptoms, on the other hand, when we refer to a patient's *communications about himself, others, and the world about him*. He might state that he is Napoleon or that he is being persecuted by the Communists. These would be considered mental symptoms *only* if the observer believed that the patient was *not* Napoleon or that he was *not* being persecuted by the Communists. This makes it apparent that the statement that '*X* is a mental symptom' involves rendering a judgment. The judgment entails, moreover, a covert comparison or matching of the patient's ideas, concepts, or beliefs with those of the observer and the society in which they live. The notion of mental symptom is therefore inextricably tied to the *social* (including *ethical*) *context* in which it is made in much the same way as the notion of bodily symptom is tied to an *anatomical* and *genetic context*.

To sum up what has been said thus far: I have tried to show that for those who regard mental symptoms as signs of brain disease, the concept of mental illness is unnecessary and misleading. For what they mean is that people so labelled suffer from diseases of the brain; and, if that is what they mean, it would seem better for the sake of clarity to say that and not something else.

The term 'mental illness' is widely used to describe something which is very different than a disease of the brain. Many people today take it for granted that living is an arduous process. Its hardship for modern man, moreover, derives not so much from a struggle for biological survival as from the stresses and strains inherent in the social intercourse of complex human personalities. In this context, the notion of mental illness is used to identify or decribe some feature of an individual's so-called personality. Mental illness—as a deformity of the personality, so to speak—is then regarded as the *cause* of the human disharmony. It is implicit in this view that social intercourse between people is regarded as something *inherently harmonious*, its disturbance being due solely to the presence of 'mental illness' in many people. This is obviously fallacious reasoning, for it makes the abstraction 'mental illness' into a *cause*, even though this abstraction was created in the first place to serve only as a shorthand expression for certain types of human behaviour. It now becomes necessary to ask: 'What kinds of behaviour are regarded as indicative of mental illness, and by whom?'

The concept of illness, whether bodily or mental, implies *deviation from some clearly defined norm*. In the case of physical illness, the norm is the structural and functional integrity of the human body. Thus, although the desirability of physical health, as such, is an ethical value, what health *is* can be stated in anatomical and physiological terms. What is the norm deviation from which is regarded as mental illness? This question cannot be easily answered. But whatever this norm might be, we can be certain of only one thing: namely, that it is a norm that must be stated in terms of *psychosocial, ethical*, and *legal* concepts. For example, notions such as 'excessive repression' or 'acting out an unconscious impulse' illustrate the use of psychological concepts for judging (so-called) mental health and illness. The idea that chronic hostility, vengefulness, or divorce are indicative of mental illness would be illustrations of the use of ethical norms (that is, the desirability of love, kindness, and a stable marriage relationship). Finally, the widespread psychiatric opinion that only a mentally ill person would commit homicide illustrates the use of a legal concept as a norm of mental health. The norm from which deviation is measured whenever one speaks of a mental illness is a *psychosocial and ethical one*. Yet, the remedy is sought in terms of *medical* measures which—it is hoped and assumed—are free from wide differences of ethical value. The definition of the disorder and the terms in which its remedy are sought are therefore at serious odds with one another. The practical significance of this covert conflict between the alleged nature of the defect and the remedy can hardly be exaggerated.

Having identified the norms used to measure deviations in cases of mental illness, we will now turn to the question: 'Who defines the norms and hence the deviation?' Two basic answers may be offered: (*a*) It may be the person himself (that is, the patient) who decides that he deviates from a norm. For example, an artist may believe that he suffers from a work inhibition; and he may implement this conclusion by seeking help *for* himself from a psychotherapist. (*b*) It may be someone other than the patient who decides that the latter is deviant (for example, relatives, physicians, legal authorities, society generally, etc.). In such a case a psychiatrist may be hired by others to do something *to* the patient in order to correct the deviation.

These considerations underscore the importance of asking the question 'Whose agent is the psychiatrist?' and of giving a candid answer to it. The psychiatrist (psychologist or non-medical psychotherapist), it now develops, may be the agent of the patient, of the relatives, of the school, of the military services, of a business organization, of a court of law, and so forth. In speaking of the psychiatrist as the agent of these persons or organizations, it is not implied that his values concerning norms, or his ideas and aims concerning the proper nature of remedial action, need to coincide exactly with those of his employer. For example, a patient in individual psychotherapy may believe that his salvation lies in a new marriage; his psychotherapist need not share this hypothesis. As the patient's agent, however, he must abstain from bringing social or legal force to bear on the patient which would prevent him from putting his beliefs into action. If his *contract* is with the patient, the psychiatrist (psychotherapist) may disagree with him or stop his treatment; but he cannot engage others to obstruct the patient's aspirations. Similarly, if a psychiatrist is engaged by a court to determine the sanity of a criminal, he need not fully share the legal authorities' values and intentions in regard to the criminal and the means available for dealing with him. But the psychiatrist is expressly barred from stating, for example, that it is not the criminal who is 'insane' but the men who wrote the law on the basis of which the very actions that are being judged are regarded as 'criminal'. Such an opinion could be voiced, of course, but not in a courtroom, and not by a psychiatrist who makes it his practice to assist the court in performing its daily work.

To recapitulate: In actual contemporary social usage, the finding of a mental illness is made by establishing a deviance in behaviour from certain psychosocial, ethical, or legal norms. The judgment may be made, as in medicine, by the patient, the physician (psychiatrist), or others. Remedial action, finally, tends to be sought in a therapeutic—or covertly medical—framework, thus creating a situation in which *psychosocial, ethical*, and/or *legal deviations* are claimed to be correctible by (so-called) *medical action*. Since medical action is designed to correct only medical deviations, it seems logically absurd to expect that it will help solve problems whose very existence had been defined and established on nonmedical grounds. I think that these considerations may be fruitfully applied to the present use of tranquillizers and, more generally, to what might be expected of drugs of whatever type in regard to the amelioration or solution of problems in human living.

*   *   *

While I have argued that mental illnesses do not exist, I obviously did not imply that the social and psychological occurrences to which this label is currently being attached also do not exist. Like the personal and social troubles which people had in the Middle Ages, they are real enough. It is the labels we give them that concerns us and, having labelled them, what we do about them. While I cannot go into the ramified implications of this problem here, it is worth noting that a demonologic conception of problems in living gave rise to therapy along theological lines. Today, a belief in mental illness implies—nay, requires—therapy along medical or psychotherapeutic lines.

What is implied in the line of thought set forth here is something quite different. I do not intend to offer a new conception of 'psychiatric illness' for a new form of 'therapy'. My aim is more modest and yet also more ambitious. It is to suggest that the phenomena now called mental illnesses be looked at afresh and more simply, that they be removed from the category of illnesses, and that they be regarded as the expressions of man's struggle with the problem of *how* he should live. The last mentioned problem is obviously a vast one, its enormity reflecting not only man's inability to cope with his environment, but even more his increasing self-reflectiveness.

By problems in living, then, I refer to that truly explosive chain reaction which began with man's fall from divine grace by partaking of the fruit of the tree of knowledge. Man's awareness of himself and of the world about him seems to be a steadily expanding one, bringing in its wake an ever larger *burden of understanding. This burden, then, is to be expected and must not be misinterpreted.* Our only *rational* means for lightening it is *more understanding*, and appropriate *action* based on such understanding. The main alternative lies in acting as though the burden were not what in fact we perceive it to be and taking refuge in an outmoded theological view of man. In the latter view, man does not fashion his life and much of his world about him, but merely lives out his fate in a world created by superior beings. This may logically lead to pleading nonresponsibility in the face of seemingly unfathomable problems and difficulties. Yet, if man fails to take increasing responsibility for his actions, individually as well as collectively, it seems unlikely that some higher power or being would assume this task and carry this burden for him. Moreover, this seems hardly the proper time in human history for obscuring the issue of man's responsibility for his actions by hiding it behind the skirt of an all-explaining conception of mental illness.

I have tried to show that the notion of mental illness has outlived whatever usefulness it might have had and that it now functions merely as a convenient myth. As such, it is a true heir to religious myths in general and to the belief in witchcraft in particular; the role of all these belief-systems was to act as *social tranquillizers*, thus encouraging the hope that mastery of certain specific problems may be achieved by means of substitutive (symbolic-magical) operations. The notion of mental illness thus serves mainly to obscure the everyday fact that life for most people is a continuous struggle, not for biological survival, but for a 'place in the sun', 'peace of mind', or some other human value. For man aware of himself and of the world about him, once the needs for preserving the body (and perhaps the race) are more or less satisfied, the problem arises as to what he should do with himself. Sustained adherence to the myth of mental illness allows people to avoid facing this problem, believing that mental health, conceived as the absence of mental illness, automatically insures the making of right and safe choices in one's conduct of life. But the facts are all the other way. It is the making of good choices in life that others regard, retrospectively, as good mental health!

The myth of mental illness encourages us, moreover, to believe in its logical corollary: that social intercourse would be harmonious, satisfying, and the secure basis of a 'good life' were it not for the disrupting influences of mental illness or 'psychopathology'. The potentiality for universal human happiness, in this form at least, seems to me but another example of the I-wish-it-were-true type of fantasy. I do believe that human happiness or well-being on a hitherto unimaginable large scale, and not just for a select few, is possible. This goal could be achieved, however, only at the cost of many men, and not just a few being willing and able to tackle their personal, social, and ethical conflicts. This means having the courage and integrity to forgo waging battles on false fronts, finding solutions for substitute problems—for instance, fighting the battle of stomach acid and chronic fatigue instead of facing up to a marital conflict.

Our adversaries are not demons, witches, fate, or mental illness. We have no enemy whom we can fight, exorcise, or dispel by 'cure'. What we do have are *problems in living*— whether these be biological, economic, political, or socio-psychological. In this essay I was concerned only with problems belonging in the last mentioned category, and within this group mainly with those pertaining to moral values. The field to which modern psychiatry addresses itself is vast, and I made no effort to encompass it all. My argument was limited to the proposition that mental illness is a myth, whose function it is to disguise and thus render more palatable the bitter pill of moral conflicts in human relations.

Further Reading :   **Health**

F. BAKER, P. J. M. MCEWAN and A. SHELDON, *Industrial Organisations and Health*, London, Tavistock, 1969.

H. S. BECKER and B. GEER, 'Medical Education' in H. E. FREEMAN, S. LEVINE and L. G REEDER, eds., *Handbook of Medical Sociology*, Englewood Cliffs, New Jersey, Prentice-Hall, 1963.

ANN CARTWRIGHT, *Human Relations and Hospital Care*, London, Routledge and Kegan Paul, 1964.

B. E. COATES and G. W. RAWSTRON, *Regional Variations in Britain*, London, Batsford, 1971.

A. COMFORT, *The Process of Ageing*, London, Weidenfeld and Nicolson, 1965.

A. LINDZEY, *Socialised Medicine in England and Wales*, Chapel Hill, University of North Carolina Press, 1962.

G. MCLAUGHLAN, *Portfolio for Health*, London, Oxford University Press, 1971.

† W. R. SCOTT and E. H. VOLKART, *Medical Care*, New York, Wiley, 1966.

† M. W. SUSSER and W. WATSON, *Sociology in Medicine*, London, Oxford University Press, 1962.

† Reference

Chapter Seven Education

Many of the features of our educational system are involved in the study of social problems. The most publicised relate to those in which educational deprivation is seen as one part of cumulative deprivation for those who live near the centre of the larger towns and cities or suffer disadvantages because of their social and economic positions. The reading from the Plowden Report, which puts the school into its social context, is concerned with these.

There are, however, other connections between education and social problems. The whole question of what the syllabus provides in our educational institutions has a bearing not only on its relevance for jobs but on the kinds of social attitudes that are current. More than one of the readings has something to say about the organisational rigidities which affect the system and the ways in which teachers are prepared for the tasks in hand. If the syllabus is concerned with less rather than more relevant subjects and preoccupied with questions of social control then it will have consequences for society at large.

The educational traditions within the present system, which are experienced at different stages, are at variance in significant ways with regard to their assumption about processes of learning, values, goals of education and the relationships between teacher and student. The emphasis on group experience and socialisation in the early years of school can give way, when competitive pressures are introduced, to an approach which stresses individual achievement to the exclusion of many other relevant considerations which it might be argued are more important to performance in the real world.

The debate on race and intelligence, dormant for some decades, is now being raised again with arguments that roam uneasily between the disparate realms of science and ideology. The relative significance of heredity as against environment, meaningless though we may be told these simple distinctions are, has returned to the forefront of debate.

The assumptions and information provided by the educational system influence those who have passed through it even if what has been provided is largely rejected; it provides a view of something which may be seen as a sham or as irrelevant. Discussions about freedom and authority, relevance and appropriate organisational and representative structures, of the kind begun in part by the so-called Campus Revolution, need to go on, as some of the authors quoted in the chapter recognise.

The Plowden Report, on *Children and their Primary Schools*, produced in 1967, was one of a number of significant reports on the educational system produced within the past fifteen years. Its importance from our point of view is that it draws attention to the problems which arise in the deprived areas of towns and cities and it provided suggestions for improving the situation which found expression in the plans for Educational Priority Areas. The reading does, however, point out the enormous range of circumstances which helps to bring about and perpetuate the inequalities and adverse conditions which exist. The formulation of educational policy and the call for a new distribution of educational resources is set firmly within the broader context of priorities within society.

The consideration given to the training of teachers, and the kinds of attitudes and experiences they are likely to find during their training, is the subject of Michael Duane's article. He suggests that this area of education, among other things, is contradictory in its theories and incompetent in relating practice to precept. It is too easy to assume that because numbers in training are increasing the situation is improving and educational standards are getting better. Equally, it is misleading to assume that if teachers are given background in particular subjects, of relevance to society, that this will have any influence on the enormous majority of already qualified teachers who have not progressed through such courses. So there is much more of a need to be critical than complacent with what is provided. The educational system is a most sensitive index of the most important assumptions in our society, and the unsatisfactory place that those who are not middle class have in it are spelled out. Authoritarian views of relationships are illustrated, notably in the paradoxical example of the college, like so many, dedicated to child-centred education, which in its organisational form remained effectively authoritarian.

Most discussion about the organisation of education goes on with reference to the schools, but as with the previous reading, that by Dr. Georgiades has been selected from elsewhere in the educational structure; in fact from the field of further education. He considers why change is essential in its administrative structure because, for example, of growth in size, lack of agreement as to the nature of the task to be accomplished and the need for a developing view of objectives and tasks. The objectives of educational institutions and the development of strategies appropriate to changing conditions are viewed in relation to the new understanding of what man demands from work which takes into account personal needs. The criteria on organisational health which is presented can be considered in other contexts and the awareness that informs the article is of the inevitability of pressures for change, and the irrelevance of some often-used methods of maintaining effectiveness.

Graduate unemployment is something that has had little impact historically in Britain. One of the most significant differences between Britain and Germany during the depression in the inter-war period was the low proportion of white-collar workers in Britain who became unemployed as compared with the large numbers in Germany. This had important political consequences which could be relevant to Britain in the future. With examples from the experience of particular people, Chris Phillips talks about the relevance of the syllabus and the general approach of students to their work against the background of industrial recession, graduate unemployment and a still rapidly expanding university population. He examines the relatively inflexible structure of some industry against the desire of many graduates for a socially relevant and satisfying career, which can lead to people dropping-out of employment. Finally there is the question of how far there are going to be jobs for all the aspiring technocrats who have been brought into universities or to take degrees but who cannot command the confidence or the money within industry to employ them.

Children and their Primary Schools

Reprinted with permission from *Children and their Primary Schools*, A report of the Central Advisory Council for Education (England), Volume 1, (the Plowden Report), HMSO, 1967, pp. 50–5.

The task of abstracting and measuring the impact made by the principal influences that shape the educational opportunities of children, and to assess and compare their importance when 'all other things are equal' is the continuing concern of research workers. But policy makers and administrators must act in a world where other things never are equal; this, too, is the world in which the children grow up, where everything influences everything else, where nothing succeeds like success and nothing fails like failure. The outlook and aspirations of their own parents; the opportunities and handicaps of the neighbourhood in which they live; the skill of their teachers and the resources of the schools they go to; their genetic inheritance; and other factors still unmeasured or unknown surround the children with a seamless web of circumstance.

In a neighbourhood where the jobs people do and the status they hold owe little to their education it is natural for children as they grow older to regard school as a brief prelude to work rather than an avenue to future opportunities. Some of these neighbourhoods have for generations been starved of new schools, new houses and new investment of every kind. Everyone knows this; but for year after year priority has been given to the new towns and new suburbs, because if new schools do not keep pace with the new houses some children will be unable to go to school at all. The continually rising proportion of children staying on at school beyond the minimum age has led some authorities to build secondary schools and postpone the rebuilding of older primary schools. Not surprisingly, many teachers are unwilling to work in a neighbourhood where the schools are old, where housing of the sort they want is unobtainable, and where education does not attain the standards they expect for their own children. From some neighbourhoods, urban and rural, there has been a continuing outflow of the more successful young people. The loss of their enterprise and skill makes things worse for those left behind. Thus the vicious circle may turn from generation to generation and the schools play a central part in the process, both causing and suffering cumulative deprivation.

The educational needs of deprived areas

What these deprived areas need most are perfectly normal, good primary schools alive with experience from which children of all kinds can benefit. What we say elsewhere about primary school work generally applies equally to these difficult areas. The best schools already there show that it is absurd to say, as one used to hear, 'it may be all very well in a nice suburb, but it won't work here'. But, of course, there are special and additional demands on teachers who work in deprived areas with deprived children. They meet special challenges. Teachers must be constantly aware that ideas, values and relationships within the school may conflict with those of the home, and that the world assumed by teachers and school books may be unreal to the children. There will have to be constant communication between parents and the schools if the aims of the schools are to be fully understood. The child from a really impoverished background may well have had a normal, satisfactory emotional life. What he often lacks is the opportunity to develop intellectual interests. This shows in his poor command of language. It is not, however, with vocabulary that teaching can begin. The primary school must first supply experiences and establish relationships which enable children to discriminate, to reason and to express themselves. Placing such children in the right stance for further learning is a very skilled operation. But those who have done remedial work will be aware of the astonishing rapidity of the progress which can be achieved, particularly in extending vocabulary, once children's curiosity is released. The thrust to learn seems to be latent in every child, at least within a very wide range of normality. But however good the opportunities, some children may not be able to take advantage of them. Failure may have taken away from them their urge to learn.

A teacher cannot and should not give the deep, personal love that each child needs from his parents. There are ways he can help:

(a) He can relieve children of responsibility without dominating them in a way which prevents them from developing independence. Deprived children may have been forced into premature responsibility. They are often given the care of younger children and are free to roam, to go to bed or to stay up, to eat when and where they can. This produces what is often a spurious maturity. Confidence can be encouraged by tasks which are fully within their capacity. A measure of irresponsibility has to be allowed for: it will pretty certainly come later, and in a less acceptable form, if not permitted at the proper time.

(b) A teacher can do much by listening and trying to understand the context of the questions the children ask. It will be much easier if he knows the child's family and the neighbourhood surrounding his home.

(c) Children in deprived neighbourhoods are often backward. There is a risk that an inexperienced teacher will think there is not time for anything but the three Rs if the child is not to be handicapped throughout his life. This is quite wrong. These children need time for play and imaginative and expressive work and may suffer later if they do not get it at school.

(d) Teachers need to use books which make sense to the children they teach. They will often have to search hard for material which is suitable for down-town children.

(e) Record keeping is especially necessary for teachers in schools in deprived neighbourhoods. There is so much coming and going by families that a child's progress may depend very much on the amount and quality of information that can be sent with him from school to school.

Hope for the future

In our cities there are whole districts which have been scarcely touched by the advances made in more fortunate places. Yet such conditions have been overcome and striking progress has been achieved where sufficiently determined and comprehensive attack has been made on the problem. In the most deprived areas, one of H.M. Inspectors reported, 'Some heads approach magnificence, but they cannot do everything ... The demands on them as welfare agents are never ending.' Many children with parents in the least skilled jobs do outstandingly well in school. The educational aspirations of parents and the support and encouragement given to children in some of the poorest neighbourhoods are impressive. Over half of the unskilled workers in our National Survey want their children to be given homework to do after school hours; over half want their children to stay at school beyond the minimum leaving age. One third of them hoped their children would go to a grammar school or one with similar opportunities. The educational aspirations of unskilled workers for their children have risen year by year. It has been stressed to us that the range of ability in all social classes is so wide that there is a great reservoir of unrealised potential in families dependent on the least skilled and lowest paid work. A larger part of the housing programme than ever before is to be devoted to rebuilding and renewing obsolete and decaying neighbourhoods. The opportunity must be seized to rebuild the schools as well as the houses, and to see that both schools and houses serve families from every social class. It will be possible to make some progress in reducing the size of classes in primary schools in these areas as well as elsewhere. Colleges of education which have taken a special interest in deprived areas report that their students respond in an encouraging fashion to be the challenge of working in these neighbourhoods. Most important of all, there is a growing awareness in the nation at large, greatly stimulated, we believe, by our predecessors' Reports, of the complex social handicaps afflicting such areas and the need for a more radical assault on their problems. These are the strengths on which we can build. How can they be brought to bear?

We propose a nation-wide scheme for helping those schools and neighbourhoods in which children are most severely handicapped. This policy will have an influence over the whole educational system, and it colours all the subsequent recommendations in our Report. It must not be put into practice simply by robbing more fortunate areas of all the opportunities for progress to which they have been looking forward; it can only succeed if a larger share of the nation's resources is devoted to education. So far-reaching a set of proposals must be firmly rooted in educational grounds, yet the arguments for them inevitably extend beyond this field into many other branches of the nation's affairs. Before explaining these proposals we give a brief outline of the reasoning which led us to make them.

Education assumptions and policies

Our study of these problems compelled us to consider the process of economic and social development and the contribution made to it by the schools. Industrial development in many respects is the motor of social progress. We recognise that there are limits to the resources that can be mobilised for education and the primary schools. But it does not necessarily follow, as many have assumed, that the fruits of economic growth, together with the present pattern of public services, will in time give every child increasing opportunities of contributing to the nation's progress. It does not follow that education, because its development depends in the long run on the growth of the economy, must therefore follow in its wake, rather than contribute to the promotion of growth. Nor does it follow that a 'fair' or 'efficient' distribution of educational resources is one that provides a reasonably equal supply of teachers, classrooms, and other essentials to each school child in each area. Nor does it follow that the government's responsibility for promoting progress within the limits permitted by these resources must be confined to encouraging development in the most capable areas, spreading word of their progress to others, and pressing on the rearguard of the laggard or less fortunate whenever opportunity permits. Though many of these assumptions are already being questioned or abandoned, our own proposals are unlikely to convince those who still accept them, and we must, therefore, challenge each in turn.

During the Second World War there was a considerable improvement in the living conditions which bear most directly upon children in deprived groups and areas. In spite of this there has not been any appreciable narrowing of the gap between the least well off and the rest of the population. This is most obvious among children, particularly those in large families. 'It is ... clear that, on average, the larger families in all classes, and also those containing adolescents and children, constitute the most vulnerable groups nutritionally.' Signs of rickets have recently been reported again from the slums of Glasgow; mortality among children during the first year of life has fallen sharply since 1950, but the difference between social classes remains great. Much the same goes for stillbirth rates which, in different social classes 'despite a dramatic wartime fall, were as far apart in 1950 as in 1939'. Meanwhile 'class differentials in perinatal mortality are as resistant to change as those of infant mortality. The results of the (Perinatal Mortality) Survey suggest, indeed, that the gap may be increasing rather than narrowing'. The Milner Holland Committee's study of housing conditions in London covered a period in which this country probably achieved a faster rate of economic growth than it has ever experienced before, and an area in which conditions are generally better and improving faster than elsewhere. But it showed· that progress has been most rapid in those parts of the town where conditions were already best. In less fortunate neighbourhoods there has been less improvement and in some respects an appreciable deterioration. Families with low incomes and several children were among those who suffered most.

If the fruits of growth are left to accumulate within the framework of present policies and provisions, there is no assurance that the living conditions which handicap educationally deprived children will automatically improve—still less that the gap between these conditions and those of more fortunate children will be narrowed.

The contribution made by education to economic development poses complicated questions, upon which systematic research has only recently begun, and we cannot present firm conclusions about it. Comparisons with other countries—all of them more recently industrialised than Britain but all now at a similar stage of economic development—suggest that we have not done enough to provide the educational background necessary to support an economy which needs fewer and fewer unskilled workers and increasing numbers of skilled and adaptable people. One example can be drawn from a pioneer piece of research in comparative educational achievements. This compares mathematical skills at several stages of secondary education. It shows that in the early stages England was distinguished from other countries not by the average standard attained (which was closely similar to the average for the other countries compared) but the scatter of its results. English children achieved more than their share of the best results, and more of the worst results. Our educational system, originally moulded by the impress of Victorian economic and social requirements, may not yet have been fully adapted to present needs. In the deprived areas with which this chapter is concerned too many children leave school as soon as they are allowed to with no desire to carry their education further and without the knowledge to fit them for a job more intellectually demanding than their father's or their grandfather's. Yet they face a future in which they must expect during their working life to have to change their job, to learn new skills, to adapt themselves to new economic conditions and to form new human relationships. They will suffer, and so will the economy; both needlessly. It should not be assumed that even the ablest children can surmount every handicap. They may suffer as much as any from adverse conditions.

If the schools are to play their part in resolving and forestalling these problems much of the action required must be taken at the secondary and higher stages of the system. But this action cannot be fully effective if it does not touch the primary schools. Recent research has shown how early in the lives of children the selective processes begin to operate. There are primary schools from which scarcely any children ever take a secondary school course which leads them to 'O' level in G.C.E. Children of good potential ability enter them, but the doors to educational opportunity have already closed against them when their schooling has scarcely begun. Reforming zeal and expenditure directed to later stages of education will be wasted unless early handicaps can be reduced.

The schools unaided cannot provide all the opportunities their pupils deserve, or create the labour force this country needs. Industry, and the authorities responsible for housing, planning, employment and other services must also play their part. But, from the earliest stages of education, the schools enlarge or restrict the contribution their pupils can make to the life of the nation. Money spent on education is an investment which helps to determine the scope for future economic and social development.

Our argument thus far can be briefly summarised. As things are at the moment there is no reason why the educational handicaps of the most deprived children should disappear. Although standards will rise, inequalities will persist and the potential of many children will never be realised. The range of achievement amongst English children is wide, and the standards attained by the most and the least successful begin to diverge very early. Steps should be taken to improve the educational chances and the attainments of the least well placed, and to bring them up to the levels that prevail generally. This will call for a new distribution of educational resources.

The Training of Teachers
Michael Duane

Reprinted with permission from Michael Duane, 'The Training of Teachers', *Technical Education and Industrial Training*, 10, 3, pp. 92–3, 96.

If ever there was an area in education almost totally lacking in coherent form, befuddled and contradictory in its theories and chronically incompetent in relating practice to precept, then it can be seen in that part of education concerned with the training of teachers.

Such a statement will make some lecturers in departments and colleges of education feel resentful or hurt, or will cause them to dismiss it as a gross over-simplification. Some, however, will recognize that there is enough substance in it to prevent easy acceptance of the complacent 'All's well!' that accompanies every announcement of a steady rise in the number of students being trained. Too many teachers leave the profession within the first year, just as too many fail to complete their courses.

From one college alone in the year 1967–8 six students fell into the first category and five into the second. Within the two-year period 1966–8 I myself encountered 40 young teachers who had gained high marks in both theory and practice but had left teaching within months of starting. Among the reasons given for leaving were (a) that they had found the formality of staff and pupil relations to be more than they could stomach, (b) that they were prevented from putting into practice what they had gained from their training and because over-large classes prevented individual treatment of children, (c) that the specialist bias in the timetable prevented them meeting their own forms for more than two hours a week, (d) that the training they had received in understanding problems of 'discipline' had no relevance to the actual problems encountered . . .

Unsatisfactory conditions or attitudes in schools used for teaching practice may not easily be susceptible to change by the colleges, but those colleges are surely not compelled to send their students to such schools? One young man whose main subject was craftwork had to spend a month in a secondary modern school. When he was allowed a period of unsupervised teaching the regular teacher took himself off to the staffroom for a smoke. The student found the storeroom in a muddle so that he had to allow the boys to look for their own work from the previous week. As most of that work had not been marked, squabbles followed about ownership.

Instead of a set of tools at each work bench he found a couple of files worn to the state of uselessness. The usable tools had been locked away for 'safety', but the teacher refused to release more than four files and a hacksaw. I asked the student whether he had complained to his tutor. He had, but the tutor had replied that the college could not complain to the school for fear of losing places for teaching practice!

A woman student, giving experience of finger painting and water play to a group of five-year-olds in an East End school in the restricted space of an old-fashioned room and a corridor, was loudly rebuked in front of the children when they accidentally spilt water in the corridor, even though when the headmistress arrived they were helping the student to mop it up. 'These children come to school to work, not to play, and the sooner they learn that, the better. They will get on only by hard work, not by play!'

The tutor in question is still fondly under the impression that this is a 'progressive' school and speaks highly of the children's work in the hall. When I looked at this work I found that it consisted of outline drawings of various spring flowers done by the teacher, with the stems painted green and small pieces of coloured paper to represent petals stuck on by the children. Some of the reasons for disillusionment lie in the colleges themselves. One widespread complaint is that students are compelled to attend lectures to hear material more lucidly presented in books or on film. I have met this complaint very often among older men and women who have already brought up their own families and have fallen out of the habits of systematic study.

*   *   *

Many colleges preach the doctrine of child-centred education but fail to implement this in the form of student-centred education within their own domain. One college which proclaims its belief in freedom for students as an essential prerequisite for the development of personal responsibility neatly divides certain functions between the Principal and the Vice-Principal so that the latter carries the burden of 'disciplining' the students as required, and has set himself the task of 'stamping out lechery' in the mixed residential block and 'persuading' undesirable students—i.e. those who are suspected of smoking 'hash' or of consorting with people who do—to leave the college. The Principal makes a point of being 'approachable' to students and creating an atmosphere of relaxed rationality associated with her Quaker beliefs. Students who attempt to have the more restrictive disciplinary activities of the Vice-Principal modified or, at least, made the subject of joint staff-student discussion, find that the Principal refuses to involve herself in the duties delegated to her colleagues since she has 'complete faith' in them. The result is a mounting sense of frustration among the more socially conscious students.

In matters of personal distress, as when an unmarried student is found to be pregnant, staff action is sympathetic and helpful, but largely confined to closing stable doors after the horses have bolted. Student attempts to anticipate such disasters by making public the names and location of doctors or clinics ready to give contraceptive advice are gently dissuaded.

At another college a student was told that he could either wear a tie to main lectures or leave the college. He left and is now teaching at a private school, running a science laboratory cum workshop that is always alive with children busily absorbed in their various interests.

In all this it is the element of 'double-think' that the students so strongly resent. A recent example of this was provided on television by the headmaster of a large London boys' 'comprehensive' school who refuses to accept that corporal punishment is a form of physical violence. What on earth he thinks it to be no one has yet discovered! Perhaps he believes that the weals raised by the cane are a kind of spiritual stigmata springing from the intensity of guilt experienced by the sufferer rather than from the energy expended by the beater.

It is, perhaps, a recognition that the 'practical' advice they so often feel compelled to tender to their students in the privacy of their rooms cannot be reconciled with the theoretical abstractions that flow so easily from the platform, that makes many lecturers unable or unwilling to consider in depth fundamental topics such as 'discipline' or 'interest'; or to examine why it has been found possible to outlaw corporal punishment for young people in the army and the navy, whereas teachers insist on its retention in spite of the mounting evidence that it is associated with sexual perversion. The 'double-think' becomes blatant when the majority of people now accept that homosexuality must be confined to consenting adults in private but teachers seek to maintain legal authority for their perversion under the canting guise of 'character building'.

It is not enough, however, to list the absurdities, the muddles, the eccentricities or the plain dishonesty that bedevil teacher training. Most lecturers, however pedestrian the quality of their teaching, are actuated by a genuine concern for their students. They are more than normally preoccupied with questions of human value and purpose. The causes of the disharmony, typified by the few examples I have quoted, lie in the character-structures of both lecturers and students. The character-structures that give rise to self-deceit, timidity, lack of principle and a terror of non-conformity are themselves the product of personal relationships created by the forms of mass-production that dominate not only this country but the whole Western world.

Every society seeks to perpetuate its own values, beliefs and the forms of its social relationships—its culture. Its education system is a most sensitive index of its most important assumptions. In this country grammar schools and modern schools, at secondary level; universities and colleges of education or of further education at tertiary level, reflect the basic division of working class and middle class. In teacher training the university departments of education cater for grammar schools and the colleges of education for the rest. The mad scramble to get on the BEd wagon is an index of the sense of academic inferiority felt by the staffs of those college vis-à-vis university departments.

Our society, grossly inefficient by the standards of America, Germany or Japan, has, in common with all other capitalist countries, geared all activities and all valuations to its central drive—profitability. Money has become the index of effectiveness or value. But whereas the processes needed in production are now immensely complex, requiring the participation of thousands and sometimes of millions of people from raw material to finished product, the ownership and control of these vast social activities are vested in individuals or small groups not subject to the control of their workers. The Beeching formula applied to the railways was primarily whether particular lines were making a profit, not whether they were satisfying a human need in linking small or remote villages to larger towns.

But the further effect of the application of power to industry, seen particularly in the system of mass-production, has been to break down the complex and far-sighted skills of the old craftsman into the 'thinking' activities of the designers, planners, directors and managers on the one hand, and the routine, machine-like activities of the skilled and the unskilled workers on the other. Divisions in the education system reflect this basic division in productive function. The grammar school and the university produce the 'thinkers' while the modern school produces the workers who, more and more, are regarded as appendages to machines, to be replaced as quickly as possible by increasingly complicated forms of automatic control.

The function of the old elementary schools was to train the workers in habits of industry, sobriety and, above all, of unquestioning obedience. That of the newer modern schools started on much the same lines, but since the last war, as job-mobility increased through the introduction of new machines, new materials and new forms of organisation and control, teachers have found themselves more and more at a loss to know *what* to teach. They have, therefore, been thrown back on the idea of educating 'for leisure', or 'for life' rather than simply 'for work'.

The grammar schools and the universities have had no such problem. Their function has always been and will, for the foreseeable future, be concerned with communication, whether scientific, mathematical or linguistic. This is what for the upper middle class life is all about. And since they are the controllers and the executors of policy at the higher levels they have always accepted the values of capitalism and have, therefore, regarded workers as wayward, if necessary, extensions of the machine and the production line. The scorn for manual labour, so often associated with Greek philosophy and culture, is also an inescapable by-product of the division of labour.

A further by-product of the division of both labour and education is authoritarianism; the high valuation of power and the exercise of power not only for the useful results that follow, but for the feeling of importance or of self-justification that it gives.

The academic system evolved for the selection of the 'thinkers', those destined to control the economy, but in an increasingly technical society education has come to mean the amassing of facts and technically useful knowledge. Since knowledge has, within the last 100 years, multiplied at an accelerating rate, entrance to the limited amount of higher education available has become steadily more competitive. Inevitably, therefore the ambitious student has to eschew distractions in the interests of amassing facts. Less and less time is free for the leisurely pursuit of his own interests. Books—second, third, fourth, nth-hand information and opinion—become his central preoccupation. He comes to depend on 'experts' and 'authorities' rather than on his own experience. His own opinions are discounted in favour of the regurgitated opinions of others. By the time he is an adolescent his own natural impulses, feelings, judgements and opinions have been largely stultified. He has ceased to have confidence in the validity of his feelings and so comes to devalue himself as a person. Therefore he turns to authority—in religion, in politics. He needs a Leader to know what to believe and what to do. He is, psychologically, a budding fascist who, given certain political or economic conditions, will become a full-blown fascist. The persistent negation of his impulses and the invalidation of his sense of personal worth compel him to depend on the opinions of others, the possession of property or the exercise of power to create a sense of self-esteem.

So, in the teacher, at whatever level, this inbuilt authoritarianism conflicts with the urge to accept the child or the student for himself. Child- or student-centred education, resting on whatever traces of respect for the individual survive the ruthless academic process, is repeatedly swamped by panic reversions to authoritarianism as the heavily conditioned behaviour reasserts itself whenever authority looks critically at the teacher.

Further, this internal conflict, seen in nearly all teachers, however authoritarian or however liberal, is intensified by, to use Suttie's phrase, our 'taboo on tenderness' or by the taboo on sex. By making sex a matter of guilt and anxiety there is created in every individual in our culture a conflict between his own natural drives to satisfy *all* his impulses, and the fear of what society, or God, will do to him if he does so, and since such conflict is about the most important thing in our lives—love—the conflict is long and intense.

So in industrial society increasingly we see apathy (lack of energy for creative purposes), neurosis (substitute gratifications for a full sexual life) and violence (the reaction to the overt and covert violence used by adults in the conditioning of the young into the character-structures required to make people accept their part in the machine without undue protest). It is, therefore, hardly a matter of surprise that it is in education and especially in teacher training that gimmicry, duplicity, and lack of principle are only too obvious and that the unending conflict between the conditioning of the lecturers and their natural respect for persons manifests itself in the lack of coherence and direction in their work.

The New Organization Men
N. J. Georgiades

Reprinted with permission from N. J. Georgiades, 'The New Organization Men', *Education and Training*, January 1972, pp. 6–8.

This is a tough time for the bureaucrats. The pressures on the traditional administrative structure of further education are immense yet, surprisingly, the need for reform is not yet widely recognized. There are three basic reasons why change is essential.

First, there is the continuing growth in the size of our educational institutions. While in theory there need be no limit to the height of a bureaucratic pyramid, in practice greater complexity is introduced along with an increase in size. The problem is already serious ... What is required to deal with this phenomena are new management strategies.

Secondly, there is still a total lack of agreement as to the nature of the task that has to be accomplished in further education. Contrast the extent of current graduate unemployment with the past pronouncements of the Committee on Scientific Manpower which has consistently prophesied a continuing shortage of scientists and techologists. Naturally enough, the concept of vocationally orientated education is now under heavy attack and strong arguments are advanced for broadening course bases.

But whatever the views for those who determine the corporate objectives of educational institutions, one thing is clear. Staff will not readily commit themselves to changes in objectives which are handed down in the traditional demanding bureaucratic manner. As Mager has pointed out: 'Exhortation is used more and accomplishes less than any behaviour changing tool known to man'. To achieve commitment to new objectives and new tasks, educational authorities must turn away from the traditional practices of bureaucracy and replace them with strategies more appropriate to new and changing demands, both from external pressures like the Department of Education and Science and the local education authorities and from those within the institutions (ie the students and staff).

The third threat to bureaucracy is a new understanding of what man requires from work. Bennis suggests that 'there is a subtle but perceptible change in the philosophy underlying management behaviour'. He believes that the change rests upon three new concepts:

1. An idea of man based on increased knowledge of his complex and shifting needs, which replaces an oversimplified, innocent push button concept of man.

2. An idea of power, based on collaboration and reason, which replaces a model of power based upon coercion and threat.

3. An idea of organizational values, based on humanistic democratic ideas, which replaces the depersonalized, mechanistic value system of bureaucracy.

These three concepts derive from observations of commercial and industrial organizations whose leaders, no less than the leaders of educational organizations, need to discover and to optimally mobilize human resources and energy to achieve corporate objectives. At the same time they recognize that they must maintain a viable, dynamic and developing organization, which is responsive to internal demands for change, and at the same time is responsive to employees' personal needs for self-worth, growth, and work satisfaction.

Today most industrial managers are deeply concerned with the problem of developing strategies appropriate to changing conditions. They recognize the need for a flexible organization which can move with changing requirements, which can be 'pro-active' rather than simply reactive. They are seeking ways to establish a work climate in which increasingly complex decisions can be made by people who possess the appropriate information regardless of their rank in the pecking order. They are looking for means by which increasingly complex technologies can be managed by people with an advanced sense of freedom and autonomy.

Such problems occupy many hours of management thought and many chapters of management text-books. Has this in any way influenced the policies of the college administrators? Are they even aware of what is being taught in their own departments of management studies? It can only be hoped that some interchange does exist. But if we accept Eric Robinson's comment that 'Heads of Department are often virtually out of touch with what goes on in their colleagues' classrooms', then perhaps the educational administrators do have something to learn from the teachers of management science, particularly those concerned with the impact of behavioural science in management.

The immediate temptation is to conclude that a few management training courses for educational administrators is the easy solution. Katz and Kahn summarize the weaknesses of assuming that changing individuals by training can lead to a change in organizations. They say: 'The essential weakness of the individual approach is the psychological fallacy of concentrating upon individuals without regard to the role-relationships that constitute the social system of which they are a part. The assumption has been that since the organization is made up of individuals, we can change the organization by changing its members. This is not so much an illogical proposition as it is an oversimplification which neglects the interrelationships of people in any organizational structure and fails to point to the aspects of individual behaviour which need to be changed.'

The assumption that a newly trained administrator (whether Director, Registrar, Bursar or Head of Department) will return from a management training course and adopt the role of 'hero-innovator' has long ago been disproved by researchers. As Katz and Kahn suggest, more attention must be paid not to selected individuals within the organization, but to the organization as a whole.

In recent years behavioural scientists have talked of 'organizational health' in much the same way as we would talk of the health of a living organism. In attempting to define the parameters of healthy organizations the work of Miles is of immediate importance. Briefly, Miles outlines 10 major characteristics:

1. *Goal focus.* The goals are tolerably clear and acceptable to members.

2. *Adequate communication.* In a healthy organization there

is distortion-free communication 'vertically' and 'horizontally'. In other words, people have the information they need without chatting-up the Director's secretary or reading it in the local paper.

3. *Optimal power equalization.* The distribution of influence is relatively equitable. A subordinate (if there is a formal authority chart) can influence his boss and, even more important, he sees that his boss can do likewise with *his* boss. Thus, wherever an individual is placed in a hierarchy, or whatever his degree of personal charisma, he may influence a particular issue, providing he has the information which is relevant to the problem.

4. *Resource-utilization.* A healthy organization is one in which optimal use is made of all available human and physical resources. The overall feeling is that people are neither overloaded nor idle. They may be working very hard indeed, but they feel that they are not working against themselves or against the organization.

5. *Cohesion.* Members want to stay with the organization, be influenced by it and exert their own influence in the collaborative style suggested above.

6. *Morale.* In a healthy organization the majority of the individuals express sentiments of well-being, satisfaction and pleasure. This would involve, for instance, abandoning the assumption that the sole source of job satisfaction for college staff is that derived from working with students. The implication of the concept of 'morale' places far greater responsibility for overall job satisfaction upon the administrative heads of department.

7. *Innovativeness.* There is always scope for new procedures and moves towards new goals. Contrast the concept with Eric Robinson's recent comment: 'We don't take enough notice of the inertia of the system, it is always easier to get something conventional . . .'

8. *Autonomy.* A healthy organization, according to Miles, responds constructively to external demands for change while retaining its independence.

9. *Adaptation.* The implication behind this concept is that when environmental demands and organizational resources do not match, a problem-solving restructuring approach evolves in which both the environment and the organization becomes different in some respect. As Miles points out 'Explanations for the disappearance of dinosaurs vary, but it is quite clear

that in some way this criterion of adapting was not met'.

10. *Problem-solving adequacy.* This is linked closely with the organization's ability to adapt. The issue is not the presence or absence of problems since these exist in all organizations, but the *manner* in which the organization copes with its problems. A healthy organization has well-developed structures and procedures for sensing the existence of problems, inventing possible solutions, deciding on the solutions, implementing them and evaluating their effectiveness.

There are clearly a number of difficulties in applying these general concepts to educational institutions. First, there is the problem inherent in the use of the word 'health'. As Miles admits educational administrators have enough difficulties without being accused of 'being at the helm of pathological vessels on the stormy seas in innovation'. The image of 'sickness' tends to divert attention away from the notions of growth and development. Secondly, educational institutions possess a number of characteristics which differentiate them from industrial and commercial organizations. For instance, there is the difficulty of specifying precisely the nature of their output; the problem of defining precise corporate objectives; the variability of the input both in terms of students and staffs and the high level of autonomy and low interdependence of the teacher which tends to reinforce pyramidal 'man-to-man' supervisory styles by heads of departments.

In all these and other respects educational institutions do not conform to traditional industrial and commercial organizational patterns. However, it can reasonably be argued that the state of health of an educational organization can tell us more than anything else about the probable success of that institution in coping with pressures for change. Moreover, looking at the state of an organization's health, and trying to improve it, is preferable both to extensive management training programmes for selected individuals and to a series of one-off simply-mix-with water solutions to organizational problems.

Graduate Unemployment
Chris Phillips

Reprinted with permission from Chris Phillips, 'Mike Hammond, Road-sweeper, B.Sc.', *Industrial Management*, February 1972, pp. 14–20.

The aftermath of industrial recession and a rapidly expanding university population are not the only reasons for the disturbingly high number of graduates joining Britain's dole queues or taking menial jobs.

There is a third factor which is vitally significant because it apparently brings into question the whole purpose of industry in society. It would seem that a highly significant number of bright young academics are deliberately opting out of the long-established custom of going from school to higher education, and then on to a career job because they are simply disenchanted with the idea. With almost impudent disregard for degree qualifications, they are swapping laboratory test tubes for a road sweeper's brush and slide rules for a bus conductor's ticket machine. It is their way of showing disapproval of what one student describes as 'the educational sausage machine'.

It would be wrong to ascribe this attitude as being responsible for most of today's graduate unemployment or 'misemployment'. Thousands of young people who left university last summer are either out of work, or doing jobs way below their ability because of the labour shake-out generally.

The latest figures published by the University Grants Committee (UGC) show that a total of 5.4 per cent or nearly 2,500 graduates, were out of work six months after leaving university —more than double the figure for 1965. However, this was for 1969–70, and unofficial, but reliable, estimates indicate that the jobless figure has nearly doubled again in just a year, to about 10 per cent.

The refusal to go into status jobs is not a new phenomenon. The attitude has always existed amongst a tiny minority. But the majority of those people intimately concerned with graduates, and noticeably those whose work is connected with the stage when they actually make their first move after obtaining degrees, see this growing at a disproportionate rate to the ever increasing number of those graduating every year.

Industry has not given undue recognition to this development because of the large recruitment pool. With only a limited number of jobs available, companies can afford to be selective, choosing only those candidates who play by the rules, and who genuinely want to find work matching their qualifications.

But the Confederation of British Industry is calling for steps to counter 'graduates' suspicions and criticisms of industry'. It supports the growing belief that young people ought to have some sort of experience in jobs between leaving school and going to university. It also advocates planned vacation work and projects between school and industry.

The Confederation welcomes 'a significant increase' in collaboration between industry and universities over the past five years, but says there is still the need for a more active approach in many sectors of industry.

It is mainly university staff and students, however, who have noticed the non-conformist thinking and its potential.

Digby Jacks, president of the National Union of Students: 'There is a growing tendency, for two reasons, to question this automatic process of going straight from university into a career-type job. There are more students around with certain qualifications and not the jobs to absorb them, and the *more important* aspect—which has been particularly noticeable over the past five years—to question the value of the whole business.'

But Jacks believes that this could ultimately benefit British industry—especially in the field of labour relations. 'If you end up as a person of some importance, it doesn't do any harm to have spent some time in situations of people you eventually employ.

'The trouble with business in the past has been the old public school, Oxbridge, company boardroom cycle with all the cossetting and blinkered thinking that this as brought.'

But whatever industry may think of his analysis of graduate recruitment, it is clear that the situation of drop-outs does exist and has yet to be fully recognized.

Mike Hammond, 23, left Luton College of Technology in the summer of 1970 with an external degree in geology. For the past nine months his hippy-like appearance of shoulder-length hair, beard, faded Levis and blanket poncho has been seen around the streets of Luton where he works—for Hammond, BSc, is a roadsweeper.

He turned down a £1,000-a-year job with the National Coal Board as a geologist after leaving college. 'I think my lecturer made up my mind for me. He said "The NCB may need you, but do you need the NCB?" I decided I didn't.'

He made what he admits were several half-hearted attempts to find other jobs with industry before 'chucking it in' and collecting his road-sweeper's cart. Until a few weeks ago, he was averaging more than the £20-a-week he could have got from the NCB collecting fallen leaves. Now he is on night shift, nine hours-a-night, seven-days-a-week—at £70 a week.

'I wouldn't say that the job I'm doing is ideal. I've been trying to get a job as a driver, but they are soon snapped up,' he says. 'Quite honestly, I've got no clear idea of what I want to do. At the moment I can go where I please. With this job I can wear what I like, and I'm free to think.

'Later on I might try and get a job with the Forestry Commission, but if it's a nine-to-five thing where you have to wear a suit I'm not interested in that or any other work.'

One of Hammond's college friends also holds a degree—and is also roadsweeping. 'I think he wanted to go into teaching, but his ideas aren't exactly in accord with the system,' said Hammond with a smile.

And anyone who is prepared to dismiss Hammond as a hippie drop-out should consider the case of Valerie Brand.

After more than five years swotting over law books, she qualifies this month as a fully-fledged solicitor—and she's thinking of then taking a job as a bistro waitress.

Naturally, it is impossible to gauge how many graduates reject good jobs. Indeed, the whole subject—viewed in relation to the country's jobless crisis—can only be a well-informed guess.

Neither the Department of Education nor the UGC, which looks after university spending, keep an up to date file of national statistics. To review the situation on a monthly basis, like the Department of Employment does generally, would entail contacting each of 43 UK universities. Their appointments boards are the principal agents for arranging jobs, but even here statistics are misleading—many students find work without consulting them, or tell the boards they are out of work and don't bother to notify them when they find a job.

* * *

Hardest hit are the engineering and science graduates, who view their position with a good deal of irony. For nearly 20 years science courses in the universities and polytechnics have been expanded enormously to cope with the expected technology boom.

Higher education has now reached a bulge in these fields—and government policy, unless altered quickly, will make the situation even more chronic. Latest unofficial figures from the universities show that the number of science and engineering vacancies—about 5,500—are nearly 30% under-subscribed, while there are more than 10,000 prospective students jostling for little more than 2,000 arts and social science places.

Nevertheless, both the UGC and the Department of Education recognize that some alteration has to be made to end the imbalance. From now on, more arts places will be made available, but with the present university population totalling well over 200,000 this will not make any immediate impact. Sir Kenneth estimates that it will take until the end of the present decade before science and arts courses have equal presentation.

If the country's economic slump has done anything, it's to bring home to graduates the CBI working party's point about the need to be more flexible. The days when a degree was the passport to a good job are long since past—the past few months have proved that in many cases it's not a passport to a job at all. Digby Jacks: 'Graduates are no longer a privileged elite with easy access to top jobs, and socially this is a damn good thing. The reason for the fall-off in demand for science and engineering places at universities is because students realize there is a glut.'

He knocks down the view that higher education should prepare students for tailor-made jobs. 'It's no good basing it on the needs of industry and commerce because they tend to be extremely fickle. Requirements of the labour market change so quickly and it's foolish, indeed impossible, to adjust courses to keep pace. One year the demand might go out for more chemists, and the following year industry finds it has too many of them.

'Industry could probably absorb more graduates, but not in the sense that someone with certain qualifications could fit into a particular slot,' says Jacks. 'The general unemployment position has accentuated the tendency for higher education to be too specialized. The emphasis should be placed on a more general education, with the facilities for specialization if desired.'

While there are those who argue that too much specialization can result in a graduate being 'too academic and less adaptable outside the range of his subject', others fear that a more general education will produce, as one observer put it, 'jacks of all trades and masters of none'.

Another aspect was put to me by a professor with close industrial links. 'With all the publicity about student unrest and so on, there's not a lot of sympathy for them when there's a job shortage. The public both here and in America tend to take revenge on students, and their publicly-expressed left-wing sympathies, by bringing pressure on governments to cut down on grants. And a few companies no doubt react in the same way over employment.'

The professor commented on another aspect of graduate employment which, if it is becoming common, presents an obstacle to the CBI aims of bringing in university-educated labour at shop-floor level to train for managerial positions. 'An increasing number of engineering graduates who have been on the shop floor are fed up with the lack of any sort of intellectual climate. They have switched to careers in economics, accountancy, marketing and other professions. I think the principal bone of contention is this sergeants' mess atmosphere, where you have to do six months' basic training before you can touch a rifle. They want responsibility, but are not being given it.'

Far from cutting back on recruitment at the present time, he argued that industry would benefit by stepping up its intake. 'The time to take on graduates is when you have the time to absorb and train them, and slackness in past months would have suited this. But a company takes the view, understandably, that you can't hire young people at the same time you are making long-standing employees redundant.'

*   *   *

What of those who, like Mike Hammond, shun the whole concept of the university-career job system? According to the anonymous business school professor, that very idea is very much a reflection and rejection of thinking bred in the depression of the thirties. 'Father has impressed on son the need to get a "good job" because in his day there were no jobs going, full stop.

'But parental influence, in this respect, is lessening. Young people are no longer prepared to accept a way of life which they don't particularly enjoy.'

*   *   *

Stephen Perry, president of the students' union at University College, London, told me: 'Taking a job in industry is to conform to hours of work and behaviour which many students find unacceptable. While at university, they have been taught to question accepted attitudes and have worked when it suited them. Contrary to the popular view, this position of being your own boss doesn't make you workshy. I maintain they work as hard as anyone else.'

Perry, who worked as a warehouse packer before going to university to take a law degree, feels that courses are too academic and insufficiently vocational. Citing his own experience, he said: 'For three years I did nothing but take notes and absorb lots of facts so that I could spill them all out at exam time. You tend to lose sight, never going into magistrates' courts, for example, that law is to do with people.'

He believes the same shortcoming applies to engineering and the sciences; too much academic theory and too little—if any—first-hand involvement of industry actually at work.

On the question of student drop-outs, he said: 'It's the whole disillusioning set-up of massive unemployment, stop-go policies and political incompetence generally.

'Every day dozens of students come to University College through Euston station and they see the meths drinkers. They hear about the plight of the homeless and see racial discimination. It's these things that interest them—not big business where your sole aim is to make more profit.'

The equation of a number of different social problems which are then related to the industry demonstrates the mixed-up picture that students have of company activity and is hardly likely to bring a sympathetic understanding from boardrooms.

But if Britain is to keep pumping millions of pounds into higher education, some hard thinking needs to be done as to what it's all in aid of. Is it economically acceptable to produce scores of aspiring technocrats without the money or confidence from industry to make full use of their talents? And is it right that graduates, either through choice or necessity, should take a menial job which could be taken by a not-so-well qualified man in the dole queue?

The country's 'university bill' has gone from £58 million to £222 million in 10 years, and the Government has provisionally set aside another £26 million for this year. Purely in cash-saving terms, the disgruntled taxpayer argues 'Why should I have to pay for graduate education (the cost of a three-year science or engineering course is roughly £3,000) when there aren't the jobs for them?'

The same was said when secondary education became compulsory for all. 'Why teach so many children to read and write when there aren't enough jobs needing literacy?'

Further Reading: Education

w. g. BENNIS, *Organisational Development: its Nature, Origins and Prospects*, London, Addison-Wesley, 1969.

R. R. DALE and S. GRIFFITH, *Down Stream*, London, Routledge and Kegan Paul, 1965.

J. W. B. DOUGLAS, *The Home and the School*, London, MacGibbon and Kee, 1964.

* E. H. ERIKSON, *Childhood and Society*, Harmondsworth, Penguin, 1963.

D. KATZ and R. L. KAHN, *The Social Psychology of Organisation*, New York, McGraw-Hill, 1966.

R. S. MAGER, *Developing Attitude Towards Learning*, Palo Alto, Fearon, 1968.

J. B. MAYS, *Education and the Urban Child*, Liverpool, Liverpool University Press, 1962.

M. B. MILES, 'Planned Changed and Organisational Help' in R. O. Carlson (ed.), *Change Processes in Public Schools*, Eugene, Oregon, Centre for the Advanced Study of Educational Administration, 1965.

* F. MUSGROVE, *The Family, Education and Society*, London, Routledge and Kegan Paul, 1966.

S. WISEMAN, *Education and Environment*, Manchester, Manchester University Press, 1964.

* Available in paperback

Chapter Eight   Crime

In order to understand what 'crime' is we need to determine
how it comes about that certain forms of behaviour are defined
as fit and suitable targets for the system through which the
law operates—the system of criminal justice. Why are some
things defined as crime whilst others are not? Because, says the
facile response, crime is what is 'harmful to society'. But are all
things that are defined as 'harmful to society' to count as crime?
Certainly not. Is crime, then, behaviour which is typically the
prerogative of those whom we define as criminals? But what
do we know about 'criminals'? The answer, unfortunately, is
next to nothing.

In the metropolitan police area which comprises most of
London, the police claim at best to 'clear' one in three of
crimes which would conventionally be regarded as serious. But
this does not, of course, mean that for every crime known to
the police one individual is found to be uniquely responsible.
It is true that many crimes *are* cleared by arrest when the
offender is subsequently prosecuted for that crime. Others may
similarly be regarded as cleared if the police have the evidence
to prosecute someone but don't because he is being charged
with a more serious crime. But more important than either
of these are the crimes which are 'taken into consideration'.
In some parts of Britain about half of the crimes which are
'cleared by arrest' are in fact 'cleared' on the basis of the
T.I.C. This may mean that only about one in *six* of the crimes
which are known to the police are cleared in a uniquely
identifiable way.

But many crimes don't become 'known to the police' at all.
There may be good reasons for this of course. In some cases,
particularly those involving behaviour which is socially
stigmatised, the victim himself may be rather unwilling to go
to the police with a complaint; in others the victim and
criminal may be members of the same family. For some crimes
we can only at best make a wild guess at the numbers that are
'really' committed. Surveys of stock losses in retail trade

indicate that if one were to take, for example, the three
largest stores in a city the size of Manchester and calculate the
value of the stock written down by the management over a
period of twelve months because of shop-lifting or 'shrinkage'
due to suspected abstraction by members of the staff, the value
of the stock thus written down would be equal to the value of
the total sum of thefts reported to the police from domestic
premises and shops combined, for the whole city over the same
period of time. Even the 'major' crimes are not free from a
sneaking suspicion that we know only about the tip of the
iceberg. For every murder cleared by arrest, tracked down by
patient detective work in the manner of the best crime novels
and pinned on some identifiable murderer, there may
be a dozen names on missing persons records which could
quite conceivably be the subject of murder enquiries.

This kind of suspicion and scepticism might lead us to put
forward the proposition that we know nothing about 'crime'.
If we set out to test even the simplest of hypotheses, for
example that low intelligence is a cause of crime, our sample of
'criminals' is almost inevitably bound to be drawn from those
who have been *convicted* of some crime—in other words very
likely those who are at present in prison for such crimes, that
is not *criminals*, but convicts, or prisoners. It is very possible,
and researchers have of course done just this, that we may find
a reasonably clear and valid correlation between, say, a
measure of intelligence and crime. We could compare our
criminal group with the same age group, sex, social class and
so on in the population of 'normals' in the world outside the
prison gates. But what would we have proved if we were to
make such a discovery? Need it be anything more than the
much simpler proposition that we only catch stupid criminals?

Let us go back for a minute to the question with which we
started out. How does it come about and, more to the point,
why does it come about that certain kinds of behaviours are
defined as suitable targets for the system of criminal justice?
Why are certain types of behaviour prohibited by law? Why
are certain kinds of people treated in certain ways? It is
becoming clear that the 'facts' that we appear to have about
crime are a product not merely of the amount and distribution
of a given sort of behaviour, of a sort that we conventionally
regard as criminal, but are also to do with the seriousness with
which the behaviour is regarded in society at large. We have
to bear in mind as well the fact that some kinds of behaviour

are far more *visible* than others. There are crimes of high
visibility like assault, burglary, robbery and murder. There are
crimes of low visibility like fraud, embezzlement, certain types
of investment swindles and those interesting practices which
are only regarded as legitimate between consenting adults in
private. There are crimes where visibility is rather variable like
shop-lifting, certain forms of sexual offence like rape, and
crimes where the visibility may be concealed as much by the
victim as the criminal, like abortion.

Again, not all societies treat the same kind of behaviour as
crime. Adultery, that is fornication between unmarried persons,
is still a crime in some American states although admittedly
seldom prosecuted. Prostitution is not in itself a crime in
Britain but certain modes of organisation of the practice of
prostitution, in particular soliciting for custom in the streets,
have often been subject to the criminal law. From 1854 to 1961
attempted suicide was a crime in England although not in
Scotland. Even behaviour that may be regarded by the
majority with abhorrence, such as incest, has not always been
criminal. Incest, in fact, only became a criminal offence in
1908 as a result of pressure from the established Church of
England.

To the general reader of the popular press, there seems to be
no doubt at all about the 'facts' of the matter: crime, and in
particular violent crimes, is 'obviously' on the increase.
Moreover, the measures that are being taken seem impotent to
control this tidal wave of violence, promiscuity, permissiveness,
in fact each and every kind of unbridled lust, which is sweeping
the country. One imagines that some newspapers have an
all-purpose headline permanently set up in type on the lines of
'Immigrant Rapes Policeman, Thousands Homeless'. But in
fact crimes of violence account for only 2 per cent of all the
arrests in Britain: 70 per cent of arrests are made for
drunkenness, disorderly conduct, driving whilst under the
influence, motoring offences and various degrees and kinds of
petty theft. The specific implications of the all-purpose headline
would be misleading also. Whilst it is certainly the case that
immigrants tend to live in areas which have significantly higher
rates of crime than other parts of the city, it is also almost
certainly the case that immigrants themselves have a *lower*
rate of crime than that of the members of the host or native
population who live in the same areas. That is, immigrants are
less not more criminal than members of the host society,

despite living in a situation in which their exposure to crime is rather higher. In other words, they appear to resist the temptations of crime more successfully than do their native neighbours. (The inference that policemen are particularly liable to become victims of a rape attack would equally be a rather dangerous conclusion to draw from the facts as they are known to us.)

The fact is that when we are talking about crime we are not talking about something that is done *to* society as is implied by the unwise use of such phrases as 'the war of society against crime', or 'society against the criminal', or even such currently fashionable theories as those of 'social defence'. Crime is something that occurs *within* society, crime is part of the structure *of* society. Crime is a form of social behaviour that is governed by rules, precedents and conventions as any other kind of social interaction is. Whenever people interact with one another rules exist, rules may be broken and sanctions may be imposed on those who break the rules. We must ask questions about who is particularly liable to break the rules, who is particularly liable to make the rules, who tends to enforce the rules, and in whose interests the rules are made. Crime may therefore be regarded as a particular set of behaviour patterns identified by the operation of a particular social institution—the system of criminal justice.

Crime in the real sense, therefore, is something that is created by the law; crime is something that cannot exist, even conceptually, outside of measures that deal with it, measures to contain it, measures to produce it.

The operation of the criminal law does seem to identify a certain group of people as most liable to become involved in crime. They tend to be poor, to be ill-educated, to be relatively unsuccessful in interpersonal relations, to have unstable job records and so on and so on. *These are the people we catch.* And it is from people like these that we generalise the meagre knowledge we have to cover the whole complex field of crime.

We can draw one rather important inference from the kind of knowledge we do possess and that is that, regardless of the mechanisms, process or etiology that account for a person's *initial* involvement in the kind of behaviour that we call crime, once he has been apprehended, convicted and punished for it, his involvement in such behaviour in the future is more probable than is the involvement of others. In other words, once an individual has passed over some invisible but none the less significant barrier that demarcates the area of what is criminal, from what is normal, he becomes a different person, someone who is labelled, stigmatised and identified in more or less permanent fashion as a 'criminal'. The consequences of such stigmatisation may be particularly invidious. The *Sunday Express* of 11 March, 1971 carried a story of a man who was debarred by a local authority's social services department from adopting a child because of an incident that had led to his being brought before a Juvenile Court some twenty-two years previously. Despite the fact that the case had been discharged, and he had had no further blot on his record apart from a minor motoring offence during the intervening twenty-two years, he was felt to be an unsuitable person to adopt a child in the care of a local authority.

We argued just now that the war against crime is not a war of society against something being done to it by outsiders. Most social scientists, in seeking the causes of criminal behaviour, would look to the same social structures and to the same value systems as produce behaviour which is approved by members of society. Moreover, it would seem that the extent to which behaviour is regarded as a suitable subject for criminal sanctions depends equally as much on the social position of those who are making this judgement as it does on the objective harm that such behaviour does to society. If society, therefore, is creating crime, society also creates criminals. And the status of being a criminal is one that is ascribed. As Howard Becker says, 'social groups create deviance, by making the rules whose infraction constitutes deviance, and by applying those rules to particular people and labelling them as outsiders. Deviance is not a quality of the act but a consequence of the application by others of rules and sanctions to an offender. The deviant is one to whom that label has successfully been applied: deviant behaviour is behaviour that people so label.'

If we accept this orientation to the problem of crime we need to pay attention to the criminal career. If it makes little sense to ask what *causes* crime, it maybe makes much better sense to look for the points in an individual's career at which through a 'transformation of identity' he becomes more or less unequivocally criminal. What are the important turning points in such a process? The first of course is being caught. We have already seen that the odds against being caught are remarkably high. Certainly, the criminal may expect to have a better than one in ten chance of evading capture for any particular crime.

But once he is caught and has gone through the ritual process of being charged with an offence, being put through the courts and finally being identified unequivocally as a wrong-doer, he goes through a series of steps which amount in total to a ceremonial degradation. Through the degradation process the 'true' identity of the wrong-doer is revealed. The individual who is thus labelled as deviant now has a choice to make. Society has rejected him, but a group already exists which can offer him a new and viable identity. It can offer him a certain degree of social support and buffer him against the consequences of his degradation in the eyes of the rest of society. He can find a place in a cultural underworld which offers him the solidarity of the membership of a group and, moreover, a viable and acceptable moral career. Several writers have traced the consequences of this process which Lemert has called 'secondary deviation'.

But if we accept the kind of re-orientation to our approach to the problems of crime that would seem to be indicated by this thinking, what are we to do about the 'facts', presented daily through the mass media, of the enormous and apparently uncontrollable increase in crime of all kinds? Does this increase exist? If so, why? Some commentators on the problem refer to the escalation of violence and trace it back to the presentation of violence in the mass media. But are the protagonists of this point of view seriously suggesting that it is in fact less safe to walk down the streets of a major British city than it was fifty or a hundred years ago, or is it simply that, as in many other areas, our *tolerance* of what behaviour we will accept in public has changed? Is it not possible that the balance of the community level of tolerance has shifted back and forth over the centuries? The Victorians maintained a strict sexual morality supported, however, by the largest army of prostitutes that any society, civilised, or uncivilised, had ever known. It maintained a comfortable and secure existence for its middle classes on the basis of a vicious and brutal penal code based in the first half of the nineteenth century on transportation and in the second on penal servitude, oakum-picking and the Pentonville System. Is society really that much more in danger today? Again, the fair-minded social scientist would have to reply that he doesn't know.

One thing that we know all too little about is the field of professional crime. There is no doubt that some criminals, successful and professional, do exist. There is no doubt either that the machinery of law enforcement appears to cope most successfully only with the least successful criminals. Many *major* robberies in fact go undetected. Moreover, nobody knows the extent of many other kinds of (possibly successful) crime. One of the most disturbing possibilities of the present day is the prospect of a rapid growth in crimes associated with the introduction of advanced electronic data-processing systems. Computer crime, a horrendous new growth of the data-processing business, is becoming the least detectable and therefore just possibly the most successful form of crime. The alteration of one code on one document can lead to the systematic misappropriation over a long period of time of money, goods, materials and, by no means least, computer time itself. Because of its very nature computer crime is almost untraceable. Some of the favourite theories of sociologists seem bound to appear irrelevant to the understanding of this type of activity. Computer crime is not 'subcultural'. It seems to have little to do with 'differential association'. It seems that the 'focal concerns' of the underworld are irrelevant to it. Computer crime is crime committed by gentlemen (and ladies), in pin-striped suits and button-down shirts, with impressive qualifications and inevitably large bank balances. Their behaviour is intelligent and it is motivated. It is the archetypal example of what Edwin Sutherland, writing in 1939, referred to as 'white-collar crime'. Possibly this and not the granny attacked by a yobbo with a bicycle chain represents the most serious challenge to society over the next few decades.

Some statistical information on crime in England and Wales is provided by McClintock and Avison. Our discussion earlier in this introduction and throughout this collection of readings as a whole have sensitised us to the need to be wary, if not downright suspicious of official statistics of crime. And this point is developed at some length by Box in his book, suggested for further reading, on *Deviance, Reality and Society*. As Erikson has argued 'deviance is not a property inherent in certain forms of behaviour; it is a property conferred upon these forms by the audience who directly or indirectly witnesses them'. So McClintock and Avison's account of the increase in crime over the past few years provides the *start* of a series of questions and not the answer to them.

We have agreed that it makes little sense to talk of crime, still less of the causes of crime in abstract and general terms.

J. A. Mack's study is one of the very few which attempt to achieve an understanding of professional crime. While there have been studies of the Mafia and other American criminal organisations, there have been rather few attempts by British social scientists to study those criminals who are relatively successful in their activities. As Mack points out, statistically, the able criminal may not be very important. In terms of cost to the community, however, he may have an importance out of all proportion to his numbers. Mack argues that the able criminal is a member of a distinctive occupational tradition. It is difficult to achieve any very precise estimate of the numbers who fall into the category of 'able criminals', but Mack suggests that it may be as low as one to every ten thousand of the normal population. But it was only the 'text book criminals,' as Mack describes them, that had suffered from bad home circumstances and a lack of parental care, whose behaviour showed some emotional disturbance and who were judged to be of low intelligence, who had spent time in prison. The more normal the criminal, and the more he conformed to the stereotypes of acceptable behaviour, in every respect other than the fact that he lived a life of crime and earned a living from crime, the more likely it was that he would be *normal* in the respect that he had spent rather little of his adult life in penal institutions. Mack argues that a large proportion of major full-time criminals are both able and successful in their occupations.

Another species of law-breaking which does not normally figure in the annual criminal statistics is discussed by Carson, who studied a particular type of white-collar crime, the infringement of factory legislation. He points out that it is only recently that sociologists have investigated the way in which agencies, like the factory inspectorate, actually operate in enforcing the law. He studied the factory inspectorate's file, relating to a sample of 200 firms of all sizes and kinds of industry, in one district of south-east England from mid-1961 to 1966. During this period a total of 3,800 offences were recorded by the factory inspectorate as being committed by the 200 firms. The minimum number for any firm was 2, the maximum was 94. The largest number of offences, by far, dealt with the need to achieve adequate and secure fencing of dangerous machinery. However, under 5 per cent of these infringements were followed up by a prosecution. As Carson concludes 'the pattern . . . is one of substantial violation countered almost exclusively by formal administrative procedures other than the prosecution of the offenders'. He argues that this pattern does not necessarily provide evidence of conscious bias in the implementation of the law by the factory inspectorate, but it may rather derive from a historical and traditional view of their role in relation to employers and in their view of which sanctions are likely to be most effective, as a means to the end of obtaining compliance with the legislation.

It is partly because of the lack of a thorough and adequate analysis of the role of the policeman in *our* society that we are reprinting the important and influential analysis of Skolnick on the origins of professionalism in American police work. Skolnick argues that several features of the policeman's occupational situation tend to induce him to regard a concern for the rule of law as rather less significant for the actual practice of his job than would appear formally to be the case. 'These features derive,' the author argues, 'from the view of the policeman as a craftsman rather than as a legal actor. One of the most important of these factors is the "pressure to produce" which induces the policeman to perceive possible criminality according to the symbolic status of the suspect; he also develops a stake in organised patterns of enforcement.' Young goes further and examines the role of the policeman as a negotiator of reality. He examines the police view of the drug 'pusher', which tends to act as a self-fulfilling prophesy in his relations with the drug user.

Crime is therefore not a simple phenomenon, as these extracts indicate. We could have focused attention on one particular type of participant, a criminal who is repeatedly caught, repeatedly sentenced to institutional punishment and whose existence allows other participants in the system to commend themselves silently for the acumen in discerning the danger to society from these desperadoes, and their courage and persistence in finally having them brought to book. Our aim in this chapter is to direct attention to areas in which the knowledge and understanding of the situation is less evident.

Crime in England and Wales

F. H. McClintock and N. H. Avison

Reprinted with permission from *Crime in England and Wales*, Heinemann, London, 1968, pp. 272–9.

While it has been well recognized that in recent years there has been a very great increase in recorded crime, it has not been so fully appreciated that the upward trend has been fairly continuous, at least since the 1920s. In the two decades preceding the Second World War, the annual average growth-rate in crime was approximately 5 per cent, while by the middle fifties and early sixties it had accelerated to 10 per cent. There may be some indication that the spread of lawlessness is now being restricted in that, since 1965, the annual growth-rate in crime is down to 6 per cent. But even so, since 1955 the number of indictable crimes annually recorded by the police has almost trebled: increasing from some 400,000 in 1955 to 1·2 million in 1966.

There is no evidence to suggest that the main increase in crime can be directly attributed to the change in size or demographic structure of the population, although the increase in the number of known offenders among young males indicates that this group has made a substantial contribution to the upward trend in crime. However, the theory of the existence of a particularly delinquency-prone generation—directly resulting from the Second World War—has been found to be unproved, as it cannot account for the high incidence of crime among young males in the 1960s. It is interesting to note that by 1966, the number of recorded indictable crimes per 100,000 of the population was as high as 2,496, in contrast with 986 in 1955. This would indicate that, during the last twelve years, the incidence of crime within the general population has more than doubled.

Throughout the present century, the vast majority of indictable crimes annually recorded by the police has consisted of larcenies and breaking offences. Offences against the person have remained a very small proportion of all crime, accounting in recent years for less than 5 per cent of the total, and although there are indications that there has been some increase in serious crimes of violence, the murder rate has remained relatively stable and firearms are rarely used, even if today they are more frequently carried. However, while this can be taken to indicate that the general criminal population is not particularly violent in its lawlessness against the community, it cannot be assumed that the problem today is merely that of dealing with an increase in the volume of crime. In fact, there are clear indications that, in recent years, there have been important changes in the circumstances, nature and seriousness of offences against property, and that this applies particularly in relation to the increases in robbery and in certain breaking offences. These two classes have increased at a much greater rate than other crimes, and in 1966 there were more than a quarter of a million robberies and breaking offences, which represented almost a quarter of the total volume of indictable crime recorded by the police. Many of these offences would appear to result from the activities of well-organized and professional offenders, and a considerable porportion of them resulted in the stealing of money and goods of a high value. It was found that between 1955 and 1965 major indictable crime increased at more than twice the rate of other indictable crime.

While many larcenies are known to be committed by juveniles and involve articles of low value or small sums of money, there is, even in respect to common thefts, a clear indication of an increase in seriousness, as indicated by the value of property which is stolen. A general estimate of the overall total value of property stolen throughout the country for recorded thefts in 1966 approaches £50 million. Many of these offences may reflect a growing attitude of carelessness toward property resulting from a greater material prosperity in the general population, and while some of these offences may be preventable, the ways in which this could be brought about would have to be the subject of separate studies.

The national upward trend in crime from 1955 onwards has been reflected in all police areas and regions throughout England and Wales. As might be expected, the increases have been greater in urban areas, as contrasted with county police forces, but even in the more rural districts, there are indications of increases in criminal activity. Forty per cent of the crime occurs in London and the large provincial towns and cities, and in 1965 the incidence of crime per 100,000 of the population was 3,000 in the urban areas as contrasted with 1,700 in the rural or county forces. Furthermore, as indicated by the value of property stolen, it would appear that in London and the large provincial towns and cities there is a higher proportion of the more serious offences against property. However, criminal activity has been spreading, in recent years, to the commuter belts and larger country houses. On the other hand, contrary to what might have been expected, the proportion of violent crime and sexual crime to the total of recorded crime was lower in conurbations than in the rest of the country.

Detection rates can be taken either to indicate the effectiveness of the police in apprehending offenders whose criminal activities have not been prevented or as some indication of the immunity of offenders whose crimes have been reported to and recorded by the police. But when used for either of these purposes, considerable caution has to be exercised, due to the lack of standardization in police recording practice and to the very limited nature of the information available on the crimes and on the ways in which they are cleared up.

From 1954 onwards the annual overall detection rate went steadily downwards from 49 per cent to 39 per cent in 1965. It is perhaps a hopeful sign that in 1966, the rate returned to 40 per cent. A study of the crime in local police forces indicated a general downward trend in detection rates for the period 1954 to 1965, although considerable variations existed from one area to another, and in 1965 the range in clear-up rate was still from 28 per cent to 74 per cent. The variations from one force to another seem to be more closely connected with differences in police procedure and recording practices than to variations in the kinds of crime committed or the social and economic conditions of the areas. However, the detection rates in the conurbations were generally lower than in the rest of the country. But it is difficult to make comparisons with these kinds of data and it has been indicated that in order to assess the relative effectiveness of different kinds of police units, it will be necessary to construct an analytical model that would take into account the differences between actual and expected detection rates. Such a study clearly lay outside the scope of the present survey.

Fairly constant variations in detection rates occur from one class of offence to another. As regards offences against the person, it approximates to 80 per cent. This relatively high detection rate reflects to some extent the greater police attention given to dealing with most of these crimes because of the natural anxiety caused when violent and sexual offenders remain at large in the community, but it also reflects the fact that many offenders are known at the time when such offences are reported, so that no genuine problem of detection arises. Detection rates for robbery and breaking and entering offences were, in 1965, well below 40 per cent and the decrease in detection rates in recent years may reflect the skill and organization with which an increasing proportion of these crimes are carried out. Detection rates for most classes of theft are low. This was particularly so for larcenies in houses, or from the person or unattended vehicles, for which in 1965, the rates were all below 25 per cent. Some evidence suggests that the majority of crimes of theft, if not immediately detected, are unlikely to be detected subsequently, and that perhaps the most effective way of controlling these kinds of crime is by taking direct preventive measures.

The total volume of unsolved crime has increased from 1·3 million during the 1951–5 to 2·8 million for the period 1961–5, and this continuous growth in the number of unsolved crimes has occurred notwithstanding the fact that the annual number of crimes solved per policeman has risen from 3·3 to 5·3 in the period from 1955 to 1965. The increasing volume of unsolved crime is a good indication of the extent to which crime pays. And, clearly, a considerable improvement in the detection rates will have to be made before any substantial change in the annual volume of unsolved crime is obtained. Thus, in 1966, although there is an improvement of 1 per cent over the detection rate for 1965, the number of unsolved crimes in 1966 was nevertheless some 28,000 higher than in 1965—due, of course, to the relatively greater increase in the total number of indictable crimes known to the police.

The problem of assessing the immunity of offenders from detection is difficult. It is probable that the immunity has increased not only for people who commit one or only a few offences, but also for the regular and professional offenders. Detailed comparative studies of criminal careers are, however, required if the basic information is to be provided for making reasonable estimates of the trends.

The vast majority of offenders dealt with in the courts are first offenders, and only a minority of these are reconvicted, thus becoming recidivists. Naturally, the problems presented by this minority of offenders are likely to be far greater than those relating to first offenders. From 1955 to 1965 the number of recidivists convicted in each of the years rose from some 35,000 to an estimated 90,000, indicating an increase of almost

160 per cent. In recent years there has been a growing proportion of young recidivists aged 14 to 21, although it is still found that some 6 in 10 of the recidivists in each year are aged 21 and over.

Three groups of recidivism have been distinguished: primary recidivism, with one previously proved indictable offence; 'medium' recidivism, with 2 to 4 such previous offences; and 'serious' recidivism, with 5 or more such previous offences. Together, the latter two groups have been referred to as 'high' recidivism. One-third of the recidivist population fell into each of the groups. The proportion of recidivists with a 'high' degree of recidivism was largest among those convicted of robbery and breaking offences, although among adult recidivists there was also a significant group found guilty of theft who were in this category of 'high' recidivism.

It was estimated on the basis of a continuation of the present conditions that 5 per cent of the total male population would become primary recidivists at some time during their lives. This estimate gives some indication of the size of the problem, but it has to be borne in mind that many of such offenders would become recidivists during their school years and would be law-abiding citizens throughout the adult part of their lives.

All areas have experienced a substantial increase in the annual rate of those convicted who were recidivists. However, urban areas were found to have higher, and rural areas lower, rates of conviction of recidivists than would be expected on the basis of the population.

A study of a special sample of recidivists found guilty in 1955 and 1959 indicated that the majority of recidivists in each age-group had committed no more serious an offence than one of larceny, but among those recidivists with a 'serious' degree of criminality as many as 7 in 10 had at least one conviction for a serious crime such as breaking and entering. Among the older age-groups, no less than 9 in 10 of the 'serious' recidivists had served at least one sentence in a penal or reformative institution. Clearly, such a group presents an important challenge to the effectiveness of the penal system. Some information on the place of birth and the background of the recidivists indicates that the vast majority were native-born, and that few offenders were convicted outside their home area.

The penological implications of the increase in crime are related firstly to the police, secondly to the courts and thirdly to penal institutions and other treatment agencies. In recent years there has been a considerable increase in the actual police strength as well as a re-organization of the police into larger administrative units, and the development of such specialized services as the Police Research and Planning Branch and the Regional Crime Squads. The actual police strength increased from 65,000 in 1955 to 84,000 in 1965. However, despite this increase the actual strength in 1965 was calculated to be still 14 per cent below the authorized police establishment, as assessed in terms of the tasks that have to be faced. In most forces a considerable amount of indoor clerical work is being transferred to civilian staff, and Traffic Wardens are taking over a great deal of routine work in respect of the control of motor vehicles in urban areas. These are all promising beginnings towards greater efficiency, but the task of preventing crime and detecting offenders continues to grow annually and it is as yet too early to assess the impact of these developments on the control of crime.

During the last decade the courts have been facing a growing volume of work each year in respect of criminal cases. Some of the burden on the higher courts was transferred to the magistrates' courts by the Criminal Justice (Administration) Act 1962, and the establishment of the Crown Courts in the industrial north of England has taken some of the strain off the higher courts in those cities. However, it is clear that the pressure remains high at a time when the courts have been required to undertake the additional task of obtaining and evaluating pre-sentence reports upon the background of offenders. At present, a Royal Commission is sitting under the chairmanship of Lord Beeching to consider whether improvements can be made in the arrangements and organization for dealing with offenders at the higher courts and the time may not be far off when it will become essential to make a similar enquiry into the working of the magistrates' courts. In the higher courts approximately 6 in 10 of the convicted offenders are sentenced to institutions and there has been little change in this proportion throughout the period since 1955. The main change as regards non-institutional methods has been the increase in the number and proportion of those fined. However, among those sentenced to imprisonment there has been an increase in the number and proportion who are given very long sentences. In the magistrates' courts that deal with adult offenders, the main change has also been the much more frequent use of the fine. The indications are that the fine is today becoming the principal penalty for dealing with the majority of adult offenders found guilty of indictable offences, but there is also some evidence to indicate that changes in sentencing practice result from the inability of the probation system and penal institutions to expand sufficiently rapidly to meet the demands that the courts would wish to place on them.

This survey has indicated the need for further information on the phenomenon of crime, and clearly this needs to be paralleled with the development of more closely co-ordinated research into the workings and effectiveness of law enforcement and the penal system.

The Able Criminal
J. A. Mack

Reprinted with permission from *British Journal of Criminology*, No. 12, January 1972, pp. 44–9.

The inquiry sketched in this paper makes no attempt to elucidate the 'causes' of crime. It is primarily descriptive, classificatory and typological, directed towards one and one only of the many and heterogeneous phenomena lumped under the general title of crime. We are concerned with those criminals who make a full-time job of crime, and who establish relationships, including networks, in the pursuance of their common occupational interests. This is a distinctive criminal group, and its existence is to be traced in general literature, so far as the United Kingdom is concerned, from Elizabethan times on.

How important are these full-time criminals? Statistically, not very important. They account for only a small part of the crime totals. The main burden of police work in the field of crime control is the great mass of criminal and near-criminal offences committed by offenders mostly not known to the police, including not only myriads of casual minor offenders but also quite high-level operators, 'substantial incomers' not hitherto known to the police. But the full-time criminal system operates at a very high *pro rata* economic cost to the community. It is also the case that when these operations are successful, not only in avoiding conviction or imprisonment, but also in getting away with large hauls, the effect on the morale of the vast lesser-criminal population, and for that matter the effect on the morale of the police, is profound. Moreover these full-time criminals carry on a distinctive occupational tradition. For the group we are studying, crime is a way of life as well as a trade: the popular expression is a 'profession'. It is composed of those full-time criminals who are of more than average competence, and who carry considerable weight in their own circles. They will have other occupations or descriptions, but their interests are bound up with and their income derived from criminal pursuits. They are not all 'top criminals', although they include the few top criminals who are going about. They are simply a group of individuals of some substance whose lives are organised round a criminal way of behaving. There are a large number of others, equally involved as regards interest and use of their time, but smaller fry; these might number about twenty or thirty times the total of heavyweight or middle-weight full-time operators.

A pilot study carried out some years ago, the Worktown study, was made possible by full information from two police forces. The question put to them was—'What, in this urban area of somewhere between 80,000 and 90,000 people, is the strength, the establishment so to speak, of full-time, comparatively heavy-weight, travelling criminals?' An initial list of about twenty was scrutinised and fined down to twelve; after further discussion it was agreed that four could be discarded as not heavy-weight enough. The residue of eight could be regarded as the full-time criminal output of this area. This gives a rough and ready ratio of one fairly considerable full-time operator for every 10,000 inhabitants.

The pilot study at once produced a distinctive feature which has shaped our inquiries ever since. The small group of eight full-time operators divided itself neatly into two equal and opposite parts. Four of the eight corresponded with fair accuracy to the criminal as found in many textbooks. They came from a deprived neighbourhood. They had bad home circumstances in early life, and suffered from a lack of parental care and affection. Their behaviour showed some emotional disturbance, sometimes considerable. They were of low intelligence. They had juvenile records.

The other four were different in all respects but one, namely that they came from much the same social background as the previous four. But three had no juvenile records, and one was recorded as having only one minor juvenile offence. Their early home circumstances were either not known or not notably bad. They gave every appearance of being psychologically well-balanced, and were quite well thought of by the police as individuals; 'you can pass the time of day with them'. Their behaviour, particularly their criminal performance as known to the police, gave strong ground for supposing that they were above average in intelligence.

A further striking difference between the two groups came out when their full criminal records were compared. They divided neatly again into the same two groups of four. The first group, the textbook criminals, had spent on the average over 60 per cent of their adult life in prison, not allowing for remission. They were of the type which might fail to earn remission. The other four had very little prison record. They averaged 12½ per cent. of their adult life from the age of 17, not counting remission (which they would probably earn).

The present study is on a larger scale, and is centred on an industrial city of about 1 million population. Among other things a sample of between 100 and 150 specified full-time miscreants is being documented and analysed. This group comprises all or most of those in whom the detective forces of the area are specially interested. The present paper is concerned with a group of 102 drawn from this larger total, consisting of those operators considered by the research team, in consultation with the police, to be continuously active.

So far the results are in line with those of the pilot study. For example the present study tends to confirm that the ratio of major full-time criminal operators in the general population is in the region of one in 10,000. This is of course a highly speculative figure. A 'major full-time operator' in Worktown, with 80,000 population, would rank comparatively low in a city of 1 million population; similarly a 'major operator' in such a city might rate fairly low on the standards of the Metropolitan Police District; standards ratified not only by the police, but also by the criminal occupational sub-culture.

The second pilot study finding is also confirmed, namely that a large proportion of major full-time criminals are both able and successful in their criminal occupation. Success in this field is not easy to estimate by the usual criteria of profit and loss. A successful criminal generally makes a lot more money than he would make in such law-abiding occupations as are open to him. But how much, and how often, and how continuous, is very difficult to determine. It seems also that his expenses and expenditures are very high by ordinary standards. But the group we are studying is notably successful in another sense. While it is known to the police that they are persistently engaged in fairly large-scale criminal enterprises, they contrive to avoid imprisonment or conviction or even, at the top of the scale, appearance in court.

There is one notable difference between the two studies in respect of imprisonment. Whereas the very small pilot study population divided into two polarised groups, 'habitual or full-time criminals' at one end of the spectrum and 'habitual or full-time prisoners' at the other, the population now under review form a continuum, a continuum crowded towards the 'successful' end, so that the proportion of those who manage to keep out of prison most of the time is higher than in the pilot study. In the following calculation five of the group of 102 are excluded as having had less than ten 'years at risk' of imprisonment—that is, they are under 27 years of age. The average age of the 97 remaining subjects is 38: the scatter is as follows:

N	Age at mid-1969	Years at risk
7	27–30	10–13
27	31–35	14–18
34	36–40	19–23
14	41–45	24–28
7	46–50	29–33
6	51–55	34–38
2	56–60	39–43
—		
97		

In the following table the subjects are classified, very roughly, according to their *main* type of criminal activity, into six groups:

1. Organisers (O) or background types, who also tend to enjoy especially high status.

2. Resetters (R); this, like the others, is a versatile group, and includes a number who combine resetting and other activities, specially fraud, sometimes of the '*long-term*' variety.

3. Thieves (T); including sneak-in merchants, shoplifters,

and a number of thief fraudsters who sell commodities like non-existent advertising space and invisible whisky.

4. 'Heavies' (H); *i.e.* housebreakers, safebreakers, bank robbers, wage-snatch operators, explosives experts, tie-up merchants, and so on.

5. Violents (V); the few in this category, while showing some

---

Proportion of 'years' at risk', i.e. since age 17, spent in prison, remission deducted, in period ending mid-1969.

Proportion (%)	O	R	T	H	V	P	Total
0	1	3	1	—	—	2	7
0·1–5	—	5	5	4	—	—	14
5·1–10	1	3	3	—	1	1	9
10·1–15	—	1	3	4	—	—	8
15·1–20	1	1	4	1	1	—	8
20·1–25	—	1	2	1	—	3	7
25·1–30	1	1	2	3	1	—	8
30·1–35	—	—	1	6	—	—	7
35·1–40	1	—	3	4	—	—	8
40·1–45	—	—	1	4	—	1	6
45·1–50	—	—	1	2	—	—	3
50·1–55	1	—	—	4	—	—	5
55·1–60	—	—	—	5	1	—	6
Over 60	—	—	—	1	—	—	1
	6	15	26	39	4	7	97

---

degree of pathology, are included because their violence is employed for acquisitive purposes.

6. Providers (P); providers of services of different kinds.

The data as regards juvenile crime bear some resemblance to those of the pilot study. More than one-third, to be precise 36 out of 102, have no juvenile record, and a further twelve have one juvenile entry only. All of the seven who have no prison record have no juvenile record. Although a fair proportion may not have taken up crime until they passed 17 or 21, or even much later, it may be safer to infer, in some cases at least, that the essential skill exhibited in the avoidance of detection was developed early in life.

It will be seen from the table that resetting is a safer criminal activity than that pursued by the 'heavies'. But the main finding is that almost half of this group of persistent major criminal operators can well accept the occupational risk of incarceration since they have in fact kept out of prison for four-fifths and more of their time at risk; while no less than 78 per cent have been able to move freely about their avocations for at least three-fifths of their adult life. Of particular interest is the select group of the seven non-incarcerated. If one adds those who kept clear of prison in the ten years ending mid-1969 the seven become thirteen: three 'organisers', six 'resetters', one 'thief' and three 'general providers'.

These figures are not quite so alarming as they may sound at first hearing. While it is true that a sizeable proportion of persistent criminals, including a fair number of direct predators—thieves, robbers and housebreakers, as distinct from the backroom operators—are remarkably skilful in avoiding arrest and conviction, it also appears to be the case that their freedom of action is fairly drastically controlled. All of these major operators have a strong distaste for the consequences of being caught, and the majority of them take very badly to imprisonment. Moreover the continuous vigilance maintained by the police limits considerably the risks they are prepared to take. A closer scrutiny of this aspect of crime control will be made at a later stage in the research. In the meantime it can be said that this fact of immunity from police and legal process provides a main focus for the present inquiry. The emphasis of the research has shifted to the study of the able or successful criminal. He is of course a highly elusive figure, for criminologists as well as for detectives. Some have even argued that the 'successful' or 'able' or 'professional' criminal is a myth invented by the police to enhance their 'image' in the eyes of the public. But no one who has broken through the barrier of police reserve in these matters can maintain this proposition for long in the face of the evidence which the C.I.D. can provide in any large conurbation. It is not of course the kind of evidence that will immediately convince a court. But this is the very heart of the problem of the study of successful full-time crime. The first condition of such a study is the abandonment of the proposition that a conviction, or finding guilty, is an essential element in the definition of criminality. The principle that these full-time operators should not be considered to be criminals until they are proved to be such in a court of law is good law and will remain so for as long as the present general ignorance on the subject of full-time criminals and criminal networks continues to be unrelieved by systematic research. It may even be good practical civics, though this is arguable. But it is indubitably bad sociology.

White-Collar Crime and the Enforcement of Factory Legislation
W. G. Carson

Reprinted with permission from *British Journal of Criminology*, No. 10, 1970, pp. 383–98.

The study of white-collar crime

In one of his essays on 'Crude Criminology' George Bernard Shaw attempted to dispel a common illusion about crime by pointing to the close similarities between the socially reprehensible behaviour of criminals and the ostensibly reputable behaviour of the military gentlemen of his day. The difference between the two was no greater, he suggested, than that between a jemmy and a bayonet or, more pointedly, than that between a chloroformed pad and a gas shell. Nor, apart from the wholesale and therefore more massive scale of the gentleman's depredations, were the results of the two kinds of behaviour distinguishable to Shaw's not unperceptive eye:

> 'Gild the reputable end of it as thickly as we like with the cant of courage, patriotism, national prestige, security, duty and all the rest of it: smudge the disreputable end with all the vituperation that the utmost transports of virtuous indignation can inspire: such tricks will not induce the divine judgment ... to distinguish between the victims of these two bragging predatory insects the criminal and the gentleman.'

At a more general level very similar views are frequently expressed by academic criminologists, though rarely with anything approaching Shaw's eloquence. Since the publication of Edwin Sutherland's controversial book on *White Collar Crime*, a literature of growing theoretical and empirical sophistication has slowly accumulated around the central theme of the criminal behaviour of persons who, if not gentlemen, are at least members of the upper socio-economic class. Although a disagreement about basic definitions has continued unabated, degenerating at times into what one writer regards as 'a futile terminological dispute', white-collar crime today usually takes its place alongside all the other standard topics in any criminological text-book.

In broadest outline Sutherland and his disciples argue cogently that the behaviour of persons of respectability and upper socio-economic class frequently exhibits all the essential attributes of crime but that it is only very rarely dealt with as such. This situation emerges, they claim, from a tendency for systems of criminal justice in societies such as our own to favour certain economically and politically powerful groups and to disfavour others, notably the poor and the unskilled who comprise the bulk of the visible criminal population.

Attempting to underpin these claims with the strongest possible support, Sutherland himself set a dangerous precedent when he expanded his definition of crime to include socially injurious behaviour which is legislatively proscribed under any kind of penalty as well as behaviour specifically prohibited by criminal law. His motives in doing so were to show that under such a definition the white-collar criminal would figure much more prominently and that legislatures themselves are not precluded from the possibility of bias in their determination of the limits of criminal justice. However defensible on these grounds, or indeed on grounds of social justice, this expansion of the concept came closer to throwing the entire subject of white-collar crime into academic disrepute. Opponents were not slow to see here the intrusion of subjectivity into criminology:

> 'One seeks in vain for criteria to determine this white-collar criminality. It is the conduct of one who wears a white collar and who indulges in ... behaviour to which some particular criminologist takes exception.... A special hazard exists in the employment of the term, "white-collar criminal", in that it invites individual systems of private values to run riot in an area (economic ethics) where gross variation exists among criminologists as well as others. The rebel may enjoy a veritable orgy of delight in damning as criminal most anyone he pleases...'

Another and a conceptually less problematic possibility than that of legislative bias is that even when the behaviour of the white-collared is defined as crime by 'the law in books', even when it is technically subject to criminal sanctions, it nonetheless enjoys substantial immunity at the operational level of 'the law in action'. Such immunity may certainly operate to some extent when white-collar people or their children engage in 'ordinary' criminal activities, but this nebulous form of bias, if such it is, has only a tangential relationship to the main argument about 'white-collar crime'. As Sutherland himself pointed out, a more crucial issue is the possibility of 'bias in the administration of justice under laws which apply exclusively to business and the professions and which therefore involve only the upper socio-economic class'. Restricted to the occupational activities of the allegedly favoured groups, the enforcement of these laws might reasonably be expected to display the most acute and most systematic form of bias if the theory of white-collar crime is correct.

As originally conceived, the theoretical significance of these ideas lay principally in their implications for the development of a general theory of criminal behaviour. For too long, Sutherland argued, criminologists had ignored the criminality so effectively though not conspiratorially concealed by the reluctance of legislatures and enforcement agencies to employ criminal sanctions in controlling business and professional behaviour. By accepting too blithely the *modus operandi* of the system the theorists had unconsciously colluded in perpetuating the myth that law-breaking is a primarily working-class phenomenon. As a result, their general theories had all too frequently been evolved on the basis of samples which were not truly representative of the behaviour they purported to explain. Thus, while Sutherland's avowed object was to reform criminological thinking, his ambition in this respect remained a comparatively modest one. He wished, indeed, to draw attention to the legislative and procedural differences between white-collar crime and ordinary crime, but only so that these conceptually false demarcations might be swept from the path of general theorisation about the causes of criminal behaviour. As C. R. Jeffrey puts it, 'he accepted the Positivists' emphasis on the criminal while rejecting their definition of crime'.

Today, of course, criminologists tend to be much less concerned with seeking general explanations for criminal behaviour, having abandoned this ambitious quest in favour of more modest, if not notably more successful investigations into particular types of offence. This tendency to abdicate from generalisations about criminal behaviour is not, perhaps, to be regretted, but there is certainly one respect in which the potential of a generic approach to the socially homogeneous phenomenon of crime has by no means been exhausted. However wide the variety of behaviour which may be involved, all crimes possess the common denominators of proscription under the criminal law and the at least hypothetical possibility of a punitive reaction by the state. These formal characteristics of the phenomenon require explanation just as much as any others if our theories are not merely to rank as hypothetical statements about behaviour rather than about crime as such. They constitute a field in which valid generalisations can and should still be sought:

'We will have to scrutinise more carefully the process by which the criminal law is formed and enforced in a search for those variables which determine what of the total range of behaviour becomes prohibited and which of the total range of norms become a part of the law.'

Such a perspective is slowly winning popularity among sociologists of deviance, particularly in the United States. In recent years a substantial literature has accumulated around the related problems of how society selects certain forms of behaviour—and subsequently some, but not all of the individuals engaging in them—to be 'labelled' as deviant or criminal. With regard to the specific issue of selection at the legislative level, it is ironic that recognition of these problems should have been implicit in Sutherland's approach even if he did not, himself, pursue their theoretical significance to its logical conclusion:

'... this newer emphasis on studying the law itself has (also) received major impetus from the theoretical issues raised by an interest in white-collar crime. The very differences between the set of laws regulating occupational behaviour and other statutes embodying legal proscriptions and sanctions have raised questions about how and why they were enacted —not just why they have been violated.'

This is an area in which much remains to be done from a historical as well as a contemporary standpoint. It is an area, moreover, in which the student of white-collar crime may legitimately engage without arraignment for the apparent heresy of extending his basic definitions to embrace behaviour which is not contrary to the criminal law. Where necessary, he can accept such behaviour as 'non-crime' and with theoretical justification attempt to isolate the factors operative in keeping it outside the confines of the criminal law despite its marked similarities to 'real crime'.

In connection with the second major problem—that comprising the processes whereby subsequent to the enactment of criminal legislation some and not other law-breakers are formally designated as criminal—the study of white-collar crime is potentially just as fruitful. If the proponents of this subject are correct in their view it is an area distinguished by a peculiarly systematic form of 'non-labelling' at the operational level. Symptomatic of 'more pervasive and generalisable features of the social structure', its investigation may serve to underline some of the crucial variables involved in this sifting process over a wider range of law-enforcement. Such research would focus primarily upon the specially constituted, administrative agencies to which the enforcement of criminal laws governing business and professional behaviour is frequently entrusted. Not only are these boards, commissions and inspectorates invested with an inevitable discretion about the use of prosecution, but also not infrequently with a range of administrative alternatives to enforcement through the criminal courts. In the exercise of these discretionary powers, however extensive, it is possible that a pattern of enforcement corresponding to what Aubert has characterised as the 'slow, inefficient and highly differential implementation' of laws relating to white-collar crime may emerge.

Records pertaining to the enforcement of law by such agencies in this country remain almost totally uninvestigated by criminologists. Along with examination of legislative processes, scrutiny of these records is one of the more pressing items on the criminological agenda. In undertaking such research the criminologist can move further towards the sociology of law—a subject from which he has for too long been estranged—and also, perhaps a little lamely, towards recognition in his error in accepting too uncritically the aphorism that 'justice should study men rather than men study justice'.

The remainder of this paper describes and interprets some empirical data concerning the enforcement of Factory Legislation. This is an area of social control which conforms in several respects to the broad configurations of laws relating to white-collar crime. Mainly, though not exclusively directed towards regulation of employers' occupational roles, the Factories Acts impose legal constraints upon one of the most important aspects of white-collar behaviour in an industrialised and highly differentiated society. Over a period of more than a century and a half the state has gradually increased the level of its intervention in the industrial sphere by stipulating the minimum standards of safety, health and welfare which factory-occupiers should observe. In doing so it has sought to ensure that the legitimate economic objectives of manufacturers are not pursued at the expense of the persons who are employed; to alter what R. W. C. Taylor called 'a method of economy which subordinated immediate human interests to the blind discretion of employers filled with the most pitiless of all passions, the pursuit of gain . . .'

While discussion of the legislative background to these enactments lies beyond the scope of the present paper, there is one aspect of the statutory provisions which is particularly germane to the subject of enforcement. Factory Legislation expressly provides for its enforcement by means of criminal sanctions. Offenders can be tried summarily and may be fined up to £300 in instances where the contravention was likely to cause death or bodily injury. With a fine eye to the integrity of the law's administrative machinery and personnel, imprisonment for up to three months is permitted to offences such as personation, forgery of documents and making false declarations. In terms of 'the law in books' therefore, little difficulty attaches to the definition of violations as crime unless, of course, one ventures down the more tortuous paths of legal argument about mala prohibita and absolute liability.

Originally vested in 'visitors' appointed by the Justices of the Peace, responsibility for the enforcement of this legislation rests today with the Inspectorate of Factories. This body is immediately answerable to the Secretary of State for Employment and Productivity and has an authorised staff of inspectors numbering approximately 600. Its various enforcement activities involve around 380,000 premises of different kinds and in 1967, inspectors paid more than 170,000 visits to factories alone.

While this enforcement agency has received considerable attention from students of social and administrative history, it has received little or none from criminologists. Nor is the kind of information required by the latter very easily accessible. Although the reports submitted annually by the Chief Inspector give details of all prosecutions, they do not specify what proportion these constitute of the total violation which is known. Even more important in the context of white-collar crime, they do not provide any details about the Inspectorate's use of methods other than prosecution in its dealings with those factory-occupiers who are found to have offended.

To obtain information on these and related issues the Inspectorate's files relating to a randomly selected sample of 200 firms in one district of south-eastern England were examined. The area chosen for the research was selected for its relatively wide range of different industries and different sizes of firm. The files which were examined contained data on all contraventions formally recorded against the firms, the means whereby the offences were discovered, the enforcement response which was made in each instance and a vast amount of less quantifiable information in the form of the written reports and comments of individual inspectors. Since the Department's programme was operating on the basis of a four-year inspection cycle, data covering the four and a half years from mid-1961 to the beginning of 1966 were collected.

Analysis of the 'harder' among these data revealed a high level of offending among the firms in the sample. During the period covered by the survey, 3,800 offences were recorded against them, every firm contributing at least some violations to this total. The minimum number for any single firm was 2; the maximum was 94. Detailed discussion of the nature of these offences lies beyond the scope of the present paper but, as can be seen from Table 1, the vast majority cannot be dismissed as trivial violations of the law's administrative requirements.

Knowledge of these contraventions reached the Department in several different ways. Chief among these and central to the entire system of enforcement was the Inspectorate's ongoing programme of general inspection. A relatively detailed examination of every factory operated by firms in the sample was carried out under this programme during the $4\frac{1}{2}$ years and these visits accounted, in all, for the discovery of around three-quarters of the recorded offences. A much smaller percentage —around 5 per cent of the total—came to light in the course of investigations into complaints which emanated from a variety of sources, mainly employees or persons connected with them. Investigations consequent upon the obligatory reporting of industrial diseases, dangerous occurrences and accidents accounted for an even smaller proportion of the total. The last of these did reveal, however, a relatively high incidence of contravention, approximately two-thirds of the relevant visits resulting in the detection of at least one offence directly related to the occurrence of the accident. A final and by no means insignificant source of information about violation was a special type of visit paid with the express intention of following-up matters which had already come to light in any of the foregoing ways. Nearly 13 per cent of the contraventions were discovered in the course of such visits.

Table 1. Nature of offences recorded against 200 firms during period of 4½ years

Type of offence	Number	%
Lack of secure and properly adjusted fencing at dangerous machinery	1,451	38·2
Inadequate precautions against fire and explosion	460	12·2
Other safety requirements	380	10·0
Failure to examine, test or treat plant and equipment	162	4·3
Failure to provide proper training, supervision or medical examination for employees	108	2·8
Offences against health and welfare requirements	317	8·3
Offences against administrative requirements	917	24·1
Other	5	0·1
Total	3,800	100·0

With reference to the pivotal issues of the law's enforcement, the survey revealed the use of six major methods which can be arranged on a continuum running from 'no formal action', at one end, to prosecution, at the other. The procedures intervening between these self-explanatory extremes comprise formal and relatively standardised communications of differing forcefulness. Least threatening of these is a form which merely notifies the offender that at a recent visit to his premises it was observed that the matters mentioned required his attention. Barely more forceful, though clearly differentiated in the Inspectorate's standing instructions, is a letter which appends a rider to the effect that the matters in question require 'urgent' attention. In neither of these communications is any mention made of legal proceedings under the Factories

Act. Reference to such action makes its first appearance in another type of letter which concludes by reminding the occupier that 'failure to comply with legal requirements can lead to prosecution'. Distinguishable as an 'indirect threat' since it explicitly mentions legal proceedings without suggesting that such action will necessarily result from further contravention, this procedure differs from a final type of communication which directly threatens the offender with prosecution. In its mildest form, the latter indicates that failure to comply will leave the inspector no alternative but to consider or institute

Table 2. Types of enforcement decision taken
in respect of recorded offences

Enforcement decision	Number	%
No formal action	36	5·5
Notification of matters requiring attention	494	74·5
Notification of matters urgently requiring attention	79	11·9
Indirect threat of prosecution	30	4·5
Direct threat of prosecution	12	1·8
Prosecution	10	1·5
Total	661*	99·7*

* There were two instances in which a seventh method – threat of issuing a certificate of unsuitability against underground rooms – was employed. (Sec. 69.) In neither case was the certificate issued and in these tables the two decisions are excluded.

proceedings; in its strongest form, the offending firm is given a very clear indication that prosecution has already been actively considered and that although no further action is being taken on this occasion, further violation will result in prosecution.

In processing the 3,800 recorded offences 663 specific enforcement decisions were made by the Inspectorate, all of the offences detected at a visit normally being dealt with by means of one communication. As can be seen from Table 2, these decisions displayed a pronounced tendency to concentrate around the least threatening procedures short of taking no formal action whatever.

All of the ten decisions to prosecute, shown in the above table, followed the occurrence of industrial accidents involving machinery in motion. Surprisingly, however, they did not represent the most serious accidents which were found to have involved contraventions. A plea of guilty was entered in every case and the average fine imposed after conviction was £50.

Another matter of particular relevance in the context of enforcement was the Inspectorate's response to those occupiers who either repeated specific contraventions (or failed to

Table 3. Types of enforcement decision taken in respect of recorded offences, distinguishing those which involved repeated offences from those which did not

Type of decision	Repeated Offences Involved		
	None %	Detected for second time %	Detected for third or more time %
No formal action	3·0	7·8	19·3
Notification of matters requiring attention	92·5	38·7	17·5
Notification of matters urgently requiring attention	0·9	35·2	43·9
Indirect threat of prosecution	1·9	11·3	8·8
Direct threat of prosecution	0·4	4·2	7·0
Prosecution	1·1	2·1	3·5
Total	(99·8 = 463)	(99·3 = 141)	(100·0 = 57)

remedy defects) in spite of having received formal notification about them. Nearly 10 per cent of the recorded offences fell in this category and although there was a noticeable trend towards greater severity in dealing with them, the concomitant enforcement-decisions still remained heavily weighted towards the less threatening forms of action (Table 3).

The pattern which emerges from the above findings is one of substantial violation countered almost exclusively by the use of formal administrative procedures other than the prosecution of offenders. Superficially compatible with the findings of earlier studies in other areas of law relating to white-collar crime, this does not however point inexorably to the conclusion that the enforcement of factory legislation exemplifies a conscious bias in the administration of criminal justice. Such a conclusion would impute motives to the Inspectorate which would ultimately only be verifiable by reference to the intentions of its members both collectively and individually. Without corroboration of this kind motives could only be attributed on a 'post' hoc' basis and need not bear any resemblance to those which were actually instrumental in generating the pattern of enforcement which was observed.

The crucial component in this motivational background is the inspector's interpretation of his own function, since it is from this that his decisions about how to enforce the law derive their immediate contextual meaning. In the course of the survey it quickly became evident that regardless of the role in which they might be cast by the sociologist, the inspectors in the District did not see themselves as members of an industrial police force primarily concerned with the apprehension and subsequent punishment of offenders. Rather, they perceived their major function to be that of securing compliance with the standards of safety, health and welfare required and thereby achieving the ends at which the legislation is directed.

A similar preoccupation with the 'ends' of law-enforcement has been observed in other agencies of this kind and has received some theoretical attention from Edwin M. Lemert and F. E. Hartung. In the present context, however, its significance lies primarily in its profound effect upon the way in which inspectors selected appropriate modes of action in specific situations. Concerned with securing the offender's compliance rather than his punishment, they tended to choose methods of enforcement as much for their functional efficiency in attaining this objective as for their appropriateness as punitive responses. There was, moreover, substantial agreement among them that in normal circumstances regular inspections, repeated check-visits, formal communications and occasional threats together constituted the most efficient means to this end.

This belief in the efficacy of maintaining consistent pressure upon employers has been endemic in the Inspectorate since its inception. Well-founded or not, it is a cultural tradition which induces resistance to anything defined as an interference with the routine process of inspecting factories and following up matters which give rise to special concern. The fact that the inspectors in the District tended to view the prosecution of offenders as one potential intrusion of this kind is crucial to an understanding of the data which have been presented. To them, the additional time and paper-work inevitably involved in such action rendered it a method of enforcement to be used sparingly and, in the words of one of their superiors, 'as a tool of inspection'. This latter phrase accurately portrays the functional role which legal proceedings were perceived to play in relation to the enforcement process as a whole; whether utilised for their predicted effect upon an individual occupier or upon other employers in the area, they were seen as a means to an end rather than an end in themselves.

The Working Policeman, Police 'Professionalism' and the Rule of Law
J. Skolnick

Reprinted with permission from J. Skolnick, *Justice Without Trial: Law Enforcement in Democratic Society*, John Wiley & Sons Inc., 1966, pp. 230–5.

The traditional concern of criminology and of writers on 'social control' is the maintenance of order in society. This study suggests that such a view is limited both philosophically and sociologically. 'Social control' must deal not merely with the maintenance of order, but with the quality of the order that a given system is capable of sustaining and the procedures appropriate to the achievement of such order. Thus, a given set of social and legal conditions may lead to order in a stable democracy but not in a stable totalitarianism. Meaningful sociological analysis of order cannot, therefore, be value-free, because such a posture falsely assumes the equivalence of all types of order.

This research rejects the 'value-free' approach, and concentrates instead upon the social foundations of legal procedures designed to protect democratic order. In the workings of democratic society, where the highest stated commitment is to the ideal of legality, a focal point of tension exists between the substance of order and the procedures for its accomplishment. 'The basic and anguishing dilemma of form and substance in law can be alleviated, but never resolved, for the structure of legal domination retains its distinguishing features only as long as this dilemma is perpetuated.' This dilemma is most clearly manifested in law enforcement organizations, where both sets of demands make forceful normative claims upon police conduct.

In addition to this fundamental dilemma, there are further complications. Neither form nor substance, law nor order, is an entirely clear conception; and what it means for police to use law to enforce order is also somewhat problematic. The empirical portion of this study looked into the question of how the police themselves conceive the meaning of 'law' and 'order' to find out how these conceptions develop and are implemented in police practices. Social conditions in the varying assignments of police heightened or diminished the conflict between the obligations of maintaining order and observing the rule of law.

First, we summarize findings about these issues and suggest that the dilemma of the police in democratic society arises out of the conflict between the extent of initiative contemplated by nontotalitarian norms of work and restraints upon police demanded by the rule of law. Second, we consider the meaning of police professionalization, pointing out its limitations according to the idea of managerial efficiency. Finally, we discuss how the policeman's conception of himself as a craftsman is rooted in community expectations, and how the ideology of police professionalization is linked to these expectations. Thus, we focus upon the relation between the policeman's conception of his work and his capacity to contribute to the development of a society based upon the rule of law as its master ideal.

Five features of the policeman's occupational environment weaken the conception of the rule of law as a primary objective of police conduct. One is the social psychology of police work, that is, the relation between occupational environment, working personality, and the rule of law. Second is the policeman's stake in maintaining his position of authority, especially his interest in bolstering accepted patterns of enforcement. Third is police socialization, especially as it influences the policeman's administrative bias. A related factor is the pressure put upon individual policemen to 'produce'—to be efficient rather than legal when the two norms are in conflict. Finally, there is the policeman's opportunity to behave inconsistently with the rule of law as a result of the low visibility of much of his conduct.

Although it is difficult to weigh the relative import of these factors, they all seem analytically to be joined to the conception of policeman as *craftsman* rather than as *legal actor*, as a skilled worker rather than as a civil servant obliged to subscribe to the rule of law. The significance of the conception of the policeman as a craftsman derives from the differences in ideology of work and authority in totalitarian and non-totalitarian societies. Reinhard Bendix has contended that the most important difference between totalitarian and non-totalitarian forms of subordination is to be found in the managerial handling of problems of authority and subordination.

Subordinates in totalitarian society are offered little opportunity to introduce new means of achieving the goals of the organization, since subordination implies obedience rather than initiative. As Bendix says, '. . . managerial refusal to accept the tacit evasion of rules and norms or the uncontrolled exercise of judgment is related to a specific type of bureaucratization which constitutes the fundamental principle of totalitarian government.' By contrast, in non-totalitarian society, subordinates are encouraged to introduce their own strategies and ideas into the working situation. Bendix does not look upon rule violation or evasion as necessarily subverting the foundations of bureaucratic organization, but rather sees these innovations as 'strategies of independence' by which the employees 'seek to modify the implementation of the rules as their personal interests and their commitment (or lack of commitment) to the goals of the organization dictate.' In brief, the managerial ideology of non-totalitarian society maximizes the exercise of discretion by subordinates, while totalitarian society minimizes innovation by working officials.

This dilemma of democratic theory manifests itself in every aspect of the policeman's work, as evidenced by the findings of this study. In explaining the development of the policeman's 'working personality', the dangerous and authoritative elements of police work were emphasized. The combination of these elements undermines attachment to the rule of law in the context of a 'constant' pressure to produce. Under such pressure, the variables of danger and authority tend to alienate the policeman from the general public, and at the same time to heighten his perception of symbols portending danger to him and to the community. Under the same pressure to produce, the policeman not only perceives possible criminality according to the symbolic status of the suspect; he also develops a stake in organized patterns of enforcement. To the extent that a suspect is seen as interfering with such arrangements, the policeman will respond negatively to him. On the other hand, the 'cooperative' suspect, that is, one who contributes to the smooth operation of the enforcement pattern, will be rewarded. Accordingly, a detailed investigation was made of exchange relations between police and informers, in part to ascertain how informers are differentially treated according to the extent to which they support enforcement patterns, and partly to analyse how the policeman creates and uses the resources given to him.

In attempting to enrich his exchange position, the policeman necessarily involves the prosecutor in supporting his enforcement needs. The prosecutor, of course, also has a stake in the policeman's work performance, since the policeman provides him with the raw materials of prosecutorial achievement. Our observations suggested, however, that although he is ultimately the policeman's spokesman, the prosecutor performs a quasi-magisterial function by conveying a conception of legality to the policeman.

Most interesting, of course, is the basis on which the prosecutor's greater attachment to legality rests. We may point here to pertinent differences between policeman and prosecutor. One, of course, has to do with socialization. The prosecutor is a product of a law school, with larger understanding and appreciation of the judiciary and its restraints, especially constitutional ones. The policeman, on the other hand, generally has less formal education, less legal training, and a sense of belonging to a different sort of organization. Such differences in background go far to explain the development of the policeman's conception of self as a craftsman, coupled with a guild-like affirmation of worker autonomy. The policeman views himself as a specialist in criminological investigation, and does not react indifferently either to having his conclusions challenged by a distant judiciary or to having 'obstacles' placed in his administrative path. He therefore views the judiciary, especially the appellate courts, as saboteurs of his capacity to satisfy what he sees as the requirements of social order. Each appellate decision limiting police initiative comes to be defined as a 'handcuffing' of law enforcement, and may unintentionally sever further the policeman's attachment to the rule of law as an overriding value. In addition, the policeman is offended by judicial assumptions running contrary to probabilistic fact—the notion of due process of law staunchly maintains a rebuttable presumption of innocence in the face of the policeman's everyday experience and of an administrative presumption of regularity.

Although the prosecutor is legally accorded a wider area of discretion than the policeman, the setting of the policeman's role offers greater opportunity to behave inconsistently with the rule of law. Police discretion is 'hidden' insofar as the policeman often makes decisions in direct interaction with the suspect. The prosecutor typically serves at most as advisor to these dealings. Whether it is a question of writing out a traffic citation, of arresting a spouse on a charge of 'assault with a deadly weapon', or of apprehending an addict informer, the policeman has enormous power; he may halt the legal process right there. Such discretionary activity is difficult to observe. By contrast, prosecutorial discretion frequently takes place at a later stage in the system, after the initial charge has been made public. The public character of the charge may restrict the prosecutor's discretion in practice more than the policeman's, even though the scope of the prosecutor's discretion is far wider in theory.

Internal controls over policemen reinforce the importance of administrative and craft values over civil libertarian values. These controls are more likely to emphasize efficiency as a goal rather than legality, or, more precisely, legality as a means to the end of efficiency. Two analyses were made along these lines. One was of the clearance rate as an internal control process. Here it was suggested that the policeman operates according to his most concrete and specific understanding of the control system, and that the clearance rate control system emphasizes measures stressing the detective's ability to 'solve' crimes. It was further shown how it is possible for this control system to reverse the penalty structure associated with substantive criminal law by rewarding those evidencing a high degree of criminality. Thus, persons with greater criminal experience are frequently better 'equipped' to contribute to the 'solution' of crimes, thereby enhancing the policeman's appearance as a competent craftsman. The introduction of this control system into police work was analysed to illustrate a response to the difficulties experienced by organizations that produce a fundamentally intangible service, or at least where 'output' is subject to a variety of interpretations. Such an organization requires internal measures of the competence of employees, plus a set of measures (which may be the same) for assessment by outside evaluators.

The dilemma of democratic society requiring the police to maintain order and at the same time to be accountable to the rule of law is thus further complicated. Not only is the rule of law often incompatible with the maintenance of order but the principles by which police are governed by the rule of law in a democratic society may be antagonistic to the ideology of worker initiative associated with a non-totalitarian philosophy of work. In the same society, the ideal of legality rejects discretionary innovation by police, while the ideal of worker freedom and autonomy encourages such initiative. Bureaucratic rules are seen in a democracy as 'enabling' regulations, while the regulations deriving from the rule of law are intended to constrain the conduct of officials.

The conflict between the democratic ideology of work and the legal philosophy of a democracy brings into focus the essential problem of the role of the police. The police are not simply 'bad guys' or 'good guys', authoritarians or heroes. Nor are they merely 'men doing their jobs'. They are legal officials whose tendencies to be arbitrary have roots in a conception of the freedom of the worker inhering in the non-totalitarian ideology of the relation between work and authority, a conception carried out in the context of police work. Seeing themselves as craftsmen, the police tend to conduct themselves according to the norms pertaining to a working bureaucracy in democratic society. Therefore, the more police tend to regard themselves as 'workers' or 'craftsmen', the more they demand a lack of constraint upon initiative. By contrast, *legal actors* are sympathetic towards the necessity for constraint and review.

The Drugtakers: The Role of the Police
J. Young

Reprinted with permission from *The Drugtakers*, Paladin, 1971, pp. 187–97.

We live in a world which is segregated not so much in terms of distance but in terms of meaningful contact and empirical knowledge. The stereotype of the drugtaker–drugseller relationship is available to the public via the mass media. This stereotype is constructed according to a typical explanation of deviance derived from absolutist notions of society. Namely, that the vast majority of individuals in society share common values and agree on what is conformist and what is deviant. In these terms the deviant is a fringe phenomenon consisting of psychologically inadequate individuals who live in socially disorganized or anomic areas. The emergence of large numbers of young people indulging in deviant activities such as drugtaking, in particular areas such as Notting Hill, would seem to clash with this notion as it is impossible to postulate that all of them are psychologically inadequate and that their communities are completely socially disorganized. To circumvent this, absolutist theories invoke the notion of the corrupted and the corruptor. Healthy youngsters are being corrupted by a few psychologically-disturbed and economically-motivated individuals. Thus the legitimacy of alternative norms—in this case drugtaking—arising of their own accord in response to certain material and social pressures, is circumvented by the notion of the wicked drug pusher corrupting innocent youth. This allows conflicts of direct interest and moral indignation to be easily subsumed under humanitarianism. The policeman—like the rest of the public—shares this stereotype and his treatment of individuals suspected of drugtaking is couched in terms of this stereotype:

(i) The police, the courts and the laws themselves distinguish between possession and sale of dangerous drugs.

(ii) The individual found in possession of marihuana is often —and in Notting Hill frequently—ignored by the police. They are after the real enemy, the drug pusher. To achieve this aim they are willing to negotiate with the individual found in possession. Thus they will say, 'we are not interested in you, you have just been stupid, we are interested in the person who sold you this stuff. Tell us about him and we will let you off lightly.' Moreover, if the individual found in possession of marihuana actually finds himself in the courts he will find himself in a difficult position, namely, that if he tells the truth and says that he smokes marihuana because he likes it, and because he believes that it does no harm and that therefore the law is wrong, he will receive a severe sentence. Whereas if he plays their game and conforms to their stereotype, namely that he had got into bad company, that somebody (the pusher) offered to sell him the stuff, so he thought he would try it out, that he knows he was foolish and won't do it again, the court will let him off lightly. He is not then in their eyes the true deviant. He is not the dangerous individual whom the police and the courts are really after. Thus the fantasy stereotypes of drugtaking available to the police and the legal profession are reinforced and re-enacted in the courts, in a process of negotiating between the accused and the accusers. The policeman continues then with evangelical zeal to seek the pusher, the forces of public opinion and the mass media firmly behind him. As a result the sentences for possession and for sale become increasingly disparate. In a recent case the buyer of marihuana received a fine of £5 whilst the seller received a five-year jail sentence. A year previously, the same individual who in this case was buying, was selling marihuana to the person who was sentenced in this case for selling.

The negotiation of reality by the policeman is exhibited in the widespread practice of perjury. This is not a function of the machiavellianism of the police, but rather a product of their desire in the name of administrative efficiency to jump the gap between what I will term theoretical and empirical guilt. For example, a West Indian who wears dark glasses, who has no regular employment, and who mixes with beatniks, would quite evidently satisfy their notion of a drug pusher. If he is arrested, then it is of no consequence that no marihuana is found in his flat, nor is it morally reprehensible to plant marihuana on his person. For all that is being done is aiding the cause of justice by providing the empirical evidence to substantiate the obvious theoretical guilt. That he might actually have only sold marihuana a few times in the past, that he mixes with hippies because he likes their company, and that he lives in fact from his National Assistance payments is ignored; the stereotype of the pusher is in evidence, and the reality is unconsciously negotiated to fit its requirements.

With time the effect of police action on the marihuana smoker in Notting Hill results in

(a) the intensification of the deviancy of the marihuana user; that is, the consolidation and accentuation of his deviant values in the process of deviancy amplification.

(b) a change in the life style and reality of marihuana use so that certain facets of the stereotype become actuality. In short, a translation of fantasy into reality.

I wish then to go through the various aspects of the social world of the marihuana user which I outlined earlier, and note the cumulative effect of intensive police action:

1. Intensive police action serves to increase the organization and cohesion of the drugtaking community, uniting them in terms of a sense of gross injustice felt at harsh sentences and mass-media distortion. The severity of conflict necessitates theories evolved by bohemian groups to explain the nature of their position in society, and in this process they heighten their consciousness of themselves as a group with definite interests over and against those of the wider society. Conflict welds an introspective community into a political faction with a critical ideology. Thus deviancy amplification results.

2. A rise in police action increases the necessity of the drugtaker hiving off and segregating himself from the wider society of non-drugtakers. The greater his isolation the less chance that the informal face-to-face forces of social control will come into operation, and the higher his potentiality for further deviant behaviour. At the same time, the creation by the bohemian of social worlds centring around hedonism, expressivity, and drug use makes it necessary for the non-drugtaker, the straight person, to be excluded not only for reasons of security, but also to maintain his own definitions of reality unchallenged by the outside world. Thus, after a point in the process of exclusion of the deviant by society, the deviant himself will co-operate in the policy of separation, and deviancy amplification occurs.

3. The further the drugtaker evolves deviant norms, the less chance there is of him re-entering the wider society. Regular drug use, bizarre dress, long hair, lack of workaday sense of time, money, rationality and rewards, all militate against his re-entry into regular employment. To do so after a point would demand a complete change of identity; besides, modern record systems would make apparent any gaps which have occurred in his employment or scholastic records, and these might be seen to be indicative of a personality which is essentially shiftless and incorrigible. Once out of the system and labelled by the system in this manner, it is very difficult for the penitent deviant to re-enter, especially at the level of job opportunities which were initially available to him. There is a point, therefore, beyond which an ossification of deviancy can be said to occur.

4. As police concern with drugtaking increases, drugtaking becomes more and more a secret activity. Because of this, drugtaking in itself becomes of greater value to the group as a symbol of their difference and of their defiance against per-

ceived social injustices. Simmel, writing on the Sociology of Secrecy, has outlined the connection between the social valuation of an activity and the degree of secrecy concerned with its prosecution.

This is what Goffman referred to as overdetermination. 'Some illicit activities,' he notes, 'are pursued with a measure of spite, malice, glee and triumph and at a personal cost that cannot be accounted for by the intrinsic pleasure of consuming the product.' That is, marihuana comes to be consumed not only for its euphoric effects and as a sign of membership of an exclusive bohemian élite, but as a symbol of rebellion against an unjust system. As a result, drug argot changes from description to metaphor: the ideal person is turned on, the unpleasant experience is a bringdown, the enlightened man a head. Reaction welds marihuana into the backbone of the subculture: it is the prerequisite of group membership; the joint passed around the circle of heads becomes the ubiquitous ritual of the new bohemia. Thus the stereotype begins to be realized and fantasy is translated into reality.

5. As police activity increases, the price of marihuana rises. This, together with the increase in the size of the market, makes the business more attractive both for the professional importer and full-time pusher. The small dealer, motivated by social and subsistence living considerations, does not disappear but he becomes more of a rarity and his career is considerably shortened. For it is the street-level pusher who fits the model of marihuana selling held by the police. His long hair, lack of economic or criminal rationality, make him an easy target. He is subject to a process of deviancy amplification and—as he is the focus of police attention in his corruptor role—takes the main brunt of harassment. Intrinsically part of the subculture, his imprisonment represents to heads the most overt example of social injustice. As risk increases, large profits are more likely to motivate people to enter marihuana distribution than the lure of a prestigious community job or the ideology of turning people on. Hippie, West Indian and Pakistani entrepreneurs become more systematic: the business becomes economically rational. Small-time criminals, previously peripherally involved, are more likely to see it as a possible full-time occupation. Elaborate organizations begin to evolve. At this point, significant external events have intervened and hastened this process. For the Nixon Administration's Operation Intercept, which attempted to cut supplies of grass entering the

United States from Mexico, had the effect of increasing the consumption of hashish in North America. The resin is more easy to smuggle and derives from the Far East, the Middle East and North Africa. London became, as one perceptive underground commentator on the drug scene pointed out: 'a major staging post in the world's drug traffic: every day large amounts of hash are smuggled direct from London to the USA ... as much as half of the hash arriving in London is forwarded direct to the USA where shit fetches between 4 and $4\frac{1}{2}$ times its London price'. The augmented national organization meshes with international networks which stretch from Pakistan to San Francisco. Not that this is centralized *to any extent* like the heroin market, but it is considerably more organized and professional than before. Violence and rumours of violence emerge; an embryonic drug pyramid begins to settle out of the confused sporadic market of the rest. At the same time, increased customs vigilance reduces the proportion of marihuana (usually grass) brought in by amateurs largely for their own consumption. Grass becomes less available and hashish the staple form of marihuana. As the organization of smuggling becomes more complex, in order to meet the demands of an international market with high risks, the number of hands through which the resin passes increases. Profit maximization involves the progressive dilution of the resin. These impurities lead to hangovers (although of a mild and soporific nature), which rarely occurred with hashish and grass previously available. Once again, on several scores, the fantasy stereotype begins to be translated into reality.

6. As police activity increases, the marihuana user becomes increasingly secretive and suspicious of those around him. How does he know that his activities are not being observed? How does he know that seeming friends are not police informers? Ugly rumours fly around about treatment of suspects by the police, long terms of imprisonment, planting, and general social stigmatization. The effects of drugs are undoubtedly related to the cultural milieu in which drugs are taken. A Welsh Rugby Club drinks to the point of libidinousness, an academic sherry party unveils the pointed gossip of competitiveness lurking under the mask of a community of scholars. Similarly, the effects of marihuana smoked in the context of police persecution invites feelings which are paranoid and semi-psychotic. The drug subculture, by institutionalizing drug use, initially minimizes and controls psychotic

episodes. But when the subculture itself has to become clandestine and cautious, paranoid episodes become written into the taken-for-granted nature of marihuana.

Thus stereotypical effects become in part reality.

7. As police activity increases, the marihuana user and the heroin addict begin to feel some identity as joint victims of police persecution. Interaction between heroin addicts and marihuana users increases. The general social feeling against all drugs creates a stricter control of the supply of heroin to the addict. He is legally bound to obtain his supplies from one of the properly authorized clinics. Lack of trained personnel, or even adequate theoretical knowledge of dealing with the withdrawal problems of the heroin addict, result in the alienation of many from the clinics. The addict is either kept on maintenance doses or else his supply is gradually cut. Either way, euphoria becomes more difficult to obtain from the restricted supply, and the 'grey market' or surplus National Health heroin which previously catered for addicts who required extra or illicit supplies disappears. In its place a sporadic black market springs up, often consisting of Chinese heroin diluted with adulterants. This provides a tentative basis for criminal underworld involvement in drugselling and has the consequence of increasing the risks of over-dosage (because the strength is unknown) and infection (because of the adulterants). But the supply of black market heroin alone is inadequate. Other drugs are turned to in order to make up the scarcity; the precise drugs varying with the availability and ability of legislation to catch up with this phenomenon of drug displacement. Chief of these is methadone, a drug addictive in its own right, which is used to wean addicts off heroin and freely-prescribed barbiturates. As a result of displacement, a body of methadone and barbiturate addicts emerge, the latter drug being probably more dangerous than heroin and causing even greater withdrawal problems. For a while the over-prescription by doctors creates, as once occurred with heroin, an ample grey market of methadone and barbiturates. But pressure on the doctors restricts at last the availability of methadone, and the ranks of saleable black-market drugs are increased in the process. Because many junkies share some common bohemian traditions with hippies, that is, they often live in the same areas, smoke pot, and affect the same style of dress, the black market of heroin, methadone, barbiturates *and* marihuana will overlap. The heroin addict, seeking money in

order to maintain his habit and, perhaps more important, his life style at a desirable level, and the enterprising drugseller may find it profitable to make these drugs available to marihuana smokers.

Some marihuana users will pass on to these hard drugs, but let me emphasize *some*, as, in general, *heavy* use of such drugs is incompatible with hippie values. Full-blown physical addiction involves being at a certain place, at a certain time every day; it involves an obsession with one substance to the exclusion of all other interests; it is an anathema to the values of hedonism, expressivity and autonomy. But the number of known addicts in this country is comparatively small (just over 2,000 heroin addicts in March 1970) whilst the estimates of the marihuana-smoking population range up to one million and beyond. Thus, it would only need a minute proportion of marihuana smokers to escalate for the heroin addiction figures to rise rapidly. Besides, the availability of methadone and barbiturates gives rise to alternative avenues of escalation. Methadone, once a palliative for heroin addicts, becomes a drug of addiction for individuals who have never used heroin. To this extent, increased social reaction against the drugtaker would make real the stereotype held by the public about escalation. But the transmission of addiction, unlike the transmission of disease, is not a matter of contact; it is a process that is dictated by the social situation and values of the person who is in contact with the addict. The values of marihuana smokers and the achievement of subterranean goals are not met by intensive heroin use. Escalation to heroin (or methadone and the barbiturates) will only occur in atypical cases where the structural position of the marihuana user changes back insufficiently to necessitate the evaluation of values compatible with heroin use as solutions to his newly emergent problems. But, on the other hand, escalation to other, more dangerous, drugs, for instance methedrine, is a much more likely occurrence. Methedrine, or speed, is a powerful amphetamine whose effects are particularly appropriate to hedonistic and expressive cultures. It is usually to drugs such as these that the deviancy amplification of marihuana users will result in escalation in the type of drugs taken. Fortunately, tight control of the legitimate supply of methedrine and propaganda against its use in the underground press have stemmed this particular escalatory path.

8. As the mass media fan up public indignation over marihuana use, pressure on the police increases: the public de-

mands that they solve the drug problem. The number of marihuana users known to the police is, as I have mentioned previously, a mere tip of the iceberg of actual smokers. The police,
then, given their desire to enact public opinion and legitimize
their position, will act with greater vigilance and arrest more
marihuana offenders. All that happens is that they dig deeper
into the undetected part of the iceberg, the statistics for marihuana offences soar; the public, the press and the magistrates
view the new figures with even greater alarm. Increased pressure is put on the police, the latter dig even deeper into the
iceberg and the figures increase once again, public concern becoming even greater. We have entered what I term a fantasy
crime wave which does not necessarily involve at any time an
actual increase in the number of marihuana smokers. Because
of publicity, however, the notion of marihuana smoking occurs
for the first time to a larger number of people and by virtue of
experimentation alone some actual empirical increase occurs.
We must not overlook here as well that this moral panic over
drugtaking results in the setting up of drug squads which by
their very bureaucratic creation will cause a regular contribution to the offence figures which had never been evidenced
before.

Police action, then, has not only a deviancy amplification
effect in the formal sense of the unintended consequences of
the exclusion of the marihuana smoker from 'normal' society;
it has also an effect on the content of the bohemian culture
within which marihuana smoking takes place.

I have discussed a process which has been going on over the
last three years, to some extent accentuating the contrasts in
an ideal typical fashion in order to make more explicit the
change. The important feature to note is that there has been
change, and that this has been in part the product of social
reaction. For many social commentators and policy makers,
however, this change has merely been indicative of their initial
presumptions about the essential nature of the drugtaker. That
is, that a minority are individuals with new psychopathic personalities having weak superegos, unrealistic egos and inadequate masculine identification. Inevitably these people, it is
suggested, will pass on to heroin, and lo and behold the figures
show that this has actually occurred. Similarly, the police, convinced that drug use is a function of a few pushers, will view
the deviancy amplification of the bohemian and the emergence
of a drug pyramid as a substantiation of their theories that we

have been too permissive all along. Thus false theories are evolved and acted upon in terms of a social reaction, the result of which are changes, which, although merely a *product* of these theories, are taken by many to be a proof of their initial presumptions. Similarly, the drugtaker, evolving theories as to the repressive nature of the police, finds them progressively proven as the gravity of the situation escalates. Diagramatically:

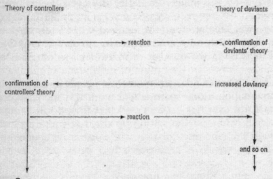

Figure 2

That is, spiral of theoretical misperceptions and empirical confirmations can occur, very similar to the spiral of interpersonal misperceptions described by Laing, Phillipson and Lee in *Interpersonal Perception*.

What must be stressed is that we are dealing with a delicately balanced system of relationships between groups, and between values and social situations, which can be put out of gear by over-reaction of public and police. It is my contention that the tendency for unnecessary over-reaction is part and parcel of the nature of modern large-scale urban societies, and that a proper understanding of the nature of deviancy amplification and the moral panic is a necessary foundation for the basis of rational social action. My feeling, here, is that we could quite easily launch ourselves, through faulty mismanagement of the control of drugtaking, into a situation which would increasingly resemble that obtaining in the United States.

Further Reading: **Crime**

†* S. BOX, *Deviance, Reality and Society*, London, Holt, Rinehart and Winston, 1971.

†* W. G. CARSON and P. WILES, *Crime and Delinquency in Britain*, London, Martin Robertson, 1971.

* M. B. CLINARD and R. QUINNEY, *Criminal Behaviour Systems*, London, Holt, Rinehart and Winston, 1967.

K. T. ERIKSON, *Wayward Puritans: A Study in the Sociology of Deviance*, John Wiley & Sons, Inc., 1966.

* D. GLASER, *Crime in the City*, London, Harper and Row, 1970.

* R. HOOD and R. SPARKS, *Key Issues in Criminology*, London, Weidenfeld and Nicolson, World University Library, 1970.

†* N. JOHNSTON, L. SAVITZ and M. E. WOLFGANG, *The Sociology of Punishment and Correction*, Chichester, Wiley, 1970.

†* M. E. WOLFGANG, N. JOHNSTON and L. SAVITZ, *The Sociology of Crime and Delinquency*, Chichester, Wiley, 1970.

* Available in paperback
† Reference

Chapter Nine Minorities

Britain is usually considered to be a relatively homogeneous
society and much of the discussion about the entry of
minorities, especially minorities from the Commonwealth
within the past twenty-five years, has centred on the extent to
which such a society can take groups whose ways of life are
different in so many respects. On closer viewing the assumption
of homogeneity is misleading. In all kinds of ways people differ
in their attitudes, their position in life, their styles of life and
their experience of it.

What is a minority? Why is it so important to examine the
experience of minorities in any society? The problems faced
by minorities are not simply those to do with size, and being
a small group is only a starting point. Minorities can be, as in
South Africa, majorities in numerical terms. The denial of
equal rights does not of itself make a minority, otherwise
women and children would be regarded as minority groups.
Crucial to the definition is the possession of recognisable
physical or cultural characteristics which are discernible and
set minorities apart from the dominant group and distinctive
ways of being treated.

It is common to regard minorities as creating problems for
the society in which they live, but this is more likely to be a
consequence of certain attitudes and practices by the majority.
The process is not a simple one: stereotyped opinions about
the minority are widely held, and distinctions between 'our
people' and them, familiar to the students of the situation in
Britain, are made. The feelings developed in the minority may
lead to a strong sense of grievance against the majority and an
increased determination to retain their identity.

A minority group is a subordinated group, therefore,
which is in a relatively weak position of power, in terms of
being able to affect decisions made about it. It is in a weak
position with regard to prestige in the system of social grading,
and its members will have low positions in the economic
structure. Changes may take place over time. For example, the

Jewish community in Britain has moved rapidly within a century from a minority status to one where its members have considerable power in all parts of the social structure. Considerable changes are taking place today in the situation of some other minorities in Britain. The factor of colour in a former imperial power, is of great significance for recent arrivals to this country from the old Empire but it is not the only one that needs to be taken into account in the examination of the position of minorities in Britain. That is why material on gypsies and the situation in Ulster is presented.

The need to consider the experience of minorities, whether indigenous or of recent arrival, should take us beyond the simple causal connections often made between minorities and social problems to a view of what it is like to be disadvantaged in the key areas of life, and to an appreciation of the complexity of the issues involved. There is probably no area of life in which there is a greater gap between the facts and what is believed than this. The themes that follow provide information and comment on some of the relevant issues.

A great deal of attention about the entry of immigrants during the period since the last war has centred upon the groups from the tropical countries of the Commonwealth or from dependent territories. In fact only one in three of the immigrants to Britain since the war has been coloured and there are large numbers of people from Ireland and other parts of Europe who have settled here. Indeed, the Irish are the largest single group of immigrants to Britain over this period.

The entry has risen in the main because of the employment opportunities that exist. In certain cases, as with the West Indians, the increase has also been linked with the restriction of opportunities of migration to traditional places, such as the United States. The motivation to come here is an economic one in almost every case but since the restriction on entry by Acts of Parliament since 1962 there has been an increasing tendency to bring over families as well. This was not the original intention of many of them, who had planned eventually to return home for good. The numbers entering Britain have been significantly lower in recent years than those of Britons leaving this country. Increasing unemployment and the possibilities of tension make the present situation more fraught with danger and difficulty and capable of being exploited for political ends.

The term 'immigrant' seems to denote a person who is alien,

probably unable to speak English, with different and possibly inferior ways of life and, perhaps implicitly, a threat to the existence or the continuance of the 'British way of life'. The gap between the beliefs about minorities, and particularly those which concern race and colour, and the facts of the situation is often wide. We bring to the situations of contact all kinds of attitudes and assumptions which tend to be validated by what we experience. The first reading in this chapter looks at some of the attitudes which are common and their component parts. Attitudes are predispositions on the part of individuals or groups, which are learned, to evaluate objects or another group in a consistent way. One way of dealing with the problem of prejudice and discrimination, which is touched upon briefly, is to ensure that the situations where groups meet each other are structured so that individual attitudes do not play an important part. Certain types of personality are prone to prejudice and those who are prejudiced about one minority group are more likely to be prejudiced about others. At the same time, it is reassuring for many others to be able to believe that the entry of coloured people into Britain has meant a decline in certain standards, an increase in crime and all kinds of other inevitable social ills. The implication is that there is something innately inferior about these groups and that is the reason for such consequences. That this is not the case is less important than that it may be believed : responsibility for the state of affairs can be offloaded on to socially less acceptable groups.

Although prejudice and discrimination towards certain minority groups is very much a subject of debate at the moment other groups which experience them may be forgotten. The second reading considers, from a government survey, the attitudes towards what are variously described as gypsies or travellers. The term 'gypsies' often include travellers who do not necessarily have a tradition of wandering but who are attracted by the kind of life it offers. The complaints are considered against some of the evidence in a way which shows the extent to which groups such as this can be scapegoated and their needs ignored.

Stuart Hall, in the next reading, looks at the problems of adjustment which face newcomers to any society, with particular reference to black people. He makes the point that the process of adaptation is likely to be phased across the generations and that change will be difficult. He discusses the factors which affect adjustment from one group to another and shows the relevance of the historical experience for the presence of the issues. Brian Lee, in an article on the language of Enoch Powell, shows the way in which Powell's effective use of communication faced particular inferences and conceals the doubtful logicality of the argument. Since race has become part of the political debate and there is great sensitivity about it, in particular in relation to the political support that could arise from its exploitation, the techniques of persuasion require to be examined in detail. Ethnic minorities are distinct from others by their language, ways of life, religion and experiences. Usually one thinks of various minority groups within a larger society distinguished to a greater or lesser degree by the culture that they share with the majority, or the extent to which their culture appears to be antipathetic to it.

In Ulster the tensions which exist between minority and majority are polarised on religion and area. They have been used as a pretext for a heightening of the political and emotional temperature over a long period of time, in fact, since 1912. The situation of the majority there, too, is unusual in that it forms a minority within the whole of Ireland. Elliot and Hickie provide a view of the social background of the conflict in Ulster which, among other things, emphasises the perspectives which the communities hold and the attitudes they have to each other which make the resolution of the present conflict very difficult.

Finally, John Lambert considers the question of police–coloured relationships and emphasises on the one hand the enormous pressures which the police have in fulfilling their role and on the other the difficulties that can arise which could be a source of enormous tension. It may be argued that the very moderation of policemen and other officials within the structure of government is of great importance in the consideration of what is likely to happen in the future. If those parts of the system are or become violently antagonistic then this has all kinds of consequences for the position of the minorities.

Racial Discrimination in Britain
Eric Butterworth

Reprinted from *Human Rights*, Heinemann Educational Books, 1967, pp. 88–93.

Attitudes are important but they do not invariably determine our actions. We might be restrained from doing certain things, or encouraged to do others, by the climate of opinion in the group of which we were a part. Traditionally, in the United States, lynchings were started by the criminal elements and later joined, after the emotion of the crowd had taken over, by the 'respectable' people. Conversely, people are often inhibited from expressing prejudice when they are in the company of those who have a more liberal view of race relations.

Thus, it is the situation which tends to determine how we respond. If there is a lot of prejudice against immigrants in our society then obviously the tendencies to respond adversely will be more common. What evidence is there about attitudes? Estimates vary, but all the surveys so far show a majority of the population prejudiced against certain minority groups.

In a society changing so quickly prejudice often reflects the original frame of reference which we have been given. Subjectively at least, the majority of people in Britain have been brought up to believe in, or at least view with respect, certain myths which lead to prejudice. The fundamental attitude underlying them is ethnocentrism. This is the belief in the unique value and 'rightness' of one's group and one's actions (or 'what I do is natural' and 'what you do—if it is different— is peculiar, wrong or immoral'). This attitude enables the majority group to exploit, or keep down, minority groups and retain a clear conscience by suggesting it is in the best interests of the minorities.

There are many myths but all embody ideas in the three main ones described here:

1. *The superiority of some 'races'*. In the past it was possible to believe in differences between races in a simple kind of way and that some races were superior to others. Because of the evident fact that coloured people were in inferior positions to white people it was assumed that this was because of their basic inferiority. This is no longer believed by scientists. People liv-

ing in poverty will attain less and will have less intelligence than those living in affluence, but when standards of living rise so does attainment. There is now considerable evidence to show that the range of ability within particular groups is fairly similar.

Race is, however, not just a figment of the imagination and scientists can identify major categories of mankind. Even so, there are considerable variations within each racial group.

2. *The inferiority of children of mixed marriages.* This proposition has been generally believed. The evidence shows that children of 'mixed' marriages are likely to be physically and mentally stronger because biological weaknesses, which tend to occur more in parents from the same 'race', will do so less in their cases. In many respects this idea has been a rationalization of attitudes which identify coloured people with low social status.

3. *Temperamental differences between races.* Beliefs about innate racial and national temperament have a long history. Obviously certain groups develop characteristics because of the situation in which they are placed. For example, the Jews were restricted to a number of occupations for centuries and this, together with the insecurity of their position in the countries in which they lived, had some bearing on what was taken to be a 'Jewish' personality type. So far this idea of temperamental difference and a naïve view about the effects of climate are not proved and are likely to depend far more on life experiences and opportunities than on race. This proposition is usually advanced in order to explain bad behaviour on the part of minority groups.

Prejudice is an emotionally rigid attitude towards particular groups of people or representatives of those groups. It is a predisposition to respond to a certain stimulus in a certain way. Prejudices are thus attitudes of mind which contain the element of prejudgement. Thus it is possible to form an impression of a West Indian or a Pakistani without ever having seen one or been in contact with one: the facts which we see are fitted into existing frames of thought, and the individual develops a vested interest in believing certain things. He may need to hate a particular group, and nothing that can be said in favour of that group will shake his determination. This is because facts which are favourable can always be countered by particular instances which reflect unfavourably on the group.

Prejudice is not a rational exercise of judgement. It may be compounded of all kinds of irrational elements. Thus it is possible to believe at one time that immigrants present a threat to the jobs of workers in our society, and believe at another time that immigrants come here purely to live off state benefits. West Indians may be unacceptable because they are noisy, strong and boisterous and Pakistanis may be unacceptable because they are quiet (and therefore somehow sinister).

The embodiment of the tradition of prejudice may be found in stereotypes. These are propositions with a purpose. They tell us more about the social group using them than the people they are supposed to describe. Stereotypes are of two kinds. One describes a subordinate group, with the object of keeping them in their place. Thus negroes have often been described as lazy, irresponsible, dull, 'instinctive' and so on. The implication is that there is little possibility of improvement. The second describes a competitive group, which may be suspected of trying to take away the livelihood of the majority. The Jews were often viewed in this way, so their qualities had to be defined in such a way as to make them un-British. 'Hard work' has been an important cultural value of our society and is regarded with favour, but where it is practised by the minority group it can be explained with reference to their grasping mentality and as unfair competition. Saving for the future is explained, for the British, as being highly worthy, but for the minority group as being a stepping stone to further exploitation. The high prestige of brain work as opposed to manual work may be acknowledged for those British people who are successful at the former, but for the successful minority group member this could be explained as being a parasite on the larger body of manual workers. An agitation for certain basic rights by British people may be seen as a reinforcement of the values of our society, but where it arises from minority group initiatives, it may be characterized as subversive.

One of the consequences of the existence of these unfavourable images of minority groups is that members of these groups may come to accept them themselves. Thus, the individual may not apply for a job or a house *because he knows he will not get them*. On the surface there is no discrimination because he has not been refused, but in reality he does not apply because of the potential strength of discrimination and his expectation of being treated as a second-class citizen.

Prejudice may be mild or violent. It may or may not express itself in discrimination. Thus discrimination may be prejudice in action. It means treating people differently because they are members of a particular group. It is possible to discriminate without being prejudiced, like the businessman who will not deal with, or employ, immigrants because he fears the effects on his business. He acts as he does because he thinks *other people* are prejudiced. If a person has a house in an area into which immigrants move, he may well develop hostile feelings, and attempt to keep other immigrants out, even though he may express extremely liberal views on the racial situation. If a person works in a factory where there are immigrants present, he may be in favour of immigrants being dismissed first, in the event of redundancy, because of the loyalty he feels towards his fellow workers or because of his own self-interest, rather than because he is prejudiced against immigrants.

This is an interesting aspect of prejudice in Britain today. Very few admit to prejudice (although a great number begin: 'I'm not prejudiced, but . . .'), but most act as though there was a lot in it. So the technically unprejudiced are able to discriminate.

Some people are prejudiced because of the mistaken facts presented to them. These may derive from the 'received ideas' of school text-books. Most people have no formal education after leaving school and the ideas they carry with them, unless modified, are often inappropriate to new situations and more-over have been disproved. The 'myths' mentioned earlier, and many like them, were respectable beliefs, with what appeared to be some scientific evidence for them, sixty years ago.

There is a danger that the immigrant (or minority group member) may be used as a scapegoat, by which the individual off-loads his fears, guilt or frustrations (caused by other factors) on to an easily identifiable object. Certain types of personality appear to be prejudice-prone, and it seems that those prejudiced against a particular minority group are also likely to be prejudiced against other minority groups.

Apart from jokes about immigrants, which are generally derogatory, the most usual source of current information about immigrants is through the press and the other mass media. It is significant that very few people obtain their main impressions of immigrants from the immigrants themselves. The main concern of the press is not with the presentation of a balanced view of British life but rather with information which is 'newsworthy'. There is a widespread misconception that if the press reports objectively, much of the prejudice against immigrants will be diminished. This is probably untrue since in any event by far the greatest number of references to immigrants will be in connection with their wrong-doings, or other aspects of life where they come into conflict with British institutions. There is a tendency to believe what is stated in the press and to assume that this is a fair representation of the lives of immigrants.

Apart from the press, other mass media are also channels of communication about immigrants. With only a small number of exceptions, the programmes about immigrants have stressed the areas of conflict, although some of these have been pro-immigrant in their general orientation. Even so it is important to recognize that people take what they want from programmes such as this and many will be able to identify themselves with prejudiced statements which are made during such programmes.

In general, therefore, there has been far too little emphasis on the positive aspects of the contribution of immigrants and the possibilities of integration, and far too much on the social costs of integration. Thus, the average person, including the official who deals with immigrants, will not be in a position to make an accurate assessment of the situation. In a great majority of cases he will be likely to hold views which are relatively hostile or which certainly do not reflect the more important realities.

Attitudes Towards Gypsies

Reprinted with permission from *Gypsies and Other Travellers*, HMSO, 1967, pp. 43–6.

Attitudes towards travellers vary from friendly sentimentality mixed with condescension at one extreme, through various degrees of tolerance and disapproval, to the other extreme of open hostility. The latter attitude was expressed by one city alderman who is on record as saying of the worst elements among the gypsies '... one has to exterminate the impossibles'.

The most widespread attitude is typified by the following comment: 'I've no objection to the real Romanies, the true gypsies, but these people are not true gypsies and they must be prevented from living this sort of life in this area.' It is certainly unlikely that many of the travellers today are pure-blooded descendants of those wandering people of Indian origin who first came to this country some five hundred years ago, since a considerable amount of 'marrying-out' has taken place. When speaking favourably of 'real Romanies' the house-dweller seems to have in mind a handsome olive-skinned gypsy family living in a gaily painted horse-drawn caravan hidden away deep in the woods, where the family, proud and resourceful, spend their time on rural crafts and draw their water from a stream, without contact with the house-dweller. Such families do exist, but our enquiry suggests that they are a negligible proportion of all the so-called gypsies, the great majority of whom have now turned to motorised transport, modern caravans and the more profitable occupation of scrap dealing and roadwork. Nevertheless, it is probable that most of today's travellers have some Romany blood. And all, irrespective of the extent of their Romany blood, experience the same difficulties in carrying on their way of life in our society.

There are four main headings under which the most common complaints against travellers can be grouped: fear of criminal acts including theft and physical assault; damage to amenities; fear of hazards to public health; and a belief that gypsies and other travellers are 'social parasites'.

Children still repeat the rhyme, 'My Mother said I never should play with the gypsies in the wood', and a popular legend exists that gypsies actually steal children. Anyone wishing to validate this fear that gypsies or other travellers may do violence to children from the settled community who stray near their camps would find any evidence difficult to obtain. Nevertheless, the fear of violence is often one of the reasons put forward by local residents to explain their objections to nearby traveller encampments. In some cases this fear may have been caused by the abusive or threatening manner adopted by certain travellers, in others it may have been aroused by the sight of occasional fights among travellers. In the Ministry files, the single alleged instance of 'violence' by travellers against a member of the settled population was when a local councillor who was inspecting an encampment was pushed off his motor scooter. More recently there have been reports in the Press of travellers' attempts to resist eviction.

Serious thefts are equally unlikely to be the work of gypsies or other travellers, although petty pilfering is not uncommon. Stealing, indeed, is often restricted to items which appear to be 'unwanted' by their rightful owners. The late Norman Dodds pointed out that, in his experience, the arrival of gypsies in an area could be the signal for local petty thieves within the settled community to begin operating, knowing that the itinerant visitors would be blamed. A Hampshire general practitioner who has had many years experience of travellers had said, 'Their standards of honesty are high among themselves. The "rogues" of their community may strip a garden of flowers if they don't know the person. They never do wanton damage. They poach as much as the average countryman, more skilfully and more humanely than the suburban car poacher.'

According to information provided by Chief Constables in 1950, out of seventy police authorities who had any gypsies or other travellers in their areas, only twenty reported that they were suspected of criminal offences; in all these cases, without exception, these were restricted to minor offences such as petty thefts and poaching. The remaining fifty police authorities did not suspect travellers in their areas of any crime. The survey showed that damage to fences and trespass on farmland, often by straying animals, were an important source of complaint although, with the rapid decline of horse-drawn transport, it may be expected that this problem has been reduced and will soon disappear. Apart from complaints about Irish tinkers, more recent information confirms this general picture. A detailed analysis of gypsy crime in Leicestershire between 1961 and 1963 shows the same general pattern, with motoring and camping offences predominating.

It is often the despoiling of beauty spots and of the countryside generally, as well as damage caused to trees and hedgerows, which give rise to the strongest disapproval among those who campaign against travellers' encampments. The sight of roadside verges and fields covered with scrap or unsaleable material is a constant cause of friction between the travellers and the settled population. The traveller, who generally has less respect than the house-dweller for rural or urban amenities, sometimes cannot understand the annoyance which his behaviour causes. Some claim that they are not allowed to stop long enough to clear the site. Many traveller families, in fact, do take care to clear up their sites before departure hoping this might make their eventual return more acceptable.

Inevitably, however, these families suffer from the bad reputation of others. The Irish tinkers have a particularly bad reputation for leaving litter on their sites. But there can be no doubt that many camping places, especially those of the families dealing in scrap metal, are extremely squalid. Scrap metal was found stored on half of all the sites where traveller families were recorded in the census and where the presence or absence of scrap was noted. It remains to be seen how the provisions of the Civic Amenities Act will affect travellers.

The popular reaction to this problem is to call for the total removal of the travellers concerned into another area (where the same situation is likely to recur) rather than to put forward constructive suggestions for solving it. The general tendency is to imply that those areas with the best amenities have the least responsibility for travellers, who would be more acceptable in areas which already have their quota of dereliction and ugliness. All too often, travellers end up on sites close to rubbish tips and the like, because there they make no noticeable addition to the existing squalor. The cleansing superintendent of one city proposed that travellers might be offered permanent sites on the municipal refuse tips. It is perhaps not surprising that living in conditions of this kind travellers take little interest or pride in their environment. Where tidiness has been encouraged, as on the better local authority caravan sites, the families have responded well and in some cases have set up fences and established gardens round their caravans. We have also noted how those families on farmland sites live in generally better conditions, possibly owing in part to the relative security they enjoy.

Objections made by local residents against travellers' uncontrolled camps are often based upon the possible hazards to public health caused by their primitive sanitary arrangements. Epidemics are expected to break out and children are warned not to go to the encampment. The litter, including remains of derelict cars and lorries, frequently forms an attractive playground for local children when the travellers have moved on. The principal source of anxiety is the travellers' habit of using hedgerows and ditches instead of W.C.s or other closets. The vicinity of the site is frequently left in an aesthetically revolting condition but a danger to health only exists when faecal matter has been deposited by some person who is either suffering from, or is a carrier of, the organism of some form of enteric disease such as typhoid or paratyphoid fevers, dysentery, salmonella or other food poisoning, or certain virus diseases. Human infection may then result either by direct contamination of the hands, by fly-borne transmission or by the contamination of food or water with the infected faecal matter. The risk from any one camp site is small but is nevertheless real and everything possible should obviously be done to prevent the fouling of the environment.

Travellers do not fit into the neat categories of our settled society. They are not householders and so do not pay rates. Because they are nomadic it is difficult to collect income tax or national insurance contributions from them—a difficulty which is intensified by their illiteracy and social isolation. Most make a living by collecting what others throw away. These characteristics of the traveller way of life—the common non-payment of taxes and the trading in waste materials—are sometimes labelled as 'parasitic'. This label suggests that travellers choose to 'live off the backs' of others, whereas, on the contrary, they strongly desire to be independent and self-employed, despite the immense handicap of illiteracy. The extent to which they are forced to depend on the goodwill of the settled population is the result of changes in society for which they cannot be held responsible, and over which they have had no control. Neither is it just to condemn dealing in waste materials as a parasitic means of earning a living since scrap collecting of all kinds serves an economic function in that it recovers useful material for which there is a demand. However, the traveller scrap dealer is often guilty of leaving behind a great deal of unwanted material which someone else has the expense of clearing. Many travellers also do agricultural work for part of the year and provide a valuable mobile labour force for farmers and market gardeners.

The antagonism between the house-dweller and the traveller is not confined to the house-dweller. The travellers' attitude towards authority arises from the difficulty he experiences in dealing with officials and bureaucratic processes. Being illiterate, he rarely knows the law. It is difficult for him fully to understand the officials who move him out of their area knowing full well that there is nowhere he can legally stop in the next area. He fails to understand why, if he is breaking the law everywhere he camps, there is any point in constantly moving him on. Many of the rights exercised by local authorities such as the power to close his traditional stopping places, he sees as an attack on his way of life and as an attempt to prevent his making a living. He also resents the attempt to prevent him from collecting together quantities of scrap metal in unauthorised places, the requirement that as a scrap metal dealer he must be licensed, and the serving on him of nuisance abatement notices under the Public Health Act.

The result, over the years, of these continual brushes with authority is that the traveller has developed a deep distrust of other people, a suspicion and resentment that will not be easy to break down. When, for example, the local authority site at Llanelli was established, despite frequent preceding consultations between officials and travellers, the latter were so sceptical about the council's intentions that, late on the appointed day, they sent along a small advance guard to see whether it could really be true that they were to be allowed to live in peace on a permanent site. The closing of stopping places and consequential extreme shortage of them has probably caused more hardship and more bitterness than any other act of the settled community. The reaction of some families has been in effect, 'Since you do nothing for me, I'll do nothing for you', and they have deliberately made no attempt to leave their unauthorised stopping place clean and tidy.

Travellers have a strong feeling of identity with their own community. They have their own particular pride about the nomadic way of life; the free life of the traveller where time is not the master is still an ideal and some shame is felt on abandoning it. An elderly traveller who had settled in a house reported that other members of his family had offered to club together to buy him a caravan; it was assumed that he would prefer to be on the road again. A permanently settled life is considered by many to be extremely restrictive and living in a house positively unhealthy. Nevertheless, possibly because of the increasing difficulties involved in travelling, and also because motorisation enables families to cover a large area from one base, the majority of families now wish to settle.

The traveller is also proud of his ability to make a living independently, without having to work for a boss. 'Put a gypsy down anywhere in the world and he will make a living' is one of their boasts. Those who take jobs at a weekly wage sometimes lose prestige. The factory worker who must clock in every morning, who can take a break only when permitted and who must work until an appointed finishing time is considered less than a man. In Hampshire, even the travellers who have been successfully introduced to wage-earning jobs are said to have a slightly furtive air compared with those remaining self-employed.

The traveller believes that he is despised as an inferior creature and tends to hold aloof from the settled population. He resents the fact that many employers will have no dealings with him, that many publicans refuse to serve him and that other customers object to his presence. Frequently, he suspects that his children are discriminated against at school. In return, he often retaliates by despising the house-dweller.

To compensate for the many humiliations of his daily existence he derives great pleasure from such minor triumphs as the besting of house-dwellers in a deal, or from using abusive language against officials who are trying to shift him, or from moving out of an area without answering a summons or without paying a fine. These sins of omission not unnaturally lead to further police activity, which only increases his sense of being persecuted.

There is little evidence of any general wish by the settled population to improve the primitive living conditions of the travellers, to free them from the injustice of being constantly moved on, to raise them from the position of a despised and isolated minority or to educate their children. On the contrary, the settled population has almost invariably objected whenever measures for the benefit of the gypsies have been proposed (the community of Llanelli was one honourable exception), and many individuals have been discouraged from constructive action by the hostility of the settled population. It is clear, unfortunately, that the attitude of hostility between the settled population and the travellers is so firmly established and so widespread that attempts to alleviate their material conditions are unlikely to enjoy majority support unless a great deal of prior publicity and explanation is given to local residents. Equally it is clear that it will not be easy to break down the travellers' mistrust of the settled population since this is the result of ill-will experienced over many generations.

Black Britons
Stuart Hall

Reprinted with permission from 'Black Britons', Part 1, *Community*, Quarterly Journal of the Community Relations Commission, Vol. 1, No. 2, April 1970, pp. 3–5.

The socio-cultural and psychological pressures on individuals or groups which are involved in moving from one culture to another so closely interpenetrate, that it is impossible to make any clearcut distinction between them. The stresses involved are multiple and have a multiple impact both on social environment and on individual personalities. The problems of adjustment are of a long-term, rather than a short-term, nature. In the United States—the classic instance of a 'melting pot society' where the elements have failed to melt—the experience of immigration is still being played out into the fourth and fifth generations. I do not believe that the vast majority of black immigrants to Britain are going to return to their countries of origin unless they are sent, although almost all of us will want to keep alive the possibility of 'going home' as an escape clause, just in case the society does decide in the end to push us over the side. The stubborn fact is—*pace* Mr. Powell —that a substantial majority of black immigrants, whether they came here as adults, at an early age or were born here, are going to remain. This does not mean that they are necessarily going to be *happy* Black Britons, but they are certainly going to be citizens of this society for a long time to come.

The problems for immigrants and the 'host' community will not necessarily be the same over a long period. Our experience of previous immigration in other countries suggests that the problems are staged or phased across the generations. The process of adaptation for people who make the transition from one society to another in adult life is also quite different from that of the first new-born generation (often called 'the second generation'), which is our central focus here. So far we have been preoccupied in Britain by the problems of the 'first wave', and all too little research has as yet been done into the problems and adaptation of the second wave.

The process of change on both sides is bound to be difficult, and may be painful or even socially disruptive. In some ways it will be as hard for adult West Indians, Indians or Pakistanis to accept the fact that their children and grandchildren will be progressively 'at home' in a different country, as it will be for white people to accept that the presence of considerable numbers of second and third generation black people will irreversibly alter *their* culture and social patterns. The question is therefore: are we prepared for the inevitable changes on both sides? Can we tackle change or will we allow it to tackle us?

To 'belong' to any society is to know it from the inside, to be inward with its forms of social organisation and its modes of personal expression, to inhabit its universe of meanings and values, habitually and instinctively, even to share its prejudices. The moment people move to a new cultural situation, they inevitably become 'strangers'. It does not matter how quickly they adjust, how well they know 'the language' or how successfully they learn to master the gestures of social interaction: there is all the difference in the world between a gesture which is correctly, but externally, performed and one which is performed instinctively. It is this sense of being strange to the entire pattern of behaviour, the whole complex of meanings which unify the society around one, which makes the actual experience of immigration so problematic. Time is perhaps the only way of overcoming the barriers.

Rather than drawing generally optimistic or pessimistic conclusions from past experiences of immigration, it is perhaps more profitable to look briefly at the background of the different cultural groups which have emigrated to Britain in recent years, the situations into which they have moved, their expectations, the expectations which confront them, and the existing context which frames the whole experience—composed largely of a stable/unstable balance between tolerance and intolerance in the host community. Very different patterns of adjustment emerge as one moves from one group to another in the current British situation. And especially where the second generation is concerned, West Indians and Asians face very different problems. In this matter, we have to take into account three different factors.

First, the cultural and social background of the immigrants themselves in their home communities. Second, the cultural attitudes, values and forms of social organisation in the country to which they move. And thirdly, and most significantly, the actual situation on the ground where black immigrants and white natives confront one another. In my view, although it is necessary to understand as well as we can the background contexts both for immigrants and for the host community, the most crucial factor is certainly how these attitudes and values operate in the actual situation where the two groups confront one another. We might express this in a diagram:

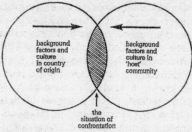

Figure 3

Immigrants from the Asian sub-continent come largely from an integrated and cohesive pre-European, rural culture with its own distinctive values and ways of life, often expressed through and maintained by powerful social and religious sanctions. Marriage, the position of women, the status of children, social habits of dress, food, etc., are all regulated by religious and social codes. Such groups have their own distinctive patterns of family life and their own language or sets of language. Incidentally, it seems to me important for the maintenance of the morale of immigrant groups that they do have access to a 'different language', even when this is simply a variant of the dominant language spoken in the new society. There is nothing like being able to swear at someone in your own private language for keeping yourself afloat in a difficult situation.

The situation for West Indians is radically different. Their culture is in some crucial respects a fragmented one. The original Arawak inhabitants of the Caribbean islands were decimated in the early years of Spanish conquest. The West Indian society which emerged after the European discovery of the New World is a highly artificial concept created largely out of economic and historic drives. The society is crucially a post-slave society, evolving within the distinctive culture of the colonial/imperial nexus. Into this cauldron, the most diverse cultural influences have been poured. Influences coming from the African past, from slave society itself, from British, American and other European influences. All of these have been absorbed, and come to their distinctive form, within the confines of a poor, tropical and largely rural society.

The basic social patterns thus represent a kind of compromise between the African past, the post-slave context and an imposed English colonial system. Religion is important, but it does not play the kind of cohesive role which it does for immigrant groups from the Asian sub-continent. As in other post-slave societies religion is very largely an expressive medium, through which men live out and express their protest against current deprivation and their aspirations for the future. This does not mean that Asian teenagers have it easy and West Indian teenagers confront difficulties. There are both advantages and disadvantages in having a relatively stable cultural background. While the Asian pattern offers a degree of personal and social stability and a sense of family and group cohesiveness, there is the danger that this very cohesiveness can become too constricting and confining a context for the second and third generations. Once again, the question of whether a cohesive background can serve as a secure baseline for future adaptation, or whether it becomes a defensive mechanism, is largely determined by the actual situation in which immigrant groups find themselves.

The West Indian pattern is far less stable. The European forms of Christian marriage and the family are recognised as the 'ideal' pattern, to which the vast majority of the working people subscribe but do not ascribe. This conflict or split in values is indigenous to the West Indian situation. It reflects the fact that the ideal value system has been transferred, through colonialism, from another and foreign culture and is critically at odds with the real, emerging pattern of life in the society. In fact, the slave situation, compounded by the rhythms of plantation life, etc., has yielded a much wider range of *types* of family as compared with the typical European *family*.

The patterns range from the typical European patrilocal family, which is especially common among middle-class West Indians, through a pattern of stable 'common-law' association to the more fragmented types of matrifocal/patrilocal units. In this last type of family, the children reside with the mother (or grandmother), the mother is the stable unit in the universe of the family, whereas the father is a wandering star—although a crucial figure of authority when he is there. Immigration transposes any one of these types of family units from the West Indian context, where work, environment and occupation provide their own natural supports, and sets it down in a society shorn of the connections and supports of extended kinship—grandmothers, aunts, older sisters, cousins and related cousins —in a society where the family is typically father, mother, two point five children, a car and an insurance policy. Whether belonging to or deviating from the classic European family pattern, the West Indian family in Britain does not have access to the natural network of relatives and friends which is common in its own home situation. The family is developing inevitably in a truncated context.

The Language of Controversy
Brian Lee

Reprinted with permission from Brian Lee, 'Enoch Powell's Language', *New Society*, 23 January 1969, p. 119.

In a controversy, it is often the scrutiny of the language in which the controversy is expressed that comes last. This is natural: one is more interested in what is being said than in the way in which it is being said. But a glance at the phraseology of commitment may be valuable. It gives us a further test for objectivity. Although we distort language (to say which is hardly to say more than that we use it), it is still our first measure of impersonal judgment. Language is part of us, but it is also apart from us.

The following notes on Enoch Powell's Eastbourne speech were made to introduce a discussion with engineering students in one of the new polytechnics. The students, at the end of a hard term's work, my own part of which was to introduce a course in 'Communications', asked for a discussion on some broader social or political issues. Powell it had to be.

However, I did not feel that I was politically conscious or knowledgeable enough to tackle this theme frontally, so to speak. I also felt that the continuity of the course on communication should be maintained. I sought a compromise; and agreed to discuss only the linguistic aspects of Powell's speech. A further contributory motive to this was my own uncertainty about my precise position on Powell. Was it possible to stay free of the anti- and pro-Powell polarity; to stay in the middle?

One had heard in argument semi-justifications of Enoch Powell's views on the grounds that at least he, in contrast to most politicians, could speak, at least he could write; and that this superiority was perhaps the guarantee of a superior ability to see and express certain facts. Though conscious that the same had been said of other political figures, one could, up to a point, agree: Powell had a power of rhetoric which seemed to exceed that of other politicians. Not for him, indeed, cliche, circumlocution, hesitancy and cant, the deft and amiable avoidance of the point, the mumbled platitude or the float upwards into abstractions and generalisation. What a relief! Given the relief, the attraction might follow.

But the listener might be imagining clarity where, in the extended extract, it did not exist. And there was another grave fact; was there not something sinister about Powell's linguistic power?

Here we come to the language in which Powell's ideas are expressed, as opposed to those ideas themselves. For what had first aroused my doubts about the morality of the Eastbourne speech was, simply, the metaphor, applied to the Briton (itself an interestingly archaic usage—more of that later) of the 'toad beneath the harrow'. One's response to it, as a lover of frogs and toads, was prompt and painful. It was first broadcast on television, and though unexamined, produced a sensation of shock. On examination, I think that the shock is due to the contrast between the very softness, vulnerableness and tenderness even of the physique of these animals (a bit slimy, certainly, but that is irrelevant) and the metallic, brutal, harshness of the harrow. There is too the connotation of size: the giant harrow, the tiny toad. And all this is applied to the position of 'the Briton ... in the areas where the immigrant population is taking root'. (Later Powell says that immigrants don't become part of English society—don't 'take root'.)

Powell half guards himself against analysis of the kind I have offered. He would perhaps answer that the metaphor is a very old one, indeed is not his at all. In his speech he recognises this by using inverted commas round the phrase (at least as quoted in *The Times*). He is conscious, that is to say, of the provenance of the metaphor, and perhaps of its power. In highly emotive writing this kind of intellectual awareness is rare—and it might be said that it is the distinguishing characteristic of Powell's language. Before going on to examine other examples of this tug between reason and emotion, I would like to point out that by putting the metaphor in inverted commas Powell is able to have it both ways—to get his use out of the metaphor at the same time as he combines with it a touch of repudiation. While he was speaking, it would have been difficult to hear the inverted commas.

The same technique is employed towards the end of the Eastbourne speech where the highly emotive phrase about 'England's green and pleasant land' is used. Of course, the case is different—but how different? It is still true that the speaker is making use of something that is not his, taken from a context carrying totally different implications. Blake's Albion, Blake's England even, are different places from our England; and Wolverhampton might stand in gloomy contrast to what *is* green and pleasant. Perhaps this is more a comment on fact than on language.

Some of Powell's uses of language are obvious enough; what may be slightly less so is his tendency to set up opposites, to assume that groups have finite boundaries, and to speak as if class-words referred to some real entity. Two examples will suffice:

1. The gulf which exists between 'the overwhelming majority of people on the one side and a tiny minority' who have almost a monopoly of the channels of communication and who 'seem determined' not to know the facts.

2. The group Mr Powell calls 'indigenous' or the 'host population', and the group he calls 'immigrants'. The word *indigenous* seems to be another case of a careful choice of terms, for it sounds socio-scientific, and therefore unemotional and factual; and it thus avoids the kind of scorn that would be poured on such a notion as that of the 'pure-bred Englishman', ridiculed by Defoe two and a half hundred years ago. The word *host* is a little more difficult to deal with. Although it too sounds scientific (medicine) it has connotations which are of dubious advantage to Powell's technique; it is on the host body that various parasitic organisms grow. Did Powell intend this implication or not?

These language uses remind one of another popular opposition in the public mind: between the 'older generation' and the 'younger generation'. What is the result—that one has a 'generation gap'. Does it exist? Who knows, now? And what journalist cares? What kind of a hope do any of these phrases offer of a reasoned solution? They merely threaten collision, as does the subsequent polarisation of pro- and anti-Powell.

And what kind of 'facts' are the facts that Powell talks about? Some are measurable. These Mark Bonham-Carter analysed in *The Times* of 18 November 1968. There are other kinds of facts—events and narratives—related in the speeches. One might think that the three examples of these in the Eastbourne speech are insufficient on which to base a generalisation—that this is the all-and-some fallacy again. Powell characteristically forestalls one: 'ask those who know, and they will tell you whether all that is exceptional.' Well, one test of the value of the statement in general semantics is verifiability. To verify it, one would have to ask those who know, and more likely than not go from statement of opinion to statement of opinion. It was into this morass of non-verifiability that the reporters who followed up the one name mentioned by Powell (that of Dr Bamford) staggered.

The central tension in Powell's rhetoric is between the emotional tow and the apparently dispassionate construction of his speech, where paragraph is linked to paragraph, in a way that the most stringent stylist would approve of, by the required formulaic phrases. The listener appears to be led logically from idea to idea in this way:

'Of course, there are many cases where individuals have uprooted themselves to come here . . .' (Connection by qualification.)

'A recently published study of one of the West Indian islands puts it thus . . .' (Connection by learned reference, reinforcement by sociology.)

'Against this background . . .' (Preparation for generalisation.)

'Under an agreement between Ceylon and India . . .'

'A cursory survey carried out by a national newspaper . . .' All these move steadily, by requisite academic progression, towards:

'The West Indian or Asian does not, by being born in England, become an Englishman. In law he becomes a United Kingdom citizen by birth; in fact he is a West Indian or an Asian still.'

Simple, well-constructed, memorable sentences; each nicely balanced, with their weight falling at the full stop. The final sentence, especially, has the kind of finality one associates with the Johnsonian couplet, or at least with Doctor Johnson. There is a delicately archaic weight about Powell's diction. It is there in the word 'still' at the end of the final sentence. The placing is a slight modification of standard usage. We would normally say 'he is still a West Indian'—which is a different matter. 'Still' at the end reminds one, *just*, of the bible; and perhaps one is led there by the Churchillian associations ('the people of England will not endure it') that are so beguiling to the people of this country. It is not crude Churchillianism. Harold Wilson's 'at the end of the day' rapidly became a cliche. What makes it more subtle, as it made the use of metaphor more subtle, is the extent of intellectual awareness with which it is all done. What the precise extent of that awareness is, one must remain uncertain. At what point could one say that it became calculation?

Ulster: Social Background of the Conflict
R. S. P. Elliott and John Hickie

Reprinted with permission from R. S. P. Elliott and John Hickie, *Ulster: A Case Study in Conflict Theory*, Longmans, 1971, pp. 32–5.

It is impossible, as always, to try and decide the rights and wrongs of the conflict from an inspection of the historical data; nevertheless several things are apparent. The first is that there is a long legacy of strife from which both sides can draw ammunition to support their own cases. Not only do they draw on different events but each side has a different interpretation of the same events. For the Catholics most of the period of English rule represented outright colonial repression. For the Protestants it was a noble attempt on the part of the English Parliament to support a besieged but civilising community inside Ireland. Again, Connolly's socialism was probably a natural response to the repressive tactics adopted by Protestant landlords, most of whom were resident in England. To the Protestants it represented only a development of the cancer of the French Revolution. Lastly the aid given by the Southern Irish community to the Central powers during the First World War could not be accepted by loyalist Protestants. The Southerners saw it only as a vindication of their inalienable right to choose their own side in war.

The conflict was made the more intractable since the hostility and opposition fell along well demarcated social and cultural lines. There was a gulf between the two social structures as well as between cultural beliefs. It is difficult for an Englishman to understand the extent to which such differences can affect two communities' perceptions of each other. Groups in a plural society may be marked by various differences, only some of which strike us as natural grounds for mutual opposition. For example, the Greek and Turkish communities in Cyprus have different religions, which means that they end up with different rules about marriage, diet and inheritance; they also have different languages. They have hundreds of years of political contact and opposition. The only obvious difference they do not have is physical appearance. The Ulster situation is in many ways similar. Although the English language is used by both groups, the Irish language and the illegal tricolour flag is something special to many Catholics. From the religious differences come crucial rules about marital and sexual behaviour, and dietary rules. An awareness of Cromwell's massacres at Drogheda and Wexford and of the decisive Protestant victory at the Boyne is socialised into school children and it becomes as much a part of the consciousness of belonging to each faith as being black is for an American Negro. The fact that such aspects of group identity are invisible does not make them any the less powerful in determining lines of cooperation and cleavage.

Even where differences between groups seem quite trivial to outsiders, to participants they may be crucial. In the Mediterranean countryside people often speak of the next village or the upper part or the lower part of a town as if the dwellers there illustrated an encyclopaedia of the vices. Not only are they the biggest liars, cheats, thieves and cuckolds, but they also sleep with their sisters. Sometimes there is a traditional annual confrontation between the villagers or the town sections which leads to fights, just as often and inevitably as do Ulster parades. Boys who come from the other place are beaten up if they try to court local girls, obscene rhymes are invented and sung lustily on feast days. With all the apparent hostility, the curious thing is that people actually are pretty civil to each other when they meet. Such opposition probably plays a part in damping down hostility within the community; the moral characteristics attributed to the enemy group are plainly untrue, there is a level at which people know they are not describing their neighbours accurately, but at times they act on the information they know to be inaccurate.

What we are describing here is a situation where two communities eventually end up needing their mutual opposition in order to maintain their own values and beliefs about themselves. It is also a situation where a multitude of different little signals serve to make the native aware of the foreignness of a member of the opposite community. In such a situation political interdependence and geographical proximity become factors which militate towards danger. It is true that both communities have to develop rules which allow them to live together in the normal course of events, whether they be rules concerning all the allocation of rewards in the political system or how one addresses a member of the Protestant community at the local shop. However, this is a very different kind of coexistence from that which, for example, people from Yorkshire have with people from Lancashire. In the Ulster situation any interdependence the two communities may have (and at the most basic level they depend on each other if only to keep the peace) becomes a matter of vulnerability. It is always important not to expose one's weaker points; one must always keep one's defences up. In such a situation, given the perspectives held by the two communities, it is rational to maintain a defensive and suspicious posture towards the other side. In the British press we often read editorials which state that the situation in Ulster would be completely calm if only the two sides could be more rational about their behaviour towards each other. Such statements overlook the subjective nature of rationality. The Protestant feels he is faced with a threatening Papist conspiracy and the possibility of a repressive rule by a Catholic majority in a united Ireland. In this light, his tactics with regard to maintaining his influence, status and prestige in Northern Ireland are entirely rational, the more so since the people against whom he is defending his position appear to him in every way foreign.

Such relationships take on the nature of self-fulfilling prophesies—the other side is treated as hostile and aggressive and therefore responds in that fashion, precisely because the other side is also keeping up its guard. Almost any move the other side makes is treated with suspicion: if the other side tries to increase its autonomy or become more independent, this is regarded as a threat. A Catholic-controlled free Londonderry would be a decided threat to the Protestant ascendancy, and any attempt to establish such a political situation would meet with extreme resistance from the Protestant side. If either community looks elsewhere for aid it is immediately accused of seeking imperialist help. Thus when the Ulster Irish look for help from the Catholics in the South the Protestant ascendancy treats this as one more proof of their seeking to overthrow the Constitution of Northern Ireland. When the Ulster Protestants look to Britain for help to the Catholics this is one more indication of the fact that the Protestant Irish are a small minority supported by an imperial power. This atmosphere makes it almost impossible for the two sides to negotiate meaningfully, even if there were this intention on either side. However, in global terms, this almost exhausts the possibilities of the different relationships that the two communities might have between themselves. If they cannot increase their autonomy, or look elsewhere for help, or negotiate with each other, the only option that they have left is to attack each other. This is of course a vast simplification, but it may, nevertheless, turn out to be a true description of recent events.

Of course, the disparity in size is also crucial. It allows both sides to feel embattled: the Catholics against the Protestant majority in Northern Ireland and the Protestants against the Catholic majority in the whole island. In terms of the situation inside Ulster it leads to a deadly cycle. Because the Catholic community is small and vulnerable, it is concerned primarily with its own security. The Protestant community is not so much concerned with its security as with control over the whole of Protestant Ulster. In simplified terms, what happens when both sides try to make a deal? If the Protestants make an offer that they perceive to be generous, how will it be received by the Catholic community? First, it will be treated with extreme suspicion; the reaction from a community that fears for its security is one of wait and see; it is up to the larger side to make concessions. However, such a response is only likely to build up pressure on the larger side, because there is always a group of people who can say there was never any point in making concessions in the first place, and that the lack of response from the smaller community bears this out. This inhibits the chances of making further concessions and also makes sure that the next reaction from the majority community will be all the more violent. This is a syndrome that has been only too apparent in Cyprus in recent years. It was also readily observable in Northern Ireland over the course of 1969 and 1970. Every time the Protestant community made any concessions, they were never enough for the Catholic minority, yet every concession made by the Protestant side was used as ammunition by the Protestant militants for vowing they would make no more.

Thus the two communities, loaded with a long history of mutual opposition, are also faced with a situation where there is a very low level of information flowing between them, which only alienates them further. As we have mentioned, there are rules which govern the day to day relationships between the two sides, but should there be any substantial shift in the social balance, or should anything happen to upset those rules, then there is every reason to be pessimistic about the future of such a society. It was just such a shift in the social situation and just such a breakdown of the rules between the two communities which led to the violence which erupted in 1969, and to worse violence subsequently in the years to come.

Coloured Immigrants and the Police
John Lambert

Reprinted with permission from *The Listener*, 13 November 1969, pp. 663–4.

Good relations between police and public are as important for the police as for the public because the police do far more than enforce the law: they are advisers and protectors, representatives of a system of justice, keeping traffic moving, as well as keeping the peace. They also do less than enforce the law, for full enforcement is impossible: law-breaking is too common, too pervasive. The law itself is too blunt an instrument for the control of human behaviour, so there must be a selection of what the law is to enforce and whom to prosecute. The police exercise discretion—the essential technique of policing our sort of society.

Good relations between police and public imply a confidence that this discretion is used wisely and fairly, that police powers are not exceeded and that the police are themselves adequately policed. This confidence has never been easily won, particularly not from those most in contact with the police, those most affected by crime and disorder, those with least confidence in the central values and institutions of our society: the working class, the urban poor, the young. Recently, the minority group whose relations with the police have caused most concern is the racially and culturally diverse group of peoples we call 'the coloured community'. There is little doubt that relations between police and coloured minorities have been deteriorating. Jim Rose's report, *Colour and Citizenship*, makes the point strongly that all organisations connected with civil liberties and race relations have files full of complaints about police practice. The police have not ignored the criticism. Liaison officers of various kinds have been at work for some years. An authoritative Home Office letter was sent in July 1967 to all Chief Constables, stressing the need for better information and training and better use of liaison officers. More recently, a Community Relations Division has been set up within Scotland Yard.

In 1967 I carried out some research for the Survey of Race Relations in Britain, part of which tried to explain this state of affairs. I started by looking into crime rates among immigrants. It was soon apparent that coloured immigrants, young and old alike, were to a marked extent less in trouble with the police than their English and Irish neighbours. Although high crime areas overlapped with areas of coloured concentration, low crime rates characterised the coloured immigrants themselves. But this low involvement in crime did not mean slight or insignificant contact between police and coloured minorities: on the contrary, it was clear that here was a significant point of contact where, quite literally, race relations in Britain were made.

What struck me most forcibly about policing was the amazing diversity of demands and calls made on the police service. A uniformed officer is called on to help, advise and assist far more often than to effect an arrest. They have to deal with all kinds of people in all sorts of situations—not just with crime and criminals—so law enforcement is a poor description of police work, and crime statistics a worthless indicator of their effectiveness. But it was clear that crime work is what the police currently regard as their proper task. Many of the service tasks and peace-keeping functions are seen as tiresome and time-consuming. The good policeman is out to make a good arrest. His promotion chances depend on that, so all incidents tend to be looked at for their crime content. This at least seemed to be the view of the police authorities seeking an image of professionalism for the police, and it clashed with what the policeman on the beat had to do. There, the calls for advice and assistance continued. Few of the situations the uniformed officer confronts are clear-cut: the policeman has to choose what to do. He continually needs to judge a person and a situation very quickly. He's bound to use stereotypes and labels to be able to anticipate what the client will do, and modify his own behaviour and action accordingly. In keeping one step ahead, as master of the situation, he is highly sensitive to the respect he is shown. So the drunk who doesn't curse but mumbles 'sir', the penitent speeding motorist, the anxious and deferential parent or youthful delinquent, the cooperative petty thief who pleads guilty—these can expect something of a square deal from the police. The arrogant, the argumentative, the youth who answers back, the man who asserts his rights—those who challenge the moral authority of the police can expect a legalistic, officious response from the policeman, for they deny him the choice, the descretion, the respect he needs.

It was clear that relations with coloured citizens were not easy. The attitudes displayed by the police were various; but, frequently critical and even hostile, their prejudices, not surprisingly, were the same as those of most white citizens. It was clear, too, that the coloured citizen was also frequently uncertain about the extent of the powers of the British police, and he might anyway have been taught a wise suspicion and distrust by experience of policing in his homeland. This distrust explains, I think, the 'arrogance' policemen frequently find in their encounters with coloured citizens. I remember an instance where a youngish West Indian was brought to a police station because an English girl of about 18 had complained that he was taking her to his home against her will. After the girl had told her story, from which it was clear that there was no offence involved, the man stated, somewhat emphatically, that the police should listen to both sides of the story, not just the girl's. One of the policemen, clearly incensed by the man's manner, went up to him and almost shouted: 'Who do you think you're talking to? You'd better show more respect than talk to a policeman like that.' The West Indian replied with equal fervour: 'You're not going to frighten me—don't think you can beat me up in a police station and get away with it.' There followed an angry and incoherent exchange which ended abruptly with the West Indian saying: 'Why pick on me for this? You only do so because I'm black.' 'Oh,' replied the policeman, 'thanks for telling me—I hadn't noticed.'

More serious complaints were recently documented in the television programme *Cause for Concern*: cases where appeals against conviction by coloured citizens were upheld, and in-

stances of police malpractice shown up. The allegations typified what happens when the police system fails and police
powers are exceeded or abused: planted evidence, perjured
statements in court, brutality in a police station, trumped-up
charges. There were complaints, too, of 'don't care' attitudes,
of an inclination on the part of the police to pay scant regard
to complaints by coloured citizens. The programme asked just
how extraordinary and atypical these instances were. When
policing goes wrong, complaints of violence, perjury and
harassment are just what one should expect, reflecting as they
do the occupational hazards that face the police. Confidence in
the police means a confidence that such abuses and excesses
are controlled and checked, that the occasional scandal is
atypical, that normal policing is supervised, legal and just.
More important, it seems to me, is the credibility of such cases
—credibility, that is, for the coloured population. At the
moment, I believe it to be the case that serious complaints,
rumours of malpractice, suggestions of impropriety, which
should be thought of as incredible and extraordinary, are considered by large sections of the coloured population to be definitely credible, just one sign of the equivocal welcome meted
out by the host society. A basis for confidence which rests on
the daily routine tasks of policing has not been achieved.

The Rose report on *Colour and Citizenship* makes a number
of recommendations: the need for improved police training;
for clear recruitment policies whereby the police themselves
become a multiracial institution; the value for the police in
developing a community relations function; the need for better
information about the role and powers of the police, and
clearer instructions about the rights of prisoners and the nature
of police procedures in police stations. The report also points
to perhaps the most corrosive element in the problem: the
present system of handling complaints against the police. At
present, the police themselves investigate all complaints. Their
definition of what is trivial or serious, what is substantiated or
unsubstantiated, is difficult to question. If there is a crisis in
confidence about the police, resulting in normal practices, as
well as specific abuses being challenged, a system whereby
police are judge and jury in their own case can only contribute
to that crisis. So the report argues for a system of external
review.

Of course the police are not alone in these problems. A
Parliamentary select committee on race relations has been tak-

ing evidence recently in several towns and cities, hearing something of the ambiguities and conflicts, hopes and fears of many people involved in race relations. It is clear that they heard complaints and criticisms about the shortcomings of a great many services and institutions, not only about the police. What is necessary is a shift in emphasis in the way we analyse and study the colour problem, away from the differences and idiosyncrasies of the racially and culturally distinctive minority, and toward the capacity of our existing institutions to cater for the needs of a multiracial society. The police are in a particularly difficult situation. By their continual and visible presence in the neighbourhood, they symbolise much more than law enforcement: too easily they can become convenient scapegoats for a variety of ills and shortcomings. In addition, since their very purpose is to conserve the *status quo*, the police are less likely to shed traditions easily. But so long as the police continue to feel that for them the old ways are the safest and best, and that policing can be given a narrow professional definition of law enforcement, criticisms and complaints will not diminish.

Further Reading: **Minorities**

* N. DEAKIN and A. LESTER (Eds.), *Policies for Racial Equality*, Fabian Tract No. 262, Second Edition, 1970.

  C. DUKE, *Colour and Rehousing. A Study of Redevelopment in Leeds*, Oxford (Institute of Race Relations Special Series), 1970.

* P. FOOT, *Immigration and Race in British Politics*, Harmondsworth, Penguin, 1965.

  J. GOULD and S. ESH (Eds.), *Jewish Life in Modern Britain*.

* B. HEPPLE, *Race, Jobs and the Law*, Harmondsworth, Penguin, 1971.

  J. A. JACKSON, *The Irish in Britain*, London, Allen and Unwin, 1965.

  C. JONES and Others, *Race and the Press*, London Runnymede Trust, 1971.

* A. LESTER and G. BANDMAN, *Race and the Law*, London, Penguin, 1972.

* J. REX and R. MOORE, *Race, Community and Conflict*, London, Oxford University Press, 1966.

  E. J. B. ROSE and Associates, *Colour and Citizenship*, London, Oxford University Press (for Institute of Race Relations), 1969.

  U. SHARMA, *Rampal and his Family*, London, Collins, 1971.

* H. STREET, *Freedom, the Individual and the Law*, Harmondsworth, Penguin, 1967.

*Available in paperback

Chapter Ten Work

The problems of 'work' are the problems of industrial society itself, and discussion leads into a consideration of the capacity of contemporary British society to satisfy and sustain some of the basic needs of its members. The problem of work is thus a multi-faceted one. For some in the North, in the one-industry towns set in a pattern of apparently irreversible decline, the problem is that there is no work. Or at least the work that may be available is unsuitable, perhaps because of traditions that only certain types of employment are consistent with the dignity of the working man. For the car worker at Luton or Dagenham, the problem is not the absence of work, it is rather that in order to meet his own and his family's expectations of what constitutes a suitable wage, he has to undertake work which is intrinsically dissatisfying, unrewarding and perhaps even degrading, even though the material rewards may be relatively high.

Technological change, of course, means that many old jobs do just fade away. The skills of a lifetime, perhaps hard won by apprenticeship and long use of experience, may suddenly and apparently quite irrationally lose their relevance. The official explanation may be couched in such terms as 'redeployment' or as a 'shake-out', and the greater glory may be the continued expansion of the gross national product, but the unemployed man has to cope with a new burden in contemporary Britain as well as the fact of his apparent lack of usefulness to an employer. While in the 1930s unemployment was generally widespread and persistent over practically a whole decade there was little stigma attached to being out of work and there was moreover a collective support of one's fellows to mitigate the psychic wound. Today's unemployed man has had his expectations of working life moulded by the affluent fifties and early sixties, his horizons elevated by the consumer philosophy embodied in the gospel according to Harold Macmillan: 'You've never had it so good'.

If, for many workers, the problem of work is its absence, to the hypothetical middle-Englander addressed by the *Daily Express*, the problem is not that the workers *cannot* work but that they won't. Absenteeism, it is argued, has become such a characteristic feature of the British economy that to the hard-working German, the efficient Swede and possibly even to the inscrutable Oriental, the syndrome has become known as the English Disease. To the manager, the chief problem facing British industry may be the threat of damaging industrial action, whether official or unofficial, by the trade union.

These are the major problems of work in an industrial society according to the participants most directly involved, but some commentators have kept their eye fixed on more distant horizons than these. To many social scientists, the problem of work is that of making work meaningful to workers. It is sometimes argued that material factors can operate only in a negative way on the experience of job satisfaction of the individual worker. If the pay is bad it may be an important source of discontent but, it is argued, no amount of tinkering with wages or fringe benefits can positively motivate men to undertake work which is inherently lacking in satisfaction. The motivation that is needed must come from the work itself, through the opportunities for self-enhancement and self-enrichment which it offers.

The increased pace of work is noticeable at all levels. The man on the assembly line complains that the management is imperceptibly speeding up the pace of the track. The secretary may perceive the future as involving her becoming a slave to the inhuman rhythm of the dictating machine rather than being at the mercy of the irrational whims of a flesh and blood manager. The doctor complains of the uncontrollable torrent of unnecessary paper work. The policeman goes mobile and thereby alerts the thief more effectively of his presence through the amplified squawking of his personal radio. The university contemplates a doubling of its student intake in the next academic year. Moreover, the change in pace and tempo produces an ever-increasing proliferation of specialised occupations. The manager becomes a corporate planner, the librarian becomes an information systems analyst, the sociologist becomes a meta-theoretician concerned with the construction of a prolegomenon to the impossibility of a rational intersubjective empirical social science. The price of specialisation may be anomie as men become threatened with incapacity in communication, and with alienation as man becomes separated from the process of work, the product of his labour, and an essential aspect of his human nature.

To others again, the problem of work is non-work or leisure. The four-day working week is a reality for many. If the real problems of western society are to do with the need to train people into simplified, less demanding, if less satisfying, work routines, so for many leisure becomes more like work. The technology of the leisure industries is ever developing and the simpler rituals of a skiffle group are displaced by the complex technology of electronic pop. Expertise is hard won even in the field of leisure nowadays.

But one group in society offers a short circuit through the problems of job security, unemployment and lack of satisfying opportunities for psychic expansion. The hippies, the flower-children, the freaks, the drop-outs, the heads, offer a life style which offers a radical, almost physical challenge to the values of conformist Protestant ethic man. For the threat which the drop-outs offer is, in Fred Davis' terms, 'partial, as yet ambiguous, evidence of a massiveness, a universality and a density of existential texture, all of which promise to transcend the narrowly segregated findings of age, occupation and residence that characterised most bohemians of the past . . . just possibly then, by opting out of making their own kind of cultural ways, the hippies are telling us more than we can now imagine about our future selves.' If these signs portend a future in which the pressure of work is eased and the immediate problems of getting and keeping a living recede, one of the first victims may be the consumer boom which has characterised post-war British society. The concern with involvement, with the products of work and with the answer to the perennial question, 'What, and who are we working for?' threaten to whip the situational and circumstantial discontents of the workplace into a tide of fundamental re-thinking that makes problematic much of what we now take for granted about the centrality of work in British society.

In their study *Strikes and the Economy*, Whittingham and Towers examine the background to the Industrial Relations Act. They examine the point of view that the pattern of strike activity in British industry represents not merely a serious and grave problem for the national economy in its own right, but that Britain has suffered from unofficial strikes to a greater extent than any other similar western society. The authors examine the pattern of strikes in the United Kingdom over the period 1931 to 1970, comparing the number of stoppages, the number of workers involved, and the total number of working

days lost. They argue that the increase in the number of
stoppages has been rather less pronounced than the increase in
aggregate working days lost, and that this was largely due to
the fact that strikes were tending to increase in duration. They
find that, if there is a British strike problem, it is far from being
of universal application throughout all sectors of British
industry. For industries such as mechanical and electrical
engineering and motor vehicle manufacture consistently ride
high in terms of all of the indices of strike activity. It may be,
therefore, that these industries are image makers because of
their importance as major exporters. They argue that the
problems that Britain has in the matter of strikes are largely
associated with particular organisations. Many of these
organisations are to be found within an industry that would
seem to be particularly strike-prone. They suggest, therefore,
that any simple-minded solution, reflecting the view that strike
activity is very widespread on a national basis, might well run
the danger of exacerbating the problem which does exist.

In their conclusion, Whittingham and Towers remind the
reader of Gouldner's conclusion that 'A strike is a social
phenomenon of enormous complexity which, in its totality, is
never susceptible to complete description let alone complete
explanation.' The analysis by Lane and Roberts of the
Pilkington Strike in St. Helens in early 1970, comes to a
similar conclusion. No two strikes, argue Lane and Roberts, are
identical. What happened in St. Helens in the spring of 1970
will never happen again, either there or anywhere else. But
the main conclusion from their analysis is that strikes are
'normal'. Very few people at Pilkingtons anticipated a strike or
indeed any dispute over the circumstances which eventually
sparked off the conflict. Similar conflicts had been localised and
contained in the department in which they originated on several
occasions in the past. What was unusual about the 1970
situation was the way this localised conflict became
transformed into a demand for a large across-the-board
increase, and the way in which workers in the firm as a whole,
in departments quite unconnected with the original cause of the
dispute, were drawn in.

Lane and Roberts are clear about one thing, however, and
that is that there is no question either before or during the
strike of its having been engineered by a group of Bolsheviks,
or other subversives, and that in fact there was no organised
plot. Moreover, the course of events that developed could not

have been predicted by anybody, nor even programmed with rough accuracy by the most knowledgeable and informed social scientist. As they say, 'drama there was ... but it was unscripted'. Such script as there was was made up by people as they went along. In other words, to over-rationalise the causal origins of the dispute and to look for clear-cut explanations might be erroneous. It was only as the situation developed that the actors and participants in it crystallised their latent discontents around a set of attainable objectives. One implication from this is, of course, that a strike can generate demands which are incompatible with the original overt reasons for the conflict. If, then, for management and workers alike the strike constitutes a problem and requires a solution, Lane and Roberts would argue that it is a problem which is maybe ineradicable in the form in which it arose at Pilkingtons in 1970. As David Matza pointed out, the idea of deviance is a simple one, for to deviate is to stray, as from a path, or a standard and such straying is as *normal* as is the act of remaining upon the path. It is the vast number of possible paths, deriving from the objective complexities of industrial society, the plurality of paths, that itself constitutes the problem. Lane and Roberts conclude that strikes generally should be regarded as *normal* features of industrial life in those sectors of the economy where large numbers of workers are gathered together under one roof.

We referred a little earlier to the view that the problem of massive, large-scale, structural unemployment such as was known in many parts of Britain during the 1930s had been largely eradicated by the economic policies pursued by successive governments since 1945 and by the ameliorating and alleviating effects of social welfare legislation. But Dorothy Wedderburn argues that there are reasons for regarding the current concern about unemployment as based on a realistic apprehension of some disturbing trends in the national economy. Some very major companies have, in recent months, got into very severe difficulties. There has apparently been a steady secular increase in unemployment from 1966 onwards and the seasonal swings in employment which bring more workers into the labour force during the summer months have in recent years apparently failed to occur. There is some danger obviously in reprinting material of this kind which may be fairly readily falsified, to all appearances, by one good year for the economy. But the analysis of underlying features of the labour market which Wedderburn presents, are, we argue, sufficiently compelling to justify reprinting the article here. Students should recognise of course that by the time the book is published some of these specific statistics and illustrations may need to be supplemented by more up to date information.

Peter Taylor examines another kind of industrial trouble. He examines the widespread belief, held by many in this country and abroad, that the problems of absenteeism are greater in Britain than in any other country. The expression 'The English Sickness', he argues, is widely used to describe a state of industrial and economic difficulty characterised by high rates of absenteeism, restrictive practices and strikes. But he finds that this problem occurs in many other industrial countries, such as Sweden, Italy, Holland and West Germany as well. While it is true that the frequency of absenteeism from some diseases, which previously had a severe impact, such as T.B. and certain kidney diseases, has decreased, other disabilities have now become more frequent. But a disturbing possibility in relation to the existence or not of the English Disease is that many of the diseases that have increased, and particularly those brief spells of illness that so afflict industry, are ones in which few objective signs of disease can be found. We are dealing, therefore, not merely with a problem of the distribution, prevalence, and frequency of disease, of an objective and physical phenomena, but of social attitudes towards disease. As Taylor argued, it is the patient himself who decides on his fitness for work ... 'Influence people's attitudes to work and you will influence rates of sickness absence.' One of the books suggested for further reading in the chapter on Health is the volume edited by Baker, McEwan and Sheldon on industrial organisations and health. This collection reprints an important paper by Hill and Trist which analyses industrial accidents as a means of withdrawal from the work situation. They argue that accidents are positively motivated forms of absence, and, moreover, that 'absence phenomena ... reflects the relationship of the person to their employing institution'. In other words, we may be dealing here with one aspect of alienation. In order to comprehend fully the dynamics of *withdrawal* from the work situation, we have to understand the basis of *affiliation* to it.

In the last reading in this chapter the basis on which male clerical workers achieve satisfaction in their work is discussed. But it is plainly too simple-minded to infer directly from the information about the satisfactions which workers claim to achieve from their work to the degrees of alienation from the process and product of work which they objectively experience. It is none the less essential to try and understand particular attitudes such as those which relate to job satisfaction, to the whole complex of social perspectives which constitutes the grid, the mesh, through which employees perceive the reality which constitutes the organisation of which they are members. It would seem that there are differences between clerks in public enterprise and private industry, in the way in which they select from their experience to re-conceptualise what they understand by the social reality of job satisfaction. The 'joy in work' of the clerical workers discussed in this study, and particularly those in private industry, is quite significantly muted.

Strikes and the Economy

T. G. Whittingham and B. Towers

Reprinted with permission from *National Westminster Bank Review*, November 1971, pp. 33–42.

The Government's Industrial Relations Act was conceived, born and reared in a period of continuous economic crisis. Thus it is hardly surprising that in the Commons debate on the bill on 15 December 1970, the Prime Minister should have stated that the legislation was necessary '... for our industrial health and for an expanding economy'. He went on to argue that it was vital for dealing with the pressures underlying the collective bargaining system which were inflation and the consequences of industrial disputes and disruptions. Hence among the major objectives of the Industrial Relations Act is the curbing of the incidence of strikes. Thus in the introductory section of the Act (General Principles) it is stated that:

> 'The provisions of this Act shall have effect for the purpose of promoting good industrial relations in accordance with ... the principle of developing and maintaining orderly procedures in industry for the peaceful and expeditious settlement of disputes by negotiation, conciliation or arbitration, with due regard to the general interests of the community...'

Earlier the Solicitor General, Sir Geoffrey Howe, pointed out that the act had much to do with curbing strike activity. Referring to the British strike pattern, he said:

> 'All the time the picture has been going from bad to worse. By the time the Donovan Commission was appointed in 1965, the number of strikes in industries, apart from coalmining, had risen from six hundred a year during the 1950s to exactly twice as many in the 1960s.'

The figure had risen to 1,700 in the year before the Donovan Commission reported that 'the prevalence of unofficial strikes and their tendency (outside coal-mining) to increase have such serious economic implications that measures to deal with them are urgently necessary'. By 1969 the figure had risen to 2,930—and that figure has been exceeded in the first nine months of this year. Donovan described the problem as serious and urgent. The gravity and urgency of the problem has certainly not diminished. More significantly, perhaps, Donovan observed that, 'the problem is peculiar to this country'. Sir Geoffrey also said that students of industrial relations had commented that Britain suffered from unofficial strikes to a greater extent than any other western democracy and that in no other did the law play such a passive part.

Given such clear indications of the thinking of the Government about strikes it is highly pertinent to examine the strike pattern in the United Kingdom. Hence, in this article, we analyse trends in strike activity on a national and comparative basis, examine some of the more important economic effects of strikes, assess the nature and importance of what is often referred to as the British strike problem and finally, offer some conclusions on this contentious and difficult subject.

It is perhaps useful initially to take a long-term view of the trend of strikes in this country. This is done in Table 1. From this Table it is clear that there has been, since 1967, a dramatic upsurge in the number of stoppages and especially in the aggregate of working days lost. This upturn is in contrast to the relative stability evident from 1933 onwards. Furthermore, this upsurge has continued in 1971. In the first quarter of 1971 some twelve million days were lost in aggregate. However, the postal workers' strike, the Ford workers' strike and strikes against the Industrial Relations Bill accounted for over 80 per cent of this total. Again, if different indicators are used it can be argued that we have now returned to what was normal three years ago.

Returning to Table 1 we can see that the recent increase in the number of stoppages has been substantially less pronounced than the increase in aggregate working days lost. The average annual number of stoppages for the years 1945–67 was 2,153. The 1968 figure showed a 1.5 per cent increase and there were increases of 44.7 per cent and 81.4 per cent for 1969 and 1970 respectively, all calculated on the 1945–67 annual average. As regards aggregate working days lost, the annual average for 1945–67 was 2,901,000 and there were increases for 1968, 1969 and 1970 of 61.0, 134.0, and 274.1 per cent respectively on this figure. Hence although there has been a marked increase in the propensity to strike this has been overshadowed by the growing economic impact of strikes as measured by the growth in aggregate working days lost. This

Table 1. Stoppages, workers involved and working days lost, beginning in each year 1931–70

Year	Number of stoppages	Number of workers involved (thousands)	Aggregate working days lost (thousands)
1931	420	490	7,010
1932	389	379	6,430
1933	357	136	1,020
1934	474	134	1,060
1935	553	271	1,950
1936	818	316	2,010
1937	1,129	597	3,140
1938	875	274	1,330
1939	940	337	1,350
1940	922	299	940
1941	1,251	360	1,080
1942	1,303	456	1,530
1943	1,785	557	1,830
1944	2,194	821	3,700
1945	2,293	531	2,850
1946	2,205	526	2,180
1947	1,721	620	1,400
1948	1,759	424	1,940
1949	1,426	533	1,820
1950	1,339	302	1,380
1951	1,719	379	1,710
1952	1,714	415	1,800
1953	1,746	1,370	2,170
1954	1,989	448	2,480
1955	2,419	659	3,790
1956	2,648	507	2,050
1957	2,859	1,356	8,400
1958	2,629	523	3,470
1959	2,093	645	5,280
1960	2,832	814	3,050
1961	2,686	771	3,040
1962	2,449	4,420	5,780
1963	2,068	590	2,000
1964	2,524	873	2,030
1965	2,354	868	2,932
1966	1,937	530	2,395
1967	2,116	732	2,783
1968	2,378	2,256	4,672
1969	3,116	1,656	6,789
1970	3,906	1,793	10,854

Source: Department of Employment, DEP, and Ministry of Labour Gazette.
Note: These figures do not distinguish between strikes and lockouts or between official, unofficial, constitutional and unconstitutional stoppages. They also exclude stoppages involving fewer than ten workers and those which last for less than one day unless the aggregate number of working days lost exceeds one hundred. Time lost at establishments other than those at which the stoppages occurred is also excluded. Other forms of industrial action, e.g. overtime bans, go-slows, etc., are also omitted. Finally, it should be noted that not all stoppages are notified to the Department of Employment.

can largely be explained by the fact that strikes are, on average, tending to increase in duration.

*　　*　　*

Equally, it is now widely accepted that many short-duration strikes are also unconstitutional. Some evidence for this is found in the Government Social Survey's study of 'workplace industrial relations', for which 1,161 shop stewards and 121 personnel officers were questioned about the duration of the last strike experienced. According to the stewards, 84 per cent of strikes lasted less than six days, and according to the personnel officers, 88 per cent. On the question of whether procedure had been exhausted within the firm or nationally before the strike (that is, was it constitutional or not?) the stewards said that in 58 per cent of the strikes it was and in 34 per cent it was not. The personnel officers, interestingly, stated that in 19 per cent of the strikes procedure was exhausted, while in 79 per cent it was not.

It is useful at this stage to summarize the statistical findings so far. The two more important aspects would seem to be:

(a) Over the last three years, the aggregate of days lost by strikes has increased much more rapidly than the number of strikes.

(b) The typical British strike is still brief, unofficial and unconstitutional.

*　　*　　*

What is the economic impact of strikes? Here it is convenient to analyse at two levels—that of the national economy and major industries and that of the single firm.

At the national level, in terms of working days lost as a proportion of total working days, the effect of strikes, even over the last three years and particularly over the first five months of 1971, appears insignificant. In crude terms, the total loss of output in 1970, as a proportion of gross national product, amounted to 0.20 per cent, and that year, as can be seen from Table 1, was exceptional in terms of aggregate working days lost. Inevitably, these calculations are imprecise and they ignore possible 'ripple effects'. These may be external or internal. Externally, our strikes record may affect foreign attitudes towards Britain both as a supplier of goods and services and as a recipient of investment. Internally, a strike in one firm or sector may affect others. The fact that these effects are difficult to quantify should not be taken to mean that they are not important. Perhaps the more important of these two types of effect is the external, given Britain's position as a trading nation. Table 2 shows our record as compared with those of other countries.

It is perhaps stating the obvious to say that international statistical data must in general be treated with caution. For example, there are differences in national official definitions of strikes. Given these problems, too much significance should not be attached to relatively small differences in the figures. However, the ten-year averages in Table 2 show that the United Kingdom has moved from seventh to ninth place in terms of working days lost per thousand workers employed. This may indicate a downward trend, especially in the light of the figures for 1970 and 1971.

Of course, differences in aggregate days lost between countries are a function of many variables. Among the more important of such variables would appear to be the industrial structure, the propensity to strike, the impact of the culture, the government and its agencies and other relevant agencies.

Despite the complexity there appears to be a kind of political consensus in Britain regarding the need for a degree of governmental intervention, in that both parties have at least attempted to use legislation as an instrument of change in the industrial relations system. Probably the major reason for such a consensus is that the centre of British strike activity is to be found in the 'key' industries serving export markets and those home markets in which there is a high propensity to import. Mechanical and electrical engineering and motor-vehicle manufacture consistently rank high in terms of number of stoppages, number of workers involved, total working days lost and days lost per thousand workers employed. These industries are, of course, key exporters. For example, in 1969, mechanical and electrical machinery and transport equipment accounted for 48 per cent of exports of manufactures and 41 per cent of all exports. In the same year the import figures were approximately 32 per cent and 16 per cent respectively. These figures underline the significance of strikes in these industries.

Such industries may also be regarded as 'image makers' in the eyes of foreign customers (that is the reliability or otherwise of firms within them as suppliers of goods, providers of services and so forth, is an oft-quoted factor underlying the

Table 2. International comparison of days lost through industrial disputes, 1957–69 (Days lost per 1,000 persons employed).[1] Annual Averages

	1957–61	1962–66	1957–66	Rank based on average for ten years 1957–66	1960–64	1965–69	1960–69	Rank based on average for ten years 1960–69
Australia[2]	306	356	331	10	350	456	403	12
Belgium	636	180	408	13	164	156	160	6
Canada[3]	596	764	680	15	460	1,556	1,008	16
Denmark[3]	700	110	405	12	708	110	409	13
Finland	248	338	293	8	340	206	273	10
France	288	322	305	9	352	243(a)	303(b)	11
Germany, Federal Republic of[4]	26	34	30	3	34	10	22	3
India	760	498	629	14	498	976	737	14
Ireland	342	1,188	765	16	686	1,350	1,018	17
Italy	676	1,386	1,031	18	1,220	1,574	1,397	18
Japan	470	250	360	11	302	198	250	8
Netherlands	61	16	38	4	62	12	37	4
New Zealand	50	170	110	5	154	242	198	7
Norway	140	98	119	6	212	4	108	5
Sweden[5]	10	26	18	2	6	28	17	2
Switzerland	—	10	5	1	10	—	1	1
United Kingdom[6]	352	230	291	7	242	294	268	9
United States[7]	1,166	792	979	17	722	1,232	977	15

[1] Industries covered are mining, manufacturing, construction and transport.
[2] Including electricity and gas.
[3] Manufacturing only.
[4] Excluding West Berlin (and the Saar up to 1958).
[5] All industries included.
[6] Owing to changes in industrial classification figures from 1959 onwards not strictly comparable with previous years.
[7] Beginning 1960: including Alaska and Hawaii. Figures cover also electricity, gas and sanitary services.
(a) Average for 1965–7 and 1969 only.
(b) Average for 1959–67 and 1969 only.

Sources: Ministry of Labour Gazette, Nov. 1967 and DEP Gazette, Feb. 1971.

decision of foreign customers to buy from British manufacturers or their competitors). Hence, strike patterns in these industries are important in the psychology of decision-making in markets for British exports.

*   *   *

It would probably be reasonable to conclude from this part of the analysis that in economic terms, if there is a British strike problem, it is sectoral rather than national. A final statistic bearing on this point is that the three key industries mentioned above contained 13 per cent of employees in employment in September 1970.

When we move to the level of the organization, there is evidence, according to Professor Turner, suggesting an even heavier concentration of strikes. He points out that in 1965, some 31 establishments experienced five or more officially-recorded strikes, and in 1966 the number was 27, several of them appearing in both lists. The statistics supplied by the motor manufacturers to the Donovan Commission imply that some 60 per cent of the time lost from disputes 'within the companies' occurred in a single firm. An unpublished study of disputes in a major shipbuilding region shows that the company which experienced most strikes over the post-war period ranked sixth in share of local output. In the metal-working trades he deduces from the Department of Employment and Productivity's summaries of 'principal stoppages' supported by press reports that nearly half the strikes occur in one hundred firms.

The danger here would appear to be that managers may develop a strike fixation which can easily grow into a more serious state of strike neurosis. This problem may often be compounded by an attitude on the shop floor which converts the use of the strike weapon from an exceptional to a normal action. This attitude may be reinforced by the knowledge that striking brings economic rewards to the strikers. The point is frequently made that striking in pursuit of inflationary wage settlements is self-defeating. However, this view fails to take into account the fact that a wage increase is certainly not immediately eroded by prices, and also that for small groups of workers gains may be made at the expense of others. Of course, in macroeconomic terms all inflationary wage increases are ultimately self-defeating, but such a global argument often fails to influence particular groups, especially when it runs counter to their own experience.

It is useful at this stage to summarize the points made in this section.

(a) At the level of the national economy and major industries in terms of aggregate working days lost as a porportion of total working days, strikes are statistically insignificant. This is true even over the last three years and the first five months of 1971. However, this statement ignores the possible 'ripple' effects. Internally these are the effects of a strike in one firm or sector upon others. Although they are difficult to quantify they are important in assessing the overall effects of strikes.

(b) Perhaps more important than the internal are the external ripple effects—given Britain's position as a trading nation.

(c) In this context it is a serious matter for the United Kingdom that the centre of the strike pattern is in industries which have great importance both in export markets and in those home markets where there is a high propensity to import. Such 'key' industries are also important as 'image makers' in the eyes of foreign customers.

Such problems as Britain has in the matter of strikes are largely associated with particular organizations. Many of these organizations are to be found within industries which would seem to be particularly strike-prone. Given this situation, any attempt to deal with the problem ought surely to reflect its nature: that is, its solution should be sought on a piecemeal, selective basis. Perhaps this suggests a role for the Commission on Industrial Relations. It could be given a strategic role in the analysis of strike-prone sectors, companies and establishments within the economy. Its specific task might be to seek out such organizations, conduct an analysis of their problems and make recommendations. Perhaps such recommendations would need legal backing. But whatever course is followed, it needs to be recognized that we are dealing with a very complex problem. Alvin W. Gouldner has reminded us of this when he notes that, 'a "strike" is a social phenomenon of enormous complexity which, in its totality, is never susceptible to complete description, let alone complete explanation'.

Strike at Pilkingtons

T. Lane and K. Roberts

Reprinted with permission from T. Lane and K. Roberts, *Strike at Pilkingtons*, Fontana, 1971, pp. 223–7.

No two strikes are identical. What happened in St Helens in the Spring of 1970 will never happen again, either there or anywhere else. But there are elements common to many strikes. The Pilkington strike was a wildcat—it was spontaneous and completely unpremeditated—and developed into a protracted struggle. These features, either taken separately or together, are far from unusual.

In this chapter we will attempt to generalise from our own study of one particular strike to other strikes having similar characteristics. While we cannot be certain that the conclusions we draw from the Pilkington strike will stand up to the sort of generalisations about to be emptied on to the reader, we nevertheless feel bound to suggest that our bucket has dredged up something of more than local importance. Just how important is for our readers to judge, and for other social scientists to confirm or dispute by further research.

Very few people at Pilkingtons had been expecting a strike. How and why the strike spread from a small beginning remained a mystery to most of the participants. Shop stewards, rank and file workers, and managers all confessed to an inability to understand the events of the first weekend. The dispute over a clerical error which sparked it all off surprised nobody, for small localised conflicts were not unknown in the Flat Drawn department or in other departments in other plants. What *was* so amazing was the way it became converted into a demand for a large increase on the basic pay and the way it snowballed right around St Helens.

In what was an otherwise extremely complex series of events only one thing stands out with clarity: there was no organised plot. The strike had not been engineered by a group of subversives who had deliberately infiltrated Pilkingtons in order to undermine the economy. Cloaks, daggers, Kremlin agents, the church of Rome, and small groups of 'politically motivated men'—all those mythical progenitors of natural and political 'calamities' belong firmly in the pages of Ian Fleming and Dennis Wheatley. Drama there was in St Helens—but it was unscripted. Such script as there was, was made up by people as they went along: the strike in its beginnings was a genuine spontaneous movement. In the early stages many workers did not know why they were striking—it was during the process of spreading through the factories that the strike acquired definite objectives.

Previous explanations of this type of wildcat have treated it as an emotional explosion following upon pent-up grievances that have not been resolved. Yet while this theory fits approximately the department in which the strike started, the same could not be said for all of the departments in all of the works. Morale in the Pilkington factories did not appear to be unusually low in the period immediately preceding the strike. If top management had been warned that they were sitting on a 'powder keg' and had noticed that they were '... getting rather less cooperation in change than (they) had in the past', they certainly weren't prepared for what they woke up to on the morning of Saturday, 4th April. There had been no sudden acceleration in labour turnover, and the incidence of localised disputes had shown no sharp upswing.

Most of the workers had not anticipated the strike either: they had seen no build-up of tensions or problems that had led them to want to strike or to believe that one was imminent. Problems and grievances certainly existed. Dissatisfaction with wage levels was widespread. In some departments there had been almost continuous friction between labour and management. Some employees (including most of those who became members of the RFSC) had felt that quite a lot of things were badly wrong at Pilkingtons. But, if it could not be claimed that the firm was purring along in a state of glorious harmony, there was certainly nothing to indicate that on the day the strike started, grievances had been more numerous or more deeply felt than they had been in the preceding months.

This means of course that workers can be drawn into a strike without being conscious of an exceptionally wide range of grievances, and without being subject to unusual stress on the shop-floor. A strike, in other words, can gather momentum under 'normal' working conditions. The prospect of a sizeable pay increase, apparent support from workmates, and advice from shop stewards, can together encourage people to join a strike and thereby add to its momentum—all without any change in the feelings and attitudes characteristic of previous months. At this stage we would merely remind readers that those people who actually set a strike in motion undergo rather different experiences from those who subsequently join it, and that a large-scale strike can be triggered off by the decisive action of only a small number of men. This, however, will not always be the case. It has to be remembered that the great majority of the Pilkington workers had never before been involved in a strike-prone work situation. In firms where workers are more strike-experienced it is much less likely that a departmental-based dispute would have a bush-fire effect— even if it were to be converted into an issue of wider application.

In contemporary Britain strikes have been defined as a 'problem', and the attachment of this label has created the allied impression that strikes are aberrations and atypical events which must therefore occur only amongst aberrant workers or under atypical conditions. It has accordingly been assumed that if certain features of the industrial landscape were remodelled the 'problem' could be buried.

This conception of strikes may well be false. The implication of our observation—that the Pilkington strike occurred in normal conditions—is that strikes generally should be regarded as *normal* features of industrial life in those sectors of the economy where large numbers of workers are gathered together under one roof.

The Pilkington workers' complaints about their jobs were mainly centred around money: 'We have to work a lot of overtime to get a decent living wage,' and of course during the strike a return to work was made conditional upon the payment of cash. This suggests that work was primarily regarded as a matter of exchanging time and labour for cash—not as a source of interest or stimulation, or a moral obligation to the employer. This attitude to work is far from uncommon amongst semi- and unskilled manual workers in large firms. Employers treat labour as a commodity and workers regard their labour-power in a similar way.

This is not to suggest that people look only for financial rewards from their work; there is in fact more than enough evidence to show that ideally workers would like to derive a much wider range of satisfactions. The suggestion is simply that as a matter of fact the nature of work is such that money is about the only reward that can be attained.

This instrumental approach towards work may have several repercussions for industrial relations. Workers with such a disposition may well use whatever tactics appear to be most effective to maximise their earning power. They may bargain through their union officials or shop stewards, they may work-to-rule, go slow, ban overtime, or strike.

From the point of view of explaining the way in which the Pilkington strike gained momentum over the first weekend, the implications of this instrumental approach to work are obvious. If there is no sense of moral obligation towards work, no feeling of personal involvement, then the possibility of a quick financial return will be sufficient to get people outside the factory gates. This certainly seemed to be one of the features in the first crucial forty-eight hours of the Pilkington strike, for, to repeat, there did not seem to have been any accumulation of tensions throughout all the plants in St Helens.

Some sections of industry are more strike-prone than others. The breadth and depth of bonds that tie individuals to their jobs and their employers will vary, and so the extent to which apparent trivia such as the miscalculation of bonuses are likely to spark off something larger will also vary. There can be no doubt that some industrial conditions are more conducive to strikes than others, but to claim that strikes can be normal is not to deny this. The fact remains that in much of large-scale industry millions of workers are employed under conditions in which periodic upsets are bound to occur, and when they do there is the continuous possibility of a wildcat strike.

Pilkington management admitted that problems did exist: clerical errors in the calculation of wages were far from unusual; anomalies did exist in the wages structure; some jobs were not particularly pleasant, and others were either distinctly unpleasant or dangerous. But management was also quick to point out that most other large firms had identical problems, and anyway what could be done about them? The answer is: very little. And this is precisely why strikes can be perfectly normal events, conducted by perfectly normal people, in perfectly normal circumstances.

Unemployment in the Seventies

Dorothy Wedderburn

Reprinted with permission from *The Listener*, Vol. 86, No. 2211, 1971, pp. 193–6.

The present concern about unemployment stems from three sources. First, there has never before in the post-war period been such a consistent run of announcements about redundancies. There have been the big shocks at Rolls-Royce and UCS. But in June, 1971, 12 leading companies each announced dismissals involving more than 200 people, a total of 4,000 workers. Second, although there have been cycles of unemployment before, the amplitude of the fluctuations has been quite small. Three times since 1950 unemployment has risen over a period of four to five years from a low point of some 1.5 per cent to a peak of 2.5 per cent. Neither the low nor the high point was particularly alarming. Since 1966, however, unemployment has crept fairly steadily upwards from 350,000 to an average of over half a million for each of the years 1967, 1968 and 1969. In 1970 it increased to 600,000, and this year to nearly 800,000, or 3.4 per cent of the employed population (well over 4 per cent of the employed male population). Third, the traditional decline in unemployment during the summer months has failed to materialise in 1971.

But the contraction in the labour market does not make itself felt only through the unemployment figures. As economic activity slows down, so groups less secure in their foothold in the labour market get squeezed out. Some, like married women, cease to appear in the statistics at all. They just drop out of paid work until the employment situation improves, without registering at the employment exchange. The over-sixty-fives retire and take their pension. Perhaps most worrying of all, the last few years have seen a decline in the number of men in employment in the age-group 25–64, the age when most people would expect to be in work. Some mystery clouds this fall. A likely explanation is that men in their late forties and fifties who lose their job find it especially difficult to get another at a time when unemployment is rising. If they have some small physical disability it will be both easier and socially more acceptable to draw sickness benefit than to register as unemployed, and the statistics of long-term sick in the older working age-groups are rising.

One of the most remarkable aspects of unemployment itself is the consistency of its main features over periods of time and between different countries. Older workers are always heavily represented among the unemployed; and although there is no conclusive evidence to support the view that age and ability to work are related in any absolute sense, we do know that social institutions and structural changes in the economy combine to place older workers particularly at risk. Redundancies occur first in contracting industries, which tend to have an older labour force. Yet it is precisely in these long-established industries that a supportive work environment for the older worker is most likely to have developed. In the railway workshops, for example, men had been working together for many years, and a system of mutual help had grown up. Older workers were relieved of the heavy tasks which they might find they lacked the physical capacity to perform, and compensated for this by contributing to the task on the basis of their judgment and experience. In addition, many employers are prejudiced against older workers and even find it cheaper to replace an older man with a younger one. At the other end of the age scale, the young school-leaver or graduate finds it hard to obtain a first job. Fear is already being expressed about the difficulty of absorbing 400,000 school-leavers this summer. Naturally enough, many companies which have to contract will cease to recruit rather than dismiss existing employees.

The number of people who have been unemployed for considerable periods of time has also increased sharply. There are now over 100,000 men in Britain who have been without work for more than a year, compared with 77,000 three years ago. The longer a person has been unemployed, the slighter his chances of getting another job. When the unemployment rate was 1.5 per cent or 2 per cent it was easy to dismiss the long-term unemployed as 'unemployable'—people with psychological or physical handicaps which prevented them from working. But it is now clear that 'employable' and 'unemployable' are not absolute conditions. What constitutes a handicap, and how much of a handicap it is, is a function of the state of demand for labour.

Anxiety about unemployment grows, but a curious ambivalence in public attitudes to the unemployed remains. There is, for example, an interesting contrast between our attitudes to the unemployed and to the old. The constant fear that the unemployed might be getting too much, that they might be better off out of work than in work, co-exists with a large body of opinion in favour of higher pensions. Perhaps it is that we all expect—or hope—one day to be old, but for most of us the prospect of unemployment still seems remote. Even after Rolls-Royce had passed into the hands of the Receiver in February this year and it was clear that some redundancies would occur, workers in Derby were saying: 'It can't happen to me. I'm a good worker. The company has invested a lot in training me.'

The belief that 'it can't happen to me' because 'I'm a good worker' is the individualised expression of a widely held general belief that a man is without a job only because of some personal fault of his own. Although the events of the last year have shown that unemployment is a consequence of Government policy, we still hear a chorus saying: 'They should move and then they'd get jobs. There are plenty of jobs in London. I can't get assistants to shampoo in my hairdressing salon.' Our television screens show us a 50-year-old Clydeside boilermaker saying with great dignity: 'You may as well shoot me, there's nae work for me to do.' The interviewer then asks him: 'Would you move to get a job?' 'Aye, I'd go anywhere,' he replies—to London to be an electrician, or to work in a ladies' hairdressers? Orwell, in *The Road to Wigan Pier*, described these same kinds of reaction in the thirties: 'When I first saw unemployed men at close quarters the thing that horrified and amazed me was to find that so many of them were ashamed of being unemployed. The middle class were still talking about lazy idle loafers on the dole and saying that the men could all find work if they wanted to and naturally their opinions percolated to the working class themselves.' We find today that the compassion of the post-war welfare state is only skin deep, that the same attitudes are re-emerging. What is worse, they are being legitimised by the philosophy of the present Government.

There have been two small but significant acts of Government which illustrate this philosophy and which will affect the unemployed particularly. In March the Government set up a commission to inquire into the extent of abuse of social security benefit. The inquiry is not aimed solely at the unemployed, although they, together with unmarried mothers or women 'cohabiting', have been most frequently cited as providing instances of abuse of supplementary benefits. It is sometimes argued that 'loafers', finding themselves better off with supplementary benefit than in a job, choose the former. But the surprising thing is not that anyone should abuse supplementary benefits in this way, rather that so few people do in fact do so. The recent report on low pay from the now defunct Prices and Incomes Board shows that there are several thousand men and women with resources little higher, and sometimes even lower, than the contemporary subsistence levels as defined by the scale rates for supplementary benefit. But so important is work to self-respect and status that these low earners continue in menial and boring jobs rather than go on the dole. On the other hand, evidence has accumulated over the last ten years to show that a major problem with supplementary benefits is to get people to claim the money to which they are entitled. Many people, who have been taught the importance of independence, object to a means test. Others find it difficult to understand the regulations. In a study of the consequences of redundancy at Rolls-Royce, it appears that a number of unemployed white-collar workers who are or have been eligible for supplementary benefit are not in touch with their local office. Thus, it would have been at least as logical, if not preferable, for a commission to inquire into the problem of failure to take up entitlement as to inquire into the 'abuse' of the system.

The second Government act has been to abolish benefit for the 'three waiting days'. Before the Second World War, a person beginning a spell of unemployment or sickness could not claim for the first three days—a deterrent to frivolous use of benefit rights as well as an economy measure. Under pressure from the trade-union movement the 1946 legislation went some way to meeting workers' deeply felt grievance about this: benefit was made payable for the first three days, but it was to be refunded only at the end of the second week of unemployment or sickness. In March this year, a new Bill was introduced to abolish these refunds, on the grounds that the economic position of the sick and the unemployed had been transformed by such things as redundancy payments and earnings-related sickness and unemployment benefits. A more cynical view would be that it was a wise economy measure to take just when unemployment was rising dramatically. Whatever the reasons for it, the change can be seen as yet another reflection of the fear that individuals might actually choose not to work when they could work, unless they are made to suffer.

But do the unemployed today suffer? In 1936 poverty caused by unemployment ranked second in importance to the main cause of poverty—inadequate wages. Although low wages are also a cause of poverty today, they are of less importance. The unemployed are now much better off in absolute terms than they were in the thirties, but that is not saying very much: everyone is. People who find themselves unemployed for the first time say that they cut back on 'luxuries'—outings, expensive foods; they 'send back the telly'. The general standard of living is such that this can be done for a time without any serious inroads on necessary expenditure for food, clothing and warmth, although it means gradual exclusion from the social life around them. For those who are still unemployed after six months, when the earnings-related supplement to unemployment benefit stops, life becomes more grim.

Average earnings of manual workers in manufacturing industries are £30 a week. Flat-rate unemployment benefit for a couple with two children is £10.70—this will go up in November, but by less than is required to compensate for the increase in prices. Family allowance will bring the family income to £11.60 and the earnings-related supplement (at a maximum for the man earning £30 a week or more) to £18.60. The subsistence needs of such a family, as calculated by supplementary benefits, total £12.50 a week, excluding rent. Many working people nowadays are paying £7 or £8 a week rent or rates and mortgage interest. (This has been one of the difficulties facing the Rolls-Royce workers in Derby, many of whom were buying their houses.) This level of housing expenditure would mean that the family was entitled to supplementary benefit, even in the six months during which the earnings-related supplement was being paid. After a year, entitlement to unemployment benefit ceases, and the family will have to rely on supplementary benefit alone. Why should there be a limit on the period for payment of unemployment benefit: there is none for sickness? When entitlement to unemployment benefit ceases, the family moves onto supplementary benefit, so the cost to the Exchequer is the same. But one is paid as of right, and the other only after a test of means with the attendant loss of dignity.

The prevailing attitude to redundancy payments is equally moralistic. When the legislation was passed in 1965 it was said that these payments were compensation to workers for loss of 'property in their job', for loss of seniority promotion prospects, pension rights. They were not intended to compensate for hardship while unemployed. Not everyone is entitled to redundancy pay, of course: people under 20 and with less than two years' service are excluded, and men approaching retirement age find their entitlement tapering off. But it is curious how many people not only feel resentful about the size of the payments (in the first quarter of this year they averaged £288 and 70,000 people received them), but presume they will be 'squandered' rather than 'saved'. For many working people a redundancy payment is the first and possibly only windfall they are likely to receive and it would not be surprising if it were used for some piece of extravagance. But the behaviour of those who receive a payment and who do not move immediately into another job does not support this belief. Most lump sums are used to supplement unemployment benefit in order to ensure that the reduction in the family's standard of living is not too sharp. They are also used to pay for major items like repairs and decoration which there is little possibility of paying for out of unemployment benefit. Another strategy is to reduce future commitments by paying off mortgages and hire-purchase debts.

The financial hardships of the unemployed may be relative, but they are none the less real. Moreover, they are accompanied by emotional hardship. The only men who refused to cooperate in a recent study of redundancy were those who had suffered so much that they felt unable to speak of their experience. These feelings tend to be stronger among older men and among those who identify closely with their occupation or place of work. Many blue-collar workers doing the most boring jobs miss the structure work gives to their lives: 'Before I used to be able to look forward to the weekend: now every day is the same.' 'It's the feeling you have: the satisfaction of having done a good day's work.' Unemployment involves not only a loss of dignity for the individual: his whole life loses meaning.

A more humane society than ours would adopt a positive approach to unemployment. The Swedes, for instance, have not only avoided the level of unemployment that we are now experiencing, but they have adopted policies which ensure that while people may be classed as unemployed, they are certainly not unoccupied. The greatest emphasis is placed on training and retraining. A wide variety of programmes are provided for all types of workers—unskilled to highly qualified—and they last from three months to two years. The philosophy is that if people have to be out of normal employment, then at least this should be an opportunity to upgrade the general skills of the labour force. To operate such a policy in Britain would, in the first place, require far more resources than our existing employment service has ever had available to it. It would also require a transformation of attitudes among those who operate the employment service, and among the candidates for retraining.

Does our society's handling of the problem of unemployment reveal a general falling back in social attitudes? The values of independence, thrift and hard work were extolled, and necessarily so, by the industrialisers, the laissez-faire capitalists, who needed a disciplined work force. Today it is still useful to emphasise these virtues because this displaces criticism which might otherwise be directed at the functioning of the economic system itself. But there are indications that a change is taking place. For instance, white-collar workers have traditionally expected security of employment and they are far less likely than manual workers to adopt the fatalistic attitude that 'you are bound to be out of work'. Even when they are anything but socialists they put the responsibility for employment policy firmly upon the Government. A danger is that both blue-collar and white-collar unemployed will turn with increasing hostility to the presence of immigrants in order to explain their own predicament.

The trade-union movement has voiced its opposition to Government policies with vigour, and individual unions have continued to fulfil their traditional friendly-society role. But with one or two exceptions relatively little has been done by the trade unions to modify attitudes towards the unemployed or to make their unemployed members politically more effective. Trade unions could usefully provide an advisory service to guide their members through the complex maze of unemployment and social security benefits. At the same time, by keeping in touch with the unemployed, they would be giving them a bridgehead to the world of work which would help to overcome some of their feelings of isolation. The associations of the unemployed, which are now springing up, are no substitute: they provide contact at the price of emphasising the distance of the unemployed from the rest of the society.

The unemployed are a statistical category—those persons who are registered with employment exchanges as seeking work. In social and economic terms, there is no hard and fast line between them and those who, like married women, have withdrawn from the labour market. But the man out of work feels different. Nor is there a hard and fast line between the hopes, aspirations and needs of the unemployed and those still at work. But we often speak as though there were. It is fashionable in management theory to describe as 'complex man' the worker who has a hierarchy of needs, ranging from simple survival through to the need for recognition and affiliation, all of which, it is argued, can and should be met in the work situation. Yet so often an unemployed worker is assumed to be nothing but an 'economic man'—and even that recognition is given grudgingly if we are to judge from the level of unemployment benefit. There is suspicion of the 'unemployed' as a category, although not of the individual unemployed man who appears in a television programme. Behind this may lurk guilt about the meaninglessness of work for so many in industrial society. The possibilities of job enrichment, or of extending workers' control, are increasingly discussed. Should we, perhaps, also be asking why a man not in work should receive any less income than a man who is in work?

The English Sickness
P. Taylor

Reprinted with permission from *Industrial Society*, July 1970, pp. 8–26.

'The English Sickness' is an expression now widely used on the Continent to describe a state of industrial and economic difficulties characterised by high rates of absenteeism, restrictive practices and strikes. Troublesome workers are said to have caught the English Sickness, and there appear to be many both here and abroad who believe that our situation is unique. Absenteeism, and its main component, sickness absence, are topics that seem to arouse strong emotions. The subject provides a fertile field for armchair critics who make dogmatic assertions about malingering—seldom based upon hard facts, or sweeping generalisations from a single example. Moreover, press and other news reports (particularly around New Year's Day), which concentrate on areas or factories with exceptionally high absence rates, tend to foster the conviction now held by many that Britain is a world leader in this unfortunate problem.

The publication each year of the latest figures of National Insurance benefit provides opportunities for headlines such as 'Over 300 million working days lost from sickness'. As the latest published figures are now over two years out of date, those for the past year are likely to be a good deal higher. Nevertheless a statement like this is inaccurate and misleading since the real situation is not as bad as this for the country as a whole, even though I believe that it is relatively worse in manufacturing industries. Such a statement needs explanation. Firstly, the national figures include all insured persons who are permanently unfit for work until they reach pensionable age. Since there are over 300,000 such people, they account for about 100 million out of the 300 million days, and few of them can be on any employers' books. Secondly, the days counted for National Insurance purposes are 312 in each year, six days a week and include public holidays; thus an absence of one calendar week over Christmas is counted as six days, even though only two or three actual working days may have been lost. In practice then, the 301 million days of certified incapacity amounted to rather less than 200 million actual working days lost by people normally at work.

These figures however probably carry little meaning for most personnel or production managers who are accustomed to measure absence in the form of a 'lost time percentage'. This is unfortunate because it is sometimes alleged that there are no national figures with which to compare a firm's rates. In fact, after allowing for the permanently unfit, the national (Great Britain excluding Northern Ireland) rate for the year 1966–7 for both certified sickness and industrial injury was about 3·6 per cent for men and 3·4 per cent for women. The latter figure is low because relatively few married women are fully insured for sickness benefit, and the rate therefore applies mainly to single women. Nevertheless how many industrial organisations can claim certified sickness and injury rates as low as this?

In the course of the past year about fifty companies have let me have their absence rates. Only four of these had rates of 3·6 per cent or less for male manual employees, although most who reported separately for male staff had figures ranging from 1·5 to 3·0 per cent for this grade. Rates for women were a good deal higher. While this can in no way be considered as a representative sample of manufacturing industry, the figures do illustrate the very wide range of absence levels that are found between companies. Table 1 shows the lost time per-

centages in male manual workers found in twelve of the firms.
It is worth noting that certified sickness and injury causes
more than two-thirds, and in one case over 90 per cent, of all
lost time among these men.

Table 1. Absenteeism and sickness in male manual workers, in
12 firms

Total absence	*Lost time percentage* Cert. sick and injured	Uncertified sickness	Employees (approx)	Type of firm
10·7	9·2	0·8	300	Engineering
10·3	7·1	0·4	1,400	Metal
9·9	7·4	0·4	4,600	Engineering
8·9	7·5	not accepted	3,600	Food
8·6	6·4	1·8	1,100	Chemical
8·1	7·5	0·2	1,900	Electrical
7·8	6·0	0·3	400	Engineering
7·8	5·1	0·4	700	Engineering
6·3	5·1	0·2	1,100	Electrical
5·9	5·2	0·3	600	Food
5·1	3·4	0·5	1,500	Chemical
4·4	3·2	0·2	1,800	Chemical

Two provisos are necessary when comparing rates in this
table with national figures. All the firms operated a sick pay
scheme and it is known that this applies to only about half the
working population of the country. Secondly the figures
obtained for women show that they usually have a much
smaller proportion of total absence attributed to certified sickness than do men. The figures of uncertified sickness absence
show that in most of these firms (and in the others not included in the table) it only causes between 5 and 10 per cent of
total sickness. This type of absence is not of course recorded in
the National Insurance statistics.

Perhaps the most disturbing trend in the past few years has
been the seemingly inexorable rise in sickness absence rates—
both nationally and in many companies. This, too, has received
much publicity, and there are many firms that have experienced a rise of about 10 per cent in the past year or two.
During a visit to Poland I was able to obtain annual figures for
their sickness absence and found that they, too, had experienced a rise not unlike our own. Enquiries from twenty

countries brought replies from all but two, although only nine
had recorded the information for each year since the early
1950s. Direct comparisons between one country and another
are almost impossible since definitions of spells and days differ
widely. Some include calendar days, some count single day
absences, others only start from the fourth day, etc, etc. Nevertheless, it seemed reasonable to compare the changes that had
occurred *within* each country to see whether there was a common pattern. All nine had experienced a definite rise in the
number of days of sickness absence per person over the past
fifteen years. The simple way to show this was to relate a
year's rate to the average for the two years 1955 and 1956
which preceeded the world-wide epidemic of 'Asian Flu' in
1957.

Britain in 1967 experienced 110 per cent of this baseline rate,
while this rise had been exceeded in Sweden (140%), Italy
(138%), Holland (135%) and West Germany (128%). Poland
and the United States have experienced rises very similar to
our own, but Czechoslovakian and Yugoslav rates have risen
scarcely at all. Only five of these countries also recorded the
frequency rate of absence (episodes), but in all of these this
measure of sickness had shown a greater proportional rise
than severity. This confirms on an international scale the
observations that have been made by industrial medical officers
in the past few years, that sickness absence is becoming much
more frequent and that this is most obvious in episodes lasting
from a day or two up to a fortnight.

The Italian analysis is particularly interesting since it shows
clearly that most of the rise in sickness absence since 1949 has
taken place in industrial employees, and that the rise in the
commercial sector has been smaller, while rates in agriculture
have changed little. I would suspect that the same thing has
taken place here, although our national figures are not broken
down in this way. It is probably true to conclude that rising
rates of sickness absence are characteristic of the industrial
societies in which we live.

Not only has there been a change in the frequency and
duration of absence from work attributed to sickness in the
years since the last war, but there has also been a dramatic
change in the pattern of disease which causes it. The annual
claims for National Insurance benefit are analysed by cause for
men, and over the past fifteen years there have been substantial
falls in days attributed to tuberculosis, dermatitis, peptic ulcers

and kidney diseases. These conditions now cause only about half as many days of incapacity as they used to do. On the other hand, conditions such as sprains and strains of muscles and joints have been responsible for a threefold increase, the now fashionable 'slipped disc', and the ubiquitous diarrhoea follow close behind, and the list also includes psychological disorders, diabetes, coronary heart disease and bronchitis. For the last three on the list, a substantial element of the increase can be attributed to improvements in treatment and medical care which prevent early death but often keep the patient alive and in indifferent health.

Many of the diseases that have increased, and particularly those brief spells that so afflict industry, are ones in which few objective signs of disease can be found. Backache is widely recognised as a condition most difficult to confirm or disprove, and it is only in the Services that proof of diarrhoea is required before a soldier is released from duty. This raises the problem of malingering (a word that some people seem anxious to avoid), and of the granting of certificates by doctors. Malingering, which the dictionary defines as the pretence of illness or the production or protraction of disease in order to escape duty, certainly does occur. While some may indeed fabricate the symptoms of a disease from nothing in order to obtain a certificate off work, this is nowhere near as common as the exaggeration of mild symptoms which actually do exist. Although this distinction may appear semantic, it is the latter variety which is much more difficult to expose and causes real problems both to employers and to doctors.

A doctor is trained to recognise when someone is seriously ill and in need of treatment, but it is very difficult for him to decide exactly when someone is well enough to work. Indeed, in almost every case he will have to rely substantially upon his patient's own opinion—and this can be coloured by matters not related to physical fitness and the demands of the job. Whether the employer likes it or not, it is the patient himself who decides upon his fitness for work in all but exceptional cases. Influence peoples' attitudes to work and you will influence rates of sickness absence—in either direction.

The whole relationship between doctor and patient is based upon mutual trust, and the doctor must accept his patient's statements at their face value, at least until he has definite evidence that they are untrue. Few of us would be content with a state of affairs where doctors disbelieved what we told them, and practised a form of veterinary medicine before giving treatment or a certificate. Fitness for work becomes more difficult to assess when the doctor has to rely upon his patient to describe the nature and demands of the job itself. It is in this respect that those factory doctors who really do know what the jobs entail (and to what extent they can be modified, can be of the greatest assistance to their colleagues in hospital or general practice. There are, however, only relatively few of these, but it may be no coincidence that the last three firms listed in the table above have comprehensive medical services including an absence control programme.

Each one of us has our own self-set standard of health which we consider necessary to allow us to work. For some, particularly but not exclusively professional or managerial workers, this standard may be dangerously low. The man who struggles to work despite a serious illness is known to all, but so too is the one who stays at home unless he feels '100 per cent fit'. The World Health Organisation has defined health as *a state of complete physical, mental and social well-being* and not merely the absence of illness or disease. How many people are that healthy at any time? Under these conditions who can call a man with a hangover healthy, is he therefore a malingerer, or is it a self-inflicted injury?

It seems that in all industrialised and therefore 'advanced' societies, there has been a definite change of national or individual thresholds in terms of the amount of ill health which people are prepared to tolerate. Increased standards and availability of medical care and social security, and in Western countries at least, the advertisements for patent medicines, all tend to increase awareness of ill health and the importance it is awarded. Some of the rise in sickness absence may thus be ascribed to people who are no longer prepared to ignore (and work with) ailments such as minor backache or bowel disturbances. This attitude certainly aids earlier diagnosis of serious or potentially serious conditions, but all too often a visit to the doctor is also used to obtain a sick note.

Finally it may be of interest to view this problem against the expectation of working life of an 'average' man. At the turn of the century the death rate was such that the 'average' man lost $6\frac{1}{2}$ years of working life between the ages of 20–60, and just over one year due to sickness and disablement. Sixty years later the productive life lost amounted to 1·8 years for death and 1·4 years for incapacity, a saving of $4\frac{1}{2}$ years. The relative importance of sickness, however, increased since it caused 15 per cent of lost time then and it causes almost half today. This change in emphasis is likely to continue and illustrates the need for well planned absence control measures to contain the inevitable rise.

Satisfactions in White-Collar Work
D. Weir

This extract was especially prepared for this volume and has not previously been published in this form.

It has been argued that 'one of the most distinguishing features of contemporary urban societies is the conscious expectation to derive meaning from work'. For 'work' is not merely the basis of one of the most significant ways in which the individual can attempt to impose some meaning on society, as a producer, an organiser, a creator; it identifies a nexus through which societal relations become crystallised in the individual's behaviour. As the occupant of a work-role, the individual actor bears the mark of a set of generalised expectations about his behaviour and performance which constrain and condition his opportunities for self-actualisation in other facets of life also.

The role of the male clerk is particularly interesting in this respect. His traditional position on the fringe of the 'authentic' middle classes has been systematically eroded in a process that started with the entry of women into the office during the first year of the century, and continued with the progressive elimination of many jobs, due to mechanisation in the 1920s and 1930s. The subsequent introduction of electronic data-processing during the last decade has represented the continuation of a trend towards complete bureaucratisation and rationalisation of the traditional clerical function.

Some older skills have been taken over by the machine; others have been absorbed by the parallel growth in specialisation in the management sphere, in particular those associated with authority, control, and the interest derived from bearing responsibility for a job all the way through.

These features of the changing clerical job have led some writers to prophesy doom and despair. Alienation from the process of work, from the product itself, from fellow-worker, and from the inexorable activity of man as a species is perceived by some as the inevitable corollary of the process by which the work of the clerk becomes more akin to that of the factory worker, and this alienation is seen by some as the general condition of man as a worker in British capitalist society.

As Alvin Gouldner writes 'we have created a mountain of objects that no one has made, that few can maintain, that fewer still know much if anything about, even though surrounded by them daily in homes and work places. The "alien" world of machines is only a special case of the alien world of objects in industrial society. We commonly know little or nothing about how these objects work, and content ourselves with knowing what they are supposed to do, that is with their supposed usefulness.'

Several researchers have criticised the facile transition made in some earlier studies between *information* about job satisfaction derived from interview and questionnaire-based studies with respondents in various occupational categories, and *inferences* about the 'degree of alienation' which apparently inheres in specific jobs.

In recent years, the greatest stimulus to research in the field of job satisfaction has come from the work of Herzberg and his associates. This approach is based indirectly on the theory of the hierarchical ordering of human needs developed by Maslow. In a series of publications, Herzberg has argued that satisfaction and dissatisfaction are not to be regarded as opposite ends of a continuum. Rather they are related to fundamentally distinct aspects of the job, relating to the *content* of the job, and the *context* in which it is performed. So the factors which are 'job-centred' and are associated with the work itself are normally associated with the expression of satisfaction. However, when these factors are *lacking* they are not strongly associated with dissatisfaction. There are other factors which are related to aspects of the context in which the job is performed which stimulate *dis*satisfaction if they are present, but which, when absent, are not associated with a high level of satisfaction.

This theory has become known as the 'motivation-hygiene' theory of job satisfaction. As Herzberg points out 'One cluster of factors relate to what the person does and the other to the situation in which he does it.' The 'satisfiers' are such factors as 'his job content, achievement on a task, recognition for task achievement, the nature of the task, responsibility for a task, and professional advancement or growth in task capability' whereas the central themes for the dissatisfiers are such things as 'the kind of administration and supervision received in doing the job, the nature of interpersonal relationships and working conditions that surround the job and the effect of salary . . .'

It is essential, therefore, to try and comprehend job satisfaction in the context of expectations about work and the satisfaction which may be legitimately derived from work. These expectations, in turn, may be conceived of as forming part of a more comprehensive and coherent way of looking at the world, a type or mode of orientation. The simple *rating* or comparison of levels of satisfaction is unlikely to prove helpful in the absence of an understanding of these social perspectives.

The chief focus of the study discussed here was on the expectations which white-collar workers have of their work and in particular of their jobs. We wished to place the question of the satisfactions derived by white-collar workers from their work in the context of *their* perceptions of what satisfactions could legitimately be expected to accrue from involvement in work. But the meaning which a job has for the clerical worker in private industry, for instance, may be significantly different from that which it has for his counterpart in a public bureaucracy. If this were the case, this would vitiate any simple attempt to compare these two groups on some overall measure of satisfaction.

We first attempted to place the clerks in the two types of organisation within the matrix of interactions in which they were involved in the course of the daily routines of their jobs. While it was impracticable, given the logistical constraints on the research, to undertake a full-scale observational study of the contacts made by clerical workers during a typical day, some understanding of the routine and processes of work was obtained. We found that all of the clerks we are now discussing, both private and public, were engaged in very similar tasks. (The main source of information about the contacts they were involved in on the job was the respondents themselves.)

There were no differences between the groups in this respect, except that the public employees were more likely to say that they had a good deal of contact with clients, customers, or the general public. Both groups reported a very high frequency of interaction with their colleagues in the same office, and with their superiors. Both reported a certain amount of contact with other clerical workers, of similar grades, in other departments. Both reported much less contact with manual workers and hardly any with management. The daily routine of the office worker is thus one which it would be apt to term 'organisationally embedded'. His major contacts are with others of his kind, rather than with superiors or inferiors, and he is unlikely to be in daily contact with members of the public. He is surrounded, then, and in fairly frequent interaction with others who share a common background, perceive common problems, and are fairly readily available to him.

Although he conceives of it as responsible, his work is not excessively demanding. He admits to being able to think of other things while engaged in his work. He tends, however, to think of it as more demanding than the manual worker's and less than that of a top manager.

Members of neither group have a consistently high opinion of their own job, the private clerks showing a slightly greater tendency to say their job is more exacting than a manual worker or than a clerk in private industry. But these distinctions are only marginal.

In terms of the job he is doing, the contacts he makes on the job, and his *general* perspective on his job as compared to that of other workers, the clerk in private industry seems very similar to his colleague in the public sector.

These similarities carry over into the area of satisfaction with the job in general terms. Four out of five of each group were able to give positive answers about aspects of their job from which they derive satisfaction. A similar percentage were settled in their jobs to the extent that they are not looking for other jobs at the present. The private clerks were slightly more inclined to rate their own jobs as 'first rate' or 'pretty good' in respect of the aspects of the job they had just identified as being important to them. They also tended to prefer their present job to previous ones they had had, more than did the public clerks.

But it was the private clerks who apparently feared the transition to a factory job less than did the public clerks. A similar number of each agreed that if they had their time over again they would go for the same kind of job. And a very small number indeed thought that office work would be a good career for someone starting out working life in today's world.

In terms, then, of these indicators of different aspects of

their *overall* satisfaction with their jobs, it is again apparent
that the private and public clerks see their situations in broadly
similar terms. Their 'satisfaction' tends to appear high when
couched in broad generalities, but to diminish when considered
in more particular terms and to evaporate almost entirely

Table 1. Contacts on the job: the pace and pressure of work

Percentage who report much contact with:	Private	Public
Others in the same office	78	86
Supervisor	78	77
Other clerical workers	31	40
Management	6	8
Manual workers	16	17
Clients and customers	14	38
Percentage who:		
Can think about other things while doing their job	62	51
Think the pace of work has increased	82	73
Think their job is more exacting than a manual worker's	59	69
Think their job is less exacting than a top manager's	64	73
Think their job is more exacting than a clerk's in the other type of organisation	46	53

when it is related to *specific* choices and decisions made by
themselves or others in whose welfare they might have an
interest.

It might be argued that the hypothetical situation of making
a choice on behalf of a generalised other represents a more
valid way of obtaining an insight into an individual's personal
priorities than asking him to answer in terms of himself. If this
is so, what a man considers to be important and to provide a
basis for action on the part of *others* is more significant than
what he claims to represent his own position.

There are, nevertheless, certain significant points of difference between the two groups. In their perception of what is
important about a job, the private clerks lay most emphasis on
'salary', 'security', and 'promotion prospects'. But while these
factors appeal to the public clerks they are not regarded as

overwhelmingly more important than are the 'interest and variety' in their jobs and the chance of exercising 'responsibility'. And this distinction occurs, though not in quite so exacerbated a form, in discussing secondary aspects of the job. But, although there is this difference between the groups in

Table 2. Private and public clerks compared on various indicators of their satisfaction with their job

Percentage:	Private	Public
Giving positive answers about aspects of the job from which they get satisfaction	89	90
Not looking for another job	84	83
Who wouldn't take a factory job at £5 a week more	71	81
Rating their own job as first rate or pretty good in terms of the most important thing about a job	65	57
Preferring their present job to previous ones	52	43
Who would go for the same job again	37	36
Who would recommend office work for a young man	26	22

their judgement of what is important, it is nonetheless the case that the tendency among both groups is to rate their own job as satisfactory in terms of its job and income security.

In fact, the public clerks are not on the whole too impressed with their own jobs from the point of view of the opportunities for the exercise of responsibility it affords. They are somewhat less satisfied again with their salary. Their counterparts in private industry are more satisfied overall with their salary, but those who rated interest and variety as most important are conscious that their job is deficient in these terms. Dissatisfaction, if we can call it that, is based then on different aspects of the job among these two groups. It seems, therefore, that the Herzberg formulation of 'motivation' factors associated with satisfaction, and 'hygiene' factors associated with dissatisfaction, is inadequate to encompass these findings.

When the focus is on jobs that have been done previously, about which a firm and consistent judgement has developed, the motivation–hygiene distinction seems even less helpful. For both groups the *good* jobs were those which had permitted varied and interesting work, the *bad* ones those in which the tasks of work, the actual content of the job, had proved un-interesting and dissatisfying.

But another distinction appeared to have more general implications for our understanding of the differences between

Table 3. Aspects of the job

Percentage who:	Private	Public
Think task factors most important	27	47
Think position factors most important	70	51
Gain satisfaction from 'doing the job well'	64	29
Gain satisfaction from 'specific tasks of work'	14	35
Gain satisfaction from contact with the public	8	22

the work of the public and private clerks. Whereas the former are able to refer to *precise and specific* aspects of their job in explaining the sources of their satisfaction, the latter resort to the vacuity of 'doing my job well'.

At first there was a tendency to probe at this point and to attempt to impel the respondent to be more specific, but it was soon recognised that, in its bland generalised implication that *no* task, *no* routine, and *no* inter-personal situation possessed enough salience to the respondent to warrant separate and discrete identification, this response was more informative as it stood. These respondents referred to 'just doing it', 'getting through the work', 'a clean in-tray at the end of the day', 'to be able to get through it as quickly as possible and efficiently, and to be satisfied that I've done it to the best of my ability', 'seeing everything completed and cleared for the day', 'just to know you've done it properly', 'to have no queries at the end of the day'. In their repeated references to the need to perform routine functions, efficiently and expeditiously, in conformance with the demands of an *externally-imposed* time-scheduling, these responses are somewhat reminiscent of those of the assembly-line workers studied by Walker and Guest, Blauner and Goldthorpe.

By contrast the public employees are less prone to invoke the vague generality of 'doing my job well' and are more than twice as likely to refer to specific aspects of the job. (True, their jobs are more precisely detailed in formal and official descriptions of the tasks appropriate to specific grades, but even so the answer to this question shows a somewhat striking disparity between the two groups.)

The affluent manual workers of Luton studied by Goldthorpe in *The Affluent Worker* achieved satisfaction in their jobs, because their expectation of the kinds of satisfaction which might legitimately be derived from work were rather low. It was the

Table 4. 'Out of all the things your job involves, what gives you most satisfaction?'

Percentage referring to:	Private	Public
'Doing my job well', and vague answers	64	29
Actual content of tasks	14	35
Contact with the public	8	22
A chance to use responsibility and initiative	12	4
Doing a 'useful' job	6	10
	100	100

extrinsic satisfactions they obtained, and these were given primacy in their orientation to work. But in terms of intrinsic factors, in relation to the objective deprivation they suffered at the workplace '... they could clearly be said to have low job satisfaction'.

We have seen that, among the public clerks at least, expressive needs appear to gain more prominence in terms of what may be expected from work. The private clerks seem more akin to the manual workers of Luton in that their present job is *accepted* rather than reacted to. It is its extrinsic aspect which provides their satisfaction; but their perspective on jobs in general, past and present, indicates that like the public clerks they see interest, variety, and the opportunity for self-expansion by exercising responsibility, as valid sources of satisfaction from work. Their lack of enthusiasm for the course of action they have chosen, as well as for recommending their job to others, indicates that to some extent they are failing to find such satisfaction in their own work.

We need to distinguish between the fact of *acceptance* of a particular job with its attendant advantages and drawbacks, and the rather more positive concept of the search for explicit *satisfactions* from that job. Thus, as 'work is the central feature of industrial capitalist society, it is impossible to be indifferent to it. To reject it completely is even more damaging to the concept of oneself as a worker, and indeed as a 'whole and proper man'. It is self-destructive and an admission of personal failure to claim that one cannot obtain satisfaction from one's work. So we expected that there would be a fairly strong positive response to questions which *assumed*, Kinsey-style, that satisfactions could be obtained explicitly from the tasks and routines of work. This expectation was bolstered by, for instance, studies like that of Morse and Weiss who found '...there appears to be a tendency for the individual to react positively to his work situation and to emphasise the favourable aspects of it'. But, in the event, although almost all respondents were able to give positive answers, the lack of explicit reference to work activities, and the rather deadening reaffirmation of the virtues of 'doing one's job' did not appear overly enthusiastic.

While there is clearly a desire among some clerks to approach the job in a craftsmanlike way, there are strong indications that, for many, the conditions under which their work is performed negate the possibility of deriving intrinsic satisfaction of this kind from it. Possibly the opportunities for deriving *intrinsic* satisfaction are greater among the public clerks, whose tasks are more minutely and rigorously circumscribed, than among the private clerks whose situation is superficially more flexible and allows greater scope for individual development.

But this does not necessarily imply that we need to accept wholesale the indictment of C. Wright Mill who claimed:

> 'the model of craftsmanship has become an anachronism ... with such a model in mind, a glance at the occupational world of the modern worker is enough to make it clear that practically none of these aspects are now relevant to modern work experience.'

It seems rather to be the case that the modern clerical worker approaches his job in a craftsmanlike way and is capable of deriving some satisfactions from it, *relative to the rather limited expectations of work which he has*. These limited expectations are matched by a somewhat *reserved* and *conditional* attitude towards his own job, illustrated by his lack of enthusiasm for recommending the job to young entrants, and his determination not to enter the same line of work again, if the chance were to arise.

These clerks do claim to achieve some kind of 'satisfaction' in their work. But perhaps 'satisfaction' is too strong a term, and it is more appropriate to characterise the responses we have just been discussing as indicative of a kind of 'acceptance' of a rather more passive kind. In general, these responses are consistent with an orientation to work which, whilst it does not see work as of all-pervading and dominating importance, nonetheless recognises it as a *possible* source of satisfaction and contribution to self-esteem. This attitude is encapsulated in the phrase 'doing one's job well'. But the lack of 'satisfaction' we noticed does not necessarily indicate a generalised disaffection or negativism towards work. This balance is struck appropriately by the respondent in an earlier survey of individual clerks undertaken by Dale who said 'I've had my lot, but it isn't such a bad lot.'

Further Reading: **Work**

V. L. ALLEN, *Power in Trade Unions*, London, Longmans, 1954.

* V. L. ALLEN, *The Sociology of Industrial Relations*, London, Longmans, 1971.

* R. BLAUNER, *Alienation and Freedom*, Chicago, Chicago University Press, 1964.

* K. COATES, *Can the Workers Run Industry?*, London, Sphere Books, 1968.

R. DAHRENDORF, *Class and Class Conflict in an Industrial Society*, London, Routledge and Kegan Paul, 1959.

† J. E. T. ELDRIDGE, *Industrial Disputes*, London, Routledge and Kegan Paul, 1968.

A. KORNHAUSER, R. DUBIN and A. M. ROSS, *Industrial Conflict*, New York, McGraw-Hill, 1954.

A. M. ROSS and P. T. HARTMAN, *Changing Patterns of Industrial Conflict*, New York, Wiley, 1960.

* Available in paperback
† Reference

Chapter Eleven Institutions

For Max Weber, the most efficient form of social organisation
was the bureaucracy, an institution in which official business
was conducted on a continuous basis in accordance with
stipulated rules. The official's responsibilities, tightly delimited,
derive from his position in a hierarchy of authority. Each act
of the official in a bureaucracy is governed by rules interpreted
through the decisions of his superior. Weber thought that such
an organisation would be technically superior to all other
forms of administration much as machine production in
factories exemplified a more efficient form of the division of
labour than cottage production, according to Adam Smith. For
the bureaucracy can offer the advantages of precision and
speed. Its decisions, if correctly taken under the appropriate
rules, would be unequivocal and of universal application.
Central to the idea of the bureaucracy is that of 'rationality' in
the sense of a calculus relating organisational means to the
desired ends of social action. The more fully the calculative
rationality of the bureaucracy is developed, the more
depersonalised the administration becomes—grace and favour,
gratuity and sympathy alike are stigmatised as irrelevant to the
efficient operation of the bureaucratic machine. But if the
bureaucracy offers these advantages it purchases them at a
price—the risk of the depersonalisation of those who served its
decision-making process and the probability of friction between
the bureaucrats and those outside its jurisdiction. Above all,
the bureaucracy should be, if impersonal, both fair and
efficient. However, subsequent analyses such as those of Robert
Merton and Alvin Gouldner, indicated the latent dysfunctions
of the bureaucratic solution. Merton showed how the
bureaucrat's internalisation of the collective need for certain
kinds of action becomes displaced and instead is used as a
basis for the bureaucrat's justification of his own position,
status and privileges. Gouldner stressed the dialectic nature of
bureaucratic rules and distinguished three types of
bureaucracy.

1. Mock bureaucracy identifies the institution in which strict rules exist and are apparently enforceable. But they are both externally imposed and considered to be totally irrelevant by both parties to the organisation contract. Consequently, their power to bind action is slight.

2. Representative bureaucracy occurs when the rules under which the organisation operates are conformable to both the overt needs of the institution and to the expectations of organisational participants.

3. Punishment centred bureaucracy occurs where the rules are not jointly initiated and only one party to the contract therefore finds them legitimate. This latter seems to identify a rather characteristic type of organisation in British society at all levels, from the secondary modern school or pseudo-comprehensive in the decaying city core to the large mental hospital, and the long-stay prison. That is not to say of course that all of these institutions are precisely similar in every aspect of their structure and functioning, only that the similarities between them may be provocative in elucidating the special problems which institutions such as these generate and have to cope with.

Institutions of this latter type, therefore, normally exemplify the following features. The rules are considered important in their own right. Any infraction of the letter of the law is considered a more heinous offence than is the infraction of the spirit. Behind the procedures for the enforcement of rules lies the sanction of coercion. There is much emphasis on routine behaviour, indeed behaviour that does not superficially conform to organisational demands may be perceived by the ruling group in the organisation as particularly threatening. Sudden and violent dislocations of the expectations of others, such as may be induced, for example, by breaking into a run down a school corridor, a hospital ward or a prison cell block, may assume fearful importance in such a setting.

The position of the lower-level bureaucrats in such institutions is particularly invidious. While the formal definitions of their work and task roles may be precise, unambiguous and apparently demanding little discretion, the practical reality of the job implies a maximisation of role-conflict and a tendency to produce apparently irresoluble difficulties over, for instance, the maintenance of discipline. But these arduous and demanding activities are little regarded by society when it comes to the lack of material rewards. The secondary school teacher, the hospital nurse, particularly in a mental institution, and the prison officer share the common understanding of their job as unappreciated by society. They are expected to treat the inmates like human beings, and to be flexible and tolerant in the every-day management of the institution, while still guaranteeing society the absolute security and discipline it feels it has a right to demand.

Community expectations, therefore, embodied in the level of material reward apparently considered appropriate for these arduous and demanding conditions, combine to produce a generalised *resentment* which, perhaps less frequently than one might anticipate, spills over in the extreme case into positive maltreatment and abuse of those entrusted to the institution's care. Those who work in institutions such as these may be sentenced in terms of career and promotion prospects to a life of employment at what is often euphemistically referred to as a career grade. The rigid hierarchical structure is crystallised in a series of promotion bars such as exist between the roles of nurse and doctor in hospital, and of prison officer and the managerial grades of Assistant Governor and Governor in the prison, and in somewhat different terms and to a much less exacerbated form between teacher and headmaster in school. Along with the belief that entry to the decision-making grades is reserved for those who come with a combination of university social science degrees, abundant confidence and implacable ignorance comes a suspicion that in a situation of real crisis support from above would be conspicuously absent. It is no wonder then that the ambiguities of the role of the first line official and his suspicion that he may, in the last analysis, be deserted by the organisation to whom he has offered his total allegiance, may sometimes drive him into an apparently unholy, and to the outsider, inexplicable liaison with those whose control society has delegated to him. Thus, the *uncertainty* of the prison officer faced with the conflicting demands that he shall control inmates but in so doing avoid all danger of contagion from them, may assume excessive importance in the problems which derive from the management of his role.

The plight of the individual bureaucrat enmeshed in a confrontation between what society wills and its incapacity to vote the means, is exacerbated by conflicts over the very goals which institutions such as these are set up to achieve. One general function performed by many such institutions is the custodial one. This generalisation is patently true of the prisons and arguably an apt, if tendentious, comment on the conditions under which long-term mental patients are treated in some institutions, but they seem extravagantly inappropriate in respect to the school. Yet it can be argued that the function (in terms of society's overt values, a latent one) of the school for working-class pupils in the inner city areas *is* that of mere custody. The pupils may certainly see it in this light and anxiously look forward to the prospect of release in order to obtain a taste of the kind of freedom offered by assembly-line work in the factory or the enlargement of personal horizons offered by a fourteen-storey block of local authority flats. The teacher too may see his role as one of 'keeping them quiet'. Certainly an apparently widespread fear of the effects of the raising of the school leaving age was expressed by those who argued that keeping under restriction for a whole year longer those who do not wish to be there in the first place and could see no valid, actual or potential benefit to themselves in remaining there, was a potentially *dangerous* exercise.

The primary goal of the penal institution is ultimately that of the protection of the community by means of the incapacitation of the criminal. The prison embodies, too, an element of social sanitation by providing a funnel by which society's most noisome effluent may be canalised into one cesspit. Sington and Playfair's book, suggested for further reading, is very critical of contemporary penal institutions. No amount of reform, no ameliorative practices, they argue, can serve to make prison a good and useful institution in the conditions of contemporary society. They show that the very concept of imprisonment derives from the expression of the need of the community for retribution. But neither the legislature nor the judiciary have control over the way prison as an institution actually operates. As they say, 'what punishment by imprisonment means, then, largely depends in practice on what its administrators want to make it mean or can afford to make it mean'. They argue that the overt purpose of committing offenders to prison for training and treatment can never be satisfactorily met in terms of the way the prison operates today.

Zeno, a former murderer sentenced to life imprisonment, examines the gap between the legal definitions of the crime for which the individual is sentenced, and the individual and personal situation of the criminal. He refers to the hopelessness of the individual convict seeking a redress for a real or imagined wrong from the impersonal and impervious prison bureaucracy.

The impact of prison life is two-sided, though. Roberts is concerned with the situation of the staff—the custodians. The disadvantageous position of this group in terms of their relations with the prisoners and their superiors is clearly brought out.

Schatzman adopts a less conventional approach to the situation of the patient in a mental hospital. His analysis of the case of one patient shows how the development of the patient's illness and the interpretation made of the illness by the psychiatrist are inextricably intertwined. A transactionalist account of the relation of the patient to staff who are treating him shows that they, *as well as he*, are acting on the basis of explanations and interpretations of his conduct which are as irrational as his own. While his religious upbringing provides the medium on which the substance of his appeal to the institutions for help is carried, his adoption of religious metaphor allows the doctor to diagnose him as a paranoid schizophrenic. He is, moreover, in a Catch-22 situation. When he asks why a particular drug has been prescribed for him, he is told that it will make him well. But he replies that in fact it makes him feel ill. However, he is told that this is perfectly all right because it is one of the symptoms of the kind of illness that he is suffering from that he does not realise that he is ill at all. Thus, whatever he offers by way of explanation and interpretation of his position is used either as ammunition by the institution in categorising and classifying him, or in devaluing his statements as irrational.

A concept that has much utility in assisting in the analysis of the way in which institutions like mental hospitals and prisons process people is that of the moral career. The final extract in this chapter utilises the concept of moral career to analyse, through the progress of a short-stay patient, the social structure of a hospital ward. The processes through which the institution manages the progress of the individual participant through various phases accompanied by transformations of identity is visible in this illustration, even if in an attenuated form.

The institution *as such* is not commonly perceived as constituting a problem in its own right. Our argument in this section is therefore that society, in seeking to solve certain problems, by means of such institutionalised specifics as the mental hospital and the prison, has merely succeeded in promoting a new type of problem, one which is admittedly out of mind because out of our sight for most of the time.

Life
Zeno

Reprinted with permission from *Life*, Macmillan, 1968, pp. 98–119.

For two years after my trial and sentence, my view remained unaltered. I had little interest in life, and the conditions of imprisonment were unlikely to instil in me a desire to survive at all cost. The influence of subjective thinking could not affect my conclusions, for what I had supported all my life had been denied me. It is the men whom I have grown to know who have changed my mind for me. They have not done this deliberately, for hardly ever does a lifer talk about his case, and rarely does he seek to excuse his act, but I have learned to know these men and to realise that, far from being the monsters so many believe them to be, they are very ordinary people who have either been overcome by circumstance or who momentarily lost their self-control. This is true of the majority of murderers, but not of all.

I have learned that many are serving life sentences for a crime which was the desperate act of an over-sensitive man. I have read the newspaper reports of the trials of many domestic murderers, but these have told me very little about the men who murdered. But after associating with them in the communal life of the prison, and watching them react to the stresses of confinement, I have learned that in a large number of cases they were ultra-thin-skinned men who were unable to cope with the mental pain of a raw domestic issue, and that when eventually they could stand the pain no longer they struck out, and in striking removed the cause of a pain which a tougher, perhaps more selfish person in the same situation would have shrugged off or walked away from. These men, and I believe they make up a considerable minority of murderers, had not a sufficiently strong armoury to deal with an emotional crisis. They knew it could not be resolved in a way which would have removed or eased their pain, and they were not strong enough to bear this knowledge. Perhaps it is an oversimplification to say that they were not adequate to handle a situation which others are able to cope with without killing the one who is dearest to them, but it is nevertheless nearly true.

I feel it would be wrong to hang these men because they had not the strength of others.

I believe too that a majority of murderers had at no time any intention of *killing*. Injury and pain they may have intended to inflict, but they struck too hard, or let go too late, and the fact that death followed an aggressive and unlawful act makes the crime murder in law, and I do not see how this could be otherwise. But I do know of many cases which leave room for a deal of thought.

Shorty and Jim had been drinking. The pubs had turned out and they were waiting at a bus stop. Three other men were waiting there as well, and they too had been drinking. An argument started and a fight followed. One of the three went down with a crash on the pavement and as a result of the injury he received he died. Shorty and Jim were charged with non-capital murder and convicted. Had Shorty or Jim been the man knocked down, and had he died as a result of the blow and his fall, the other three men would have been serving life sentences. Jim would be a free man if Shorty had been killed, and Shorty would be at liberty had it been Jim who died. The survivor would have been a prosecution witness.

Hugh had a row with his girl. For a little while it followed the pattern of a million tiffs. She smacked his face and started to kick his shins. He grabbed her and she twisted round in his grip till her back was towards him. She continued to kick back at him and he to hold her. Then she ceased to kick, and after a few more moments he let go of her. She slipped to the ground —dead. The rigid forearm of a fit and angry young man had been pressed across her throat as he held her struggling body. There had been no intention to do anything but restrain her.

Hugh is a friend of mine; I know from him the remorse he suffers to this day.

Hugh knew nothing of the law, and cared about nothing for weeks after his arrest. He had signed a damning statement. His solicitor told him later that if he had not signed it he would probably have received a three-year sentence for manslaughter. His defence was conducted under the Legal Aid scheme, and as sometimes happens he saw his counsel for the first time only a few minutes before he went up into the dock at the Old Bailey. He was told that he should plead guilty to the murder charge ... 'after all, they can't hang you—it's non-capital, and your statement makes it difficult to do anything else'.

This was the first he knew of his counsel's opinion—it was the first time he had seen him. After what his solicitor had told him, he wanted to fight for a manslaughter verdict. His counsel shrugged and left him. In the dock, the charge was read out and he was asked how he would plead. I can imagine him looking round for the counsel he couldn't see, for he has told me of the despair he felt when he recognised no one, and felt only the silence of the court. He was twenty years old and only ten months in England, his family thousands of miles away on the other side of the world. He must have felt very much alone when he made his plea of 'Guilty'.

I think sometimes of young Mickey Davies, convicted of the Clapham Common murder. Everybody who knows anything about the case and the men who were sentenced with him, and who were given comparatively short terms of imprisonment on charges of grievous bodily harm, are convinced of Davies's innocence. From the point of view of authority, Davies has made a constant nuisance of himself since his conviction in his efforts to establish his innocence, and yet although he is unpopular with the staff of the prison, they too are sure he did not commit the murder. Frank Pakenham, now Lord Longford, fought to establish Davies's innocence for years, and to some degree his efforts were rewarded, for Davies was released on licence after serving only seven years. If Davies were really guilty of the murder there could be no grounds for such an early release, and so I recall with a slightly acid amusement a conversation I heard only a few days ago between a lifer who had served many years and one who had done only a few months of his sentence. The newcomer was still in an enquiring state of mind, and he asked the old timer:

'How long is a life sentence?'

'It depends—did you do it?'

The newcomer looked blank for a second or two. 'Well, yees—yes, I did it.'

'Behave yourself then, and you might be out in nine or ten years.'

'But why did you ask me if I did it?'

The old timer grinned sardonically. 'Because it makes a difference. If you were innocent, you'd only do seven.'

Innocent men in prison—in England. My father would never have believed it, and nor should I at one time. Even now I don't believe there are a great many, but I am convinced there are far more than the public realises. But the important thing that the public does not realise is how much obstruction there is the moment a man makes a determined effort to establish his innocence. Nearly helpless, he can be blocked and thwarted in a hundred ways, and he never knows who is responsible. When he is denied a facility to fight his case, he never knows who has decided that he should be denied. It is done in the Home Secretary's name, and the decision is made known to him by a member of the prison staff, but he will never know who it was, somewhere above the prison Governor and below the Secretary of State, who decided that it would be embarrassing if doubt were cast on his guilt.

The Custodians
R. Roberts

Reprinted with permission from *Imprisoned Tongues*, Manchester University Press, 1968.

The gaoler has never been popular. Prison officers even more than policemen are often chary of mentioning their job, knowing only too well the unease it causes. Naturally they resent suspicion. Society demands that offenders be locked away, then looks darkly on those it employs to prevent their escape. Of all civil servants the prison officer is perhaps the one held in lowest esteem. The public tends to see him as a member of a paramilitary order who lives behind locked doors and only comes to light when some ex-prisoner accuses him of gross brutality. Criticism is sporadic but widespread. Recently an ex-Member of Parliament after a four years' sentence in one gaol asserted that 'ten per cent of warders are brutes and the majority of the rest unemployable'. Articles, plays, and books by released prisoners all go to darken a tarnished image still further. In reply the Prison Officers' Association writes indignant letters to the Press damning all such attacks as vicious libels on a fine body of men who do their duties with the utmost restraint and who never use force against a prisoner except in the strictest self-defence. What is the truth?

Facts about gaols, their inmates, and guardians are hard to establish, not necessarily through any concealment of truth, but simply because an observer's judgement is prone to become distorted by the abnormal circumstances in which he moves.

The layman visiting prison regularly with ideas of rehabilitation and reform soon finds his sympathies going out to the captives. Inmates generally are not slow to pour out their troubles and in complaining seldom spare the staff. Officers know this well enough and naturally take it ill. Brusque, taciturn, on the defensive, some do not go out of their way to welcome outsiders. Only later, perhaps, after getting to know staff members personally, is the visitor able to make juster assessment of the difficulties and antagonisms of prison life, and even then he should come to conclusions with diffidence.

Much has been written on prisoners, their problems, and difficulties, but almost nothing about the men who, according to their book of rules, must spend a working lifetime 'training and treating convicted prisoners so as to establish in them the will to lead a good and useful life on discharge and to fit them to do so'. What kind of people are the 'treaters' and 'trainers'? Until far more is known generally about the prison officer and *his* problems one can hardly hope to make any clear judgement on the British penal system.

Any man of proven good character between the ages of 21 and 42 ($44\frac{1}{2}$ in the case of ex-service recruits) and not less than five feet six inches in height is eligible to join the six thousand officers who form the prison service in England and Wales, provided, of course, he is physically fit and can satisfy the authorities as to his nationality. After success in interview and a pass in a simple English and arithmetic test, the entrant is sent for a month in plain clothes to a gaol or borstal to learn the elements of prison routine. This is followed by an eight weeks' course at Wakefield or at the Leyhill Officers' Training School in Gloucestershire. The course includes some tuition in elementary sociology, 'man management', first aid and a glance at the future role of the service. Practical instruction is given in the running of prison establishments. At the end those successful in a written and oral examination go to a borstal or prison for a year's probation, selection for posting taking into account a recruit's performance during the course and at the interview. Until recently the period in a training school was the only theoretical training a man received, but now officers are returning after two and five years in the service for development and refresher courses.

A large proportion of the prison staff with any length of service came in from the forces, but over the last ten years the pattern has been changing fast; most recruits are now drawn from civilian life, attracted by the security of a government post and the prospects of a pension. Some enter because they have a genuine desire to do what seems to be a worthwhile social service. But wherever authority is given to men to order the lives of others, whether in armies, hospitals, or the police force, one will always find a few who grossly abuse their powers. Staff selection boards, no matter how vigilant, can never hope to succeed in weeding out all such people; indeed, tyrants often become so only after tasting the pleasures of uniformed authority. The prison service, like all authoritarian bodies, has its little quota of bullies. To deny their existence is futile. These few would be better out of the service.

Officers live in a confined society. Those who have joined from the Army and Navy find again the same camaraderie and group loyalty they have been used to and a similar system. Outside gaol many officers and their families live in quarters— groups of houses that may form an almost socially isolated unit within the community. Usually a recreation club exists in the prison supported by many but by no means all the officers. Since staff generally may remain only a few years in any one establishment, friendships with people not in the service are often fleeting. As with any other closely knit group, criticism or attack from outside, whether justified or not, tends to be met by the common front and the united response.

Any regular visitor to prison cannot fail to be struck by the gulf which lies between those in and out of uniform. In the larger local prisons the uniformed staff is made up of (a) the chief officer (class 1); (b) 2 chief officers (class 2); (c) 16 principal officers; (d) 200 officers. Out of uniform are the governor (1st, 2nd, or 3rd class, according to the size and importance of the prison), one deputy governor, and two assistant governors, together with a welfare, medical, clerical, and trade staff.

It takes about sixteen years for a man to gain his first promotion to principal officer and another seven or so for him to become chief. As in the forces, many retire after a lifetime's service no more than 'ordinaries'. What are the chances of the young aspirant ever becoming governor (class 1)? Very remote, it seems; the staff rates it at about a thousand to one against. There are two examinations for entry into the governor grades of the prison service, one for internal, the other for external candidates. Suitability is judged on interview and written performance. Internal applicants are assessed besides on departmental reports and on their success in the 'country house' test. Here would-be governors meet socially for a few days to allow examiners to estimate their intelligence, verbal facility, and *savoir-faire*. Only about 4.8 per cent of internal candidates are promoted to governor grades. The authorities state that this is much to be regretted. They are only too anxious, they say, to promote officers from the service itself, provided that such men have the necessary qualities and education. The uniformed staff in general, however, feel that several years of practical experience, at least, should first be required from anyone who seeks an executive post in the service. They deeply resent the fact that so many from outside with no knowledge of prison are placed in authority over them 'merely through having passed an examination'.

In his more pessimistic moods the officer at a large local gaol sees himself as little better than the turnkey of a century ago. His basic daily duty is to unlock prisoners, escort them to exercise and to workshops, shepherd them to their cells, see they are fed and, in the evening, make a final check on numbers and lock them up again. In between times he becomes a 'mere fetcher and carrier' for a small elite of executives who deal with the inmates. His job is to stand outside the door, a null custodian, until business is completed, then return the prisoner to his appointed place. Day after day the mindless round continues; only the puppets change. He recalls that his duty is to help convicted prisoners to lead a good and useful life on discharge and 'to fit them to do so', and he wonders just what he is doing to make them lead the life good and useful. Long years he may serve without promotion and always in the company of imprisoned men whose qualities are seldom those which go to refine the human spirit. Eventually whatever ideals he came in with are lost. He grows disillusioned, cynical, bitter even, as institutionalized in his way as the old lag himself. After years at a local gaol any officer who can always show patience and kindly understanding in face of prisoners' demands should qualify for sainthood.

'You know and I know,' an elderly officer once told me, 'we get no violence in prison—except, o' course, for a few bastards what we got to cut down to size.' Undoubtedly in every large gaol there are always some men (bullies and thugs outside) ready to make brutal physical attack on members of the staff or other inmates, and there are officers, too, who will pay them back in kind. But what astonishes after years of experience of prison life is not how much but how little violence occurs.

'As for getting knocked about,' one old lag told me, echoing

the view of many others, 'I bin comin' in nicks now for forty
year, an' I know what's what! There's good screws an' bad
screws, an' I don't like either sort. They're like coppers—never
trust one till e's bin dead three year! But in all my time I seen
very little violence—not screws agen cons; I seen plenty o' con
carve-ups. But not one officer's ever raised 'and or stick to me.
Then again for a good few year now there's been a better sort
o' feller comin' on the job—less o' that shoutin' an' bawlin' an'
effin' and blindin' what useter go on—more quieter blokes,
see—wi' more understandin'. O' course, there's some decent
chaps among the older end, an' all, what's never lifted their
stick to nobody—not in thirty year, an' wouldn't. They got
their job to do like anyone else an' I don't blame 'em—so long
as they treat yer with a bit o' respec', like I do them—then
there won't be no trouble. But, o' course, there's allus the odd
screw—an' don't let nobody tell you there's not!—what, when
'e thinks it's safe, will give someone a good kick in the arse, or
a beltin' round the lug. But 'e makes sure it's a bloke what's too
small or too bleedin' daft to stick one back on 'im! But as for
proper voilance, I bin in all sorts o' nicks an' punishment
blocks, I seen very little of it.'

'Nicks is better today than ever they was an' I don't agree
with it! Not for a lot o' them lads what's comin' in now. It's
too easy. They oughter make it bloody stiff for 'em like what
we used to 'ave it afore the war—no mattress for a month, no
tea, an' no snout at all! That ud learn 'em. You 'ad to wait a
full twelve month afore you got yer first bit o' cheese! An' no
talkin' in them days, mind! When it wuzz brought out that we
could chat the screws wuz dead agen it!—said we'd plan all
sorts o' villainy an' riots an' there wouldn't be no discipline!
Now they're all for it!—wouldn't 'ave the no-talkin' rule back
at no price, they wouldn't. Makes it easier for them—see?
They not gotter keep bawlin' "Shurrup, you!" Aye! Dead
agen a thing, then dead for it! Christ! It just shows 'ow bloody
wrong *they* can be. It's a good job, I allus say, that there's
fellers above 'em wi' a bit more sense nor they've got, else nicks
wouldn't never alter.'

'But they should keep it rough for these young uns. There's
no discipline at all today. When I wuz a child I got chastised
proper by my parents an' it kep' me in my place; but lads
now—they do what the 'ell they like!—no respec' for religion,
nor their elders, nor decent people at all! It's not right, yer
know!'

Officer attitudes to their charges may vary, according to the individual, from the repressive to the easily tolerant with a dash of cynicism and wary indifference thrown in, yet one finds a surprising number who take a keen interest in prisoners and the social problems which beset them. Of course, the service contains a solid body of men who support the massed public demand for a return to strict discipline in prison and the re-introduction of hanging and flogging but in my experience this group is not as strong as some sociologists seem to believe. Naturally such men have seldom much time for psychology or psychiatry in the treatment of prisoners, for education or, in fact, rehabilitation in any form. They dislike outsiders who come 'pamperin' 'em with their frills and fancy schemes', and consider repressive discipline in gaol, with longer and longer sentences, the only deterrent to crime. Above all, they believe that practical experience of prison life is the sole guide in the treatment of delinquency. But these old authoritarian attitudes are steadily disappearing. One hears fewer and fewer contemptuous remarks about criminologists, social scientists, probation officers, 'do-gooders', and the rest. In recent years workers in the probation service have been spending study periods in gaol, and prison staff, in turn, now work for a week outside with probation officers—an interchange which has caused a remarkable revision of ideas on both sides. After practical experience of its activities many prison officers speak with admiration of the probation service and see their own job in a different light.

One lesson the more thoughtful officer soon learns in gaol is that all the short-cut solutions offered by the uninformed for the reduction of crime are worthless. Dealing each day with criminals, he sees men about him of every sort and condition—the feckless, the foolish, the mentally disturbed, the vicious and dangerous. Some are already too spoiled ever again to take a normal place in the community; others set social problems both subtle and profound. He realizes that emotional demands for more severity and all-round repression in prisons can only come from those who have no inkling of the complexities involved.

New thinking and new methods, he knows, are vitally necessary if we are ever to understand, even partially, the reason for criminal behaviour in our society. Fortunately, great changes are on the way in the British prison service and the ordinary officer is anxious to take on a much more active and significant role than he has played hitherto. Further responsibilities will demand from him, of course, a much higher standard of education, and many are already preparing to meet new, exacting requirements.

The hope of the Prison Officers' Association is for the eventual take-over by prison staffs of all the rehabilitative, welfare, teaching, and after-care systems of the penal service, now mostly in other hands. But such unification, it is realized, can only come about when officers in general are much better equipped educationally than they are today. Well aware of this, the modern officer, no longer content to be a mere turnkey, is already preparing for the new status that may soon be thrust upon him. In 1965, out of a complement of more than 6,000 men staffing our prisons, over 1,000 were taking courses in general education and in criminology and social studies. And none too soon the prisons of the near future will call for a new kind of staff, trained to a far higher degree than ever before.

Madness and Morals
M. Schatzman

Reprinted with permission from *Counter Culture*, edited by Joseph Berke, Peter Owen, 1969, pp. 293–300.

Mental hospitals like prisons confine 'deviant' persons, but they confuse their inmates more since they do not tell them what rules they have broken, nor even that they have broken rules. The psychiatrist in the mental hospital tries to persuade himself, his colleagues in the medical profession, the staff, the 'patients', the 'patients'' families and friends, and society, that he practises medicine, and to deny to himself and all others that any persuasion occurs or is even necessary, To frame his activities within a medical model he calls a trial, 'examination'; a judgment, 'diagnosis'; a sentence, 'disposition'; and correction, 'treatment'. If his 'patients' claim they are not ill they challenge his pretensions.

One must admire the ingenuity with which he copes with his contingency. He presumes that a basic 'symptom' of the 'mentally ill patient' is his failure to know that he is 'ill'. When a 'patient' disagrees with the doctor who says he is 'ill', the doctor does not tell him that he should not disagree, but that he does not know what he is saying, and that he does not because he is 'ill'. He hears the 'patient's' statement that he is not ill as evidence that he is 'too ill' to realize that he is 'ill', and he tells him so. If a 'patient' feels healthy despite being told by his doctor that he is not, and says so, the doctor may tell him that he is not motivated to regain his health.

The psychiatrist outwits by another twist a person who pretends that he is mentally ill to manoeuvre a social situation for personal gain. The psychiatrist who suspects a person of this 'diagnoses' him as suffering from the 'syndrome' of feigning illness which he considers to be a sickness with a poor prognosis (Ganser's syndrome). If a man knows what is going on, but pretends that he does not, and knows that he is pretending, the psychiatrist may see him as a man who thinks he knows he is pretending, but as really not pretending, and as pretending to pretend.

Kaplan, an American psychologist, says in his introduction to *The Inner World of Mental Illness*, 'a series of first-person accounts of what it was like' to be 'mentally ill':

> 'One of the salient features of the psychopathologies that are described in this book is that they are opposed to a normality which is intimately related to the major value orientations of Western society. It may be asserted therefore that abnormality [psychosis] involves a negative relationship to prevailing social normative prescriptions—perhaps the most extreme and complete form of negation that is possible. This is more than an abstract and logical conclusion. In the jargon of the moment we may call this "alienation". In this association of abnormality with a refusal to be bound by things as they are and with the striving to be different, we have what is at bottom a concern with the category of change and transcendence.'

The same is so for many of the 'mentally ill' who have not published their ideas. The dis-ease spins off a runaway feedback loop: those who negate the prevailing social norms are negated by those who uphold them, and the upholders are negated in their negations of the negators by the negators—not *ad infinitum* but ad the ascription of 'mental illness' by the upholders upon the opposers.

When Jeremiah broke an earthen vessel in the Temple courtyard to pronounce and predict the destruction of Jerusalem, the Temple police seized him, beat him and punished him publicly by putting him in the stocks. They did not, as far as we know, suspect him of 'mental illness'. Recently, a young man in the NATO military forces with a position in a chain of command authorized to push a nuclear-missile 'button', decided to refuse to obey orders related to his job. He was diagnosed as 'schizophrenic' and was hospitalized.

All that is certain about 'mental illness' is that some people claim that other people 'have' it. Epistemologically, 'mental illness' has the status of an explanatory concept or a working hypothesis. No one has proven it to exist as a 'thing', nor has anyone described its attributes with scientific precision and reliability.

Since mental hospitals regulate the behaviour and the biochemistry of their inmates to a degree unequalled elsewhere in the 'free world', 'patients' rebel and resist. Official psychiatry trains the young psychiatrist not to see what is in front of his face when it teaches him to class patients' attempts to protest against their situations as 'signs' and 'symptoms' of 'illness'. He learns to label 'patients' as 'ill' with 'personality disorders' if they make problems for others by defying the authority of the hospital or of society. He is taught to see those who openly challenge the rules of others as 'sick' with an 'illness' called 'psychopathy' or 'sociopathy', and those who inhibit their challenge due to a fear of the consequences as 'sick', with 'passive-aggressive personality disorders'. He 'treats' the 'victims' of these 'diseases' with drugs and may insist on bed-rest too. He learns to see 'acting-out', 'agitation', 'excitement', and 'withdrawal' as 'symptoms' which 'disturb' his 'patients' and not to see that they may be saying by this behaviour that he is disturbing them.

Some doctors in their first year of psychiatric training argue at staff meetings that their patients' views of the situation are valid. I have heard their teachers tell them that they have not 'worked through' their own 'adolescent personality crises' yet.

The situation is a special case of what Wittgenstein called the 'bewitchment of our intelligence by means of language'.... 'A picture held us captive and we could not get outside it, for it lay in our language and language seemed to repeat it to us inexorably.'

Laing says:

'The concept of schizophrenia is a kind of conceptual strait-jacket that severely restricts the possibilities both of psychiatrists and patients. By taking off his straitjacket we can see what happens. It has been abundantly shown in the field of ethology, that observations on the behaviour of animals in captivity tells us *nothing reliable* about their behaviour in their own natural setting. The whole of our present civilization may be a captivity that man has somehow imposed on himself. But, the observations upon which psychiatrists and psychologists have drawn in order to build up the prevailing picture of schizophrenia, have, almost entirely, been made on human beings in a double or even treble captivity.'

The power to confine people in mental hospitals, involuntarily if necessary, deprive them of civil liberties, define their limits of legal redress, and award to their medical governors licence to formulate and execute rules to regulate their management and 'treatment', derives from the State and is guaranteed by the 'Law'. The confinement of the 'mentally ill' must serve a basic homeostatic function to sustain the social and political order in Western society, since many people are confined and many work to confine them.

Here is a schematic version of an actual story. Matthew, aged twenty-three, is from a devout Christian family. When he was twelve his father died, and since thirteen he has slept in the same bed as his mother, at her request, because she has feared to sleep alone. He meets a woman of his own age whom he likes and whom he kisses one evening. That night 'vampires' attack him in his sleep. When the nightmares continue, his mother takes him to a G.P. who tells her he shows early signs of 'mental illness' and suggests he go into a hospital before his 'disease' progresses further.

Matthew enters a mental hospital as an in-patient. He says to his psychiatrist the next day, 'Please help me. You are a messenger from God. You will decide my fate: whether I will go to heaven or hell. Do I have any power to influence you? If I confess that I have masturbated, will I help my chances with God or hurt them?' The psychiatrist hears these statements as 'grandiose' and 'over-ideational', and diagnoses Matthew as a 'paranoid schizophrenic', since 'grandiosity' and 'over-ideation' are 'symptoms' of 'paranoid schizophrenia'. The staff think the 'disease' is due mainly to an inherited constitutional biochemical defect. They believe the 'illness' appears now because sexual excitement stressed his delicate state. They feel his mother aggravated his condition by her overconcern about his health, but they do not 'blame' her, especially since her husband died from an illness. The hospital is a good place for Matthew: he will have a chance to rest because the rules forbid all sexual contact.

The psychiatrist 'treats' him with a common tranquillizing drug which is thought to have an 'anti-schizophrenic' action. As the dose is raised progressively he develops a new 'symptom': he says he is 'being poisoned'. The common 'side-effects' of this drug occur at the same time: dry mouth, nasal congestion, blurred vision, constipation, drowsiness, stiffness of the muscles of the mouth and occasional dizziness. The staff realize that the drug is responsible for these effects. Since the doctor has diagnosed him as a 'paranoid schizophrenic' they see his belief that he is being poisoned as a 'progression' of his 'disease' which occurs despite the efficacy of the drug.

The doctor raises the dosage of the drug. Matthew now shows the effects of high dosage: a pill-rolling tremor of both hands, masklike rigidity of his facial muscles, a stooped posture and short quick steps when he walks. He reveals to an attendant in the ward that he has phoned the Municipal Health Department to complain that the hospital poisons its inmates, and that he has done this to protect others. He frequently says that he is frightened. The staff now believe his 'disease-process' is 'worsening'.

The doctor adds a second tranquillizing drug, administered by injection. Matthew develops a rash over a large part of his body. He says that the 'doctors' are 'in league with the Devil' to arrange that he burns in hell for his sins, and that he would 'rather die than suffer eternal damnation'.

The staff see him as 'deteriorating' rapidly despite the best modern 'treatment'. They see his 'illness' as 'unresponsive' to drug therapy. The doctor orders electroconvulsive shock therapy. 'Patients' often feel this therapy as an assault and they always suffer some memory-loss after it. The doctor knows this but he wishes to help Matthew before it is too late.

The staff do not see his behaviour as a consequence of his experience of their behaviour towards him. Here is an outline of some transactions between him and them in which I infer his experience of his situation, and interpret his behaviour as an attempt to cope with their behaviour.

1. He sees from the posture his psychiatrist adopts towards him and from what other 'patients' tell him that the psychiatrist can assume much control over him if he wishes to. He hopes that the psychiatrist will not, but fears that he may.

2. He sees that the psychiatrist does not see himself as a powerful master who controls his charges, but as a doctor who treats 'sick patients'. He fears that, if he tells the doctor he fears his power, he may offend him.

3. A nurse tells him that 'patients' help themselves when they reveal their 'innermost' thoughts to their doctor and the staff.

4. A nurse tells him he is 'ill' and belongs in the hospital. A nurse's aide tells him that although he entered the hospital voluntarily, the psychiatrist can sign a form to confine him against his will.

5. He cannot obey the claims of both (1) and (3) unless he disobeys his consideration in (2). He cannot obey (2) unless he disobeys the demands of either (1) or (3), and if he makes a move to leave the situation he will act against the advice of the staff and risk being confined involuntarily. He decides upon (6).

6. He tells the doctor, 'Please help me. You are a messenger from God. You will decide what my ultimate fate will be, etc. . . .' His religious upbringing colours the content of what he says. His dilemma imposes the *necessity* to speak in metaphor.

7. He does not realize that these statements lead his doctor to diagnose him as a 'paranoid schizophrenic'.

Although staff 'treat' patients by telling them frequently that they are 'sick' they usually do not tell them their 'diagnoses', or the data which their doctors used to diagnose them, or the criteria by which their doctors used the data as evidence for their particular diagnoses. If a 'patient' asks for this information, to which all the staff have access, the reply is generally evasive.

8. He is not sure why his doctor has ordered a drug for him. When he asks a nurse why, she tells him he is 'ill' and that the drug will make him 'feel better'.

9. He tells the staff that this cannot be the right drug for him, since he had felt well before he took it and now feels ill.

10. His doctor says that the fact that he had felt well before he was given the drug does not prove that he had not been ill then, since 'mentally ill patients' often do not realize they are 'ill'. The nurses tell him at a ward meeting that he should trust his doctor, since the doctor is trained in this field and he is not,

and that 'mistrust' is a 'symptom' of 'mental illness'.

11. He feels confused. He mistrusts those who tell him he was ill when he felt well and that the drug they give him can help him to 'feel better' when it makes him feel ill. He mistrusts them more when they tell him he is ill if he mistrusts them. How can he influence the doctor to change his 'treatment' and conceal that he mistrusts the 'treatment'?

12. He says he is 'being poisoned'. In this way he both conceals and reveals his mistrust. Since he does not know the doctor has diagnosed him as a 'paranoid schizophrenic' and has ordered the drug to 'treat' this 'disease', he does not realize that by saying he is 'being poisoned' he brings about what he most fears: an increase in drug dosage.

I leave it to the reader to complete the analysis of the story from here to the doctor's decision to administer electro-shock therapy.

Many ex-mental patients have told me of experiences in mental hospitals similar in structure to my inferences about this man's experience. I read this story to seven of them and they each confirmed that they had found themselves in predicaments like this one, with which they had found it difficult to cope in a 'sane' way. Mental hospitals entangle all their 'patients' in knots which are so constructed that the 'patients'' struggles to untie them tighten the knots.

The staff's need to translate interpersonal events within the hospital into terms of the medical model is especially bewildering for inmates who may be befuddled already before coming to the hospital. Goffman, a sociologist who studied the social world inside a large American mental hospital, says:

'... whatever else these institutions do, one of their central effects is to sustain the self-conception of the professional staff employed there. Inmates and lower staff levels are involved in a vast supportive action—an elaborate dramatized tribute—that has the effect, if not the purpose, of affirming that a medical-like service is in progress here and that the psychiatric staff is providing it. Something about the weakness of this claim is suggested by the industry required to support it ....

'Mental patients can find themselves in a special bind. To get out of the hospital, or to ease their life within it. They must show acceptance of the place accorded them, and the place accorded them is to support the occupational role of those who appear to force this bargain. This *self-alienating moral servitude*, which perhaps helps to account for some inmates becoming *mentally confused,* is achieved by invoking the great tradition of the expert servicing relation, especially its medical variety.'

The mental hospital confronts hapless wayfarers, gives them a conundrum to solve, and punishes them dreadfully if they fail. Shall we not destroy this modern sphinx before it destroys the unwary among 'us' too?

The Moral Career of the Day-Patient
D. Weir

This extract was especially prepared for this volume and has not been previously published in this form.

In his book *Asylums*, Erving Goffman analyses the progress of the mental patient through the Mental Hospital in terms of the concept of 'his moral career', 'that is the regular sequence of changes that career entails in the person's self and in his framework of imagery for judging himself and others'. He points out that the concept of career is valuable in analysing certain kinds of institutional processes because it has a two-sided nature. From the one point of view a career is something personally experienced, lived through, felt and evaluated by the individual who is progressing through the organisation: from the other side the career identifies processes, changes, outcomes which are common to the members of a social category, specified and identified in terms of the formal structure of the organisation. Of great importance in the analysis of an individual's career are the crucial turning points, circumstances and situations which mark a change in his relation to himself and others and frequently a change in his status as an organisational member. Moreover institutions such as mental hospitals, hospitals, prisons, schools and business enterprises are commonly organised so as to promote a view of certain changes, certain specific turning points as especially crucial for the individual in terms of the way the organisation manages him. More recently, the label 'people processing institutions' has been applied to such organisations as systematically set out to manage the moral careers of occupants of a particular type of organisational role. As Goffman says:

> 'Each moral career, and behind this, each self, occurs within the confines of an institutional system, whether a social establishment such as a Mental Hospital or a complex of personal and professional relationships. The self, then, can be seen as something that resides in the arrangements prevailing in a social system for its members. The self in this sense is not a property of the person to whom it is attributed, but dwells rather in the pattern of social control that is exerted in connection with a person by himself and those around him. This special kind of institutional arrangement does not so much support the self as constitute it.'

Goffman's own work pays particular attention to the relation between the role of the pre-patient and that of the in-patient, in particular the view of the inmate of the activities of those who he may come to regard as having manipulated his transition between the pre-patient and in-patient stage. Consequential on this transition is the need of the in-patient to develop a 'sad tale'—a version of himself which he can present to others by way of an apologia or justification for his presence in the organisation. Most of the examples considered by Goffman are concerned with the kind of role which is fairly well developed because the role occupant tends to be, typically, a long-term inmate of the institution in question. And subsequent research has focused on the role of the long-term prisoner, and certified mental patient, the child in hospital suffering from some relatively serious disorder, or the student at an educational institution.

But we shall argue that the concept of the moral career has a very general application and in particular may be utilised to illuminate the situation in which an individual is, as it were, projected into an institution and equally abruptly ejected from it, thus experiencing what may for the sake of argument be styled 'an instant career'. It may even be that such instant careers are of rather general application and interest themselves. For instance, although it is undoubtedly true that the bulk of the literature about the institutional career of the prisoner deals with the man serving a long sentence, nonetheless large numbers of those who are ever in prison are there for a short time only. They may, for instance, be remanded in custody awaiting trial following which they are sentenced not to prison perhaps but to some other form of disposition—they may even of course be found 'not guilty'. Similarly, while the career over three years of an undergraduate degree course may be said to characterise the typical student in British universities, it is nonetheless the case that many more aspirant students pass in and out of the university's ambience for a day or two, during the process of seeking admission to the university, than are ever finally admitted. Thus the typical experience of many in British society of the 'people processing institution' may be rather typically a short-term one. One such 'instant career' with which we shall deal with in this paper is that of the 'day-patient' in the male surgical ward of a major general hospital.

The day-patient is one who has typically been undergoing a course of out-patient treatment, either through his general practitioner, or through some specialist service of the hospital itself, and who has been assigned for an exploratory operation, or examination involving surgery under a general anaesthetic. Such an initiating experience, or introduction, to the male surgical ward may thus eventuate from a wide variety of initial medical conditions. As the possibility of undertaking the examination, or exploratory operation depends on a coincidence of the availability of the appropriate medical professionals as well as the availability of space in the ward and in the operating theatre, it is typically the case that a fairly short notice is given to the aspirant day-patient of the requirement that he attend on a particular day at a particular time. He has of course however been alerted, probably well in advance, by his G.P. or the clinic that he has been attending that 'they may send for you at any time, and you must simply give it priority because they are very busy people and if you turn it down you may well not get another opportunity for a very long time'.

As the patient will not be staying in the ward over even one night he is not routinely sent therefore a list of essential items of equipment to bring with him. He is unsure of the requirements. As he is requested to attend at 8.30 a.m. and as he knows he must be out of the ward by the early evening he will tend to leave his home as for the office, dressed in routine street clothes. He is thus instantly recognised, when he makes his appearance and presents himself at the entrance to the ward, as what he is, an intruder. Everywhere is bustle and activity, as preparations are made for the day's work of the ward. Immediately a problem is generated by the fact that as he has no long-term status in the ward, accordingly no space has been allocated for his existence. The lockers which should contain his street clothes which he must exchange for an operating theatre gown are therefore all occupied. This problem is solved by directing him to the sluice where he can change in moderate privacy if in some discomfort. This done he wanders back into the ward for classification and allocation to a space. He now enters the role of what Goffman calls 'neophyte in ... the total institution, the new in-patient (who) finds himself cleanly stripped of many of his accustomed affirmations, satisfactions, and defences, and is subjected to a rather full set of mortifying experiences: restriction of free movement, communal living, diffuse authority of a whole echelon of people, and so on. Here (he) begins to learn about the limited extent to which a conception of (himself) can be sustained when a usual setting of supports for it are suddenly removed.'

He remains in the neophyte role only a relatively short time however. He is removed fairly soon to undergo the full course of pre-operative, operative and post-operative surgical experiences for which he has been brought to the institution. These experiences are non-problematic, in the sociological sense at all events, and are therefore beyond our purpose at the present.

On his return to the ward within the hour he is normally, of course, still under the influence of the general anaesthetic, and is therefore removed, hors-de-combat as far as the routine of ward life is concerned. At this stage he may continue to be segregated from the other occupants of the ward, with whom he has so far had no acquaintance at all, by the device of having screens placed around his bed. The screens themselves have an interest however in that as well as providing a rather minimal 'private space' for the day-patient himself they also remove him from the consciousness of the real occupants of the ward, the long-stay, the serious, the 'ill' patients. In her study of 'Human Relations and Hospital Care' Ann Cartwright discusses the problem of privacy in the hospital ward. She quotes what one patient said about 'weepy patients. ... If they were screened off you would feel they weren't so near you and they wouldn't get you down.' It is clear from her findings that the need to remove from the ward patients who in some sense were felt to constitute a source of trouble, or even in some way to threaten the mental and physical well-being of other patients, was very great.

It is the formal understanding of the ward staff that the day-patient will take the rest of the morning to 'recover' from the administration of the general anaesthetic. While this may, in some cases, be necessary on medical grounds, it is possible that it has another implicit advantage for the management of the social system which constitutes the hospital ward. And that is this. As long as the day-patient is being treated in exactly the same way as other patients undergoing surgery of a more major and radical variety, he is acceptable to the routines by which the ward is managed. He does not in any sense constitute an exceptional or deviant case. He can be treated as the *type* of sick person for whom the ward is meant. But, as his recovery from the effects of the anaesthesia, not in themselves particularly long term or devastating, proceeds, he becomes more and more of an embarrassment to the ward because his role becomes a more and more ambiguous one. Efforts are therefore made to maximise the extent to which he may in fact be suffering from the effects of anaesthesia. He is told that he 'needs to sleep'; he is advised against taking liquids such as tea when the tea trolley comes round at about 11 o'clock. When he requests lunch he may be referred to the ward sister who has then to adjudicate his 'medical' condition and determine whether the administration of boiled beef, mashed potatoes, and cabbage is likely to prove fatal.

During the afternoon the ward settles down to the normal routine. Leadership in the ward is bifocal. While the Sister clearly operates as the formal leader of the ward in terms of the attainment of the official goals of the hospital, promoting the well-being and progress in medical terms of the patients, it is the Ward Orderly who functions as the expressive leader. He orchestrates the ward like the genial compere of a variety club. And like the variety club compere, beneath the facade of sexual and masculine joking a determination to maintain discipline in terms of some normative standards is fairly clearly visible. Perhaps the fact that hospital work is conventionally regarded as more appropriate for women leads to an exaggerated emphasis on the masculinity of the orderlies and their audience, the patients. A jocular debate over the respective merits of the two local first-division football clubs ends in a mock fight with the orderly instructing a bed-ridden elderly man to 'get thi' jacket off'. Football of course represents not so much a *substantive* area of discussion in itself but a universally available cultural medium for the management of interpersonal relations. In fact the Ward Orderly's knowledge of football is somewhat deficient and his references are to City and United players of a generation ago. But nobody corrects him because the purpose of his activity is visible to all for what it is. Likewise as he jocularly feels an older man's knee-cap, turns to the ward with a lubricous wink and giggles 'Ooh I do fancy him', no one is under any serious doubt as to his normal heterosexuality.

Among the patients themselves there are distinctions of status, too. In the mid-afternoon a raffle is organised by the Orderly. The draw is made traditionally, by the longest-serving resident of the ward. I observed on one occasion that he drew his own ticket, obviously quite by chance, but that whereas in the outside world this might normally be regarded as a somewhat dubious or suspicious procedure, in the ward it was greeted with great acclamation. It reinforced the status structure of the ward, and was felt to be an appropriate and indeed auspicious outcome.

The common thread which binds these activities together is a conception of the position of patients in the ward, in relation to their medical condition, that sees them as progressing through a series of 'normal' stages of ... diagnosis ... exploration ... operation ... recovery ... convalescence ... ambulation ... release. It is noticeable that once patients have progressed from one stage to the next it is regarded as a somewhat unhappy and unwelcome indication if they show signs of wishing to retrogress to some earlier stage. Of course, the clearest example of this is the patient who requires a further bout of major surgery, consequent on the apparent failure of a first operation. But mild sanctions may even be invoked to persuade a patient who wants a meal in bed, feeling somewhat fragile on a particular occasion, but who has previously been allowed the privilege of taking his meal at the table in the centre of the ward, that he 'really' feels well enough to sit up at the table with the others of the table set of which he has now become a member.

Within the limits of the daily routine of the ward it is fair to regard it as constituting a micro-system. It is noticeable that visitors to the ward are treated in one of two ways. There is a good deal of informality surrounding the entrance of visitors of the same or equivalent level, from similar wards in the hospital—off-duty nurses, out-of-hours visitors and patients from other wards, even the girl-friend of one of the most seriously ill patients, who was herself a patient in one of the female wards. But other visitors may be treated as outsiders; even the surgeon who comes to visit one of his more interesting cases may be treated in this way. And the normal activities of the ward go on as it were 'back-stage' of the doctor/patient interaction. A clerk from the administrative section may be completely ignored when he visits to collect documents and may have to approach the Ward Sister in a placatory and submissive manner for information about the absence of some record sheets which he had expected would be available for him to take.

While the personnel obviously change therefore, the social structure of the ward exhibits a certain degree of permanence, certain roles are available, and for the patient, the conception of his role which is presented to him within the context of the interaction that occurs within the ward is that of one making progress through a series of stages. It is possible then that the 'instant career' in which a patient apparently goes through all the stages within the space of about 8 hours, constitutes a very profound disruption of expectations. But during the afternoon period the day-patient comes as close as ever he may to assimilation within the ward. He is playing an acceptable role, in terms of a comprehensible stage, that of convalescence. He may be brought in by the Orderly and by the more senior members of the ward into discussion of football, sex and other major substantive issues.

Now comes what constitutes in many ways the most difficult and contentious turning point in his moral career, that is his transition back to a fully fledged 'normal' member of the society outside the ward from whence he came. One alternative immediately presents itself. In extreme cases, a patient who comes in under the dispensation of the day-patient regulations may be kept in if his medical condition is sufficiently acute to justify such an extreme course of action. It may be questioned however whether in practice such an event is ever likely to occur. And for a good reason. For the day-patient's presence in the ward is only explicable in the first place because some other patient, a member of the long-term set, is sufficiently ambulant to be allowed to spend the 'working day' in an armchair by the ward fire or pottering about the ward, so as to allow the day-patient the, strictly temporary and short-term, use of his bed. Such is the pressure on beds however that the 'real' patient who has given up his bed to the day-interloper may be only in the early stages of post-operative ambulation. He will thus tend to be tired and keen to return to his bed by the early evening. It is possible then that the implication that it may be necessary to keep a day-patient in, if his medical condition is sufficiently grave, has the function of drawing attention to a norm in terms of which his position in the ward may ultimately be justified, and to thus minimise the embarrassment felt by all about the ambiguous status of a patient, in a ward of very sick people, who is not himself, to all appearances, 'ill' at all. During this stage of the day-patient's moral career, he is brought into the ambit of discussion, by means of a sort of attenuated joking relationship, of the kind described by many anthropologists, and by Pamela Bradney in particular in relation to the industrial scene. 'You'll have to go soon, you're in *his* bed' was the general message of these 'jokes'.

Eventually, following the successful completion of a series of tests of basic bodily functioning, the day-patient is allowed to dress. He then moves to a chair by the fire. The brief flowering of bonhomie and camaraderie is over. He is an outsider again. Shortly after, he leaves the ward. Nobody mourns his passing.

This, inevitably abbreviated, account of the instant moral career of the day-patient illustrates some rather illuminating features of the social structure of the men's surgical ward of the large general hospital. Firstly the extent to which the progress of the day-patient is channelled through a series of phases, each of them marked by some fairly abrupt transition punctuated by some specific ritual. Thus the degradation of the neophyte on his induction into the ward is marked by the stripping of his ties with the outside world, in a direct and obvious way. Donning the operating theatre robe and lying naked but for this flimsy garment on a bed bare of any covering illustrates in attenuated form the mechanism of 'personal defacement' which according to Goffman usually accompanies admission to a total institution, and in which the individual is stripped of his usual appearance and of the equipment and services by which he maintains it. Moreover the embarrassment caused by the day-patient's later presence in a ward full of people much sicker than himself, is indicated by the insistent emphasis on his obtaining sleep, *which in physical terms he probably has less need of than do those around him.* The sleep has the latent function of removing him from the social system of the ward. Finally his presence in the ward constitutes an offence to the territorial order which obtains there. He has taken another's bed, his space, in a real sense his only 'private property' in the situation. When it becomes fully clear that he cannot be assimilated to the category of those 'really ill' by being kept in the ward, his stay in the ward ends not with a bang but a whimper and he is allowed to leave with no kind of ceremony as the ward closes ranks behind him.

Further Reading: Institutions

R. ATKINSON, *Orthodox Consensus and Radical Alternative*, London, Heinemann, 1971.

V. AUBERT, *The Hidden Society*, Totowa, New Jersey, The Bedminster Press, 1965.

R. BENDIX, *Max Weber, An Intellectual Portrait*, New York, Doubleday Anchor Books, 1962.

* E. GOFFMAN. *Asylums*, London, Penguin, 1968.

* A. W. GOULDNER, *Patterns of Industrial Bureaucracy*, London, Routledge and Kegan Paul, 1955.

T. MATHIESON, *The Defences of the Weak*, London, Tavistock, 1965.

R. K. MERTON, *Social Theory and Social Structure*, Glencoe, Illinois, The Free Press, 1967.

P. MORRIS, *Put Away, A Sociological Study of Institutions for the Mentally Retarded*, London, Routledge and Kegan Paul, 1969.

The Prison – Studies in Institutional Organisation and Change, New York, Holt, Rinehart and Winston, 1961.

* J. A. ROTH, *Timetables*, Indianapolis, Bobbs-Merrill, 1963.

D. SINGTON and G. PLAYFAIR, *Crime, Punishment and Cure*, London, Secker and Warburg, 1965.

† A. H. STANTON and M. S. SCHWARTZ, *The Mental Hospital*, New York, Basic Books, 1954.

J. E. THOMAS, *The English Prison Officer since 1850*, London, Routledge and Kegan Paul, 1972.

* Available in paperback
† Reference

Chapter Twelve Conclusion

The reader who has persisted this far may feel a sense of
frustration and possibly confusion by this stage. After all,
although certain of the topics with which we have attempted to
deal in this collection are recognisably and visibly social
problem phenomena, it seems rather an extension of
terminology to include some others under this heading. In their
widely-used American textbook Horton and Leslie discuss
some of the fallacies which are commonly held about social
problems. The first of these is that people in general agree on
what really constitutes a social problem that their society has to
be concerned with. The second is that problems are abnormal,
unexpected, unexplainable things which pop up where they
have no business to be 'like sand in a fruit salad'. Other
specious ideas are that social problems are caused by bad
people, ... that problems are created by talking about them, ...
that all people would like to see the problems solved, ... that
problems will solve themselves, ... that getting the facts will
solve the problem, ... that problems can be cured without
institutional changes. It should be fairly clear by now that we,
like Horton and Leslie, would disagree quite sharply with these
attempts to evade the issue.

But while we may have developed or extended our repertory
of possible explanations of specific types of social problem,
their causes, consequences and associated circumstances, we
still may have some difficulty in relating the discussion of
social problems to the general area of sociological analysis. For
it has unfortunately been the case in British society, as in
America also, over a long period of time that the greatest
amount of work in the social problems field has been
undertaken by those who are not themselves trained
sociologists. Indeed it may even have been the case in the past,
and we would argue that it very probably still is at the present
time, that many professional sociologists would tend to look
down and disparage the study of social problems. Sociology,
they argue, is not a therapeutic discipline, and nor should it be.

Moreover, who is to say that sociologists know more about the most viable solutions or even the likely consequences of attempting any particular solution than do, for instance, social workers, politicians and public officials? We have sometimes found it difficult to obtain material written from a sociological point of view but written with the needs of the non-specialist in mind. And the absence of coherent, cogent and useful material by sociologists hindered the task of selection very much.

What then is the role of sociological analysis in relation to the social problem? C. Wright Mills, in the reading included in the introduction, drew a distinction between 'the personal troubles of milieu and the public issues of social structure'. Troubles are to do with the individual self and with his interaction with other social actors. The trouble is a private matter. But issues have to do with matters which relate to the individual as a member of a category or a collectivity. An issue often involves what Mills refers to as 'a crisis in institutional arrangements', of the kind which several of the extracts we have reprinted in this volume have dealt with in particular detail. Accordingly, to understand the source and origin of problems which are felt by the individual as troubles, we have in most cases to relate these individual troubles to contradictions, antagonisms and crises in social structure. As the institutional organisation of society becomes more complex so the possibility of such antagonisms becomes more widespread. While in the 1930s there was probably one set of issues, experienced by the individual as unemployment and identified and analysed by the social scientists as a crisis of the capitalist system, today there may be no such widespread sense of crisis. Instead there may be a generalised unease, a malaise which results in a retreat from social action, and an indifference to the well-being of others, whose interests may none the less be very consonant with one's own. To the resolution of this uneasiness and to its crystallisation in a set of practical possibilities for social and political action, Mills saw the 'sociological imagination' as providing the essential catalyst. What we have tried to aim at in this collection is the illustration of this kind of sociological imagination, in relation to the real issues of our time, and specifically as these issues impinge on the individual troubles experienced by members of contemporary British society.

The following selection deals with one such issue, that of the impact of public policy in the field of housing and sanitation on the life chances of a group of individuals. The lesson of this analysis is, however, a somewhat sad one. The author implies that without a largely circumstantial coalition of interests the problem might never have been satisfactorily resolved. More particularly, it was the middle-class members of the 'problem group' who had access to the means and resources by which the problem could be solved, in their interests at least. This is not to say, of course, that there was, or is in general in such circumstances, anything morally unsatisfactory about such a state of affairs. This kind of community leadership is widespread and many may even see it as being an inevitable and indeed quite satisfactory aspect of social life. But the analysis illuminates the extent to which the same processes, the same preconditions and the same potential for a generally satisfactory solution may be generally available in *other* situations, but the crystallisation and focusing of an issue in terms of some specific proposal— the process referred to by the author as that of 'detonation'— may be lacking. In the circumstances it is probably fair to assume that, other things being equal, those people have their houses pulled down. So social problems do not merely exist in the abstract: they exist in so far as some mechanism for their resolution, and some perceived need for their resolution, can be made to appear acceptable to those who have the power and wit to carry out this resolution.

But the power and wit are of themselves an inadequate basis for action. Lemert shows in his analysis of the concept of secondary deviation how social action to alleviate or cure some social problem through a specific application of policy, may, in fact, produce the very conditions under which the problem may be fostered, albeit unwittingly. The application of severe legal punitive sanctions against forms of behaviour which are commonly regarded as acceptable or even as desirable has been shown repeatedly to have an immediate impact, not necessarily on the problem itself, but on the creation of a black-market. This market provides illicitly the goods and services which have become illegal or proscribed for conventional market channels. This market is supported by institutions and organisations which are parasitic upon the behaviour which has been initially proscribed but which, by their existence, seek to keep this behaviour in being. Thus they perpetuate the initial problem conditions which gave rise to the perceived need for social action. These constitute a class of problems which society itself creates in a very obvious way. The results of the secondary deviation are a means of adaption to the problems created by society's reaction to the primary deviation. And whereas the primary deviation may be understood in terms of the needs of individuals, the secondary deviation is only understandable in terms of the way in which deviancy is symbolically attached to individuals, institutions, groups and situations and how society reacts to the attachment of such a label. Many extracts in our present collection have dealt with this theme. To explain social problems entirely in terms of secondary deviation is, of course, impossible. At some stage we must grapple with the need to find an explanation of the distribution of primary deviation in the first place—or even to explain whether such situations and processes as are apparently identified by the primary deviation label in fact *exist* in a real sense. This problem applied to our analyses of crime and mental illness in particular.

The last extract in this volume is a summary of the final address to the jury by Richard Neville, one of the editors of *Oz*. It reveals better than any strictly sociological analysis can do the complex nature of modern society. Plurality, however, leads in many cases to misunderstanding. Neville's speech is reminiscent of the position stated by Dick Atkinson when he writes in *Orthodox Consensus and Radical Alternative* 'Contemporary social life ... can be understood as a variety of beautiful colours and forms, made grotesque only by the accumulating actions of particular men and particular action-classes. Brightly coloured patterns exist. The point is not just to construct an alternative means of interpreting them by recognizing their relation to the actions of men, but, also to seek, shape, and colour our future lives more vividly. The variety and beauty contained in such colours is like the rainbow. In the first chapter C. Wright Mills wrote of the 'sociological imagination'. The aim of this collection is to indicate some ways in which this sociological imagination can be brought to bear on the problems which arise because of the very complexity and diversity of life in our society.

The Stages of a Social Problem . . . The Story of Strawberry Gardens
Denis Tare

This extract was especially written for this volume and has not previously been published in this form.

In an article written in 1941, Fuller and Myers argued that social problems typically possess a career pattern, going through the three stages of *awareness*, policy determination and reform. In the awareness stage a group comes to identify certain of its core values as being threatened by a particular situation. The next stage constitutes a *definition of values* in terms of some concrete proposals for action, offered by one side or another. In the *reform* stage action eventuates because some group is able successfully to influence a particular course of action in terms of their own definition of the situation reflecting the core values of their group. Fuller and Myers' analysis has two main implications for the study of social problems. First of all they clearly identify the significance of values in determining what is to count as a social problem. But secondly, they demonstrate how a particular social problem goes through a unique course of development in which, however, the three different phases or stages may be distinguished. It thus appeared to Fuller and Myers to make sense to talk about the 'natural history' of a social problem.

In this paper, we shall argue that not merely are the stages of a social problem a useful way of conceptualising the way in which social problems develop and become recognisable, but that in practice groups may systematically *manipulate* definitions of what constitutes a social problem in their own interests. It thus becomes rather questionable whether the 'awareness' stage is really most accurately defined in these terms. It may be more sensible to regard it as a stage at which a social problem is *promulgated or produced by* some group in terms of some definitions of value. The value of definitions which will be used in a situation are those which correspond with the rational interests of the participants. The story of Strawberry Gardens illustrates these points rather clearly.

Strawberry Gardens comprises a group of nine dwellings in a cul-de-sac within three miles of the centre of a major British city. All the properties date from the 1830s. The properties are interesting and characteristic examples of early Victorian dwelling house construction, built to rather spacious standards of external and internal amenity, set among a group of mature trees and shrubs. While, with one possible exception, they do not constitute individually remarkable specimens of historical architecture, their age and collective aspect lend them a certain unusual attractiveness, so near to the heart of a major conurbation. Of the nine houses in Strawberry Gardens, five had been the subject of major internal and external rehabilitation during the previous decade, and the owner-occupiers had spent quite large sums of money on internal repair and improvement and on external renovation. The four remaining houses were in various stages of rehabilitation, only two of these being noticeably dilapidated from the outside. This individual rehabilitation of the properties had been carried out by the owner-occupiers in financial circumstances which were rather unfavourable as assistance was forthcoming from neither the local authority nor from the conventional agencies for obtaining finance for house purchase, the building societies. The age of the properties and the position in an area of mixed residential, industrial and commercial use made the future of Strawberry Gardens somewhat problematic, in the official mind. However, there were in fact no proposals for the comprehensive redevelopment of the area in which Strawberry Gardens was immediately situated, although the boundary of the local authority's redevelopment scheme approached within two hundred yards of the end of the cul-de-sac. Despite these disadvantages the average price of properties in Strawberry Gardens had risen over the decade and the evidence of the work carried out to improve the properties indicated that their proximity to the city centre and to several major employers made them particularly attractive, especially to professional people wishing to live near their work.

But some years previously, when the properties had reached a low point, a decision had been taken to include Strawberry Gardens in a list of properties to be surveyed by the Health Department with a view to determining whether the properties as individual dwelling units were 'fit for human habitation'. At that time it would admittedly have been difficult to anticipate any reversal of the apparently inevitable decline of the properties into a state of complete dereliction. The very act of nominating the Gardens for inclusion in a list of properties to be surveyed some years in the future, added another twist to the street's fortunes. For once it became known that the properties were liable to survey, prospective purchasers were frightened off by the discovery of these proposals by their solicitors undertaking routine searches prior to advising their clients whether or not to continue with the purchase. A second consequence was that under the rules then operated by the local authority for determining whether or not particular properties were eligible for assistance with improvement and other grants, the fact that the properties were liable to survey constituted a profound counter-indication. In other words, the properties and the street as a whole by being labelled as substandard, thereupon entered a stage of secondary deviation. Or, put another way, having identified these properties as liable to deteriorate into a derelict state some time in the future, the community by imposing this very label created the situation under which a descent into dereliction became not only possible but highly likely. The imminent threat of the survey therefore, in fact promoted a form of 'blight'. Nonetheless the strong demand from people with capital available to make their demand effective had gone some considerable way towards alleviating the blighting effect of the survey order. Strawberry Gardens, thus at the time our story opens, presented a somewhat unusual appearance, with half or over half the properties renovated and rehabilitated, some houses being inhabited by respectable, moderately well to do and highly vocal and literate professional workers, the others being in various stages of rehabilitation and regeneration. It would be quite wrong of course to give the impression that the only residents of Strawberry Gardens who were concerned about their property were the recent incomers, the professional people. For three of the other properties had been substantially rehabilitated by their owners and thus only one house, owned by an absentee landlord and let off into bed-sitters, was by now visibly substandard.

It would be unfair, though, to make too much of the differences in occupational and class background of the residents of the Gardens. All of the owner-occupiers had at various times demonstrated themselves keen and willing to put in hand improvements to their property. But the formation and subsequent activity of a branch of the Civic Society, in the late 1960s, had certainly owed a good deal to the enthusiasm and concern of members of two families which could be called 'university people'. In fact, the chairman and meetings' secretary of the local branch of the Civic Society were both residents of Strawberry Gardens. The work of the Civic Society led some residents into a heightened awareness of the position of the Gardens in relation to the local authority's plan to conduct the Health survey. So from quite an early stage there did exist what one could call 'a generalised awareness' of the problematic possibilities that existed for the Gardens and its residents. But this awareness needed to be canalised, crystallised and focused into a programme for specific action before it could become a basis for a collective initiative on behalf of the residents.

As the essential parameters of the situation had been for some five to ten years previously well established, what promoted the growth of 'awareness'? The answer is rather instructive. One of the owner-occupiers, an architect, who had personally supervised and taken a major part in the almost total re-construction of one of the properties and its neighbour (in collaboration with a colleague who had now left the district and sold his own property to newcomers) purchased some land on an adjacent site and constructed some new houses. This act was of course very consistent with his activity over the previous years in promoting the rehabilitation and regeneration of Strawberry Gardens and its immediate vicinity, an ideal to which he was plainly both personally and professionally highly committed. In order to make the construction of the new properties a viable proposition, he had at this stage to contemplate selling the house which he had ten years previously converted and which had by its existence exerted a certain symbolic influence on Strawberry Gardens as a whole. Prospective purchasers of this intrinsically highly desirable property were persistently put off by the discovery that the area was subject to survey. How could this situation be broken? An individual approach to the local authority might or might not be productive. But a collective approach, associated with the possibility of totally regenerating a micro-environment of substantial interest and quality, would have a much greater possibility of success.

A brochure, an impressive and professional piece of work, was therefore prepared. This brochure was then circulated to, and formed the basis of a series of discussions among, the owner-occupiers. It was pointed out that it was in the interests of all to resolve the situation and remove the ambiguity which surrounded the future of the Gardens. The brochure was printed as a submission to the local authority. It contained elevations, plans, descriptions of the properties, schedules of the work already completed and in hand on the individual houses and a proposal for a *modus operandi* for dealing with the need to rehabilitate the remaining properties and bring all the Gardens up to the standard at which it would meet the requirements of the survey to be undertaken in the near future by the Health Department.

This brochure formed the basis of discussions on an individual basis between the architect who had drawn it up and his neighbours. It was agreed by all that it represented a comprehensive, systematic and clear analysis of the situation of survey blight which obtained in the Gardens and contained not merely a generalised expression of goodwill on the part of the residents, but embodied a collective determination to see the job of rehabilitation through. Thus, the stage of *awareness* gave way to that of *policy determination*.

After discussions among the residents, an amended version of the brochure was forwarded to the local authority. The response was somewhat dilatory and contacts were made with the local Member of Parliament who promised to use his good offices with the local authority, and with the local press, who gave the issue some coverage. These actions appeared to release the log-jam and the residents of Strawberry Gardens were invited to meet the members of the relevant Town Hall departments with the power and responsibility for dealing with the issues made by the proposals to rehabilitate Strawberry Gardens.

This meeting took place in an atmosphere of some apprehension as far as the residents were concerned. Representatives of every property in the street, with the exception of that owned by the absentee landlord, were present at the meeting.

The Chairman, who was an Alderman and Chairman of the Health Committee, began by introducing a senior member of the Sanitary Section of the Health Department who gave a detailed and comprehensive outline of the procedure for determining whether a dwelling was fit for human habitation under the Housing Act, Part 3. He informed the residents that Strawberry Gardens had been placed as a proposal to survey under Part 3 of this Act. He also informed the residents that 'almost all our original designations have been determined to be correct by the Ministry'. He told them also, though, that in response to a 'bona fide enquiry' the Council would be prepared to comment on a scheme or proposal to make a house fit. He emphasised that the criteria of fitness were related to the twelve points of the Housing Act as stated on a publication of the local authority. The 'fitness' in question would have to be sufficient to give the house a probable life of thirty years after the twelve appropriate criteria had been met. He also told them that applications for grant aid for improvement could now be entertained for fit houses. He concluded by informing the residents that Strawberry Gardens was scheduled for inspection on that basis in the spring of the following year, some five months in the future. Another speaker from the Housing Department confirmed that the action of his department in placing Strawberry Gardens under a survey order had not been motivated by any planning requirement. He went on to say that he noted that a considerable number of the houses had been improved but that some in his view would not meet the requirements at that time. A member of the Planning Department confirmed that there were no other proposals for the area from a planning point of view and that the area was exempt from the comprehensive redevelopment scheme which had been drawn up for adjacent districts. There then followed a fairly suprising contribution from a member of the Architect's Department who pointed out that in his view the houses in Strawberry Garden were very pleasant, both individually and collectively, and well worth every attempt to save them from demolition.

A spokesman for the residents asked the Council for three concessions. Firstly, for a declaration that if the houses were put into good condition they would not then be still liable for survey. Secondly, for assistance in knowing what the residents would have to do to put the houses in such condition. Thirdly, for a declaration that if the residents undertook work to put the houses in fit condition they would be eligible for grants in aid of improvement. The spokesman for the Sanitary Section of the Health Department who had emerged as the chief spokesman for the local authority side replied that he would certainly give a copy of the twelve-point standard to the residents but was not able to give any undertaking to bring the survey forward, far less to obviate the need for a survey at all. He pointed out that it was not for the corporation to impose minimum or general standards but that if a specific proposal came back from the residents they would see if it met the twelve-point standard. It was agreed that the best advice that the Council could offer to the residents would be to obtain a surveyor who would prepare a scheme and liaise with members of the Housing Department in an attempt to make such a scheme acceptable.

In response to a question from a colleague of the architect whose action had instigated the whole chain of events (the colleague was not a resident and thus had no official *locus standi* at the meeting) the local authority spokesman gave an unconditional undertaking that if any particular house were to be represented as unfit when the survey should take place in the following spring, the local authority would give 'sympathetic consideration' to any proposal to make it good and invoke only its powers under Part 2 of the Act if it felt that demolition was the only satisfactory course of action. This, almost an afterthought to the main body of the discussions, actually represented a quite substantial advance on the position which had previously been adopted by the local authority officials. This distinction between Part 2 and Part 3 of the Act meant in fact that the houses could be dealt with individually and if any one house appeared to be unfit at the conclusion of the survey, the Council would operate its powers to order demolition or some other course of action only in respect of that specific property. This single undertaking, albeit at this stage merely a verbal one, effectively lifted the threat of survey blight from the heads of those owner-occupiers whose houses were, they felt, in a reasonable condition to meet the survey. From this moment on there was therefore a possibility of a divergence of interest between those of the occupants of the good houses and their neighbours in property who may have had more to fear from the application of the twelve point standard.

But a further point remained to be elucidated. Certain owners of properties in Strawberry Gardens had previously made application for grant assistance for such works as putting in a damp course. These grants had been refused on the grounds that such grants were not available for property which might be found 'unfit for human habitation', even though it was possibly the very absence of such works which might lead to the properties in question being determined as so unfit at a future date. Following some discussions with the officials it appeared then that the Catch-22 which had apparently prevented the offering of grants for such works as a damp-proof course was to be lifted, and that such grants might in future be given, subject to other points being met which would in total bring the houses into 'fit' condition under the terms of the Act. The meeting concluded with a declaration of support from the elected representatives of the people, the two councillors for the Ward in which Strawberry Gardens stood and advice from them that the residents would be well advised to employ a surveyor on their behalf as soon as possible.

Within the next few days a meeting of the residents took place at which it was agreed that the architect should prepare a short list of surveyors and attempt to persuade someone to undertake the work if his charges were reasonable. All present at the meeting agreed that they would be prepared to meet their share of the survey fees, which it was estimated would be within everybody's means. It was also agreed that a further attempt should be made to contact the owner of the one house which had been unrepresented at the meeting with the Council officials. It was also decided to send the local MP, whose initiative had been helpful, sets of minutes kept by the residents of their meetings. Within the month a surveyor had been found and invited to a meeting of the residents. He prefaced his remarks by warning the residents that there were still many slips between cup and lip due to other sources than the mere threat of the survey.

He outlined a course of action which would be for him to make appointments to inspect all of the properties following which he would talk to the M.O.H.'s Department to discuss what needed to be done to the houses to avoid their classification as unfit. He would assume, unless directed otherwise by the local authority officials, that improvement grants would be available for this work. It was agreed that a large part of the surveyor's task would be to negotiate with Council officials. There was a general consensus that they should try to move ahead as soon as possible so that the necessary improvements could be completed or at least put in hand by the time of the survey next spring. Although the surveyor recognised the need of the residents to take action quickly, he wanted to avoid having too much pressure put on him because the speed of progress was really limited by the availability of Council officials. It was agreed as a tactical matter to work through the senior official who had appeared at the full-dress meeting to be fairly sympathetic to the anxieties of the residents. Shortly afterwards the survey took place and negotiations were put in hand with the Council. Plans for meeting the cost for the necessary renovations were made with the residents individually. For the sake of our present analysis the story of Strawberry Gardens ends here. The stage of policy determination had been succeeded by positive proposals for reform.

Fuller and Myers had written 'Social problems do not arise full-blown commanding community attention and invoking adequate policies and machinery for their solution.' The Strawberry Gardens story illustrates this truth very clearly. Although the *pre-conditions* for the emergence of Strawberry Gardens as a social problem had existed for some considerable time, it was the coincidence in time of the impending survey, and the need for one of the residents to sell his house in order to finance some further developments, that promoted the escalation of an individual 'trouble' and a generally felt malaise, into a problem demanding a collective solution. Once the escalation had been initiated both the community and the decision-makers became aware of the existence of a problem in Strawberry Gardens requiring some action and decision at a collective level. At this stage explanations, theories and rationalisations of the 'real' genesis of the dispute became common among the residents themselves. For instance, following the initiative of the Member of Parliament, fairly extensive press coverage was given to the residents of Strawberry Gardens. This press coverage, complete with photographs of the longest-serving residents, concentrated, of course, on the theme of small man about to be crushed by the juggernaut of town hall bureaucracy. 'Strawberry Gardens Residents Fight for Their Homes. Can We Afford to Destroy this Slice of Local History?' were the themes which engaged the mass media communicators' attention. In point of fact, as we have seen, no such threat of this kind, that is of the comprehensive demolition and redevelopment of the site as a whole, had ever been contemplated by the local authority. In fact, the confrontation had, as we have seen, been to some extent engineered. But the view of the residents tended after a while to accord more with the image of themselves and the sequence of actions in which they had been involved which was being promoted by the media.

Our analysis indicates that whilst the process of awareness does 'lie in the awakening of people in a given locality to a realisation that certain cherished values are threatened by conditions which have become acute' and while the stage of policy determination, the debate over policies involved in alternative solutions, 'does promote a discussion on "ends and means" and the conflict of social interest', a solution proposed by a section can be a means of pre-empting the no-mans land that exists in advance of a specific policy decision being taken by the relevant official body. In the case of Strawberry Gardens, the middle ground of the attitudes and interests of the other residents of the Gardens was also pre-empted in this way, though doubtless to their advantage and in their interest.

Fuller and Myers identify three inter-related levels of policy determination, firstly the neighbours and other interested and unorganised groups, secondly organised groups and thirdly specialists and administrators in governmental or quasi-governmental units. They comment that the 'inter-influence and cross-fertilisation of debate among and between these three participating discussants represent the dynamics of policy determination'. It is possibly also a lesson of the Strawberry Gardens story that the *latter* group still retain influence and access to instrumentalities for effecting change desired by them even at the level of their own neighbourhood and the interested but unorganised groups in their vicinity. Indeed they may provide an essential leavening and *detonating* influence on the process of awareness itself. We would argue that awareness does not simply come about. Awareness is the *end product* of a process by which a group comes to regard its own interests as crystallised in terms of a set of values which have apparently more general viability and application and embarks on a process of creating a social problem, the purpose of which is to generate a demand for a certain type of solution. In this process of opinion formation, the same routines, instrumentalities and processes which operate in the wider society and in issues of more general salience, come into play; that is, access to the media, access to technical and professional skills and access above all to the decision-making levels at which intervention is most appropriate in view of the interests of the groups involved. A detailed, precise and up-to-date understanding of the workings of the machinery of local government is one of the essentials in this task. Perhaps a most indicative conclusion of the Strawberry Gardens affair is the comment of the Chairman of the Housing Committee who summed up the discussion between the Council officials and the residents, looking around the room with some satisfaction, by observing, 'Of course, you do appreciate that we wouldn't do this for everybody, don't you?'

The Concept of Secondary Deviation
E. M. Lemert

Reprinted from Edwin M. Lemert, *Human Deviance, Social Problems, and Social Control*, 2nd ed., © 1972. Reprinted by permission of Prentice-Hall Inc., Englewood Cliffs, New Jersey, pp. 49–52.

Law, policy, and social control

The idea that society's efforts to alleviate social problems of deviance through the establishment of public policy may aggravate or perpetuate the problems is by no means novel. The adverse consequences of the corn laws in early Roman society in producing 'sloth' and further poverty did not escape the notice of such commentators as Cicero, and beginning with sixteenth-century England, the idea that pauperization and dependency were largely the hedonistic consequences of public policy set by the Poor Laws came to be widely accepted by critics. Much of the succeeding history of public and private charity to the present time has turned on the issue of how, in institutional terms, to 'insure that people who are not provided for by the usual economic arrangements of society shall be maintained and yet not incapacitated for future participation in the organized economic system'.

While the nineteenth-century hedonistic explanations of pauperism are unacceptable from a sociological perspective, nonetheless the possible importance of calculational factors cannot be summarily set aside in a sufficient analysis of secondary deviance—particularly in those problems of deviance which have identifiable economic features. This stands out in sharpest relief where a demand is created for illegal goods and services, illustrated on the grand scale by public prohibition of the consumption of alcoholic beverages, and to a lesser degree in current legal repression of prostitution, gambling, and the unlicensed use of narcotic drugs. Stringent enforcement of laws against these forms of deviance, called 'crimes without victims' by one writer, can be presumed to make the forbidden goods and services more difficult to secure and also to raise their costs. This in turn lays a basis for the growth of an entrepreneurial sub-culture offering opportunities of status and income for criminal deviants. At the same time problems are built up for the customer seeking a supply of the goods or services; he has to participate in the criminal subculture for his purposes, and he may have to expend time and money ordinarily allocated to established or conventional claims on his budget. If he is strongly motivated, as with persons addicted to alcohol, drugs, or gambling, he may neglect his family, alienate his friends, and beyond this, engage in outright criminal activity to finance his costly habit.

A good deal has been written on the contribution which repressive laws make to the 'problem' of narcotics in the United States, especially as sources of illegal traffic in drugs and the commission of crimes by addicts in order to supply themselves with drugs. Yet it remains to be shown that the laws themselves cause addiction; more plausible are the assertions that laws and policy determine access to drugs, their forms of use, the attributes of the addict population, their degree of contact with criminals and other deviants, their involvement in other deviance, and the particular kind of self-conception held by addicts. From these must be teased out the more generic factors which underlie or sustain addiction. Needless to say, after this has been done, it would be totally unrealistic to ignore the peculiar physiological effects of the drugs in the making of an addict. Furthermore, in this and other forms of deviance there remains a knotty problem of assigning relative weights to the factors assumed relevant, determining their mutual effects and the order in which they occur. The solution for this methodological problem traditionally has been held by many sociologists to lie in the concept of process.

Process and secondary deviance

The most general process by which status and role transitions take place is socialization. As it has been applied to the study of deviants the concept has been further circumscribed to designate such processes as criminalization, prisonization, 'sophistication', 'hardening', pauperization, addiction, conversion, radicalization, professionalization, and 'mortification of self'. All of these speak in varying degrees of a personal progression or differentiation in which the individual acquires: (1) morally inferior status; (2) special knowledge and skills; (3) an integral attitude or 'world view'; and (4) a distinctive self-image based upon but not necessarily coterminous with his image reflected in interaction with others.

The earliest descriptions of deviant socialization current in sociology came from Shaw's documents on delinquent careers.

These were likened to natural histories and so titled, but their descriptive content was derived from the delinquent's 'own story', as related to an interviewer. From a present-day perspective these studies appear to have been coloured by Shaw's unconcealed interest in reform and the probable interest of the respondent in supporting Shaw's views. Valuable as the stories were and still are for certain purposes, they carried unavoidable overtones of nineteenth-century entrepreneurial ideology in reverse, resembling 'sad tales', or reminiscent of Hogarth's rake's progress, or early moral propaganda tracts which portray prostitution as the 'road to ruin'.

The deviant career concept also has been linked with or partly derived from an occupational model, examples of which are found in the descriptions of criminal behaviour systems, such as thieving, and the marginal deviance of dance musicians. The occupational parallel, of course, can be demonstrated in the professionalization of some types of thieves, prostitutes, political radicals, vagrants, bohemians (beatniks), beggars, and to some extent the physically handicapped. In contrast to these, however, there is little indication of an occupational orientation among alcoholics, mentally disordered persons, stutterers, homosexuals, and systematic check forgers.

Closer examination of the career concept suggests that its application to deviance should be guarded. I doubt, for example, that the notion of 'recruitment' of persons to most kinds of deviance can be any more than a broad analogy. While learning specialized knowledge from other deviants is a condition of some deviance, it is not so for all, and the notion that deviants serve an 'apprenticeship' may be more figurative than literal where it is applicable. A career denotes a course to be run, but the delineation of fixed sequences or stages through which persons move from less to more serious deviance is difficult or impossible to reconcile with an interactional theory. Furthermore, no incontrovertible evidence has yet been marshalled to justify the belief that prodromal signs of deviance exist—either in behaviours or in personality syndromes such as 'predelinquent', 'prepsychotic', or 'addiction-prone'. The flux and pluralism of modern society make concepts of drift, contingency, and risk far more meaningful in deviance than inevitability or linear progress.

A more defensible conception of deviant career is that of recurrent or typical contingencies and problems awaiting someone who continues in a course of action, with the added notion that there may be theoretically 'best' choices set into a situation by prevailing technology and social structure. There is some predictive value of a limited or residual nature in concepts like 'turning points' or 'points of no return', which have been brought into the sociological analysis of careers. These allow it to be said that persons having undergone certain changes will not or cannot retrace their steps; deviant actions act as social foreclosures which qualitatively change meanings and shift the scope of alternatives within which new choices can be made. Even here a caveat is necessary, for alcoholics, drug addicts, criminals, and other deviants do sometimes make comebacks in the face of stigma, and an early history of deviance may in some instances lead to success in the conventional world.

Drift, contingency, and discovery

While some fortunate individuals by insightful endowment or by virtue of the stabilized nature of their situations can foresee more distant social consequences of their actions and behave accordingly, not so most people. Much human behaviour is situationally oriented and geared to meeting the many and shifting claims which others make upon them. The loose structuring and swiftly changing facade and content of modern social situations frequently make it difficult to decide which means will ensure ends sought. Often choice is a compromise between what is sought and what can be sought. Finally, even more important, situations and the actions involved often are defined after they occur, or late in the course of interaction when formal social controls intrude. Where deviance is a possible contingency, delayed definition is more likely than early.

All of this makes me believe that most people drift into deviance by specific actions rather than by informed choices of social roles and statuses. Each of such actions has its consequence and rationale and leaves a residual basis for possible future action depending on the problems solved or the new problems brought to life. From the societal side, repetition of deviant action may be ignored or normalized by those who are thereby threatened, or it may be compounded through patronage of associates who have something to gain from it. The pimp may encourage his new female conquest in her belief that she is entertaining men for pay because she 'loves him so'. The family of the heavy-drinking man erects perceptual defences against seeing his action as alcoholism because they, like him, are distressed by this ascription of meaning. The ideological gulf between stereotypes of good and bad, acting in concert with prevalent medical conceptions of deviance as the symptom of a defective or 'sick' personality, strengthens such normalizing tendencies by inhibiting recognition of similarities between the primary deviant and stigmatized persons. Meantime they allow the drift to deviance to go on.

The Trials of Oz
Tony Palmer

Reprinted with permission from *The Trials of Oz*, Blond and Briggs, 1971, pp. 223–37.

'Sitting in this court for five weeks,' began Neville in his final speech, 'listening to the allegations and suggestions made by the prosecution, I have felt at times as though I had got caught up in one of Dr Who's time machines; that I had been transported back through time to a wonderland of wigs and starched collars, of liveried courtiers and secret passageways; that I had been deposited amidst an eternal, antique stage play where – at regular intervals – everyone bowed to the leading man, and people talked as though the outside world stood still. And most of what went on in that world, moreover, was probably irrelevant.

'In one respect, Members of the Jury, you and I have more in common with each other than those who spend their days in Court Rooms such as this and their evenings in clubs, while at weekends they whip away to country mansions and fox hunts. You and I can go to the local cinema and see films such as *Little Big Man*, *The Wild Bunch*, *A Man Called Horse* or *Soldier Blue*. *Soldier Blue* – a film which reveals, in gory close-up, details of the massacre of an Indian tribe, with children maimed and beheaded, women raped and brutalised. And you can watch in panavision – 70 mm. technicolor while a struggling Indian squaw has a breast cut off. No magnifying glass is necessary there. Personally, I have a dainty stomach; but just like you, ladies and gentlemen of the Jury, I can exercise my discretion; I can choose not to see such films. I can also choose not to buy certain books and magazines overflowing in abundance at my local newsagent.

'We have had evidence in this Court that it is not so much sexual material that seeks out the individual, but the individual who seeks out sex. And for the curious, there is ample reward at even the most respectable of newsagents. Thick glossy paper and full clear colour; the girls are not stylised or fantastic, but full, live, red-blooded gatefolds who – in the last two years – have sprouted bushes of pubic hair. In the display cases outside such newsagents and I am *not* referring to Soho, you can read all sorts of ambiguous invitations. Last night, I looked at the board outside my local sweetshop in Kensington Church Street, and was offered: "Leather wear for sale"; "Young coloured student gives French lessons"; "Riding school mistress seeks superior position – full course of instruction".

'I raise these matters because there is some doubt in my mind whether the prosecution is aware of the contemporary climate, of what's going on outside this Court Room. He seems to live in a world where people pass around something called a 'reefer', where oral genital sex is practised only within happy marriages, where venereal disease is something cloaked in dangerous embarrassment, where, all too hastily, one's fellow man is labelled a pervert, where adolescent children should be seen and not heard, where wearing an *OZ* T-shirt is somehow sinister, where rock 'n' roll is a coded plea for fucking in the streets. There are, however, West End productions in which real live people are actually naked and simulate sexual intercourse. These are plays which do no harm to anyone but help make the theatre what it's supposed to be – a varied reflection of contemporary tastes. There are some people who see all these things as part of the rising tide of pollution, and have formed committees and plan regular excursions to Soho and Copenhagen. Others defend the new sexual tolerance as though it was some sort of cultural renaissance, a new religion.

'I think that both points of view are too extreme. There is greater freedom now than ever before in entertainment and the arts, but none of it is compulsory. If you don't want to see *Oh! Calcutta*, there is a Noel Coward revival just around the corner. For every new book about masturbation, there is a new romance by Georgette Heyer or Barbara Cartland. Sex is coming into the open and we are all going to be healthier for it. Mr Leary talked mysteriously about child prostitutes; well, there were far more child prostitutes in Victorian times when everyone pretended sex was to do with storks and cabbage leaves. In Sweden, incidentally, which has a liberal attitude towards sex, there are no prostitutes at all.' It was a noble beginning. The Jury looked interested. The Judge was studying his A to Z.

'Whatever you feel about the increasingly free climate of sexual expression,' Neville went on, 'I would ask you to rely on mankind's common sense. I would like to remind you of a very famous experiment with children that is in all the textbooks on psychology. This is known as the cafeteria feeding experiment. Children of all ages were allowed to select their own food from an appetising smorgasbord available to them. For the first few days, the children stuffed themselves with cream cakes, custard pies and all sorts of goodies imaginable. But, in a surprisingly short time, the children began broadening their choices, taking fruit juices and green vegetables. Soon, the experimenters found that the children, completely of their own volition and without any help or guidance, were automatically selecting the same foods as were recommended by trained dieticians.

'This connection between freedom of choice and good health is not accidental. The price of freedom is high. But the fruits of freedom are a healthy community. Freedom demands that we trust our fellow man; and yet we have built a society which does not seem able to trust its members. Thus, the weapons we use to repress and to stifle man's natural sexuality are guilt, and the threat of condemnation by others. The pretext is the concept of an ideal, happily married family.

'I have been criticised throughout this trial for seeming to stray from the central issues; but these issues have no meaning unless understood in the context of the society around us. It is not honest of the prosecution to attempt to confine discussion to the scrap of white paper known as the indictment.

'The attacks of the prosecution have concentrated upon our personal beliefs, on the philosophy of OZ and on the integrity of our witnesses. Yet the prosecution itself has introduced into this Court Room a whole community of people who are concerned with the outcome of this case, a concern which has shown itself, for example, in the public gallery – a gallery, incidentally, which was referred to with contempt by Mr Leary as though the presence of the British public is further evidence of a conspiracy. I must also add that I noted with alarm His

Lordship's continual threats to clear the gallery, as though the handful of remaining press were any guarantee whatsoever of this trial being regarded as public. Members of the Jury, you cannot see the gallery from where you sit; but throughout this trial, people have been quite arbitrarily cleared from their seats at the slightest display of any emotion. I think we have to ask ourselves just what sort of temple is being constructed here by people in the name of a law which can expel anyone who smiles.

'We cannot confine our discussions, our beliefs, our laws, to little white bits of paper; for each man must understand the consequences of the Law, and, just like a publisher, he must take responsibilities for his decisions. Those who turned on the gas ovens for Hitler said they were merely obeying the Law, just as did those who burned witches at the stake. "I was just doing my job," said Adolf Eichmann, when asked why he slaughtered two million Jews. "We're just doing our job," say Mr Leary and Inspector Luff, when asked to consider the consequences of this prosecution.

'This case has not been without its absurdities. We are charged with debauching and corrupting the morals of young people within the Realm. And yet there have been young people – one only 14 years old – sitting in the public gallery throughout the course of the trial. Occasionally, they were expelled for an afternoon for being human, but the State otherwise made no attempt to protect them from the lengthy discussions about the homosexual headmaster or Rupert Bear. So, if we are guilty of debauching and corrupting, then the Crown, especially as it has placed a persistent and unhealthy emphasis on sex, must be double guilty of corrupting minors in the public gallery. Do you remember the day the visitors' benches opposite were suddenly filled with eleven young men in school uniforms? They arrived just in time to see Mr Leary undertake one of his dramatic re-enactments of Rupert Bear meets the Fabulous Furry Freak Brothers and finds happiness with coffee and ice cubes. The boys stayed the whole afternoon before returning to their school in Surrey. So far, there has been no reported outbreak of fucking in the school playgrounds.' In his lime-green pullover, the unlikely figure of Mr Neville pressed on with his argument.

'You may remember that in my opening speech I referred to the fairytale of the naked Emperor. It was a child who first noticed that the Emperor had no clothes and his immediate response was one of laughter. While it is no enemy of truth or justice, laughter thrives on pomposity and falsehood. It is the barometer of social sanity and the nightmare of every dictator. In this respect, I would like to remind you of Marty Feldman. Mr Leary attacked his performance in this Court Room. Let me try and put his side of the story. He thought School Kids *OZ* was funny and, like many people, he was upset by the prosecution. He is not a friend of any of us and, despite his round-the-clock work schedule, he agreed to come along and try and help. He was very nervous. The only Court Room he had ever seen before was made of cardboard and peopled with actors. So he stumbled over the ritual of oath taking; the very next minute, it was being suggested that his evidence was inaudible and that it didn't matter anyway. Suddenly, he sensed the attitude of authority, the same authority that had expelled him from all those schools for being funny, the same authority that censors his television shows for making jokes about the wrong subjects. Mr Feldman reacted, perhaps over-reacted. Humorists are highly sensitive to their environment; he is a comedian, and we had brought him to a place which does not recognise comedy. He is a laughter maker and we had brought him to a place where laughter is outlawed. He was a man who was alienated by this Court Room, because this Court Room seemed, to him, alienated from life.

'Mr Leary began his closing speech by painting a cheap stereotype: lazy, good-for-nothing hippies, who worship sex for its own sake when they are not lying around in some drug-induced stupor. Maybe this was a clever way of enlisting your prejudices, but I'm afraid we just aren't like that at all. As Felix told you, people on *OZ* work a 70 hour week. We might start at midday and end at 3.00 a.m. the next day, but it's still work. Perhaps the difference is that we enjoy our work. Mr Leary's next allegation was that because we believe the drugs laws of this country need reform, we are, therefore, inciting drug taking. Were it true that every call to reform was an incitement, then a good many lords and politicians of both sides of the Houses of Parliament, Baroness Wootton and her entire Committee, Lord Thomson and the editorial staff of *The Times* which published a full page advertisement stating that the current drug laws are immoral in principle and unworkable in practice, should all be on trial. To my knowledge, Inspector Luff draws the line at harassing people like that, despite the fact that *The Times* reaches many more homes than *OZ* ever does. Reforming drug laws, like reforming any laws, is quite a respectable activity.'

Mr Malcom Muggeridge, the commentator, was later to dismiss the whole affair in a letter to *The Times*; 'the squalid, illiterate antics of *OZ*,' he wrote.

'Another example,' Mr Neville went on, 'of the way the prosecution has sought to put on trial what it chooses to describe as the "alternative society", is its continual insistence that *OZ* promotes dope, rock and roll and fucking in the streets. This proposition was maintained in the teeth of the total disbelief of almost every witness. We have really been prosecuted therefore, for what the prosecution likes to think are our views and *not* for the written words and pictures that were published in *OZ* 28. And of all the distortions of our views, the one which concerned us most, the one which disgusted us most, was the imputation that I, we, the alternative society, *OZ*, *OZ* 28, and whatever else was within range at the time, was harmful to children.

'But if anyone is exploiting children in this case, it is the prosecution. They knew that a prosecution of our earlier issues could not succeed, because, despite the deliberately inflated claims made for them in our "Back Issue Bonanza", they pale into insignificance besides the sex material easily available in every newsagent. But they thought they could convict us – and thereby silence us – by preying upon your natural fear and anxiety for children. Throughout this prosecution, they have taken advantage of the emotional and protective feelings aroused by children – they have dangled the image of "some little boy or little girl" before your eyes, ignoring the fact that this *OZ*, like all others, was aimed, not at children, but at the normal *OZ* readership.

'Not one of the previous 27 issues had been prosecuted – an admission that none of these issues were considered obscene. So listening to Mr Leary throughout this trial, it would seem that *OZ* has been prosecuted under a misunderstanding. Had we ommitted the words "School Kids Issue" from the front cover, there would probably have been no prosecution. But these three little words, which meant to us simply that it had been edited by school kids, have been singled out as proof that this *OZ* was specially directed to, and promoted for, a readership much younger than usual. But the evidence we have called shows first, that this was not the case – it was aimed at the normal *OZ* readership; and second, that even putting

"School Kids Issue" on the front cover did not make the magazine more attractive to schoolchildren.

'Mr Leary has continually flattered me as a master of the media. And he had some elevating comments to make about the responsibility that an editor has to his reader. This responsibility I do not disown. But it was precisely that sense of responsibility to the *OZ* readership which caused me to print, uncensored, the thoughts of the school kid contributors. The *OZ* readership is not interested in censored viewpoints, and neither Jim, Felix nor I had any intention of playing a confidence trick on them. We live in a society where the mass media are, for the most part, controlled by powerful proprietors whose political affiliations determine the views expressed. The *Daily Telegraph*, for example, is solidly Conservative, the *Guardian* is solidly Labour and the *News of the World* is solidly profit. Our readership is aware of this editorial perspective in most overground papers and is very cynical about it. That's one reason why they read *OZ* – to get a variety of opinions outside the conventional political spectrum. They would cease to buy it if we wielded the blue pencil for reasons other than space. To have played the headmaster, and censored school kid's contributions would have been to have abdicated from that responsibility.

'As for sex; although we have heard so much about the sex in the pages of this magazine, the items concerning sex either written or selected by the school kids are really very few indeed. In fact, there is only one article which deals entirely with sex. Admittedly, sex is used to make points in several of the other articles, but the points involved are not themselves sexual ones, and most witnesses have accepted that sex is not the dominant message. We are left with a total of 3 pages out of 48, or 5 contributions out of 83 which deal with sex.

'Our suggestion that *OZ* had the intention of improving society has been heavily derided. But that has always been our intention and always will be. We felt it was of social value to find out what adolescents were complaining about, in the hope that when their complaints were published, someone might do something about them. Young people, as they go through this no-man's land between 15 and 18, are socially impotent. Even if some of the criticisms expressed in *OZ* 28 are crude and silly, we believe it was of sociological and educational value that they should have been openly expressed.

'It was illuminating to listen to Mr Leary also deriding our claim that our freedom to speak is on trial. The first thing he said was that every opportunity had been given to us in this Court Room to say what we wanted to say. That is true. But it is one thing to speak one's ideas in Court, and entirely another thing to be allowed to *publish* those same ideas. It is that freedom – the freedom to publish ideas – which is on trial. Perhaps now you can understand why the National Council for Civil Liberties wrote in their Annual Report last year; "The activities of the Obscene Publications Squad raise a serious civil liberty issue. For 1970 saw it in a new political role, a role that enabled it to decide which magazines can be printed and which can't, what is obscene and what isn't, what is good and what is bad for us. It is all too reminiscent of other countries, other times. It doesn't matter whether you personally liked the style of *OZ* or *IT* or agree with their content. The fact is that thousands did and are now being prevented from reading it. This is political censorship."

'Another interesting exercise in deception was Mr Leary's attempt to explain away the fact that the prosecution had called absolutely no evidence to show that *OZ* depraves or corrupts. He pleaded that this had been a time-saving device. But the only inference that we can draw from this failure is that they could obtain none to call – and certainly none of the reputation and eminence of the ladies and gentlemen called for the defence.'

*   *   *

'Those who grew up in the early fifties were known as the "Silent Generation" because they seemed to accept that the most important goal in life was to get rich as quickly and ruthlessly as possible, while ignoring those who were poor, homeless and discriminated against. But suddenly it became too dangerous to be complacent any longer. Old gentlemen with cigars and curly moustaches could push buttons which might blow up the whole world. So young people came into the streets with their duffle coats and guitars to protest. They discovered they had a collective identity, a fellowship, a brotherhood. Sometimes these people merely rejoiced in the discovery of their own identity. They sprouted bright plumage to distinguish themselves from their predecessors and gathered in large numbers to hear their particular style of music. As they searched for new values and experiences, they stumbled upon an old drug, cannabis, which would also help distinguish them from their parents' generation. Each generation has a duty to develop a new culture and new values. It faces a different world from its parents, with fresh excitements and novel dangers. Bob Dylan sang nearly ten years ago;

> "Come mothers and fathers throughout the land
> Don't criticise what you can't understand
> Your sons and your daughters are beyond your command
> Your old road is rapidly ageing.
> Please get out of the new one if you can't lend a hand
> For the times they are a' changing."

'Will you lend a hand, Members of the Jury? With your verdict, you have a chance to bridge the generation gap, the culture gap, the ignorance gap, call it whatever you like. You have a chance to demonstrate that parents are not necessarily intolerant of the young, or unsympathetic to change. Acquitting *OZ* does not mean that you endorse what is in the magazine, but it does mean that you have confidence and compassion for the tender ideas of the young, for people who, in Dr Linken's words, want to solve old problems in new ways.

'I have learned a lot from this trial. If we did School Kids *OZ* over again, I would do it differently. I would try and ensure the message came through clearer. I can see how some of the contributions are open to misinterpretation. Also, while I regard the bringing of this prosecution as dangerous and destructive, I have no personal animosity for Mr Leary. While I think he has misunderstood the magazine as well as our intentions and has been unfair to some of the witnesses, he has, overall, carried out his duty with a sense of fair play. Before all this began, a friend remarked to me that we were lucky to be fighting the trial in England. I absolutely agree. Although the atmosphere in this Court Room has not always been the most conducive for the presentation of complicated ideas, I have certainly been allowed considerable freedom of expression. There are few countries in the world which would have granted us such latitude.

'But it is cases like this which test that latitude, which test our rights of freedom of speech, which keep the tradition of tolerance flexible, alive and up-to-date, and able to cope with changing voices and changing generations. It is cases like this which see whether we just play lip-service to such high sounding notions, or whether we are prepared to act on those beliefs, even at the expense of our own ideas of taste and decorum. A free trial in an open Court Room only has any meaning if the voices of reason are listened to, if decisions are made according to evidence, if people are prepared to leave this building with different ideas from those with which they entered, if the freedom within the Court Room is extended to the society outside and if the verdict is a verdict which will confirm the values of tolerance, reason, freedom and compassion. Let it be a verdict which helps to remove the barriers between us all, which helps us understand one another even through our disagreements, which enables us to live together as many communities with many alternatives, and yet still at peace and love with one another.'

Textbook and Reader Reference

Our aim in compiling this Reader was to present students and teachers with work of quality relating to problems of current concern in British society. We hoped that the provision of material which was not otherwise easily available would add to the value of courses organised around a sociological interpretation of social problems. By the nature of the subject, textbook and other similar approaches tend to date rather quickly. We have, however, thought it useful to provide a summary cross-reference to some of the major books used on courses in Social Problems. Many of these are, of course, American in origin and refer to American material. But we hope that this indication of the *comparative* coverage of these various texts and Readers may prove useful to students and save them time which might otherwise be wasted in tedious searching through library catalogues and tables of contents.

H. S. BECKER, *Social Problems: A Modern Approach*, New York, John Wiley and Sons, 1966.

E. BUTTERWORTH and D. WEIR (eds.), *The Sociology of Modern Britain*, London, Fontana, 1970.

W. M. GERSON, *Social Problems in a Changing World*, New York, Crowell, 1969.

P. B. HORTON and G. R. LESLIE, *The Sociology of Social Problems*, New York, Appleton-Century-Crofts, 1970.

P. B. HORTON and G. R. LESLIE, *Studies in the Sociology of Social Problems*, New York, Appleton-Century-Crofts, 1971.

E. MCDONAGH and J. E. SIMPSON, *Social Problems: Persistent Challenges*, New York, Holt, Rinehart and Winston, 1969.

R. K. MERTON and R. NISBET, *Contemporary Social Problems*, New York, Harcourt Brace, 1971.

E. D. SMIGEL, *Handbook on the Study of Social Problems*, New York, Rand McNally, 1971.

P. M. WORSLEY (ed.), *Problems in Modern Society*, Harmondsworth, Penguin, 1972.

Another important book which we have not annotated in this way because it is not organised on a topical basis is: E. RUBINGTON and M. S. WEINBERG, *The Study of Social Problems*, London, Oxford University Press, 1971.

Textbook Reference

	Becker	Butterworth and Weir	Gerson	Horton and Leslie (1)	Horton and Leslie (2)	McDonagh and Simpson	Merton and Nisbet	Smigel	Worsley
2. Population and the environment	12		36, 37	9	8	9	8		1
3. The Family	1, 4	1	22, 25, 26	7	6	7	7, 10		5
4. Poverty	9			11	10	1	12		
5. Urban Problems	8, 10	2	19, 20, 21, 24	15	12			19	3
6. Health	6			18	14, 15	6	1, 4, 5, 6	10, 11	8
7. Education	2	3		10	9			8	6
8. Crime	5		7, 8, 11, 14	5, 6	5	10	2, 3	7	7
9. Minorities	7		1, 4, 30, 31	13, 14	11	8	9	12	9
10. Work	3	4	40			3		9	
11. Institutions		4	17, 18				11		2
12. Conclusion		7		20, 21	1	12		15–23	

Note: The numbers refer to the chapters of the book concerned.

Index

A Fontana Selection